A Politics of Emancipation

SUNY series in Contemporary French Thought
———————
David Pettigrew and François Raffoul, editors

A Politics of Emancipation
The Miguel Abensour Reader

Edited by

MARTIN BREAUGH and
PAUL MAZZOCCHI

Photography Credit: Yann Levy

Published by State University of New York Press, Albany

© 2024 State University of New York

All rights reserved

Printed in the United States of America

No part of this book may be used or reproduced in any manner whatsoever without written permission. No part of this book may be stored in a retrieval system or transmitted in any form or by any means including electronic, electrostatic, magnetic tape, mechanical, photocopying, recording, or otherwise without the prior permission in writing of the publisher.

For information, contact State University of New York Press, Albany, NY
www.sunypress.edu

Library of Congress Cataloging-in-Publication Data

Names: Abensour, Miguel, author. | Breaugh, Martin, editor. | Mazzocchi, Paul, 1979– editor.
Title: A politics of emancipation : the Miguel Abensour reader / edited by Martin Breaugh and Paul Mazzocchi.
Description: Albany : State University of New York Press, [2024]. | Series: SUNY series in contemporary French thought | Includes bibliographical references and index.
Identifiers: LCCN 2023050592 | ISBN 9781438498256 (hardcover : alk. paper) | ISBN 9781438498263 (ebook) | ISBN 9781438498249 (pbk. : alk. paper)
Subjects: LCSH: Political science—Philosophy. | Political science—France—Philosophy.
Classification: LCC JA67 .A24 2024 | DDC 320.01—dc23/eng/20240221
LC record available at https://lccn.loc.gov/2023050592

10 9 8 7 6 5 4 3 2 1

Contents

Acknowledgments		vii
Note on Translations		ix
Introduction: The Legacy of Miguel Abensour *Martin Breaugh and Paul Mazzocchi*		1

Part I: The Return of Political Things

Chapter 1	Manifesto for the "Critique de la Politique" Book Series, Éditions Payot (1974)	27
Chapter 2	New Manifesto for the "Critique de la Politique" Book Series, Éditions Klincksieck (2016)	29
Chapter 3	Modern Political Philosophy and Emancipation (1983; republished 2009)	31
Chapter 4	What Kind of Return? (1994; republished 2009)	37

Part II: The Critique of Totalitarianism

Chapter 5	On a Misinterpretation of Totalitarianism and Its Effects (1996; republished 2009)	43

| Chapter 6 | On Compactness: Architecture and Totalitarian Regimes (1996; republished 1997) | 67 |

Part III: Critical-Utopian Political Philosophy

| Chapter 7 | Hannah Arendt against Political Philosophy? (2001; republished 2009) | 101 |
| Chapter 8 | For a Critical Political Philosophy? (2002; republished 2009) | 127 |

Part IV: Utopia, Democracy, and Emancipation

Chapter 9	E. P. Thompson's Passion (1988; republished 2012)	171
Chapter 10	The New Utopian Spirit (1991; republished 2013)	189
Chapter 11	The Utopian Conversion: Utopia and Awakening (2013)	215
Chapter 12	Letter from a "Revoltist" to Marcel Gauchet, Convert to "Normal Politics" (2004; republished 2008)	251

Notes	261
Bibliography	287
Index	317

Acknowledgments

This book has been many years in the making and the editors owe thanks to several people who helped bring it into existence. Judith Abensour and the Abensour family generously gave us permission to translate the essays. We hope this book will lead to a wider reception of their father's work in the Anglo-American world. As consultants for Abensour's literary estate, Hubert Tonka and Anne Kupiec helped us with permissions and offered us ongoing advice and support. Antoine Chollet, Dick Howard, and Andreas Kalyvas provided invaluable advice and much support at different stages of the project. Gilles Labelle kindly gave us access to his comprehensive Abensour bibliography and helped interpret some of the more enigmatic passages in Abensour's work. Christopher Holman read a draft of the introduction and kindly offered us his unfailingly insightful comments (in bullet-point format). Our thanks to editors David Pettigrew and François Raffoul for accepting the volume in their excellent series in Contemporary French Thought. Warm thanks to Michael Rinella, senior acquisitions editor, Diane Ganeles, production editor, and everyone at SUNY Press who helped guide us through the publication process from the book proposal to the finished product. Thanks also to the peer-reviewers for their enthusiasm and solid advice on the manuscript. Thomas Kiefer completed the index and Gordon Marce the copyediting—we thank them for their meticulous work. The book cover is based on a poster designed by Maddy Phillips for the "Politics of Emancipation: Utopia, Insurgent Democracy and the Legacy of Miguel Abensour" conference held at York University in September 2022. Thanks to Maddy for her beautiful work. Our thanks to York University, and to the office of the Dean of Liberal Arts and Professional Studies, for ongoing support. Finally, we extend our immense gratitude to the scholarly translators, Asher Horowitz, James Ingram, Devin Penner, and Olivier

Ruchet, for their excellent work on the project. Translating Abensour has not been an easy task and the book is all the better for their diligence and commitment to the project.

Note on Translations

Miguel Abensour's idiosyncratic usage of the French language, and his great sense of literary style, has led us to choices that are (somewhat) unconventional. Indeed, we have translated with a view to preserving stylistic choices (in the form of sentence fragments, notably), and we have transliterated fundamental concepts of his thought into English following the original text. For example, in chapters 9 and 10, Abensour writes *"tout autre" social*, whereas in chapter 11, he writes the same expression without quotes. Here, we chose not to harmonize our translations and we knowingly followed his lead. For Miguel Abensour, writing is not the definitive expression of one's thought, but remains open to the free play of ideas and concepts.

Introduction

The Legacy of Miguel Abensour

Martin Breaugh and Paul Mazzocchi

French political theorist Miguel Abensour (1939–2017) has yet to be fully discovered in the English-speaking world of political philosophy. Despite his influence in utopian studies and democratic theory, only a fraction of his work has been translated into English,[1] and the emerging secondary literature reflects this situation. Consequently, major gaps still mar the reception of his thought, including his approach to political philosophy and his critique of totalitarianism. The present reader seeks to fill these gaps and open new pathways inspired by him in contemporary political theory. This endeavor begs, of course, the question "Why?" Why does the Anglosphere require yet another "French Theorist"?[2] Is there truly a need for Abensour's thought today? The answer to these questions rests upon his desire to provide a fresh approach to thinking politics and to his fidelity to elements of political thought that are too quickly evacuated from our politics, elements such as the impact of totalitarianism on politics today, the relationship between emancipation and utopia, and the presence of insurgent forms of democracy, which are among the core themes of the works translated here for the first time in English.

Two inseparable projects govern Abensour's approach to political theory: on the one hand, a radical critique of all forms of domination and, on the other, a desire to conceptualize the political as the realm of freedom and emancipation. For Abensour, both projects are to be undertaken together to avoid the double trap of an evacuation of conflict from politics and the reduction of politics to a form of domination. In other words, a politics of emancipation requires a "ruthless" critique of domination coupled with an analysis of politics as the domain within which human beings experience freedom and equality. While this approach does have eminent forbearers, notably Jean-Jacques Rousseau, Karl Marx, Hannah Arendt, Claude Lefort, and Cornelius Castoriadis, such a project is not widely shared. Indeed, Miguel Abensour's political theory has always been somewhat *out of season*.

For example, early in his career, while some political theorists were justifying the "Dictatorship of the Proletariat" on behalf of the French Communist Party,[3] Abensour was quietly working with other heterodox thinkers, like Pierre Clastres, Claude Lefort, and Marcel Gauchet, on the "untimely" notion of "voluntary servitude" in Étienne de La Boétie's thought.[4] The untimeliness of Abensour's work is exemplary. Instead of following trends, Abensour sought to open other horizons in political theory. By doing so, he offers us a valuable lesson, namely, that political theory can and should free itself from the chains of fashionable thought. With the possible exceptions of Jacques Rancière and Étienne Balibar, who remain likewise steadfast in their commitment to emancipation, Miguel Abensour's approach to political theory is distinctive within his generation of thinkers in France. As such, it deserves to be pursued, renewed, and expanded.

An Intimate Encounter with a Tragic Century

Miguel Abensour's trajectory was unique, and it began with the catastrophic events of the twentieth century. Born into an Algerian Sephardic Jewish family in Paris in February 1939, Abensour discovered at a very early age the perils of total domination. After the occupation of Paris by National Socialist Germany in June 1940, his parents fled the capital and sought refuge in a small village in the Pyrenees Mountains in free zone France. There, the young Abensour rapidly learned that some people should not be spoken to while others could be trusted.[5] When a contingent of SS officers visited the village looking for more Jews to detain, Abensour recalled having taken cover under a truck with his mother: the sounds of the SS's perfectly polished boots still resonated in his ears some seventy years later. The trauma of this initial experience of totalitarian terror was, however, mitigated by the kindness and solidarity of the peasants of the village. Indeed, when circumstances became too dangerous, Abensour's parents could count on the help of locals to hide the young Miguel for days and even weeks at a time. Abensour himself acknowledged that his unrelentingly critical stance towards domination derives from this direct contact with the tragedy of his times. Yet Abensour's willingness to consider politics as the realm of emancipation must equally be seen as a consequence of his unique childhood.

Abensour's lived experience of another political tragedy contributed to his wariness of the "normal" politics of postwar France: the Algerian War (1954–1962). Abensour spent a part of the summer of 1957 in Oran, where he was able to witness firsthand the ethnic hatreds in the city and how Algerians suffered daily the humiliations inflicted upon them by French colonizers.[6] In Paris, Abensour was revolted by the massacre of Algerian demonstrators by the national police under the orders of a former Nazi collaborator, Maurice Papon, on October 17, 1961. Beaten or thrown in the Seine River, more than two hundred people were killed by the French *forces de l'ordre* that day. Abensour described the period of the Algerian War as nothing less than "nightmarish" in France: the French socialists renounced the emancipatory project by participating in the "pacification" of Algeria, the French Communist Party approved the Soviet repression of the uprising in Budapest in 1956, the "counterrevolutionary" Constitution of the Fifth French Republic was adopted, and General de Gaulle returned to power in 1958.[7]

For Abensour, it is only with the period immediately following the end of the Algerian War that the nightmare began to dissipate, thanks to a "return of the repressed,"[8] that is to say, a return of the question of a politics of emancipation. The events of May 1968 played a decisive role in this return. With May '68 the "fraternal disorder" that characterized revolutionary moments reemerged. Such a disorder rests upon the joy of acting in concert with others, the freeing up of public speech, and the return of public happiness through the extension of the realm of the possible. The most important consequence of this "fraternal disorder" was, for Abensour, the destruction of the monopoly on leftism held by the French Communist Party and the concomitant emergence of an anti-bureaucratic and radically democratic left. While the former represented the Jacobin-Leninist tradition, the latter embodied the communalist tradition of the Parisian sans-culottes and the Communards of 1871, but also of the workers councils of early twentieth century Europe. The central legacy of the "lovely month of May" is the reappearance of an emancipatory politics in the form of democratic action that goes beyond the limits assigned to it by electoral and parliamentary politics, as well as by the modern state.[9]

It is during this period that Abensour began his long career as a university professor (1962–2003) at the Université de Dijon, followed by the Centre national de la recherche scientifique, where he completed his *thèse d'état* on utopia under the supervision of Charles Eisenmann and Gilles Deleuze. Received at the very top of the first French state qualifying exams in political science (*agrégation*), Abensour subsequently taught at the Université de Reims. In 1990, he became a full professor at the Université de Paris 7–Denis Diderot. Throughout this period, Abensour was an active member of experimental scholarly journals oriented towards emancipatory politics, such as *Textures, Libre, Passé-Présent, Tumultes*, and *Prismes*. In 1973, he also became the editor of a groundbreaking book series, "Critique de la politique," at Éditions Payot, later Payot-Rivages, before moving it to the Éditions Klincksieck in 2016. His series notably published the members of the first generation of the Frankfurt School, as well as the work of a new generation of French political thinkers, such as Pierre Manent, Étienne Tassin, and Géraldine Mulhmann. A devoted teacher, Abensour created in the late 1970s a graduate program at the Université de Reims in political theory taught by the rising stars of political thought in France: Claude Lefort, Pierre Clastres, and Luc Ferry lectured or gave conferences at Reims in the context of Abensour's program. At the instigation of Jean-François Lyotard and Jacques Derrida, Abensour became the president of the prestigious Collège international de philosophie (1985–1987), where he thrived as the architect of epochal conferences, such as the Martin Heidegger colloquium held at the Collège[10] and by ensuring a curriculum that focused on philosophical matters beyond what "salaried philosophers"[11] taught in the august halls of French universities.

Alongside these intensive and time-consuming intellectual and scholarly engagements, Abensour maintained a sustained rhythm of publication, initially in the form of articles and, as of the mid-1990s, of books. The present reader proposes a selection of some of the most important of these publications, in providing a somewhat systematic introduction to the oeuvre of a thinker who refuses systematicity.[12] In this direction, the book follows the central themes that structure his work: (1) the return of political things, (2) the critique of totalitarianism, (3) critical-utopian political philosophy, and (4) utopia, democracy, and emancipation. By way of an introduction, we propose a contextualized analysis of the issues and problems of each section and offer an overview of Abensour's perspective on politics. For the readers who wish to read Abensour directly, they may skip this introduction, or come back to it once they are done reading the original. For the readers seeking elements of context to better grasp Abensour's perspective, we hope that the following pages will be illuminating.

Which Return?
Challenging the Tradition of Political Philosophy

In France, Abensour is recognized as one of the instigators of the "return of political philosophy."[13] To stake out his contribution and to understand his challenge to the dominant "return" of the field, we need to turn to the specific context of this return. By the 1950s, in both the Anglophone and Francophone world, there was a seeming consensus[14] that political philosophy was, if not dead, in its death throes or in need of euthanization.[15] This was the result of a change in the methods of political research. With the rise of Weber's fact-value distinction, logical positivism, and structuralist Marxism, political thinking was dominated by scientific methodologies that eschewed value-orientations.[16] Political phenomena were thus subject to a "scientization" and "sociologization" that undermined the project of classical political philosophy, which sought to draw normative distinctions between political regimes in service of finding the good life.[17] While the growth of scientific methodologies did not eliminate interest in political philosophies or theories, thinking about them was reduced to explanatory and, more specifically, causal modes of inquiry using allegedly neutral social science methods. On the one hand, studies focused on the structures and circumstances under which particular political ideas emerged, outside of value-judgements and within purportedly neutral modes of causal explanation that reduced such ideas to a moral relativism.[18] On the other, where inquiries were not reduced to causal explanation, they were limited to either historical forms of literary criticism[19] that were divorced from the present or philosophical inquiries into the logical use of concepts.[20] Ultimately, political philosophy was either destroyed in the name of science or reduced to an obscurantist historical endeavor. If it retained the previous modes of grand normative theorizing, it was seen as drawing on discredited modes of reasoning, making it not merely unscientific but anachronistic.[21]

Yet, within a few decades, political philosophy made a miraculous recovery as normative assessment burst back into political discourse. The frequently cited catalyst for this resuscitation in the Anglo-American world was the 1971 publication of John Rawls's *A Theory of Justice*.[22] Rawls broke with political thinking's dogmatic slumber by turning to an account of distributive justice, provoking vigorous debates about normative questions and how societies ought to be ordered.[23] This was not limited to philosophy and elicited a return to normative inquiry in political science, economics, sociology, and other fields dominated by social scientific methodologies.

Less explored than its Anglo-American counterpart, the return of political philosophy in France was sparked by internal forces. While Claude Lefort's work and his 1983 call for a "restoration of political philosophy"[24] appear to have played a leading role, events over the preceding decades opened a pathway to political philosophy. Centrally, during the mid-1970s, French intellectuals "discovered" totalitarianism insofar as it became central to understanding politics. Democracy, understood as the polar opposite of totalitarianism and seemingly a stagnant catchphrase since the nineteenth century, was subject to normative inquiry. At the same time, French Marxism was experiencing a theoretical and practical crisis, undermining the political import of the structuralist Marxism that had played a leading role in the eclipse of political philosophy. In these contexts, political philosophy offered normative tools that could fill the void.[25]

We cannot simply situate Abensour within this return of political philosophy. Indeed, in "What Kind of Return?," he differentiates two opposed returns: "return *to* political philosophy on the on hand, return *of* political things on the other."[26] The return to political philosophy revives a neglected or forgotten academic discipline, intent on rephilosophizing and legitimizing "normal politics." Consequently, Abensour deems it a "restoration," playing on a double signification: the restoration of an academic discipline "as if nothing had happened" in the interregnum; the restoration of the established order through a new intellectual legitimation. As an intellectual exercise, this return represents a diversion that distracts from political events in the present that challenge the status quo. The return of political things embraces such events: "It is no longer the interpreter who chooses to turn to a provisionally erased discourse to bring it back to life, but it is rather political things that are irrupting into the present, interrupting the forgetting that affected them, awaiting a response."[27] Thus, rather than the return to an insular academic discourse legitimizing the established order, the return of political things refers to the emergence of events in the here and now that draw into question that very order on the basis of the needs of humanity. Such an irruption opens the questions of the nature of politics itself.

Leading figures in the French return to political philosophy—what can be termed the historical liberal school associated with Pierre Manent and Marcel Gauchet—took a critical distance from the Rawlsian analytical paradigm, which centered on a philosophically abstracted account in which reason contemplates the meaning of justice by itself, divorced from politics and the realm of discussion.[28] Through this procedure, Rawls displaces politics "by remaindering—punishing, ostracizing, concealing—the moments of dissonance and otherness that disrupt"[29] the order established by abstract reason. Challenging the abstraction contained in this form of "pure" or "ideal" theory, the historical liberal school developed a historically contextualized understanding of the liberal tradition, returning to its genesis in the work of Alexis de Tocqueville, Benjamin Constant, and François Guizot. Yet, this school undertook a similar restoration and displacement, attempting to normalize and stabilize the liberal democratic order. In Gauchet's words: "Two centuries of historical change have not added a single basic principle, a single fundamental rule, to those we have known since the eighteenth century."[30] By going back to a sacrosanct vision, it confines democracy to a bygone era and its bare institutional framework, occluding other forms of democracy that have challenged it in the intervening two centuries.[31] Certainly, the French return to liberalism also emerged in relation to totalitarianism. But it did so only as a means of further legitimating liberal democracy as the sacrosanct contrary of totalitarianism. In these respects, it reiterated the general response to totalitarianism that was limited to, in Samuel Moyn's words, "defining an aberrant regime for the sake of ratifying a liberal democratic norm and of stigmatizing the 'totalitarian enemy.'"[32] Consequently, the historical liberal school succumbs to an uncritical endorsement of liberal democracy, culminating in a triumphant proclamation that, despite needing to be managed and administered, liberal democracy is the inescapable horizon of all politics.[33]

Political Things and the Critique of Totalitarianism

"We were expecting a tumultuous theory of freedom, but we ended up with a fainted-hearted theory of moderation, or even worse, normalization," writes Abensour.[34] As he argues in "Modern Political Philosophy and Emancipation," political philosophy and modernity express a mutual crisis. Addressing this crisis requires reasserting the *political* status of political philosophy against the normalization of the existing order. In turning his attention to political things that challenge normal politics, Abensour adopts a phenomenology of the political, attempting to understand the return of political things "unclouded by philosophy."[35] As he argues in "Hannah Arendt against Political Philosophy?," classical political philosophy, starting with Plato, presents an opposition between philosophy (the *vita contemplativa*) and politics (the *vita activa*). Rather than representing an objective mode of knowledge, philosophers adopted a corporate gaze that reflected a "disdain for human affairs" and asserted the domination of those who know over those without knowledge. This inaugurates the sovereignty of philosophy and philosophical knowledge over politics, whereby the latter is subject to a new form of domination (the command-obedience relationship) in which philosophy dominates and commands the world of human affairs.

In the manifestoes to his "Critique de la politique" book series, Abensour asserts the need to rethink politics through the critique of domination that emerges from the return of political things, namely, emancipatory social movements challenging gods and masters. This begins with "a conversion of the gaze" such that one can "relearn to see"[36] against philosophy's clouding of political vision. Rather than the gaze of the philosopher looking down on the realm of politics and dismissing the many, it requires writing "about politics from the side of the dominated, those who are from below and for whom the state of emergency is the rule."[37] Elsewhere, Abensour refers to this as "the choice of the negligible"[38]—those excluded and neglected—which entails resisting or refusing the totalizing tendencies of classical political philosophy. In service to its contempt for the dominated, classical political philosophy imposes a totalizing logic on the people via the sovereignty of philosophical truth over the polis. This philosopher's gaze structures the narratives of identitarian totality contained in the end of history narratives, which demand a normalization of the existing order devoid of alterity or change. The choice of the negligible would allow the gaze to see otherwise,[39] opposing assimilation into the totality and allowing the dominated and politics to appear in their singularity.[40]

Through this changed gaze, political things return and draw into question so-called normal politics. Abensour argues that the events spurring this return of political things for his generation were the Algerian War and the experience of totalitarianism. The Algerian War illustrated the oligarchic and authoritarian tendencies of France's purportedly democratic regime,[41] showing that liberal democracies were not merely founded in inequality and violence but depended upon their continued deployment.[42] Indeed, far from being an open regime, France's liberal democracy sought to suppress challenges and it showed its inability to come to terms with political things except through legitimation of the established order and authoritarian repression of dissent.[43] On the other hand, the inability to inquire into the internal dynamics of liberal democracy's oligarchic and authoritarian tendencies was justified precisely by its attempts to situate itself as the peaceful alternative to totalitarianism. Hence, liberal democracy was treated as unquestionable.

At the same time, totalitarianism was not grasped as a fundamentally unique phenomenon and was instead reduced to another iteration of tyranny or authoritarianism. As Abensour argues in "On a Misinterpretation of Totalitarianism and Its Effects" and "On Compactness: Architecture and Totalitarian Regimes," totalitarianism represents a unique form of domination that discloses the nature of politics, precisely through its attempt to suppress the possibility of political things. In elaborating on this in "On a Misinterpretation," he challenges the "politicization" thesis, which sees totalitarianism as an excess of politics or a maximal politicization of life. Such a claim is predicated on the division between private and public and sees totalitarianism as invading or saturating the private sphere, making it public or political. This leads to the conclusion that we need to rid ourselves of "politics," which can be nothing other than domination. Against this, Abensour argues that the politicization thesis confuses politics with totalitarianism's transformation of everything into an ideology driven by a single-party imposing itself on the social order. He cites Rousseau to the effect that "everything depends radically on politics." Far from signifying that "everything is politics," this suggests a connection between different instances in the sense that society is instituted and thus shaped through its interrelation with the political and vice versa.[44]

In developing his understanding of the political, Abensour draws on Claude Lefort's concept of "the political institution of the social": the idea that all societies are instituted and "politics," far from being derivative or causally produced by something external to it, has a heterogenous and indissoluble character. Lefort distinguishes the political, as a realm of conflict and social division (the originary division of the social), from politics, as society's means of holding itself together and representing its unity or wholeness.[45] As Abensour elaborates: "the social and the political form an indissoluble couple, inasmuch as the political, as the 'leading framework' of a mode of human coexistence, is a response, a position-taking in relation to the originary division of the social, a division that is of the very being of the social."[46] Ultimately, the social is not a homogenous, stable, or determining entity and politics is not something that stabilizes a preexisting social.[47] Rather, the social is instituted and, in being so, is not subject to an external logic but is constantly in the process of being shaped and giving meaning to collective life, which emerges out of division and plurality. As James D. Ingram explains Lefort's formulation: "politics in the broad sense involves not only the shaping (*mise-en-forme*) of collective life, the self-production and reproduction of society, but also the staging (*mise-en-scène*), the self-representation and interpretation of those relations. Only the two together, collective relations and actors' understandings of them, give (objective) form and (subjective) meaning (*mise-en-sens*) to society."[48] Building on this, Abensour understands a political regime as a way of life, which distinguishes different regimes "by the mode of generation and the representation of power" they enact, which connects the form of government to "the ways of living in a society,"[49] including the institution of social bonds. Pace the politicization thesis, Abensour refuses to confuse the criticism of a *particular* institution of the social—and one predicated upon a novel form of domination—with political institution in general.

In explaining the political institution of the social, Lefort argued that democracy institutes itself while acknowledging the gap between society and its self-representation in the political. On the other hand, totalitarianism refuses this gap, representing society as self-same and attempting to eradicate alterity through terror and violence.[50] As Abensour argues in "On Compactness," this raises the question of the social bond and what image of society totalitarianism mobilizes. Politics exists where "paradoxical bonds of division can be formed" via a relationship of "friendship-freedom" constituted by "all ones" or a plurality and being-together within difference that acknowledges the singularity of individuals.[51] But totalitarianism's image of society and its correlative social bond is based on an identitarian totality or a fused homogeneity that eradicates plurality and individual singularity. Consequently, totalitarianism aims to suppress both the space between subjects and the public space where they can appear. Hence, it aims at "compactness" or compression of space and subjects. Compactness involves the "elimination of all in-between space and therefore also all political space for creating the new," ultimately opposing "the *porous* or *porosity* that, thanks to an incomplete fabric, would open up spaces of liberty, or rather spaces celebrating the marriage of liberty and play."[52] Totalitarianism enacts the movement of a compact and fused mass "that presses together individuals" to establish the movement of "all One" as a "unitarian totality."[53] This requires both the erasure of the space between individuals to produce an internal homogeneity and the production of a "*residual* space" that ejects or rejects "the 'parasites,' the 'waste' that it is best to eliminate because they may damage the integrity of the body."[54] Uniting the compact mass as an all One allows for their mobilization via the heteronomous power of the party-leader that seeks to create the compact mass and mobilize it through "scenes of substitution," which act as a simulacrum that replaces autonomous action. Given all of this, Abensour draws the conclusion that totalitarianism is a nonregime, because it blocks "the constitution of all political bonds as well as the constitution of a space between humans within which their double quality of being-for-freedom and being-for-beginning can appear."[55]

Towards a Critical-Utopian Political Philosophy

After the experience of totalitarianism, Abensour posits not merely the rediscovery of the political as an ineradicable domain of human life but, in its aftermath, the need to "reconstruct the political sphere that remains the condition of possibility of a new experience of freedom."[56] This does not equate with a normalization of liberal democracy. Rather, Abensour sees the emergence of post-totalitarian liberal democracy as colonized by the vestiges of the totalitarian experience in the continued apoliticism or extinction of politics that emerges with neoliberalism, which displaces politics by reducing it to a form of corporate governance or technocratic management of the economy.[57] This ignores or suppresses the return of political things, which irrupt in the here and now precisely "in the moment that totalitarian domination breaks apart" expressing "the need for politics"[58] against such apoliticism or anti-politics. Reconstructing the political requires recreating the conditions of possibility of political action and political space, including new social bonds capable of mobilizing democratic subjects and expanding the spaces within which they might appear.[59]

In "Hannah Arendt against Political Philosophy?," Abensour explores what this new mode of politics entails by sketching out an exit from the constrictions of classical political philosophy. Classical political philosophy enacts a series of transformations that destroy political action. This begins with the reduction of the *polis* to the *oikos*, which transforms "politics" into a means to the reproduction of life. Such a reduction carries within itself the transformation of action (understood both as "to begin" and "to act") into the command-obedience relationship, modeled on the relations of domination found in the household. The resulting politics institutes an inegalitarian order reducible to a means-end framework in which some command and others execute. Finally, classical political philosophy places an emphasis on the unity of the *polis*, undermining the ontological condition of plurality. Rediscovering politics—recreating the space of politics—requires recuperating the political possibilities that have been effaced by these transformations. Hence, it starts with the notion of philosophical wonderment and the possibility of action, as a new beginning and, more specifically, as a heroic birth of acting-in-concert.

Building on this pathway, "For a Critical Political Philosophy?" presents a systematic account of Abensour's critical-utopian political philosophy.[60] Critical-utopian political philosophy focuses on two areas of inquiry—the nature of servitude-domination and the possibility of emancipation—in the service of answering "the political question *par excellence*" posed by Spinoza and La Boétie: "Why do people fight for their servitude as if it is for their salvation?"[61] Indeed, natality and politics do not emerge out of nothing: they confront the situation of the existing world and its forms of domination and attempt to institute new social bonds in the service of emancipation. But, in considering a domination-emancipation coupling, Abensour confronts an intellectual impasse between critical theory, with its focus on domination, and a political paradigm, with its focus on emancipation. The problem lies in reducing politics to a binary opposition whereby politics becomes a domain of domination *or* emancipation,[62] without accounting for the interconnection between the two. To overcome this, Abensour undertakes a process of salvaging each perspective by drawing them into a critical constellation to transcend their unilateralisms.[63]

The critical theory of the first generation of the Frankfurt School undertook the project of unmasking domination in all its forms. This begins with the claim that the distinction between domination and exploitation cannot be collapsed nor can the political simply be derived from the economic, such that the transformation of the economy would eradicate domination. Even after economic revolutions, domination can remain untouched. The connected claim is the need to understand that human societies have been constituted by the political division between dominant and dominated groups or between those who command and those who must obey. While this takes on economic forms, it is not reducible to them, and domination constitutes a more expansive understanding of these relations. Domination has three overlapping levels. First, the domination of nature, including the reduction of nature to an instrumental object to be used and dominated for human purposes. Second, the domination of humans by humans, including—but not limited to—the control of human labor in the process of dominating nature. Third, the domination of internal nature, such that human subjects become acclimated to the system of domination through the internalization of existing social structures. This last form is central, as critical theorists see domination as being interiorized via "the complex interplay taking place between culture, stable institutions, and the psychic or interior apparatus."[64] But here we find critical theory's unilateralism: in breaking with Hegel's and

Marx's developmental unfolding, it sees "permanent domination, its regular repetition in history," abridging the possibility of emancipation and veering towards catastrophism. On the one hand, this catastrophism emerges in critical theory's tendency to eschew the question of emancipation in favor of the critique of domination.[65] On the other, it appears in the association of politics with domination, which internalizes the politicization thesis and the idea that "emancipation consisted not in the establishment of a free political community but in the liberation from politics."[66]

Against this, the political paradigm returns us to Lefort's account of the political institution of the social and the idea that all societies are instituted. The heterogeneity of the political indicates not its insularity but its irreducibility to, and lack of causal determinacy by, other spheres of life or by the march of a heteronomous metaphysics. As a result, the political paradigm refuses to associate politics with domination. Arendt is symptomatic. In her analysis of the Greek *polis*, she situates domination not on the side of politics but in the private sphere of the *oikos*, which is subject to multiple forms of domination-servitude (master-slave, husband-wife, father-children). By contrast, politics is associated with freedom from the realm of domination and found outside, in the realm of equals (*isonomia*) in the *agora*. Hence, Abensour argues, the political paradigm asserts a difference or antithesis between domination and politics: "where there is politics, that is to say the experience of freedom, domination tends to disappear; inversely, where domination reigns, the political is effaced from human experience and becomes the object of a project of destruction."[67] Freedom becomes possible again through the political, after totalitarianism's attempt to destroy the conditions of politics as freedom. But the political paradigm succumbs to its own unilateralism insofar as it "forgets" or "occludes" the fact of domination—it presents politics-freedom outside of domination, as though it occurs without tensions. Indeed, while recognizing totalitarian domination, after its disappearance the political paradigm risks viewing political space in idealized terms, without domination and conflict, as though regression were not possible. By ignoring the fragility of politics and emancipation, the political paradigm threatens to fall into an irenicism: in seeing politics as operating within a smoothed out, peaceful space, the political paradigm regresses into a linear intersubjectivity that effaces plurality through regression into consensus, ignoring domination and the unruly nature of political things in their challenge to the status quo.

Refusing the binary between these two positions, Abensour's critical-utopian political philosophy instead chooses "the option of articulation" asserting a permanent dialectic between domination and emancipation, with domination eliciting the irruption of political things that attempt to break its hold. This begins with the distinction between politics and totalitarianism, such that politics and emancipation are not separated, or politics and domination are not reduced to the same thing. Rather, politics involves the possibility of freedom as the institution of new social bonds predicated upon plurality and the opening of political space. But, in order to avoid the simplistic binary of totalitarianism-democracy or totalitarianism-freedom, Abensour acknowledges that political forms are subject to degeneration: that friendship-freedom is always threatened by the fragility of the political. Hence, against the political paradigm's presentation of the political after totalitarianism, democratic regimes can regress into new forms of domination that are not totalitarian. At the same time, against critical theory, we must acknowledge that far from being an iron cage, the political can be reinstituted against domination, opening new possibilities of emancipation. Ultimately, then, domination is not a single thread running throughout history: "Domination is rather thought as a complex dimension, historically specific, historically recurrent in the life of human beings, but which can be transformed, which ought to be transformed by them."[68] Abensour sees the domination-emancipation couplet as a permanent dialectic at the center of political existence, with new instantiations of domination reopening in projects of emancipation that challenge domination.

A Politics of Emancipation: Democracy and Utopia

For Abensour, the two lynchpins of emancipation are democracy and utopia, which represent modes of reinstituting and reopening the political in the face of domination's repetition and its attempt to close political space. With the 2011 translation of *Democracy against the State: Marx and the Machiavellian Moment* and E. P. Thompson's influential overview of Abensour's concept of the "education of desire" in the postscript to the 1976 edition of Thompson's *William Morris: Romantic to Revolutionary*,[69] democracy and utopia are the most familiar elements of Abensour's work to anglophone audiences. But, given the lack of English-language translations of most of his work, a full reception of his contributions to thinking democracy and utopia has been stunted, producing gaps in the secondary literature.

While much of contemporary democratic theory has focused on the institutional procedures of democracy, Abensour contributes to the radical democratic turn[70] by theorizing democracy as a mode of action that constantly challenges hierarchically imposed modes of order via permanent contestation.[71] In elaborating his theory of insurgent democracy in *Democracy against the State*, Abensour posits a fundamental antagonism between the demos, as the originary and indeterminate political subject, and the State, as an institution controlled by the Few who wield power over the demos. Ultimately, the State is a reified, hierarchical, heteronomous institution and relation (an all One)[72] that portrays itself as the universal representation of the people while holding them in subjection and fostering passivity. Against this oligarchic order, Abensour understands democracy as an insurgent action that blocks or ruptures attempts to efface the demos's indeterminacy. In the process of blocking, democracy opens an antagonism between the all One and all ones, seeking to institute an intersubjective space via "the passage from power *over* human beings to power *with* and *between* human beings, the *between* being the place where the possibility of a common world is won."[73] This distinguishes the sovereign power contained in the State as a relation of command-obedience from "the bond of division" as a horizontal relation of being-together. But, remaining attentive to the "Machiavellian moment," insurgent democracy acknowledges a permanent antagonism at the heart of political life, embracing the temporality of any political experience and the dialectic of emancipation, which battles both the old regime and the new state *in statu nascendi*.[74]

"E. P. Thompson's Passion" presents a case study of insurgent democracy and its form of plebeian politics. Indeed, Abensour reads Thompson not simply as a historian but a "political writer," whose account of "culture, ethics, and modes of sociability and solidarity could not be dissociated from the *political resistance* the working class put up against other classes." This political inflection on class—class as constituted by and in the moment of struggle—sought to combat deterministic elements that stripped the working class of agency. More specific to insurgent democracy, Thompson's *The Making of the English Working Class* shows how these forms of struggle emerge "*outside* power" in attempting to institute new modes of life and human collective action. This begins with the production of a plebeian public sphere, which constitutes not the entrance of the "uneducated people" into the public sphere, as Jürgen Habermas argues, but the attempt to produce another type of public sphere rooted in a different culture. This egalitarian and inclusive plebeian public sphere emerges in spaces of working-class existence, challenging the dominant discourse and its constitutional embodiments that seek to exclude the working class. At the same time as they challenge their exclusions, the working class formed new modes of solidarity and mutuality, beginning with the announcement of the London Corresponding Society "That the number of our Members be unlimited."[75] Challenging the appropriation of power by the propertied classes, English plebeianism sought not merely to end the exclusivity of the public sphere, but to multiply multiplicity—to open "the search for diversity" in refusing "any homogenizing unification." But this also involves expanding the plebeian public sphere or challenging the "strict separation of the political and the social" in seeing "the places of production as one of the places for expressing the political."

Thompson's introduction of Abensour's work on utopia to anglophone audiences, and the subsequent adoption of Thompson's reading by Raymond Williams[76] and other leading figures in the field of utopian studies, led the education of desire to become a foundational idea,[77] helping to inaugurate the idea of "critical utopias."[78] While critics portrayed utopia as tantamount to totalitarianism in closing off the space of the political,[79] they largely focused on "blueprint models" and the attempts to construct a "perfect" and harmonious world. Against this, Abensour discerns the emergence of a "new utopian spirit" after 1848, which internalized plurality and temporality and adopted a "heuristic" mode of thinking.[80] As a result, the function of utopian texts shifted from portraying ideal worlds to aiming at the "education of desire":

> The point is not for utopia . . . to assign "true" or "just" goals to desire but rather to educate desire, to stimulate it, to awaken it—not to assign it a goal but to open a path for it. . . . Desire must be taught to desire, to desire better, to desire more, and above all to desire otherwise; it must learn to shatter the dead weight, to alleviate the weakness of appetence, to liberate the firebirds of desire, to give free reign to the impulse of adventure.[81]

Ultimately, utopian texts aimed to open something beyond the given by inspiring the desire for a better world, as well as inspiring the subjectivities that could create it. Moreover, against the monological imposition embodied in blueprint models, the new utopian spirit maintained a dialogical core that sought to provoke a conversation about freedom and justice via nonhierarchical social bonds attuned to plurality and difference.

Because Abensour's work on Morris remained untranslated until 1999, the understanding of the "education of desire" in the Anglo-American context remained wedded to Thompson's account. But, as Christine Nadir argues, Thompson's reading led to a serious misinterpretation reproduced by subsequent scholars: they viewed desire merely as the driving force of utopian aspirations, ignoring Abensour's central political contention that attempts at emancipation produce new forms of domination, with emancipation and domination forming a persistently oscillating pair. Not only did Abensour reject seeing desire as a panacea for utopia,[82] he argued that the desire for emancipation could produce the desire for domination.[83] Abensour develops this point in "The New Utopian Spirit." The new utopian spirit internalized the dialectic of emancipation in an attempt "to identify the blind spots of emancipation, or the centers or nodes in which this reversal takes place and the repetition begins."[84] Abensour situates this blindspot in "the fear of the outside" or "the fear of otherness," which drives utopian thought towards closure. While avoiding this regression requires that we "act *as if* the catastrophe was a permanent threat," it also requires refusing the ontologization of this judgment, which would establish the permanence of catastrophe. Ultimately, against closure, utopian thinking must retain an *écart absolu* (absolute gap) embracing the idea that something else is possible—including utopia's utopia, or its transformation via the permanence of utopian striving.

We can link this to "The Utopian Conversion," which explores how desire is educated as part of the process of what Tom Moylan refers to as "becoming utopian"[85]—the production of a utopian subjectivity. The basic idea contained in the education of desire was that one needed to be taught to desire otherwise and to desire utopia. This conversion to utopia (or towards a utopian disposition) is necessitated by the established order, which appears as a "crushing force" that renders resistance "unthinkable, if not by acts immediately accused of 'madness' or 'crime.' "[86] While Abensour's work on Morris focused on how literary texts enact such a change, "The Utopian Conversion" expands this[87] in seeing two other means of being detached—via doubt and separation—from this oppressive established order. The first means, which Abensour draws from Levinas, is the phenomenological epoché that, in bracketing or interrupting the established order, gives "life to silenced voices, suppressed by the world's knowledge."[88] This involves both reopening lost horizons and turning to the intersubjective realm of proximity or the other against the sovereignty and primacy of the I. The second means, which Abensour draws from Benjamin, is the dialectical image. While this begins with the analysis of collective dreams of classless society, it requires a critical gaze to avoid falling into myth. Hence, Benjamin's dialectical image involves a moment of psychoanalytic deconstruction and interpretation, as well as the awakening that can herald a revolution via the interpenetration of Old and New. Drawing this back to embracing alterity as a means to avoiding the dialectic of emancipation, the alterity of the other and the nonidentity and recurrence of the image of the classless society act to disrupt or challenge utopia's regression into the sovereignty and identity-thinking that would capsize into new forms of domination.

Beyond the formal separation of utopia and democracy, and against accepted *doxa*, Abensour undertakes another articulation, between democracy and utopia, asserting their interconnection in theorizing emancipation as a democratic-utopian project.[89] Their seeming contradiction lies in the fact that democracy is a "form of political institution," while utopia appears to be "apolitical, even anti-political, insofar as it is a search for a harmonious, reconciled society, to the point of getting rid of the political."[90] Abensour sees democracy and utopia as having overlapping emancipatory projects, namely, the attempt at establishing a condition of nondomination. But each does so through a path that can help to correct the other, allowing for a process of "democratizing utopia" and "utopianizing democracy."[91]

In "The New Utopian Spirit," Abensour argues that utopia must distance itself from "the image or myth of a reconciled society, of a social world in full harmony with itself." The new utopian spirit emerged after 1848 through an internalization of democratic plurality, challenging the substitutionism and authoritarianism of previous utopias. By internalizing democratic plurality, the new utopian spirit turned to a dialogical mode of utopianizing, which preserved the indeterminacy and intersubjectivity at the heart of the democratic project. At the same time, democracy must be utopianized to avoid regressing into normal politics, a tendency that emerges with the binary pairing totalitarianism-democracy in which any form of the latter is justified by virtue of not being the former. Abensour raises this concern in "Letter from a 'Revoltist' to Marcel Gauchet, Convert to 'Normal Politics.'" He argues that Gauchet endorses a singular revolution, the founding of democracy as an institution from below. But Gauchet then severs the connection between democracy and revolution or revolt. Ultimately, democracy is the outcome of a revolution but then becomes normal politics, allying itself with reaction and counterrevolution and, in rejecting any further revolutions, closing the utopian gap in presenting society as reconciled with itself. Against this, Abensour asserts the need to inflect democracy with a utopian element, preserving alterity and continual innovation—the preservation of the absolute gap—so that democracy never coincides with itself, challenging its own foundations in being remade to establish new modes of democratic-utopian life that, against pacification or instituted forms, expand the realm of nondomination.

Ultimately, the democratic-utopian is a permanent insurgence that demands continual transformation towards nondomination.

Abensour's emphasis on this permanent insurgence has been the most frequently criticized element of his work. On the one hand, insurgent democracy has been subject to a criticism that is directed at radical democracy as a whole: it is episodic or "revoltist," tied to negativity without (or without theorizing) a positive moment and thus incapable of concerning itself with the creation of an institutional infrastructure. In other words, it produces a dualistic binary between insurgence and institution, privileging forms of disruption.[92] On the other hand, critics have argued that Abensour's work on utopia, and critical utopias in general, place an emphasis on unmasking or exposing the ideological contours of existing societies without positing an alternative model or new modes of living, emphasizing merely the new values that would be abided by, such as plurality and openness. This reduces the utopian project to a disruptive ideology critique that refuses a positive content or even to distinguish between "good" and "bad" utopias.[93]

These lines of criticism fail to grasp the methodological articulations—between critical theory and the political paradigm, and between democracy and utopia—that inform Abensour's thought. Hence, the claim that his work only theorizes disruptive negativity ignores that, against critical theory, the political paradigm demands that we think the possibilities of emancipation beyond the critique of domination. Insurgent democracy embodies this in demanding forms of political objectification and the production of new modes of life and horizontal social bonds, which is specifically connected to the influence the tradition of council democracy and its institutional forms have exerted on Abensour's work.[94] Moreover, the utopian moment of Abensour's thought supplies a positive content beyond the negation enacted by the demos. As Abensour states: "Utopia reconstructs the social destroyed by capitalism and the state, multiplying small communities 'behind the state's back' and against the state in order to remake the social fabric, to reconstitute it, to remake the social bond."[95] Even beyond notions of "small groups" or "laboratories of utopia," "The Utopian Conversion" asserts that revolution, and the everyday practices that contribute to it, are weapons of utopia, as seen in the French Revolution, which exhibited a utopian epoché that suspended the symbolic markers of the Ancien Régime, allowing for the flowering of "fraternal disorder"—"the open experimentation of a new being-in-the-world and a new being-together."[96]

Turning specifically to the problem of institution, we need to keep in mind that Abensour's work is informed by another articulation, this time between insurgency and institution. Critics have called into question Abensour's emancipatory project because of its insurgency. Yet, radical politics confronts the opposite problem: it can become "formal" (or "normal") rather than "extraordinary,"[97] which tends towards political alienation in depriving the demos of agency. Insurgency arises precisely because of the lack of democracy—it emerges against institutions of domination, as well as against normal politics. Drawing on Merleau-Ponty, Abensour sees institution as giving experience "a sustainable dimension" that produces "a creative, innovative (in the Bergsonian sense) duration."[98] Thus, institution constitutes not so much a resistance to change as a "launch pad" towards action, including resurrecting the originally insurgent quality of democratic institutions.[99] The "Letter from a 'Revoltist' " further elaborates this dynamic. Abensour challenges the accommodation to normal politics for accepting "institutions with openly authoritarian tendencies" as democracy becomes a framework and a state-form. This represents a de-utopianizing of democracy, which allows for authoritarian regressions. Ultimately, insurgency is necessary to expand democratic space against the order of domination, both old and new—and precisely because of the threat of new forms of domination, such insurgency must persist. In these respects, Abensour emphasizes insurgency as both a utopianizing of democracy, which never lets democracy stagnate into a framework, and democratizing of democracy, which seeks to constantly expand the horizontal relations of being-together in new spheres.

Far from lacking a "positive" framework or rejecting institutions, Abensour sees the democratic-utopian as a persistent project, never identical with itself and thus reemerging in time and space precisely because—against closure or the dialectic of emancipation—emancipation is partial, alternating between fulfillment and defeat. Every overcoming must therefore be subject to critical interrogation to ascertain the need for subsequent emancipatory forms against authoritarian regression and the passivity of normal politics. This preliminary quality is modeled on Theodor Adorno's negative dialectics: negation without regressing into an identity thinking that would occlude difference. Ultimately, Abensour acknowledges all action as contextual and situated in time, subject to an interrogation of its own conditions of possibility—with each instantiation being the condition of possibility for new instantiations. As Morris writes in *A Dream of John Ball*: "Men fight and lose the battle, and the thing that they fought for comes about in spite of their defeat, and when it comes turns out not to be what they meant, and other men have to fight for what they meant under another name."[100]

Abensour Today:
The Project of a Critical-Utopian Political Philosophy

Abensour's critical-utopian political philosophy charts out a new path—a new gaze, new points of entry, a new mode of reading—for political philosophy, one that distances itself from the classical tradition. In asserting the irreducible nature of politics, he demands that we pay attention to the return of political things that burst into the here and now, opening the possibility of emancipation against the forces of domination. While Abensour often conducted this inquiry through a subversive engagement with preeminent and marginal sources of political philosophy, his intention was to address the aporias of his own time, excavating from these sources insights as to how the resurgent needs of humanity might be addressed during times of crisis. Hence, his reading of political philosophy sought not an insular contribution to the return to political philosophy but to understand the experiences of, and dialectic between, domination and emancipation that structured seminal political moments, including the French Revolution's regression into Thermidor;[101] the suppression of the Paris Commune of 1871 in a bloody restoration;[102] the council democracy of the early days of the October Revolution giving way to Soviet totalitarianism,[103] which was in turn challenged by the rise of anti-totalitarian movements, culminating in the Hungarian uprising of 1956;[104] and the Algerian War and the increasingly authoritarian nature of the French Fifth Republic[105] paving the way for the irruption of May 68 in Paris.[106] Critical-utopian political philosophy focuses on the persistent tension between emancipation and new forms of domination, while trying to understand the gaps or spaces where emancipation might become, if not permanent, prolonged.

But what does this mean for us today? What can Abensour's work and the project of a critical-utopian political philosophy tell us about our current political moment, as well as future ones? At the more obvious level, we can turn to the continuation of the dialectic of emancipation over the past two decades. Hence, we must continue the ruthless critique of domination in all of its forms, including considering whether new forms constitute the repetition of domination or the qualitative emergence of new modes. In the contemporary moment, this directs our attention to the continuation and mutation of neoliberalism, as well as the rise of alt-right, neofascist, and authoritarian movements. But, lest we fall into catastrophism, we must simultaneously and equally look to the moments that challenge domination and open the possibility of emancipation, including Occupy Wall Street, the Arab and Maple Springs, Idle No More, Black Lives Matter, Nuit Debout, anti-pipeline protests in North America, anti-austerity movements, and endless other movements, moments, and actions across the globe.[107]

Yet, in continuing the project of a critical-utopian political philosophy, we must be mindful of Abensour's distinction between the return to political philosophy and the return of political things. We must focus on the latter and avoid the proliferation of an insular scholarly discourse and the production of an institution around the name "Abensour," divorced from political things and their continuing emergence. A fidelity to critical-utopian political philosophy requires infidelity in the form of "interpretive experiments"[108] that liberate Abensour's own texts and insights from such an institutionalization and intellectual reification—as well as from Abensour's own points of entry and concerns. By acknowledging every text as fragile and structured by an alterity or nonidentity that unseats its stability,[109] we can subject them to a hermeneutics of emancipation that goes beyond the text's original meaning. This form of fidelity-by-infidelity was the meaning Abensour ascribed to "disciples" of utopia:

> The true disciple is the one who, away from existing cultural lines, takes up the movement at the origin of the discovery of the new continent and he does not relentlessly follow the same route to take possession of the same continent. A secret thread connects initial dissent with renewed dissent. . . . The true disciple is the one who resumes the march towards the unknown, and not the one who brings the unknown into the already known. Instead of defining and trivializing the path, creating a new axiomatic, recentering what has been decentered, the true disciple accentuates the decentering, breaks with orthodoxy, reactivating the initial energy of departure and sets sail, if necessary, to a new continent. . . . It follows that true disciples are heretics.[110]

Heretical action requires a fidelity to political things and the movement towards emancipation but it also requires unsettling Abensour's thought, to more adequately contribute to the critique of domination and the project of emancipation that his critical-utopian political philosophy aims to herald.

To follow Abensour's path is to pursue the project of the merciless critique of domination and the constant search for emancipation in the context of our own return of political things. While Abensour provides guideposts for addressing these questions, guideposts can also become identitarian restrictions—they can become traffic signs that suppress the intention of the "open work." Hence, fidelity to Abensour would also involve infidelity in the sense of going beyond his work, opening up the critique of domination and the project of emancipation in places that he insufficiently addressed or that he simply overlooked, while also exploring texts and traditions that he neglected but that could contribute to critical-utopian political philosophy.[111] Ultimately, the importance of Abensour's work lies not primarily in this or that argument, but in compelling us to participate in the critique of domination and the project of emancipation. This involves seeing Abensour's work not merely as elaborating on the idea that utopian texts aim to educate desire, but that his elaboration on the education of desire simultaneously seeks to educate the desire of his readers: to teach them "to desire, to desire better, to desire more, and above all to desire otherwise," giving "free reign to the impulse of adventure"[112] so we can continue the project of decentering and set sail for the unknown place of emancipation.

Part I

The Return of Political Things

Chapter 1

Manifesto for the "Critique de la Politique" Book Series, Éditions Payot

(1974)

The critique of political economy does not and cannot include the critique of politics, which was an integral and distinct part of the young Marx's project in his great 1843 and 1844 texts. Here we aim to recover this lost, or perhaps deliberately obscured, dimension. The critique of politics is based on the essential distinction between domination and exploitation. These are two different phenomena. As a separate concept, domination cannot be reduced to exploitation, nor should it be considered a by-product of it, even if those who suggest this concede the relative autonomy of politics.

The central object of the critique of politics is the historical structures of domination-slavery. In addition, the critique of politics is defined:

- by the rejection of political sociology, which is one example of a field that suppresses the critical questions established by political philosophy: claiming to build a science of politics, it tries to make politics into a science;

- by the choice of a point of view: writing about politics from the side of the dominated, those who are from below and for whom the state of emergency is the rule;

Translated by Devin Penner. Originally published as "Critique de la politique," in Max Horkheimer, *Éclipse de la raison* (Paris: Payot, 1974). Translated from "Critique de la politique," in *Pour une philosophie politique critique* (Paris: Sens & Tonka, 2009), 49–51.

- by the brilliantly formulated question of La Boétie: Why does the dominated majority not revolt?

Aiming to break new ground, this critical effort develops in three main directions:

A social critique of domination that moves away from politicization, and, following the Frankfurt School, begins with the hypothesis of a tendency towards total domination in the contemporary world, no matter what the political regime. Going beyond ideological justifications, this critique tries to reveal the new forms of domination associated with the displacement of politics and the universal rule of bureaucracy. Because structures of domination are contingent constructions, an investigation into the genealogy of historical forms of politics is required. The resulting criticism will not limit its focus to the State, but will rather be as polymorphous and diverse as the complex structures of domination it seeks to uncover.

A critique of political reason examining the great historical texts that have constituted this reason. This effort will bring to life theoretical critiques of politics, and, moreover, will question the blind spots of Western political thought, looking at the relation of philosophy and politics and identifying the theoretical roots of domination.

A reconstruction of the practical critiques of politics, namely, those of social movements that, faithful to *neither God nor Master*, attacked the very structure of domination and, rather than installing a new coercive power, tried to abolish the division between masters and slaves during various historical insurrections and revolutions.

While many modernist currents seek to rehabilitate politics, the task of the Critique of Politics series is to listen to projects that attempt to break the "chains of slavery." The aim here is to challenge the endeavors that confuse the subversion of society with the transformation or modernization of the State, and thus under the guise of political emancipation block the path to human emancipation.

Chapter 2

New Manifesto for the "Critique de la Politique" Book Series, Éditions Klincksieck

(2016)

Established by Miguel Abensour and directed by Michèle Cohen-Halimi, the Critique of Politics series aims to highlight and deepen the opposition between the political and the state.

The series explores different forms of nonstate political relationships or political bonds that exist outside of the State. In this regard, we follow Étienne La Boétie's invaluable distinction, in his *Discourse on Voluntary Servitude*, between two forms of totalities: the *all One* [*Tous-Un*], or the State, versus the political community of *all ones* [*Tous-uns*] or the Against One.

Contra the return of political philosophy, which gave birth to a philosophy of restoration, the Critique of Politics series is dedicated to developing a critical political philosophy. It is defined by three questions:

1. The question of Spinoza, inherited from La Boétie: Why do people fight for their servitude as if it is for their salvation? This is the political question *par excellence*, and it is destined to remain as such.

Translated by Devin Penner. Originally published as and translated from the web page for the book series "Critique de la politique," Éditions Klincksieck, 2016, https://www.klincksieck.com/les-livres/collection/95-critique-de-la-politique.

2. What constitutes critical political philosophy? "Critique of Politics" proposes an articulation between the critique of domination, such as that of the first critical theory (Adorno, Horkheimer, Marcuse), and political thought that engages the formulation of Rousseau: "Everything depends radically on politics."[1] This articulation suggests that politics, as an experience of freedom, is practiced and necessarily thought of as a break with domination.

3. What are the conditions of possibility for a politics of human emancipation?

We address these questions through a double critical-utopian movement:

- A critique of new forms of domination, which are all the more misleading or fallacious inasmuch as they profess to pursue freedom and justice.

- The option of utopia, because to give up on utopia is to accept the established order, "a kind of coherence, a hellish unity" (Adorno),[2] "it is to give up on the inextinguishable thirst for justice and on the demand for it now" (Françoise Proust).[3]

Chapter 3

Modern Political Philosophy and Emancipation
(1983; republished 2009)

It might seem rather problematic, if not adventurous, to undertake a publication in political philosophy today. By doing so, aren't we indeed necessarily confronting the weightiness of traditions or the arrogance of pretentions that, stemming from different horizons, allegedly share a common desire to oppose a confrontation, or even a simple encounter between philosophy and politics? In the eyes of most philosophers, inasmuch as political philosophy is granted the right to exist, the discipline only belongs to a minor genre, seen as a sort of appendix to philosophical work, or worse, to a mixed genre where the impurity of politics would unduly trouble the serenity or the elevation of philosophy. As for a certain number of political scientists, who, in the fervor of their supposed youth, aspire to build an empirical-analytical science of political phenomena—very often akin to an unstable compound between functionalism and Marxism—they have nothing but contempt for a form of discourse they see as quaint. According to them, convinced as they are of the merit of associating philosophy with ideology, political philosophy is immediately invalidated as it fails to make the principle-based distinction between science and ideology, or it can only be, upon closer inspection, akin to a slightly inane resurgence of morality. Doesn't political philosophy indeed ignore that only a form of knowledge that is ethically neutral deserves the name of science?

Translated by Olivier Ruchet. Originally published as "Présentation," Cahiers de philosophie politique, no. 1 (1983): 3–8. Translated from "Philosophie politique moderne et émancipation," in *Pour une philosophie politique critique* (Paris: Sens & Tonka, 2009), 53–58.

Are these remarks out of place? It is true that over the past decade signs of interest, of desires oriented towards confrontation, towards opening up have manifested themselves; hence the present endeavor does deserve to be undertaken, as it is only valuable if it is heard, and therefore possibly shared.

However, a perspective on the crisis of political philosophy that would be purely institutional and restricted to the French case would be short-sighted—even if the national specificity, very likely related to the eclectic institution of philosophy in the nineteenth century, should not be neglected. The crisis is presently quasi-universal and is located well beyond the threats that assail an academic discipline. Let us listen to Leo Strauss's assessment: "Today, political philosophy is in a state of decay and perhaps of putrefaction, if it has not vanished altogether. Not only is there complete disagreement regarding its subject matter, its methods, and its function; its very possibility in any form has become questionable. . . . We hardly exaggerate when we say that today political philosophy does not exist anymore, except as matter for burial, i.e., for historical research, or else as a theme of weak and unconvincing protestations."[1]

The diagnostic becomes clearer and points to a specific era: the crisis of political philosophy is the crisis of modernity, or if we reverse the proposition, the crisis of modernity would essentially consist in the crisis of modern political philosophy. Such an extravagant, provocative statement might well induce a wave of laughter. However, let us be attentive to Straussian irony: we can already perceive that political philosophy is not fundamentally an academic discipline and remember that the great political philosophers, Socrates, Plato, Xenophon, Aristotle, Machiavelli, Rousseau, were not university professors; we can thus have the premonition that it is about "Old Adam's" destiny, that what the decline of this form of thought is about is nothing but the question of nihilism, or still, the refusal or the acceptance of the intolerable, for instance of the event of 1933.

The conclusion seems obvious: it would be fitting to restore political philosophy, and, to that end, to return to the inaugural moment of the destruction of classical political philosophy, to the beginnings of modern political philosophy, in short to reopen the Quarrel of the Ancients and the Moderns to choose, against the modern project, the party of the Ancients, that of classical political philosophy. Restoration does not mean repetition. As Strauss himself confesses, that "return to the Ancients" can only have an experimental value, since tradition is not immediately applicable, as it stands, to a form of society that is the fruit of the modern project and, as such, totally unknown to the Ancients. We must refrain from transforming into a slogan or a dogmatic program that which aims rather at opening a perspective, a place at a distance from which we can take stock of the modern world.[2]

What is more, the reference to Strauss must not lead astray. If any enterprise in political philosophy must necessarily engage with his work, or better may only establish and affirm itself in a dialogue or a conflict with Strauss—how could we forget the indelible shock that his thought induces in contemporary political theory—it in no way implies that one must subscribe to the Straussian analysis of modernity. Indeed, essential questions remain.

—Should we consider the different foundations of modernity to be homogeneous to one another; can we for instance include under a single rubric—as the modern project—the instituting figures of Machiavelli, Bacon, and Hobbes?

—Can modernity only be thought, as Strauss suggests, under the sign of the loss of the old, of decline, of pettiness—where modern society would be Lilliput—of a narrowing of the horizon? How may such resolutely anti-tyrannical thought remain indifferent to the sudden appearance of a new freedom peculiar to the modern world? Pierre Leroux, acutely aware of the political meaning of the Quarrel of the Ancients and the Moderns, identifies emancipation as the very essence of modernity—a triple emancipation carried by a new affirmation, the creative feeling of "an elevation of Humanity, a sort of divine exaltation of all its faculties"—without in any way ignoring, at the same time, that the fantasy of reconciliation threatens modern emancipation with the creation of a new servitude. What is more, can Strauss unquestionably claim that the modern era understands the human in light of the subhuman rather than the suprahuman? Couldn't a more complex but also more generous view of modernity, sensitive both to the modern opacity and to what transpires through that opacity rather approach our age, with Maurice Merleau-Ponty, as "far from explaining man by the lower as it is by the higher,"[3] and thereby not close the political unto itself but rather open it, from within immanence itself, onto another dimension, such as the dimension of the oeuvre, which confers on the political, in the fashion of the moderns, both irreducibility and relativity, severing it, thanks to that decentering, from the illusion of mastery. Other models of modernity exist, either as unfinished projects or as ambiguous projects where invention, the sudden appearance of the new, rivals repetition.

—Rather than accepting the alternative between political philosophy under the sign of a return to the Ancients or social sciences on the side of the Moderns, wouldn't it be fitting to outline and explore another alternative, classical political philosophy or modern political philosophy, with the premise that the modern project does not necessarily and uniformly lead to a "scientization" of the political? The sensibility to the collapse of a certain form of intelligibility can go hand in hand with an attentiveness to the emergence of another. Thus is the demand born of a quest for the sites or locations from which a modern political philosophy could be elaborated aside from historicism and positivism, for instance on the side of the "Machiavellian moment," or on the side of the critical tradition in German idealism.

It is thus from the perspective of a reactivation, or better of a *reconstruction* that could invent new links to tradition, that we shall pursue our reflection on the idea and the legitimacy of a modern political philosophy that would be a philosophy of freedom and not of virtue. We shall orient our investigations around four main questions.

—How can a modern political philosophy manage to think the consistency of the political without imposing on itself the teleological referent of an order of nature or of the world, but also without contributing to a reduction of the political expressed as a level of totality about which we could edify a regional science? The thesis of the "relative autonomy" that others present as a progress insofar as it would avoid the folding of the political into the economic may be interpreted differently, to wit as a strategic transaction, as a form of sophisticated censorship meant to cross out, under the guise of overdetermination, Rousseau's fundamental proposal according to which "everything depends radically on politics."[4]

Whether in the guise of a phenomenology of action (Hannah Arendt), of an emphasis on the plurality of models of socialization (Jürgen Habermas), or of political thought as instituting the social (Claude Lefort), doesn't a similar determination appear: to recover, to reconquer the irreducible heterogeneity of political matters that can be linked to no natural or material necessity, to no empirical essence, in short, thinking as we are invited to by the contrast between the two cities that inaugurates the *Republic*, the enigma of men living together beyond the reciprocity of needs, beyond the game of interests, beyond the division of labor and its effects, reveals itself by that very gap as a rapport, as the truly human bond. The enigma of human affairs, of the human social bond, which persists or even increases when the political is thought under the figure of voluntary servitude (La Boétie) or under that of the struggle by which we transition from "beasts" to "men" (Machiavelli).

—What do we mean by thinking the political and with the help of which faculty can we think the political without positivizing it and transforming it into a sociological object?

—Which relations can we establish between political philosophy and the social sciences?

—Finally, which transformation, which shift does the question regarding the best regime undergo in modern bodies of thought that, while breaking with the "noble dream" of the classics and dismissing the modern illusion of the good society, still manage to avoid falling back into the positivism of a politics of understanding or into nihilism? Isn't it in the incredible experience of new forms of society and in the attention patiently lent to the questions that emerge in relation to the totalitarian form that a site appears where the question of freedom and the question of democracy may be tempered anew?

Indeed, it goes without saying that a modern political philosophy oriented toward freedom remains inseparable from a critique of domination. Refusing any form of resignation, such a political philosophy, ceaselessly renews with the question destined to remain one, that of human emancipation.

Chapter 4

What Kind of Return?

(1994; republished 2009)

The question proclaimed by the title testifies to a growing unrest—or even a certain malaise—when faced with a certain number of phenomena registered under the label of return. Indeed, what we see reappear does not correspond to what we expected. A case of mistaken identity? That for which we all worked, in scattered fashion, continues to be awaited, or rather instead of a return we see progressively unfolding a *restoration* that might well, in turn, hinder the return we were hoping for. With the exception, it is true, of a few singular works that precisely allow us to better measure the distance between return and restoration.

Are we not indeed in the presence of two intellectual gestures that may seem similar but give rise to an extremely harmful confusion: return *to* political philosophy on the one hand, return *of* political things on the other?

There exist multiple signs of the first gesture: creation of journals, book series, organization of conferences, associations, publication of manifestos, and so on. It even seems—first alert—that this movement seamlessly slips into an almost anonymous mold that is currently very successful on the intellectual scene. The flag does not actually matter—political philosophy, moral philosophy, philosophy of law—the navigation is the same. First comes the more or less regretful assessment of an enigmatic eclipse. The intellectual discipline that one once again takes care of would allegedly have

---

Translated by Olivier Ruchet. Originally published as "De quel retour s'agit-il?," in *Les cahiers de philosophie*, no. 18 (1994): 5–8. Translated from "De quel retour s'agit-il?," in *Pour une philosophie politique critique* (Paris: Sens & Tonka, 2009), 59–63.

strangely disappeared from our contemporaries' intellectual life. Then, in spite of that uncanny realization, the analyst pursues her investigation with little difficulty and eventually encounters the infernal trio, Marx, Nietzsche, Freud, or at least one of them, considered as sufficiently evil on his own to have single-handedly provoked the nefarious effects blamed on the triad of suspicion. Third and last, a statement of intent is enunciated for a return to the neglected discipline: the statement is all the more tempered that the point is to present and to practice it as a "weak thought," or at least as a mid-range theory.

The return of political things and the response to it are both very different. Political things are back, one could say. It is no longer the interpreter who chooses to turn to a provisionally erased discourse to bring it back to life, but it is rather political things that are irrupting into the present, interrupting the forgetting that affected them, awaiting a response. At a time when totalitarian regimes, understood as endeavors that claim to put an end to the political, are disintegrating, the political is staging a comeback as if its "permanence," far from inciting us to follow paths already treaded, rather commanded us to open up new ways, since that very permanence itself elicits questions. Two intellectual gestures that we would be deeply wrong to confuse with one another or to consider as going in the same direction or responding to the same orientation, the latter only seeming more ample and destined to include and to outflank the former. In fact, it is not the case. If it may be conceivable that the return of political things may perhaps include a return to political philosophy—or more exactly to tradition, but to a broken tradition—it is not forbidden to think that the return to political philosophy may have the paradoxical effect of distracting us from political things to the point where they would be overshadowed. The paradoxical character of this hypothesis diminishes as soon as we remember that the two greatest thinkers of the political of our time, Hannah Arendt and Claude Lefort, who both articulated critiques of totalitarian domination from nonliberal perspectives, manifested the deepest reservations towards what we classically name political philosophy. Arendt preferred to self-identify as a "political writer": she was concerned about approaching political things "with eyes unclouded by philosophy," that is to say with eyes not confused by the professional distortion that affects philosophers, their suspicion regarding the political. Lefort preferred to define his work as "the thought of the political" [*pensée du politique*] rather than political philosophy, which in his view was marred by a connection to a foundation (the cosmos, nature, God, etc.). Such an initially puzzling fact—the opposition of two great political thinkers to political philosophy, both engaging in a positive, inventive relation with the break brought about by Machiavelli's work—a fact that is apparently ignored, neglected, or forgotten, deserves our full attention, as its elucidation may lead us to the core of the difficulties and of the problems we encounter. Doesn't this shared reluctance sufficiently indicate that the current eagerness to salute the reawakening of political philosophy—as the charms of Marx or of Nietzsche have apparently waned—seems, at best, to display naivete, and, at worst, trickery. We therefore need to measure the meaning and the stakes of that reluctance, and we need to understand how to practice "exercises in political thought" (Arendt) or how taking on the task of "thinking the political" (Lefort) demands that political philosophy be kept at bay, and even that we work against it in order to free ourselves from the weightiness of inherited thought, without necessarily yielding to any sort of sociological *technē*.

In order to better make out the difference between return and restoration, let us turn to Ludwig Feuerbach, an author probably seldom read by the new zealots, who in the opening to his 1842 text "Provisional Theses for the Reformation of Philosophy" invited precisely to distinguish between two types of reforms:

> There is a qualitative difference between a new philosophy that falls into a common epoch with earlier philosophies and one that belongs to an entirely new phase in the history of mankind. To be more specific, there is a fundamental distinction involved between a philosophy that owes its existence to a philosophical need, as, for example, the philosophy of Fichte in relation to that of Kant, and one that corresponds to a need of mankind. In short, there is a world of difference between a philosophy that is related to mankind only indirectly by virtue of its belonging to the history of philosophy and one that is directly the history of mankind.[1]

Thus, if we manage to tread the path opened by Feuerbach—who was saluted by Franz Rozensweig for being the inventor of a new thought—shall we learn to distinguish, under the name of political philosophy, the plain awakening of an academic discipline that, constrained by a narrowly institutional horizon, starts again as if nothing had happened and is furthermore exposed to transforming itself almost necessarily into a history of political philosophy, and, what is very different, into the post-totalitarian manifestation of a need of the political, to speak like Feuerbach, that is to say the rediscovery of politics after totalitarian domination attempted to cancel, to erase once and for all that constitutive dimensionality of the human condition. In short, evidently, the child of a need of mankind. Other question, other project, other stakes, other regime of thought, other register. We shall easily agree: to conduct a research project on Rousseau read by Kant is one thing, and asking the question of voluntary servitude as it was reactivated by totalitarian experiences—or on the basis of those experiences to ponder over the possible meaning of politics—is a very different thing. But isn't it precisely to that difference, to that source—approaching thought as resistance rather than as an academic enterprise—that the two thinkers, Arendt and Lefort, who in a similar indivisible movement described the nature of totalitarianism and have worked either towards a rediscovery of *action* as distinguished from work and of labor, or to the enunciation of the question of modern democracy, the two questions being premised by the introduction of a questioning more radical still, that is, what is the political thing, destined to deploy itself in ultimate questions such as: What is freedom, the "miracle" of freedom? What is man taken as a political being? How to operate a distinction between domination, power, and authority? How to distinguish politics from the State? What is it to think the political with an eye on the horizon of societies against the State? What is the difference between a free political regime and despotism? What is public happiness, that "lost treasure" of great modern revolutions?

Part II

The Critique of Totalitarianism

Chapter 5

On a Misinterpretation of Totalitarianism and Its Effects

(1996; republished 2009)

Does totalitarianism, as an interpretive category, suffer from a paradox? Its interpretation is developed in both a complex and a trivial perspective. In terms of complexity, the philosophical interpretations of totalitarianism seek to understand the newness of our century, its "heart" says Hannah Arendt, and in particular, the unprecedented character of totalitarianism. The task is thus to describe a novel form of domination that is neither tyranny nor despotism. This implies a comprehensive interpretation of modernity and a fresh take on political thought that rejects the idea of politics as a science. It is remarkable that the philosophers who have interpreted totalitarianism have sought both to elucidate the originality of totalitarianism and rediscover politics either as action or as the institution of the social. In short, we could say that a new political theory was born of the interpretation of totalitarianism. While this new political theory is in dialogue with the tradition of political philosophy, it cannot be reduced to it, because the totalitarian experience has opened an abyss between that tradition and us.

At the same time, the trivialization of the notion authorizes a series of equivocations, ranging from the identification of any type of dictatorship to totalitarianism, all the way to the proposal of a simulacra of philosophy of

---

Translated by Martin Breaugh. Originally published as "D'une mésinterprétation du totalitarisme et de ses effets," *Tumultes*, no. 8 (1996): 11–44. Translated from "D'une mésinterprétation du totalitarisme et de ses effets," in *Pour une philosophie politique critique* (Paris: Sens & Tonka, 2009), 167–98.

history that affirms domination as the permanent status of human history by thoughtlessly identifying domination with politics itself. In fact, one of the determining factors of this equivocation is precisely the relationship between totalitarianism and the political. An incessant wavering thus appears when discussing totalitarianism:

- either it is considered an exacerbation of politics or politics elevated to its maximal expression;
- or it is theorized as the disappearance of the political, its destruction, or even a fantastical attempt to destroy the political bond and the human political condition. It is as if totalitarianism is, in act, the most radical denial of Aristotle's thesis of man as a political animal.

Such is the interpretive knot that we must urgently and unequivocally undo. The stakes are clear:

- If totalitarianism is theorized as an excess of the political, or an exacerbated form of politicization, then the critique of totalitarianism and the exit from it implies a disengagement from the political. Ridding ourselves of politics becomes legitimate precisely because it is held responsible for totalitarianism.
- If, on the other hand, totalitarianism is seen as the destruction of the political, the critique of totalitarianism and its exit would take a completely different trajectory. The post-totalitarian moment must restore the political and rediscover its irreducible consistency and dignity. Because totalitarianism affirms itself through the attempt to destroy political things, a rediscovery of such things is therefore necessary.

Once this equivocation is clearly stated, we encounter the problem of apoliticism. Indeed, if the first hypothesis prevails—totalitarianism as an excess of the political—apoliticism becomes a quasi-legitimate or normal reaction to this excess. Apoliticism would be a withdrawal from the political after a period of political saturation. Inversely, if the second hypothesis is confirmed—totalitarianism as the destruction of the political—apoliticism appears in a new light. In a post-totalitarian society, could we then not see apoliticism as a remainder or a trace of the totalitarian attempt to destroy the political? In short, apoliticism is the sign of an irrecoverable injury done to the political. It is therefore in this sense that totalitarianism and its interpretation turn out to be a possible source of apoliticism today. Moreover, it could very well determine its meaning and orientation, even its concrete manifestations can appear to be similar; either apoliticism as a rejection of the political or apoliticism as a remainder of the destruction of the political.

Totalitarianism as an Excess of the Political, Its Effects

In order to make the thesis as clear as possible, and take leave of the equivocations of opinion, I will turn to an essayist, Simon Leys, who has written much about totalitarianism, notably in its Maoist form.[1] He later wrote an essay on George Orwell,[2] the author, as we know, of *Homage to Catalonia*, *Animal Farm*, and the acclaimed *1984*. It is as if Leys recognized in Orwell the fundamental inspiration of his own critique of totalitarian domination. In his work, which brought much critical light during a period of obscurantism, Leys analyzes totalitarianism as the ultimate politicization of society. Totalitarianism is defined by the crushing, and even the destruction, of nonpolitical elements and values in the name of politics elevated to the "supreme command post." This is how, with much talent, Leys practiced a "literary investigation," as defined by Claude Lefort, of Chinese totalitarianism by opposing small critical vignettes to the grand ideological schemes of the regime. Through the study of overlooked and even hidden details, these vignettes demonstrate that the Whole is the untruth. Totalitarianism understood as the ultimate politicization crushes the frivolous like it does the eternal. It crushes the unpredictable fabric of everyday life, that which creates newness in human life and the unforeseeable, what Hannah Arendt calls "the miracle of being."

This interpretation of totalitarianism will immediately produce its effects on Leys, notably in his essay on Orwell, the title of which is eloquent enough, "The Horror of Politics." Following Leys, there is an Orwell enigma: for some, he is the political animal par excellence; for others, including his second wife Sonia, he enjoyed living in the countryside, far from politics and his combat in Spain was an accident of history and devoid of meaning. To this enigma, Leys responds with a paradox: Orwell remained in a field of tension between the two directions, political and pastoral. Yet, Leys quickly abandons this paradox and reduces Orwell's exceptionality to a "horror of politics," not having explored the category of the impolitical. "More specifically," he writes, "his originality as a political writer comes from his hatred of politics."[3] And so this political writer, who hated politics, would give priority to the frivolous and the eternal, and politics would come after; we could qualify this attitude as an aesthetic and metaphysical variant of apoliticism. From this, Leys establishes the legitimacy of a general attitude towards politics: one should hold the same attitude with politics as one does with a rabid dog, a dog whose fury blinds him from the distinction between friend and enemy, in contradistinction with Plato's dog. "If politics must mobilize our attention, it is in the manner of a rabid dog who will leap at your throat the moment you look elsewhere. It is in Spain that he discovered the ferocity of the beast."[4] And Leys insists on the relationship between this attitude of defiance with regards to the political and Orwell's Spanish experience. "After being seriously injured by a fascist bullet, he [Orwell] was brought back from the front only to be stalked by Stalinist killers more worried about annihilating their anarchist allies than with defending the Republic against its fascist enemies. In England, after the war, he wanted to bear witness to the Communist's treason of the Republican cause, but he was met with a wall of silence and slander. . . . For the first time, he directly encountered the totalitarian lie."[5] Admittedly, Orwell discovered Stalinism in Spain, its extensions and its destructive effects. But is it not shortsighted to reduce Orwell's Spanish lesson to a hatred of politics, especially since the hatred of Stalinism can go hand in hand with a love of politics?

Admittedly, the expression "the horror of politics" is taken from Orwell's writings about Spain. But we must specify that it is related to the "internal operations of left-wing political parties." Horror of politics per se or horror of partisan politics? The question deserves to be asked, since Orwell discovered in Spain the miracle of Revolution or the Revolution as miracle, as the emergence or the invention of newness by the Many. Some of the most beautiful pages ever written about the human bond, and how that bond can be transformed during a Revolution, during what Chateaubriand called "humanity's vacation," are found in *Homage to Catalonia*. "The aspect of Barcelona was something startling and overwhelming. It was the first time that I had ever been in a town where the working class was in the saddle. . . . Waiters and shop-walkers looked you in the face and treated you as an equal. Servile and even ceremonial forms of speech had temporarily disappeared. . . . Above all, there was a belief in the revolution and the future, a feeling of having suddenly emerged into an era of equality and freedom."[6] Leys thus articulates a wonderful model of the first interpretation of totalitarianism with its two fundamental proposals:

- totalitarianism as total politicization or as an excess of politics;
- the legitimate reaction to this new form of domination, the hatred of politics that can take many forms, the aesthetic, metaphysical opposition, or, closer to us, ethical opposition.

I would like to make a few critical comments before discussing the second interpretation. If *politicism* in a narrow sense is a process of ideologization, like the term "economism" is the overvaluation of an instance separated from the totality, then apoliticism as a refusal of this process is quite legitimate. Still, can we really extract from it a hatred of politics, as if the phenomenon of politics and its ideologization, its overvaluation, should necessarily be confused? Working from this very debatable identification, is Leys's mistake not that he fails to distinguish between apoliticism and an apolitical, or even anti-political, point of view? In short, does he not unduly deduce from a legitimate form of apoliticism—understood as a refusal of politicism—an anti-politics or a hatred of politics that is problematic? This apoliticism, in the sense indicated, may have the aim not of denying politics, but of rediscovering it in order to save it.

In light of this interpretation of totalitarianism, questions remain:

- Can we not observe here a confusion between the "Everything is political" and the "Everything is ideological," that is to say, the imposition on all activities within society of a dominant model controlled by a single-party?

In any event, this "Everything is political" by way of ideology—this identification of the totality with a political-ideological model, this politicism in act—does not legitimize the discrediting of Rousseau's famous formula found in *The Confessions*, "everything depends radically on politics,"[7] which means that the political institution of the social can exercise, up to a certain point, an influence on the elements that make up a given society. Is not this proposal, when properly examined, also shared by Montesquieu in his theory of regimes and de Tocqueville in his description of democracy in America? To critique politicism in act is one thing, to appreciate the role of politics in the institution of the social is another:

- Can we not observe another confusion between "Everything is political" and the attempt to achieve total socialization, which would entail, if we follow its artisans and partisans, the disappearance of the political?

- Is the "Everything is political" interpretation of totalitarianism not a narrow perspective? Indeed, does this conception not limit itself to a declaration of intentions, without measuring the effects of the practice? Supposing that totalitarianism is the project of "Everything is political"—the identification of politics and totality—would the implementation of the project not lead to the dissolution of the substance and frontiers of the political? In other words, the accomplishment of "Everything is political" would have the paradoxical effect of dissolving the political itself, since the very existence of the political is predicated upon its difference with other dimensions of a given society.

By accentuating its traits, this interpretation of totalitarianism sensitizes us to the attitude of defiance of the political held by public opinion in the post-totalitarian era. If, in its banal and equivocal understanding, totalitarianism appears as the political unchained, an excess of the political, then we can understand the attitude of defiance of the political in public opinion, its apoliticism, which can always degenerate into a hatred of politics. Under these circumstances, we may also have to consider the return of antiquated Christian attitudes that associate the political with evil: in this case, totalitarianism is the expression, par excellence, of political evil.

Oddly enough, public opinion is here relayed and comforted by the positions taken by certain philosophers, as if in this case philosophy was not doing its critical work on opinion and did not attempt to go from opinion to knowledge. Is this a strange resignation of philosophy? Is it not rather the reactivation of the "esprit de corps" of philosophers and their traditional distrust of politics, as Arendt has eloquently denounced in her work? Following Arendt, since the initial traumatic event—the trial and execution of Socrates—philosophers suffer from a true "occupational hazard" that brings them to conceive of politics as a dangerous activity that can disrupt the calmness and serenity required for the *vita contemplativa* and put into question its primacy. We can easily observe this attitude of defiance of politics if we examine the reception of Emmanuel Levinas's work. If we believe them, Levinas is the spokesperson of the priority of ethics and the depreciation of politics, since one of the great benefits of this priority is the struggle against politics and its totalitarian ontology. This is a nearsighted and inaccurate reading. If Levinas, following Kant, distinguishes between ethics and politics, he nevertheless posits the necessary articulation between the two and thus recognizes the importance and consistency of the political. Admittedly, he affirms the priority of ethics—of the ethical fact, of the responsibility for others—but he immediately reminds us that the simultaneous appearance of the third party imposes the need for the political. With regard to the ethical relation, which is exposed to extravagance and excess, the task of politics is to reintroduce a form of measure. In other words, to introduce with the third party the comparison of the incomparable. It is thanks to this measure, and therefore thanks to politics, that a pathway from extravagant ethics to justice is cleared.

In its extreme simplification, this reception of the work of Levinas is symptomatic of the movement of opinion in the post-totalitarian era, where the phenomenon has been misinterpreted as an apoliticism that degenerates into a depreciation of politics and an overestimation of ethics. Is it not in this double movement that we can recognize the acritical valorization of humanitarian action that is the other name of the priority of ethics over politics in a disenchanted, even disoriented, world?

Need we insist? Totalitarianism constitutes an essential marker of the contemporary world from which we must orient ourselves. From this perspective, the acceptation or the rejection of this category is fundamental for the understanding of Nazism and Stalinism. For those who accept this category to think through this new form of domination that appeared in the twentieth century, it is obvious that totalitarianism totally shattered the political field to the point of making it unrecognizable. We therefore cannot be surprised that the interpretation of totalitarianism entails a set of representations that have a decisive effect on our relationship to political things, in this case on apoliticism and its possible degeneracy into the discredit of politics. Already Benjamin Constant spoke up against the reduction of politics to a game of visible forces and underscored the importance of opinions. "The empire of the world is now exclusively given to opinion. Opinions create strength, by creating sentiments, or passions, or enthusiasms."[8] Hence, the "opinion" of totalitarianism as "Everything is political," in addition to being questionable, as we have seen, carries with it, almost irresistibly, a hatred of politics and of all of the passions related to it. In this perspective, the experience of totalitarianism has revealed, or confirmed, the profoundly malign nature of politics.

Totalitarianism:
Total Domination and the Destruction of Politics

Fortunately, there are other positions on totalitarianism. Other philosophers, principally Arendt and Lefort, offered another perspective and thus another interpretation of totalitarianism. They were able, in one fell swoop, to critique totalitarian domination and work to rediscover the political. They both hence refused the equivocations of opinion and resisted the ambient depreciation of the political. They share a common philosophical inspiration; to find common characteristics, they refuse to remain at the level of empirical analysis of totalitarian domination; and they extract the essence of this form of domination from a phenomenological point of view. What is more, they reactivate, by different means, the general question of political philosophy. In the face of the totalitarian phenomenon, they ask with a fresh perspective the question of the difference between a free political regime and its opposite, without yielding to the illusion of a return to tradition. If they do not hold the same conception of politics, one giving precedence to action and the other insisting upon the institution of the social, they nevertheless share an essential thesis: far from being the excess of politics or the "Everything is political," totalitarian domination is fundamentally, as the rule of ideology, destructive of political things, of the realm of politics and of the political dimension that they consider essential to the human condition. They thus develop another position with regard to the political, to the struggle against totalitarianism, or to the exit from totalitarianism. In short, another position with regard to the possibilities of the political in a post-totalitarian world. In this analysis, I will give the priority to Arendt, as I have already devoted a long study to Lefort's work on this point.[9]

Arendt, in her critique of totalitarianism, starts with a theory of regimes taken from Montesquieu. But it is significantly modified, because she adds an additional criterion to Montesquieu's two. From Montesquieu, she retains the distinction between the *nature* of a regime, its form or its structure, and its *action principle*, the specific passion that makes it act and that permits it to persevere in its being. To these two criteria, she adds a third, namely, the definition of the fundamental experience upon which each regime rests. This experience refers, each time, to a dimension of the human condition. Hence, Monarchy rests upon the experience that humans are distinct and different one from another because of birth; Republic, on the opposite experience, rests upon the equality between all humans born equal and who are distinguished solely by virtue of their social status; this manifests itself by an equal share in power, which reflects the condition of plurality. Tyranny, finally, thrives on fear and rests upon the experience of angst that we feel in situations of total isolation.[10] Armed with the three criteria, Arendt defines totalitarianism as the following: the nature of totalitarianism is terror, and its action principle or its principle of movement, is ideology. Finally, it rests upon the fundamental experience of isolation, which is considerably aggravated by the modern experience of desolation.

Arendt's analysis shows that, at these three levels, totalitarianism destroys political life, the realm of politics as the domain of human affairs, the essence of politics, which is action, the political dimension par excellence. This judgement should not be understood as that of a journalist or of a political actor. It is rather the conclusion of a philosopher, and it acquires its full meaning with regard to the fundamental categories of her thought.

The destruction of the political means, in the first place, a violation of the condition of plurality, of the fact that it is *men* that inhabit the planet, not one man, not simply multiplicity but plurality that includes both being-with other humans and singularity. It is the true ontological condition of politics that, for Arendt, must continue to elicit wonder of a renewed political philosophy. Secondly, destruction of the political signifies the destruction, not so much of humans, but of the world as a horizon of meaning that humans construct together at the intersection of fabrication and action. The world, an intermediary space where human affairs are deployed and play out, a space of appearance where "I appear to others like others appear to me." Only the respect of the condition of plurality can ensure the possible existence of a world, and only the existence of this world is the condition of possibility of a public-political sphere as a sphere of freedom. Finally, the destruction of politics means the double negation of freedom: negation of the freedom to express and exchange opinions and the negation of the freedom to act, to begin anew, the power to create a new beginning that requires the presence of others and the ability to confront them. For Arendt, as we know, action that points to the condition of natality is always action in concert with others.

Because Arendt's concepts are so intertwined, it would suffice, in order to be faithful to her thought, to affirm that the fundamental characteristic of totalitarian domination is the destruction of politics inasmuch as totalitarianism denies the foundational fact of politics, human plurality. The case of Arendt is particularly interesting. We encounter, in her work, formulations such as "totalitarian politics" or "totalitarian State" that allow us to think that she oscillates between the two possible interpretations of totalitarianism and sometimes even partakes in the first interpretation. At the same time, does she not assume a critical distance from this first interpretation when she writes about the forms of State totalitarianism "in which the totality of human life is claimed to be so totally politicized"?[11] This hesitation, or contradiction, is only apparent. Arendt's argument is more complex. The interpretation of totalitarianism as the negation of politics is the result of a long development. She first seems to agree with the total politicization thesis and embraces it, in a certain sense, to better flesh out the prejudice that is at its origin, the confusion between domination and politics, and thus jettison it. Public opinion can see it as total politicization only because it implicitly identifies politics with domination. It is, therefore, all at once that Arendt describes totalitarianism as the destruction of politics, dissociating politics from domination, and recovers the meaning of politics, which is freedom. It is all at once that she dismisses the contemporary despair that seeks to get rid of politics and that she recovers politics as the original site of a properly human miracle, the miracle of action, of acting together, the "miracle-event" of freedom in the realm of human affairs.

If politics means freedom, then we understand that the evils of totalitarianism that we wrongly attribute to politics are, in fact, attributable to ideologization, to domination, and to an unprecedented division between those who dominate and those who are dominated. They are not attributable to the action undertaken with peers and oriented to freedom. Are we not embracing the subtle undertaking of the text "Does Politics Still Have Any Meaning?" It appears nevertheless that Arendt's concepts point to the direction of the second interpretation of totalitarianism. Already regarding tyranny, did Arendt not argue that it is a regime that self-destructs, since the fear that "flusters" or that discourages cannot be an action principle? As for totalitarian regimes, which are nonregimes, her verdict is unambiguous: "totalitarian regimes have not been content simply to squelch freedom of opinion, but have also set about on principle to destroy human spontaneity in all spheres."[12]

Firstly, the destruction of politics, at the level of the nature of the regime, by terror. The totalitarian regime as terror is defined by opposition to the constitutional or republican government. The essence of the republican government is the law and, as such, it institutes the conditions of freedom and action. Following Arendt, the laws fulfill multiple functions:

- they institute barriers, they establish and draw limits;
- as a result of these delimitations, they create a differentiated space between humans (*inter-esse*) and, at the same time, allow for the deployment of the ontological condition of plurality;

- it is also due to these limitations that the laws institute modes of communication between humans that live together in a community and act in concert;
- finally, these laws, because of their stability, allow humans to evolve within this delimited space.

In other words, it is the stability of the laws that permit humans, in a republican regime, to experience the upheavals of history, particularly in the political realm, the birth of new human beings. Thinker of natality and the conditions of natality, Arendt reminds us: "With each new birth, a new beginning is born into the world, and a new world has potentially come into being."[13] To follow Arendt, we can consider that the action of the laws, their stability, consists in the establishment of a complex game between the preservation of a common world and the opening to the potentialities contained within this beginning. "The stability of laws . . . hedges in this new beginning and assures, at the same time, its freedom; laws assure the potentiality of something entirely new *and* the pre-existence of a common world."[14]

Terror is characterized by both an absence of laws, akin to despotism, and, more importantly, a displacement of the law, of the idea of the law. The law is no longer the expression of positive law as it emerges from traditional sources. The law becomes the law of a process, either natural or historical, that is thought of as being almost completed, or to which we must contribute to ensure the completion. Totalitarianism is characterized by a constant tension between stability and change: to allow for the deployment of the law of process and to unleash its dynamic, totalitarian domination stabilizes human beings. "Terror freezes men in order to clear the way for the movement of Nature or History."[15] This fixation of humans, this inversion of the place of the static and the dynamic jeopardizes the political quality of humans as actors, as beings-of-beginnings and being-for-beginnings. Inasmuch as this form of domination seeks to accomplish a process, it must stop "all unforeseeable, free, spontaneous acts" that could hinder the unfolding of the process. This implies the abolition of political time, or of the time of politics, understood as the time of action and of newness, since the only temporality tolerated by this form of domination is the procedural, anonymous, neutral time that operates "behind the backs" of humans at the expense of their gift of action. An abolition of limits, therefore, that brings with it a whole series of destructions: the abolition of the space *between* humans that allows for the creation of a complex relationship between bond and conflict; the abolition of the modes of communication between humans and, especially, that which constitutes its root, the condition of plurality. It is at the end of this description that Arendt proposes her theory of terror as a *straitjacket* or *iron band* that, damaging the space between humans, creates an unprecedented state of unification, a novel state of confusion. "Terror substitutes for the boundaries and channels of communication between individual men an iron band which presses them all so tightly together that it is as though they were melded into each other, as though they were only one man. Terror, the obedient servant of Nature or History and the omnipresent executor of their predestined movement, fabricates the oneness of all men by abolishing the boundaries of law which provide the living space for the freedom of each individual."[16] It is not so much that freedoms are destroyed, but it is the very conditions that allow for freedom that are denied. "[The terror] simply and mercilessly presses men, such as they are, against each other so that the very space of free action—and this is the reality of freedom—disappears."[17] We can find the same analysis in the *Origins of Totalitarianism* where the abolition of plurality is linked to the emergence of the One. "It [terror] substitutes for the boundaries and channels of communication between individual men a band of iron which holds them so tightly together that it is as though their plurality had disappeared into One Man of gigantic dimensions."[18]

For Arendt, the terror-straitjacket undoubtedly destroys politics by destroying both that which makes politics possible and that which politics makes possible. It destroys the polity, this specific form of life in common, this public-political realm within which humans act and decide together by creating and staging the condition of plurality through a set of antagonistic relations. Terror also destroys the fruits of political action, the institution of a domain of human affairs, the constitution of a world, the institution of a human bond between visible and invisible human beings that is held above necessity and utility and has to do with that strange phenomenon known as "public happiness." Terror also destroys, or seeks to destroy, the human political condition. In short, the state forged by terror is a void of society and a void of politics.

Without a doubt, the origins of Arendt's critique are Aristotelian, even if she is not, per se, an Aristotelian. It is as though the struggle against terror in the name of plurality tracked, up to a certain point, Aristotle's critique of Plato's *Republic* with regards to multiplicity. Indeed, Aristotle argues that the *Republic* highly overrates unity, and this does violence to the polity as the space within which the multiplicity of humanity manifests itself. "Yet it is obvious that a city which goes on becoming more and more of a unit, will eventually cease to be a city at all. A city, by its nature, is some sort of plurality. If it becomes more of a unit, it will first become a household instead of a city, and then an individual instead of a household. . . . These considerations are sufficient to show, first, that it is not the nature of the city to be a unit in the sense in which some thinkers say it is, and secondly, that what is said to be the supreme good of a city is really its ruin."[19] Up to a certain point, this tracks Aristotle's critique, we argued. We would need to distinguish between Arendtian plurality and Aristotelian multiplicity, and also we would need to clarify that Arendt is not Karl Popper. While she professed a systematic and well-articulated anti-Platonism, she never mistook Plato for the father of modern totalitarianism.

If we consider that power is a fundamental component of the political realm, then totalitarian terror also pursues its work of destruction at this level. It is here that the full force of the originality of Arendt's analysis appears. For Arendt, totalitarianism, far from constituting itself in an excess of power—the central claim of the "Everything is political" thesis—actually defeats power, the possibility of power *between* human beings or it defeats power as the power of acting together. As we know, Arendt is one of the rare modern theorists who does not articulate a "negative" conception of power; she resists identifying power and force, power and constraint or coercion. There is, for her, a mysterious alchemy of power such that power comes to existence and allows free reign to the companionship of humans, to the "great grace of companionship."[20] Posing a link between power—the chance of power—and the fact of being-together, Arendt conceived of this phenomenon as power *between* humans, as power *with* humans and not power *over*. Power is the very manifestation of human plurality itself. "Power, insofar as it is a factor and certainly one of the chief ones of politics, springs up in between men. . . . Men together constitute the realm where power can originate and find it at the very moment they decide to 'act in concert.' "[21] Inversely, isolation ruins the very possibility of power and its manifestation; it generates the will to dominate. The tyrant, who is alone, without friends and outside of the companionship of peers, knows that everyone fears his power, and he responds to this with a will to dominate.

Having torn herself from the prejudice that confuses politics and domination, Arendt presents a mixed picture: on the side of plurality, the blooming of the power to act together, the experience of the equality of power between humans; on the side of isolation, the will to dominate of one human over all others. She describes tyranny as founded "on the essential impotence of all men who are alone."[22] It is in this sense that totalitarianism, a form of total domination and unlimited rule of *libido dominandi*, excludes, via the confusion it introduces between humans and the destruction of the human bond, the very possibility of power and of its manifestation. Threatened by unlimited domination, humans are trapped in the iron band of totalitarian domination and they are precisely without power, outside of power, outside of politics and outside of all possible action. This description obviously applies to those who are dominated but also to those who dominate, since once we enter the order of domination, we close the door, so to speak, to politics and to that upon which it is founded, the gift of action.

Under such conditions, it is unsurprising that Arendt, in a research project in 1948, argued that concentration camps are the *essential institution* of totalitarian regimes organized with a view to inducing "a state of political and social apathy" and breaking the source of human spontaneity, of the *power to begin*. But those who, strangely enough, expect to find a public-political sphere in Nazism—for, as surprising as it may seem, our reading of Arendt, as the interpreter of totalitarianism, does not appear to be prevalent—it becomes obvious for them, when they turn their attention to concentration camps, that there is no longer even a trace of the political, but rather an extreme situation of total domination.[23] The *unprecedented* nature of totalitarianism, its difference with classical tyranny, appears precisely when studying the camps. At a remove from all usefulness and political rationality, this institution seeks to create a situation that ensures the total control over a population subjected to terror. "It is characteristic of totalitarian terror that it increases as political opposition decreases and that concentration camps are expanded when the reservoir of people genuinely hostile to the regime is exhausted." For Arendt, the stakes of the terror are crystal clear: "Totalitarianism aims at the total domination of man."[24] Likewise, there exists an abyss between the classical tyrant and the totalitarian *Egocrat*; while the former exercises power with a view to breaking opposition and ensuring a form of tranquil domination, the latter, who considers himself the leader of the human species, eliminates human beings seen as superfluous to allow for the accomplishment of the laws of the movement. We could pursue the demonstration by exposing Arendt's theory of ideology and show how ideology, action principle of totalitarian regimes, damages politics and contributes to its destruction, thus marking a precious distinction between ideologization and total politicization. In this direction, we need only retain three particularly key points.

(1) Following Arendt, ideology would indeed be the action principle of this new type of regime, just as virtue is the principle of a republic or honor that of a monarchy. "We may say, then, that in Totalitarian governments, Montesquieu's principle of action is replaced by ideology,"[25] she writes. But the reference to Montesquieu must not obscure the newness of her analysis, since a close reading demonstrates that it is not the case and that this question, action principle or not, precisely reveals the specificity of totalitarianism. Within totalitarianism, ideology does not truly function like an action principle, it functions more like a principle of movement. This is Arendt's genuine thought. What does it mean?

Firstly, it recognizes that if Arendt does indeed start with Montesquieu, then being faithful to the essence of totalitarianism requires her to do a general overhaul of the initial problem. We must thus return to terror, the essence of the totalitarian regime. The strength of Arendt's interpretation is to confer consistency to the thesis of the "unprecedented" by dissociating terror and tyranny, the reign of the arbitrary and the absence of the law. Terror obeys a higher legitimacy than that claimed by positive laws, because terror invokes the law of movement, that of Nature or of History, which is destined, in its accomplishment, to produce nothing less than humankind. If terror crushes humans against each other in an iron band or in a straitjacket by abolishing the condition of plurality, it also seeks to accelerate, to accomplish the law of the movement by denying human spontaneity which is linked to the condition of natality. "Terror is the realization of the law of movement; its chief aim is to make it possible for the force of nature or history to race freely through mankind, unhindered by any spontaneous human action."[26] We can go one step further and argue that terror as the essence of the totalitarian regime is itself a process, a movement—terror is the law of History or of Nature in movement. "Under totalitarian conditions, this essence has itself become movement—totalitarian government *is* insofar as it is kept in constant motion."[27] This immediately results in a modification of the idea of essence that is no longer to be thought of on the side of permanence and stability—like the beautiful animal at rest in the *Republic*—but must be apprehended as the deployment of a process, like the beautiful animal in movement in *Timaeus*. It is because of this modification of essence, of the idea itself, in the case of the totalitarian regime, that Arendt can arrive at the surprising declaration that terror fills a dual function, that of essence of the totalitarian regime and that of principle, stating immediately that it is not an action principle but a principle of movement. Yet terror cannot carry out this dual function, it cannot possess this dual quality, because in a totalitarian regime, as an essence, it is already in movement, it is already a process, since a confusion appears between the essence of the regime and its principle marked by the movement. From there, as we have already observed, an inversion of the poles of the static and the dynamic. In a classical regime—republic or monarchy—the essence confers, via its authority, a stable framework within which humans can give free reign to action in its unpredictability and spontaneity. Inversely, in a totalitarian regime, the law as law of movement, terror as the accomplishment of this law, as movement, stabilizes humans, immobilizes them in order to hinder and stop action and thus permit the essence to deploy itself and the movement to accomplish itself. Now, what works for terror in a totalitarian regime works *a fortiori* for ideology; by this, we must understand that the law of movement, the imperialism of movement, expands its grip not only on the essence of the regime but on its principle. With regard to the essence, it renders it dynamic; as for the principle, it reduces it to the sole rank of principle of the movement. In the totalitarian situation, the law of movement rules like a master, transforming all it touches into movement. The essence of the totalitarian regime does not need, or no longer needs, an action principle, since it contains within itself a principle of movement that, in this instance, acts as a substitute to all possible action. The movement having become the essence of the regime itself, a solution has thus been found to the problem encountered by classical theory, which consists of knowing how to put into movement a permanent structure that privileges stability and how to respond to the requirement of the movement of a political body. Hence in Montesquieu the idea of an action principle that, with different names depending on the essence of the regime, responds to this requirement. The specificity of the totalitarian regime is that a solution has been found for this problem, not through the discovery of a new action principle, but by the discovery, in this case, of the uselessness of all action principles. The essence, being itself dynamic, is henceforth no longer in need of an action principle to dynamize it. "In a perfect totalitarian government . . . under conditions where terror can be completely relied upon to keep the movement in constant motion, no principle of action separate from its essence would be needed at all."[28] But, despite its desire to take leave of the limits of the human condition, the totalitarian regime encounters the imperfection of human things. As soon as it aims at total, planetary domination, terror even transformed into movement does not suffice "to inspire and guide human conduct." Terror is thus constrained to call upon an auxiliary, ideology, that, following the logic of the totalitarian regime in the grip of the law of movement, comes to reinforce the essence. It does not function like an action principle but only like a principle of movement, aiming either at accelerating the process or achieving its total accomplishment. Ideology, understood as the logic of an idea applied to history, is there to prepare individuals to participate in the process by unveiling the law of the movement, by teaching them, by preparing them to play either the role of executioner or of victim.

Thus, despite the reference to Montesquieu, Arendt's answer is inscribed in a distinctly modified framework, even if she still defines, here and there in her work, ideology as the action principle of totalitarian regimes. Her real answer is without doubt: the unprecedented character of the totalitarian regime holds to, on the one hand, the fact that its essence is movement, process, and, on the other hand, that the principle that animates it, ideology, is not an action principle but a principle of movement. Moreover, this distinctly totalitarian principle of movement renders superfluous all action principles. In other words, it is in the name of this principle of movement—ideologies state the law of movement—that totalitarian leaders mercilessly eliminate everything that resembles, directly or indirectly, human action. "No guiding principle of action taken from the realm of human action—such as virtue, honor, fear—is needed or could be used to set into motion a body politic whose essence is motion implemented by terror. In its stead, totalitarianism relies upon a new principle, which, as such, dispenses with human action as free deeds altogether and substitutes for the very desire and will to action a craving and need for insight into the laws of movement according to which the terror functions. . . . What totalitarian rule therefore needs, instead of a principle of action, is a means to prepare individuals equally well for the role of executioner and the role of victim. This two-sided preparation, the substitute for a principle of action, is ideology."[29]

Principle of movement, action principle? The debate is not scholastic; it is not only about applying the right analytical category; it is about the very existence of politics. Indeed, to define ideology as the principle of movement is to show that the totalitarian regime—inasmuch as it seeks to accomplish the law of Nature or History destined to produce the human species—is permanently mobilized against everything that could hinder its course. Therefore, in the first instance, against the gift of action, against acting in concert with others, against the existence of a political realm, against the very possibility of politics. Humans turn away from mutual understanding with others, rendered superfluous, in order to focus on the knowledge of the law of movement, which may eventually be accessible only to the understanding of the One: "not the concert of human minds, but only one man would be needed to understand these laws and to build humanity in such a way as to conform to them under all changing circumstances."[30] In its enslavement to the movement, totalitarian ideology, far from politicizing everything, is the figure of the destruction of the political realm, since the total ideologization of society (which must be distinguished from the idea that "everything depends radically on politics") aims at permanently substituting the ideological "solution" corresponding to the internal law of the movement, to the unpredictable beginnings that are the proper of acting in concert with others. In this sense, destruction of the political is insufficient to describe the full effect of totalitarianism. It aims at purely and simply denying the human political condition by undermining the possibility of new beginnings, that is to say, by undermining the condition of natality.

(2) Beyond the auxiliary role played by terror, ideology, whatever its content, puts the masses into movement. It manages to impel the masses, in one direction or another, thanks to its power of attraction. What is this power? Where is it located? How can we understand it? Turning her attention to the "shirt-changers," Arendt writes, "no matter what content they accept—no matter which kind of eternal law they decide to believe in—once they have taken this initial step, nothing can ever happen to them anymore and they are saved." She immediately asks the question: "Saved from what?"[31]

As the logic of an idea, ideology is a form of doctrine that claims that the key, the elucidation of the mysteries of life and of the world, holds to a single formula referring to a unique element that determines the natural or historical process. Therefore, ideology, and those who share it, emancipate themselves from reality as it is perceived by our five senses by invoking a "truer reality," which is hidden and to which we have access precisely via an ideology that functions as a sixth sense. As such, it corrects and replaces judgements born of common sense. As well, Arendt insists that the proper of ideology is to organize facts following an absolutely logical procedure that starts from an axiomatic premise and deduces the whole process, the logical succession of cause and effects that unfolds like an alphabet. The power of attraction of ideology on the masses is found in this logical form that replaces thought and remains more attractive than any promise of a paradise on earth. When the intercalary world between humans collapses, when humans live in the desert, beset by desolation, the only remaining compass is ideology, as the logic of an idea, which produces certainty and thus redemption—"this familiar terrain and absolute certainty of the Law"—

even against the evidence produced by our senses. As we can see, Arendt is drawing closer, but only closer, to La Boétie's hypothesis of voluntary servitude, without subscribing to its counterfeit version, the repugnant and authoritarian thesis of an "obedience instinct": the masses under the conditions of totalitarianism, are neither deceived nor manipulated, they are attracted, that is to say that they participate, to a certain extent, in their own domination, inasmuch as they find in the pure logic and ensuing certainty a salvage or, better yet, the illusion of a salvage.[32] As Remo Bodei pointed out, from this perspective, Arendt attempts to understand modernity's opacity without relinquishing to the desire for intelligibility that is the proper of a political philosophy that questions the workings of a free political regime and its contrary. The very existence of voluntary servitude (as understood by La Boétie in contrast with friendship in a political sense) in a totalitarian context shows the extent to which the regime is located at the exact opposite of the political relation and of the form of human bond that the relation can forge.

(3) At another level we can measure how much, despite appearances, ideology as principle of movement, is not political. To do so, we need only to confront it with judgment, an essential component of action and of the political realm for Arendt. With ideologies, we adhere to an internal law of movement, more to "stick" to a doctrine that claims to be exhaustive and rests upon the illusion that only one person suffices to understand the laws of Nature or History and produce Humanity. By contrast, the ability to judge, understood as enlarged thought or open thought, calls for thinking that puts "ourselves in the position of everyone else." To put oneself in the position of everyone else, thanks to a relation to understanding and imagination, is what makes possible a "thinking together," so to speak, or a thinking that virtually supports a "judgement from a *universal standpoint.*"[33] The work of the imagination allows for this enlarged thought to deploy itself in a virtual public sphere and such as the thought adopts the point of view that Kant attributes to the citizen of the world.[34] Ideology, "captive thought," or passive thought that tends towards nonthought, demands obedience and submission to the internal law of the movement, by capitulating to the instances that, via an identity game, are supposed to incarnate the movement. Judgement, by contrast, has as its first maxim to *think for oneself.* From this perspective, we can consider that the totalitarian experience modified, as a repercussion, the meaning of this maxim. It is no longer, as in Kant's thought, a thinking without prejudice. Thinking without ideology results in a new definition of *Aufklärung* [Enlightenment]: Aufklärung is the liberation from ideology.

Finally, totalitarianism destroys politics and, worse, it destroys the conditions of possibility of politics, at the level of the fundamental experience of the human community that, following Arendt, constitutes the common breeding ground of terror and ideology.

As we have previously noted, it is the situation of human isolation that allows us to understand the power of attraction of ideology. But the Arendtian analysis goes even further: beyond isolation, that we can already find in tyranny and that still leaves marginal possibilities of action, totalitarianism, if only through fear, rests upon the fundamental experience of *desolation*, that is to say, "the dangers of loneliness and superfluity."[35]

Whatever the real differences between solitude, isolation, and desolation, a continuity and worsening is nevertheless clear: the lack of companionship proper to each of the three states, the absence of peers and equals destroys all possibility of power—of power *with* and power *between*—this essential reality of the political sphere. Regarding this, Arendt, as we have seen, never ceases to recall the existence of a relation between power and the fact of being together, or, inversely, between the absence of power and isolation. If tyranny bears the germ of its own destruction, since fear, its action principle, is anti-political, totalitarianism appears to be a nonregime, since desolation blocks, by its very existence, which is negation of plurality, the constitution of all political bonds as well as the constitution of a space between humans within which their double quality of being-for-freedom and being-for-beginning can appear.

Like tyranny, totalitarianism corresponds to an experience of the desert, but it is considerably aggravated. When tyranny creates a desert, it is following the model of the type of peace found in a cemetery; "peace reigns" because the tyrant's objective is to topple all opposition, to discourage it in the precise sense of the term, in order to enjoy "in peace" the fruits of their domination. When totalitarianism produces the desert, it takes the form of desertification, a never-ending process of extension of the desert, as if the desert had to absorb, blanket, and devour the spaces that remain distinct from it and that thus offer possible spaces of resistance. Desertification is a dynamic process that incessantly gains terrain; in this sense, under the sway of the movement, it turns away from peace and experiences what Arendt calls "sandstorms," "in which false or pseudo-action suddenly bursts forth from deathlike quiet."[36] Mobilization campaigns, Hundred Flowers Campaign, and so on, "the desert in movement" is what threatens to blanket the earth in its entirety. Such is the power of Arendt's vision, since it is truly a vision that she articulates. Furthermore, the totalitarian desert not only destroys the faculty of suffering and of action but it endangers the existence of oases, that is to say, the fountains of life that exist independently of politics, as exemplified by the love between Winston and Julia in *1984*. To follow the metaphors of Arendt, totalitarian desertification threatens all the more the oasis because it allows us to live in the desert "*without reconciling ourselves with it*," that is to say endure the desert, the conditions of the desert while waiting for the new arrivals, those who begin, to take leave of the desert and edify a human world.

Once again we can observe that Arendt is far from the classical liberal critique that conceives of totalitarianism as a submission of the private to the public, even as the confusion between the two, thus drawing closer to the first interpretation. Arendt's vision is completely other. Indeed, totalitarian domination cannot submit private life to public life, since it is first and foremost a destruction of the latter and of its possibility. It is rather in the context of the destruction of the public-political realm, obeying the movement of desertification that wins over, that totalitarian domination proceeds to the destruction of private life and thus pursues the destruction of human community.

"Totalitarian government, like all tyrannies, certainly could not exist without destroying the public realm of life, that is, without destroying, by isolating men, their political capacities. But totalitarian domination . . . is not content with this isolation and destroys private life as well. It bases itself on loneliness, on the experience of not belonging to the world at all, which is among the most radical and desperate experiences of man."[37]

The fundamental experience that precipitates totalitarianism (the uprooting and the feeling of uselessness afflicting the modern masses), and that it institutes and generalizes, is specific. Desolation opens to a new mode of being, being-abandoned by everything and everybody, which is constituted by a triple loss: loss of self, loss of others, and loss of the world. Desolation, as the ordeal of the destruction of experience, harms the human condition itself; being-abandoned falls into the vertigo of being-superfluous.

If we knot together the different threads we have just pulled—terror, ideology, desolation—Arendt's diagnostic can only be reinforced. Totalitarian domination is truly this unprecedented experience of the destruction of politics, of its realm, of its conditions of possibility. And, beyond, in its attempt to produce a humanity that incarnates the law of the movement, a will to put an end to the human condition, as a political condition, in such a way that the implicit formula of totalitarianism could be: fundamentally, humans are apolitical animals or, even more, anti-political, that is to say, destined to live apart from the polity and against the polity or, if we wish to confer to the totalitarian break its maximal sense, countercurrent to the invention of politics and to the rupture represented by the emergence of a community of citizens. Against the slope of this "miracle-event," to quote historian Christian Meier, "For the first time in the history of the world, men acquired the possibility of deciding for themselves the type of political community they wished to live under. In truth, they could only do so by transforming themselves and by assuming a political identity. The constitutional concepts that end with *archia* and *kratia* are commonplace today. They represent however a revolution in world history."[38] If we follow Arendt in her study of Walter Benjamin, language itself is what gives to this past, this revolution, its ineradicable foundation. "The Greek *polis* will continue to exist at the bottom of our political existence—that is, at the bottom of the sea—for as long as we use the word politics."[39] But we would still have to know how to pronounce the word, what its enunciation entails, and not confuse it with its opposite, domination.

Indeed, if we knot together the three threads, we can measure the extent of the misinterpretation of totalitarianism understood as an excess of politics. We can measure how each time this misinterpretation rests upon a set of prejudices and misunderstandings—confusion between politics and domination, power and violence, action and movement—and we can envisage more than we can measure the unending ravages done to our relationship with politics produced by this misinterpretation; how that which should bring us to salvage politics tends to, on the contrary, turn us away from it because of our inability to resist the traditional and totalitarian prejudices that, in post-totalitarian times, communicate to us the horror of politics.

To orient our reflections *after* the totalitarian experience—for example, what applies today to the countries of Eastern Europe—Arendt warns us that totalitarianism can survive the downfall of totalitarian regimes. The perils of totalitarianism "by definition, will not be overcome merely by victory over totalitarian governments."[40] That our experience of totalitarianism is direct or indirect, it leaves us in "a true field of ruins." Ruins of politics, ruins of the world. In addition to politics, totalitarianism destroys the world, this horizon of meaning, "namely, the thing that arises between people and in which everything that individuals carry with them innately can become visible and audible."[41] The imperialism of the movement, so unchained that it extends right to the desert, has destroyed the intercalary space that constitutes itself at the intersection between labor and action and that allows for a sort of permanence. The totalitarian experience leaves us prey to a new type of acosmism, fruit of desolation.

What is now in question is the existence or not of a world and, with regards to this problematic existence, the existence or not of a political domain for human affairs, the possibility or not of a political existence, which remains a preliminary question to all reconstruction of a public-political sphere. Politics has not made us ill because we abused it, because we were overpoliticized. It is politics and the world that are ill from the totalitarian experience, the former having lost its very consistence and the latter, its texture. From here proceeds the strange yet legitimate expression "rediscovery of politics," as if this continent had disappeared from our horizon. But such is the effect of totalitarian domination that it forces us to search for the politics lost as if, like a screen, it covered politics, occulting the dimension of the political, to the point where we lose the memory of it, its meaning, and our desire for it. It requires us, "pearl divers," to wager on a politics regained. Whomever deals with totalitarianism deals with apoliticism and its consequences, the conditions of apoliticism and its possible genesis. The totalitarian experience, as we should understand it, is the often-overlooked blind spot of apoliticism, of all forms of political disinvestment. Inversely, whomever deals with apoliticism, yet refuses the necessary detour via totalitarian domination, can grasp it only empirically, narrowly, with recognizing the historical and philosophical thickness that it calls for.

Let's return to the conflict of interpretations. If we persist with the first interpretation, we add to the confusion and will end up sinking deeper in an inhuman world, in the desert, maintaining a defiance with regard to politics, seen at best as a necessary evil or as an instrument used to manage the problems born of human coexistence. Is this horror of politics so pure? Does it not unknowingly partake in the hatred of action on which totalitarian domination is edified? Does the recurring theme of the end of politics not reproduce *nolens volens* the totalitarian illusion of a disappearance of politics once the goal of the movement has been achieved? Blind to the modern democratic revolution, this return to liberty is seen as the liberty of liberating ourselves from politics. Before brandishing the flag of the hatred of politics, it may be important to partake in a moment of salutary suspicion: Is this hatred not the resumption of the hatred of action, does it not bear the mark, the stigmas of the desert that it has crossed? More than a watchword, we must see it as the sign of a symptom, a survival in the post-totalitarian world of the experiences that nourished the totalitarian experience.

If, on the contrary, we accept the second interpretation, we can, in a post-totalitarian world and in line with the analysis proposed above, develop the question: Does politics still have meaning? We can encounter in this interrogation a golden opportunity; would this meaning not be a "miracle-event" of freedom? And maybe in this direction, having measured the earth-shaking nature of totalitarian domination, we can see pointing, like a modest sunrise, a renewal of left-libertarian thought, or a reorientation of this inspiration that has ceaselessly influenced modern politics? It is as if, having withstood the test of totalitarianism, its accumulated ruins and the radicality of the destruction, revealed, in a sort of after-effect, the new requirements for a theory of freedom: how freedom can no longer be thought of against the law but with it, in accord with the desire for freedom that gave birth to it? How freedom can no longer be conceived of against power, but with power, as the power of acting in concert? Especially how freedom can no longer rise up against politics, but how politics is now the very object of the desire for freedom? A politics thought and desired, away from all idea of a solution, practiced like a never-ending interrogation on the world and the destiny of mortals on Earth. Of the two interpreters of totalitarianism that we have analyzed, does Lefort not help us discover a left-libertarian idea of democracy, that he calls "savage democracy"? Does not the other, Arendt, participate in an "anarchy principle"? Does not the deconstruction of the political that she calls for liberate action from the domination of principles, of theory, and of ends? Does she not conceive of action as free of all *archē*?

Chapter 6

On Compactness

Architecture and Totalitarian Regimes
(1996; republished 1997)

> Architects do not represent a Dionysian or an Apollonian state: for them it is the great act of the will, the will that moves mountains, the intoxication of the great will that demands to be art. Architects have always been inspired by the most powerful people; architects have always been under the spell of power. . . . Architecture is a way for power to achieve eloquence through form, sometimes persuading, even coaxing, at other times just commanding.
>
> —Friedrich Nietzsche, *Twilight of the Idols*[1]

Has the disturbing shadow of Albert Speer returned to haunt us? It seems that some people have such a strong aversion to modern architecture that they have been misled to feel admiration for—or even to worship without scruples or remorse—the monuments and the work of Speer. If we believe them, the work of Hitler's architect constitutes a model of public architecture for our time and for times to come. Speer's National Socialism, his participation in the highest ranks of the Hitlerian enterprise (Hitler even considered

---

Translated by Devin Penner. Originally published as "Architecture et régimes totalitaires," *La part de l'oeil*, no. 12 (1996). Translated from *De la compacité: Architectures et régimes totalitaires* (Paris: Sens & Tonka, 1997).

making him his heir apparent), are merely contingent, secondary elements that we could easily put aside, or in parentheses, in order to rediscover the authentic architectural core under the ideological shell.

It is known that Speer was an expert liar. For example, he denied any participation at the Posen Conference (October 1943), where Himmler made a murderous speech about the so-called "Final Solution to the question of Jewish people in Europe," that is to say, about the intended removal of the Jewish people from the surface of the Earth. The complexity of his denials does not matter to us. What matters is that he claimed to be completely ignorant of the Jewish genocide and asserted that he had never visited a concentration camp. But it is undeniable that he knew about the Jewish extermination, and, in the exercise of his duties, he visited at least one camp. In the later stages of his life, after he left Spandau Prison, Speer began a new "literary" career, which he used to dispense himself in broadcasts, interviews, and conferences in Germany and many European cities, especially London. So Hitler's architect succeeded in transforming his renowned participation in Nazi barbarism into an object of curiosity, into an interesting experience belonging to the history of civilization. As if it was possible and justifiable to dissociate the architecture of Speer from the power of Hitler. We still know that, in an unrestrained moment of jubilation, Speer dared to arrogantly rejoice for being so free and having successfully fooled the public. Are Speer's maneuvers about to succeed unconditionally? Does the name Speer now solely belong to the history of architecture? Would a discourse with aesthetic pretentions be enough to softly reintroduce Nazism on the cultural scene? In Berlin, some nonrepresentational modern sculptures—"degenerate art" according to Nazi criteria—skillfully arranged in front of the Japanese-German Centre, the former Japanese embassy under the Third Reich, hide or try to hide Speer's architecture by presenting the spectator with an eclectic cultural ensemble that appears typically modern. As if these sculptures were the admission ticket Hitler's architect had to pay to hold his place in twentieth-century art history.

Without a doubt, the appearance of art books on the architecture of Speer suggests the triumph of Hitler's architect. Will his self-justification and self-rehabilitation efforts eventually win? Will his connection to culture allow him to succeed in erasing his connection to power? With this in mind, we must take up the critical question of Nietzsche: under the influence of which power did Speer work, at the suggestion of which power did he obey or submit? We should recognize in Speer's work an architecture that gives orders, that aims to dominate, or, worse, seeks to crush its link to Nazi power. Rather than seeing it as public architecture, we should recognize an oeuvre "in the nature of the musical accompaniment with which the SS liked to drown out the screams of its victims."[2]

I. The Strategy of Disjunction: Five Propositions

As the subtitle of this essay indicates, the idea is to interrogate and explore the relation between certain forms of architecture and totalitarian experiences in this century. It is to clearly problematize some strategies of dissociation or disjunction between these two orders of phenomena.

Certain recent works on the architecture of the Third Reich make it seem that the encounter between architecture, in this case neoclassical architecture, and Nazi totalitarianism is the contingent result of Hitler's passion for architecture.[3]

Without knowing the intention of historical actors, we must nevertheless note that this relation between art and politics was explicitly claimed by the Nazis. This is the spirit of the article "Art as Foundation for the Creative Force of Politics" (*Völkischer Beobachter*), according to which the political works of Hitler were the sublimation and transfiguration of his artistic dispositions:

> Today we know that it was not by chance that Adolf Hitler did not at the time become one of the many students studying painting at the Academy of Vienna. He was destined for a greater task than simply becoming a great painter or perhaps a great architect. His gift for painting is nevertheless not an aspect of his personality that is simply due to chance, but is a fundamental characteristic that touches the very kernel of his being. There is an internal and indissoluble link between the artistic works of the Führer and his great political undertaking. Art is also the root of his development as a politician and a statesman. In the case of this man, his artistic activity is not simply an occupation of his youth, due to pure chance. It is not a deviation from his political genius, but is the primary condition of his creative idea of totality. . . . The Führer has given the concept of politics a constructive content, and he was able to do so only because his political ideas developed from his understanding of an autocreative artistic activity.[4]

It is thus appropriate to question the purpose of the strategy of disjunction, which consists of rescuing neoclassical architecture and dissociating it from National Socialism. Five propositions encapsulate this strategy of disjunction.

(1) To successfully reappropriate classical architecture, it would be important to distinguish the "noble cultural means" from the "vile," racist political ends. This distinction is all the more legitimate when one puts forward the following thesis: if, historically, a detestable political regime appealed to noble cultural means to attain its ends, it turns out that the means mobilized always ended up, because of their "nobility," transcending the reprehensible political goals.

Thus, according to Léon Krier, who insists on using the "transcendence" argument, the architecture of Albert Speer was the "civilizing facade"—and as such salvageable—of an empire of lies.

(2) This distinction leads directly to the *thesis of the neutrality of architecture*, or even its agnosticism or its political indifferentism.[5] As Krier writes, "There can no more be authoritarian or democratic architecture than there can be authoritarian or democratic Wiener Schnitzels."[6] Without even interrogating the soundness of this comparison between cooking—food—and architecture, it could be remarked that Krier hardly troubled himself with conceptual categories, since he blithely confounds authoritarianism, dictatorship, tyranny, and totalitarianism; since he indiscriminately uses one of these terms, which he clearly regards as synonyms, to allow for an economy of repetitions!

(3) The thesis of the political indifferentism of architecture rests on an instrumental conception of architectural phenomena:

> There are good and bad constructions, humane and inhuman forms of producing, using or exploiting architecture. . . . Architecture is not political. It is an instrument of politics, for better or worse.[7]

(4) The next proposition is the justified denunciation of the false syllogism. Following Krier's analysis, all events would be due to the implementation of a false syllogism:

- Hitler liked classic architecture, *and* Hitler was a tyrant; *therefore*, classic architecture is tyrannical.

If it is indeed true that we cannot logically leap from Hitler's passion to the necessarily tyrannical nature of classical architecture, then it also does not follow that we can be saved from an *interrogation* of the possible relation between architecture as "sovereign art," "tyrannical art"—in the theocratic age it is true (Victor Hugo)—and the totalitarian regimes of our century.

(5) Finally, the strategy of disjunction highlights the *indeterminate* relationship between totalitarian regimes and architectural style. National Socialism is indeed most often associated with neoclassical architecture, Italian fascism with modernist architecture, and, from the middle of the 1930s, Stalinism is equally guided by neoclassical architecture. We could thus conclude by simple logic that architecture and politics are autonomous realms: since the same architectural styles appear in different political regimes and, conversely, structurally similar regimes base themselves on different architectural styles.

But, to take this further, have we really understood the essence of a totalitarian regime? Is it enough to invoke this logic and superbly ignore the logic of the totalitarian institution of the social and, at the same time, the relationship it is able to establish through the institution of a singular space and time?

The sole interest, for us, of this *strategy of disjunction* is to direct attention to the dangers that result from the dogmatic thesis of conjunction. But, as we know, using a thesis is another way of conserving it, of remaining *willy-nilly* under its control.

II. The Three Critical Demands

Our task is therefore defined in this way: How do we critically think about the relationship between architecture and totalitarian regimes?

The word *critical* implies satisfying a number of requirements.

1. Research Hypothesis

It is about putting a research hypothesis to the test rather than affirming a dogmatic thesis, and this hypothesis is based on the following questions: Has totalitarian domination given birth to a specific architectural logic? Are there one or a number of architectural forms proper to the totalitarian experience, or else—the counterhypothesis—are the architectural productions and the totalitarian experience separable and therefore independent from the political-ideological unities in which they appear?

In order to be relevant, these questions must be operationalized; that is to say, it is appropriate to distinguish many types of architecture at the center of the same historical-political unity. Hence, what counts for public architecture does not necessarily count for industrial or private architecture. By the same token, what do we mean by totalitarian domination? Barbara Miller Lane writes:

> Nazi architectural policy was not the product of a monolithic totalitarian system, but of feuds and power struggles. The Nazi building program reflected not a new totalitarian ideology, but a series of conflicting ideas which were themselves rooted in and conditioned by the architectural controversies of the Weimar period.[8]

If it is true that we must take into consideration the jumbled, eclectic nature of Nazi ideology, is Lane's conclusion not impaired by a rather banal conception of totalitarianism as a monolithic structure; a conception that ignores Hannah Arendt's celebrated analysis of the "onion"-like structure of this regime (if it can be called a regime)? Also, works as remarkable as that of Lane's often suffer from a lack of reflection on the nature of totalitarian domination and a failure to situate themselves on the most important point of observation, namely, the political institution of the social bond.

But the relationship, if there is a relationship (again, do the precise terms of the relationship need to be specified?), must be considered in its *reciprocity*: totalitarian regimes feel a particular attraction, a fascination with architecture. How can we interpret this fascination?

2. Philosophical Interpretations of Totalitarianism: Unity and Diversity

The point is to interrogate and problematize existing research on totalitarian architecture, beginning with philosophical interpretations of totalitarianism (especially those of Hannah Arendt and Claude Lefort) rather than sociological and legal typologies that base their analysis on instances of correlation. The main concern with bringing together these two objects—totalitarian domination and architecture—is that it might lead to overlooking the diversity of each phenomenon: different architectures and different totalitarian regimes. If one of the research presuppositions is that totalitarianism is a novel form of domination, originating in the twentieth century, then it is clearly distinct from dictatorship, tyranny, despotism, or authoritarian regimes. But the fact remains that, despite this interpretation, which privileges the unity of totalitarian domination, it is necessary to consider the diversity of totalitarian regimes.

This means, in part, questioning the origins and nature of the unity: Is massive architectural investment a distinctive criterion of totalitarianism? As Krier recognizes about architecture, but without drawing a conclusion, "recent dictatorships all over the world fare all too well without it."[9]

At the same time, it is necessary to take diversity into account: What role does architecture play in the process of differentiating totalitarian regimes? Is architecture at the center of a unitary constellation, a distinguishing element for such regimes? In other words, can we locate the effects and signs of the process of differentiation at the level of the architectural?

3. Political Intelligence

Finally, the fundamental critique developed here addresses the strategies of disjunction from the perspective of *political intelligence*, that is to say, an approach that attaches primary importance to the question of the political *regime*. We use regime not in the narrow sense—the legal or constitutional sense—but in the larger sense as "the way of life of a community as essentially determined by its 'form of government.'"[10] By this, we admit to putting forward a double hypothesis:

- A society is distinguished from others by its regime, whose principle is shaped by the mode of generation and the representation of power;

- there is a relationship between the ways of living in a society—in this case, architecture—and the form of government.

How, in the light of political intelligence, do we understand the relationship between architecture and totalitarian regimes? Beyond the very question of totalitarianism, we must stop thinking of politics as a derived element, but rather restore it to the status of a mode of institution of the social. If, therefore, politics, which institutes the social, is comprised of three constituting moments—the *mise en forme*, *mise en sens*, and *mise en scène* [shaping, giving meaning, and staging][11]—what is the relationship between the totalitarian regime, its principle of interiorization, and the singular constitution of the social bond? And how does architecture intervene in the totalitarian institution of the social bond? In essence, it is from the point of view of the social bond—the form of community—that we try to understand the articulation of the aesthetic and the political.

A political intelligence approach to the question of architecture invites us to work on the category of totalitarianism using the contributions of Arendt and Lefort, but at the same time attempting to reflect more deeply on totalitarian domination through a connection with other theories. For instance, George Mosse's invaluable work *The Nationalization of the Masses*[12] puts forward the thesis of a "new politics," which aims precisely to articulate the relationship between the aesthetic and the political, or, in Benjaminian terms, the aestheticization of politics. Is Krier's characterization of Speer's work as "an architecture of desire" not a response to a hypothesis of this nature?

An equally valuable source is Weber's theory of charismatic authority. It is used by Franz Neumann, in *Behemoth*, when he invokes the Weberian typology to better understand, in a critical fashion, the specificity of National Socialism.[13]

Next and above all, a political intelligence approach is about interrogating the political subject in question. But how should this expression be understood? Contrary to Krier's argument, which seeks to salvage Speer's neoclassical architecture, we are not here in the universe of citizenship, nor in that of *res publica*. Rather, we are in the universe of a "disturbing strangeness," a universe enchanted by what Elias Canetti calls "the mass and power."[14] The political subject in question here is the mass, an ambiguous subject (which allows us to play on the word "subject") that can be clearly dissociated from the ideas of action and autonomy, but that is close to the ideas of submission and "total mobilization." The mass is a subject that is paradoxically constituted by an experience of radical heteronomy: the moment when the *movement*, the putting into action, is substituted for the individual. This leads to the most extreme form of subjection. The mass as a political subject leads us to a political problem obscured by the tradition, but that is reactivated and recuperated because of the necessity of interpreting the totalitarian enigma of our time. I am referring here to the enigma of "voluntary servitude," as La Boétie magnificently developed it. According to his interpretation, the "political subject" embraces servitude as if it were their salvation in Spinoza's terms, and they surrendered their autonomy and liberty for the enchantment of nonliberty and the charm of subjection. Architecture, approached in this light, would not then be an arcane instrument of domination (*arcanae dominationis*) but instead a new face of voluntary servitude. Consequently, the question is: What is the relationship between the magical power that goes by the *name of architecture* and the charm that goes by the *name of One*?

III. Grand Position

1. No Univocal Relation: The Necessity of Displacement

With these critical requirements in mind, how do we preliminarily define the broad guidelines of this essay?

It is necessary to accept the disconcerting thought that there is no univocal relationship between totalitarian regimes and a given architectural style,[15] since it seems that a totalitarian regime can equally appropriate neoclassical, modernist, or futurist styles, or even practice the eclectic coexistence of many styles.

Furthermore, it is wrong to reduce the question of architecture and totalitarianism to a matter of style, whether there is a relation or whether it should be denied. The question should rather be broken down into the two following lines of interrogation.

a. The Question of the Status of Architecture

We need to shift from architectural style to architecture itself, understood as the identifying self-representation of a given historical community. What is the status of architecture in a specific totalitarian regime? The status of architecture is the same as the *name of architecture*, if we take into consideration the fascination that architecture exercises on totalitarian power. This was suddenly discovered by Speer, to his benefit, when he outlined a project for the First Congress of the Nazi Party in July 1933. He writes:

> Preparations were being made for the first Party Rally of what was now the government party. The victorious spirit of the party was to be expressed even in the architecture of the background.[16]

And on this occasion Speer met the Führer, the one who held the power to make all decisions in this domain, for the first time:

> For the first time I had *an intimation of what the magic word 'architecture' meant under Hitler*. . . . But in those days few people were acquainted with Hitler's hobby.[17]

The question of the status and the name of architecture could provide a discriminating criterion for totalitarian regimes: we could, in essence, distinguish between the regimes that reveal a congruence between architecture and totalitarian domination, where architecture becomes a constitutive element of this form of domination (e.g., National Socialism), and the regimes in which we only see a *tropism* towards architecture, where architecture serves a function that is more ornamental than constitutive.

In any case, having given reason to the strategy of disjunction in *style*, but rejected its analysis regarding the *status* of architecture, the question remains: Why does the logic of totalitarianism lead to such a strong investment in the architectural? At this level, which is addressed in Speer's *Memoirs*, it is worth posing a new question: How do we explain the singularity of the relationship between the architect who enjoyed an exceptional status and the Führer? Is the relationship one of attraction, fascination, or reciprocal rivalry? What distinguishes or brings together the relationship between the philosopher and the tyrant, as it is described by Alexandre Kojève?[18]

Following the analysis of Barbara Lane, we can determine the point at which architecture acquired an exceptional status in the Nazi regime. In the beginning of the 1930s, an increasing number of articles in the Nazi press attacked the new architecture, equating it to "cultural bolshevism." This campaign intensified in 1933, according to Lane—from this point on "architecture . . . took the most prominent place" in the press.[19] In general, while there was no homogenous view in the Nazi camp as to what the style of architecture should be, there was nevertheless agreement that the place and importance of architecture should be recognized. We see this in the reappearance of the age-old comparison between the statesman and the architect—or to put it in a more plebeian way, the stonemason—and in the simultaneously constructivist and conservative nature of statist intervention. It was also expressed in July 1933, during a reunion of *Kampfbund*, in the parable of the unknown stonemason, which makes a clear allusion to Hitler:

> During the last generation, a "wonderful old building" (the German Reich) had been allowed to decay. But then came an unknown stonemason (Hitler), who gathered together . . . the good old workmen who had earlier been unable to protect the

old building. Together "they chased out the false masters and shored up a firm scaffold around the building and began to clear away its fake decorations and vain tinsel, so that the old pure form could arise again."[20]

The Führer did not hesitate to present himself as "the Architect" or to declare that, without war, he would very likely become, one of the greatest or even the premier architect in Germany.[21]

The status accorded to architecture was all the more prominent insofar as the issue of architecture became an essential part of ideological warfare, especially because this issue assembled and condensed all the themes of Nazi ideology—anti-modernism, anti-bolshevism, and anti-Semitism.

For example, consider this comment regarding the *Bauhaus*:

> The Bauhaus—that was "the cathedral of Marxism," a cathedral, however, which damned well looked like a Synagogue. To the "inspiration" of this "model school" we owe not least those oriental boxes which we have described before, [and] which are repugnant to good taste. . . . These men reveal their character as typical nomads of the metropolis, who no longer understand blood and soil. . . . Now their secret is known! The new dwelling is an instrument for the destruction of the family and the race. Now we understand the deeper sense of that architectural nonsense which built housing developments in the style of prison cells, and perpetuated an Asiatic interlude on German soil. . . . Bolshevism, the arch-enemy of all mature culture, works toward the victory of this [architectural] desolation and horror![22]

b. The Question of the Threshold?

Given the Nazi regime's indifference to the *only architectural style* that would be permitted, the question can henceforth be expressed as follows: What becomes of neoclassical architecture when it is *mobilized* in the constitution of a totalitarian regime? Evidently, the same question could be asked of futurist or modernist architecture. In short, the idea is to locate and describe the mutations and metamorphoses that appear in a given style of architecture when it becomes a constitutive piece of a totalitarian regime. Are there signs or markings of totalitarian influence? Monumentality, colossality, excessiveness, giganticness? As only an initial indication of totalitarian influence, we only need to look to the question of space, the institution of space. This focus allows us to formulate a more specifically political question: Does the way in which space is constituted suggest it is valued as public space—as political space—or not? That is to say, does it permit a plurality of humans, a condition of politics, to assemble and display themselves, to appear; or, is architectural space instead constituted as the negation of plurality and therefore as the negation of the political? In this regard, it seems necessary to recall a more precise definition of public space, for instance that given by Arendt, as that which dares to occur beyond the protection of the household.

Public space is a space of equals—of citizens linked by a principle of equality where each can pay attention and listen to another—and an agonistic space within which paradoxical bonds of division can be formed. Arendt still hastens to add that this conception of public space is not yet political: it only becomes political when it manifests itself in the heart of a free *polis*, which is not dominated by a tyrant and where people can gather together to act in concert.[23]

Following this conception, if the observer adopts a single criterion to judge the architecture of public space, it could be described as the question of the threshold: At which point does an ensemble of signs cross a threshold and an architectural work is henceforth subject to a totalitarian influence? Speer sketches some responses in his *Memoirs*:

> Whenever, nowadays, I look through the plans and photos of the models, even these varied parts of the avenue strike me as lifeless and regimented. . . . Our plan completely lacked a sense of proportion. . . . The entire conception was stamped by a monumental rigidity that would have counteracted all our efforts to introduce urban life into this avenue.[24]

Again, it would seem that this influence is best marked by a will to total domination; consider in this light the project of a central station:

> The station, its steel ribbing showing through sheathings of copper and glass, would have handsomely offset the great blocks of stone dominating the rest of the avenue. It provided four traffic levels linked by escalators and elevators and was to surpass New York's Grand Central Station. State visitors would have descended a large outside staircase. The idea was that as soon as they, as

well as ordinary travelers, stepped out of the station they would be overwhelmed, or rather stunned, by the urban scene and the power of the Reich.[25]

It is at the level of the totalitarian influence that we could refine our analysis by adding the question of *idola fori*, the idols of the marketplace: Could we not distinguish between the *idola fori* privileged by architecture according to the totalitarian regime? For example, consider the immensity of natural phenomena for National Socialism, or the machine for Italian fascism. These can in all likelihood be traced back to divergent models of community.

2. Totalitarian Regimes, Architecture and Social Bonds

Not only does the point of view of political intelligence allow us to go beyond the simplified disjunction thesis based on a univocal relationship between architecture and totalitarianism, but it also suggests that the fundamental question is that of the political institution of the social bond. Or, to put it in Arendtian terms, the question is, What is distinct about the fundamental experience of human community that permeates a totalitarian regime?

In order to understand the totalitarian institution of the social bond in its complexity, it is necessary to rework the main categories discussed: the new politics, charismatic domination, the totalitarian logic, and social space.

a. Totalitarian Regimes and New Politics; or Architecture and the Mobilization of the Masses

Rather than oppose the concept of "new politics" to the politics of totalitarianism,[26] it appears, on the contrary, more constructive to integrate the contributions of this new conceptualization with analyses of the totalitarian experience. With the term "new politics," George Mosse intends to distinguish the form of politics appearing at the end of the eighteenth century, especially in the French Revolution and the wars of liberation in Germany. This "new politics" opposes the liberal focus on the composition of elites—those of "superior capacity," according to Guizot[27]—with the idea of the "nationalization of the masses," where masses are integrated into the national body. Reformulating the idea of popular sovereignty and the transformation that leads to the appearance of the people on the political scene, this new ambition is a deliberate metamorphosis, in spite of the modern separation between religion and politics, into a new secular religion that defines itself as such (the Saint-Simonians, for instance). Against representative government, which is criticized as favoring atomization and separation, the new politics, as "democracy of the crowd," searches for new institutions that will establish other types of mediation or communication between the rulers and the ruled, and also elaborates new forms of social control. In shifting to modern political reason and the choice of limited forms of participation, as emphasized by Benjamin Constant in his famous opposition between ancient and modern conceptions of liberty, this new form of mobilization creates a style of politics focused on myths and symbols, liturgies, even cults, through which "the people" acquires its identity by undergoing a series of intense emotional experiences.

Political action is transformed into a drama with the ascendance of speech, the supremacy of oral over written propaganda. Permanently integrating the arts, in practice this new politics develops at the intersection of the religious dimension and the aesthetic dimension. We witness an unprecedented aestheticization of politics.

In short, the dominant characteristic of this new politics is the formation of a type of human community that regards itself as superior to the modern democratic community. It is superior because it opens access to a specific form of unity, one that could be overcome in the passage from *all ones* [*Tous-uns*] to the *all One* [*Tous-Un*], the distinctly modern form of alienation.

To put it another way, it is characteristic of totalitarian regimes to take note of the emergence of the people at the beginning of the new politics in order to better deny them: it is in the very process of *demobilizing the people* as a political actor that there is a *mobilization of the crowd* as a "subject." The totalitarian regime, which shifts from nationalization to the organized mobilization of the crowd, is oriented around a fusional social bond that presses together individuals to a degree seldom achieved in the new politics. A new political regime that destroys the very conditions for politics, totalitarianism operates through terror and ideology, but also, one could say, through the exasperation of the new politics. It is by beginning with this exasperation that we can interpret the place of architecture in this form of domination.

Krier, who wrongly associates totalitarianism only with terror, himself recognizes the "magical power" of the architecture of Speer:

Classical architecture is incapable of exerting terror by the force of its internal laws. The grandeur, elegance and solidity of these monuments was in no way designed to frighten. Their purpose was, on the contrary, to raise enthusiasm and *seduce*, to *impress* and *overwhelm* the masses, to offer protection and ultimately to deceive the captivated souls as to the final intentions of the industrial-military system.[28]

But rather than proceeding once again to the dissociation of the "civilized and respectable facade"—architecture—from the empire of lies, it is necessary instead to pose a continuity, a connection between the two, between the seduction of architecture and the process of the constitution of the crowd, between capturing souls (not by deceiving them about intentions) and the shaping and staging of a magical and fusional social bond.

Architecture appears then as a moment and as a fundamental device for organizing the mass. It works through the institution of a sacred, magical, and specifically structured space, attributes which come to form a constitutive piece of this regime. The totalitarian regime is a paradoxical one in the sense that the disappearance or destruction of the political, an aim it requires, is tantamount to its self-destruction as a regime. In this regard, it is worth reemphasizing that totalitarianism is a new form of domination, which is distinct from despotism, an absolutist State, or a super-Leviathan. The latter of these is the model that Franz Neumann follows, giving the title *Behemoth* to his study of National Socialism. Another name for a biblical monster that ruled the desert, "behemoth" had the merit of joining the idea of totalitarian domination to a Stateless and lawless situation of "anarchy" and chaos. With this reminder, we see how the problem at hand is far from an empirical study of statist intervention in the cultural field, or of the administrative, bureaucratic ordering of architectural politics.

Instead, what is necessary is to find the meeting points where the logic of total domination (well beyond law, the conscious administrative organization) becomes inseparable from a definite representation of the community, of the social bond. These points emerge in architectural devices, and more specifically in a certain structuration of space, and, in this regard, it is legitimate to speak of a specifically totalitarian space that, by its very nature, is apolitical or—better yet—anti-political. This totalitarian space is destructive of all cities, of the "geometry" proper to the organization of a city per se.

Elias Canetti's analysis of crowd dynamics helps to better perceive these meeting points. In essence, he points to a strange alchemy at work in a mass *in statu nascendi*: "It is only in a [mass] that man can become free of [his] fear of being touched."[29] In the mass, not only is this fear surmounted, but it turns into its inverse, the search for contact, the fusion into a unity or a compact body. Canetti continues:

> That is the only situation in which the fear changes into its opposite. The crowd he needs is the dense [mass], in which body is pressed to body; a [mass], too, whose psychical constitution is also dense, or compact, so that he no longer notices who it is that presses against him. As soon as a man has surrendered himself to the [mass], he ceases to fear its touch. Ideally, all are equal there; no distinctions count, not even that of sex. The man pressed against him is the same as himself. He feels him as he feels himself. Suddenly it is as though everything were happening in one and the same body. This is perhaps one of the reasons why a [mass] seeks to close in on itself: it wants to rid each individual as completely as possible of the fear of being touched. The more fiercely people press together, the more certain they feel that they do not fear each other. This reversal of the fear of being touched belongs to the nature of [the mass]. The feeling of relief is most striking where the density of the [mass] is greatest.[30]

Canetti bases his analysis by attaching the name "discharge" to the process that unfolds at the interior of a mass and that constitutes them free of the charges of distance:

> During the discharge distinctions are thrown off and all feel *equal*. In that density, where there is scarcely any space between, and body presses against body, each man is as near the other as he is to himself; and an immense feeling of relief ensues. It is for the sake of this blessed moment, when no-one is greater or better than another, that people become a [mass].[31]

Canetti's writings tell us about the meeting point between architecture and totalitarian regimes through their account of the "effect of compactness," of compactness itself. In other words, the constitution of compact spaces has the distinct character of making the intervals between people disappear, or of reducing and abolishing the burdens of distance.

It is Canetti himself who, in his reading of Speer's memoir, *Inside the Third Reich*, provides extremely valuable insights about the possible relationship of architecture and the organization of the mass. Rejecting what he sees as the wrongheaded analytical perspective of Krier, Canetti characterizes the architecture-mass relation as a type of animation.

By doing so, it offers a very rich hypothesis, according to which the *organization of the mass, their animation, is the true mediation between architecture and totalitarian domination*. This is exactly the thesis that he puts forward in the essay "According to Speer," which carries the significant subtitle, "Grandeur and Permanence":

> Hitler's constructions are meant to attract and to hold the greatest [masses]. The creation of such [masses] is what brought him to power, but he knows how easily great [masses] tend to fall apart. Aside from the war, there are only two ways of preventing that. One way is their *growth*, the other their regular *repetition*. As an empiricist of [the mass], such as few have existed, he knows both their forms and their methods. On huge squares, so big that they are hard to fill, the [mass] has the possibility of growing, it remains open. Its passion, which he is especially aiming at, increases with its growth.[32]

Canetti very sharply reinforces this hypothesis of mediation by affirming a relation between the type of animation and the type of building, as if the type of building is destined to determine the form of animation:

> For the regular *repetition*, he wanted buildings of a cultic nature. Their model is the cathedral. . . . These edifices and areas, which are so large as to seem cold and standoffish even on paper, are filled—in their builder's mind—with [masses] that behave differently according to the nature of the vessel holding them, according to the nature of their delimitation. . . . It should [be our task] to generally emphasize the way those buildings and areas would be animated.[33]

As evidence, this "mobilization of joy"—the future place Hitler would assemble a million men—goes alongside a demobilization of political actors. As

Siegfried Kracauer wrote in 1927, in *The Mass Ornament*, "the production and mindless consumption of ornamental patterns divert [people] from the imperative to change the reigning order."[34]

b. Totalitarian Regimes and Charismatic Domination

ARCHITECTURE AND THE DIRECTION OF THE DAEMONIC

In similarly critical ways, Roger Caillois (*Quatre essais de sociologie contemporaine*, 1951) and Franz Neumann (*Behemoth*, 1944) invite us to think together totalitarianism and charismatic authority, even going so far as to suggest that this form of authority is a constitutive moment of the totalitarian logic. The *daemonic* is a key element, in the strong sense of the term, of this form of domination. That is to say, it is a form of power that is steeped in the irrational—in ways that seemed to escape the common man, the *daemon* of the Führer itself would be allowed to decide the division of friend/enemy. The Führer's power would be endowed with superhuman qualities, *numinous*, of a nature that generates at the same time terror and fascination. It is based on the constant staging of a *mysterium tremendum*.

According to Max Weber's definition,

> The term "charisma" will be applied to a certain quality of an individual personality by virtue of which he is considered extraordinary and treated as endowed with supernatural, superhuman, or at least specifically exceptional powers or qualities. These are such as are not accessible to the ordinary person, but are regarded as of divine origin or as exemplary, and on the basis of them the individual concerned is treated as a "leader."[35]

The mark of a totalitarian regime is that it operates at the junction between the qualities of the new politics—the aestheticization of the political—and those of charismatic domination. It is characteristic for this form of domination to arouse an intense *emotional community*. The organization of rites, of congress (processions, marches, parades, and according to Canetti "creeping masses"), or similarly that which we could call "living architecture," aim to represent this *magic vibration* between the Führer and the crowd, to set the tone of the "movement." It is in this sense that we can consider architecture as the staging of the Führer's *daemonic* power.

With regard to the new chancellery, Speer reports these words of Hitler:

> I stand here as representative of the German people. And whenever I receive anyone in the Chancellery, it is not the private individual Adolf Hitler who receives him, but the Leader of the German nation—and therefore it is not I who receive him, but Germany through me. For that reason I want these rooms to be in keeping with their high mission. Every individual has contributed to a structure that will outlast the centuries and will speak to posterity of our times. This is the first architectural creation of the new, great German Reich!³⁶

We have already seen the effects of this mixture of terror and fascination, how it aroused faith and subjection.

TIME AND POLITICS: ARCHITECTURE AND ENTRAPPING CHARISMA

The reason we introduce the question of charismatic authority, envisioned in a critical way, is to understand its relationship to architecture in the institution of a specific time. For is not the principal concern of Max Weber's typology of authority to show how each form of authority institutes a singular experience of time, a determinate form of time? From this point of view, the distinguishing feature of charismatic authority is the extraordinary privileging of the power of the extraordinary, exceptional only in the sense of what breaks the usual course of things; of its anti-economic, anti-everyday character. Revealing in this regard is the antagonism that opposed Hitler, the charismatic leader, to Speer, the bureaucrat-architect who became the Minister of Armaments in 1942. As he explains in his *Memoirs*,

> Nevertheless, I considered these official buildings as subsidiary to the total plan; Hitler did not. His passion for building for eternity left him without a spark of interest in traffic arrangements, residential areas, and parks. He was indifferent to the social dimension.³⁷

The charismatic leader is caught in an aporetic situation. Like all forms of authority, charismatic authority tends to persevere in its being, and therefore must be carried out in time. But, at the same time, this carrying out in time destroys the charismatic character that founds and legitimates it. This is the aporia of the routinization of *charisma*: its execution in humdrum, everyday time dissolves the *primum movens* of this domination, namely, the very charisma or epiphany of an exceptional, non-everyday time. The inscription of charismatic authority in time, in short its success, paradoxically opens the door to its failure, the disappearance or dissolution of charisma.

This dissolution is an aporia of the type that Canetti has in mind when he insists on the "Egyptian" character of Hitlerian architecture. Considered again in terms of the animation of the mass, Canetti writes:

> It is an animation that continues *beyond the death* of the builder. "Your husband," [Hitler] says solemnly to Speer's wife on the first evening they meet, "will erect buildings for me such as have not arisen in four thousand years." He is thinking of Egypt, particularly the pyramids, because of their size, but also because they have always existed during these four thousand years. . . . It is as though they had stored up their millennia, for which they were meant, as permanence. Their public character and their permanence have deeply impressed him. . . . For these constructions . . . are the symbol of a [mass] that cannot crumble.[38]

The hypothesis is then that the task of architecture under this form of authority is to provide a "solution," a response to the aporia that results from the routinization of charisma. It is as if the architecture—by virtue of its grandeur, its monumentality, its giganticness—aims to immobilize or to *fix* (in the sense of a static shot, but also in the sense of an inscription) the charisma of the Führer. It seeks to retain that "elusive quality"—that which defies capture—in time and always *in statu nascendi*. As Canetti explains, "[Hitler's] buildings . . . were not pyramids and were to take over only their size and permanence."[39]

Contrary to Krier, who does not hesitate to summon Arendt's theories for the occasion, it is not about using a public architecture as a remedy for the fragility of human things, the "whirlwind of all things human."[40] It is rather about using a totalitarian architecture to institute totalitarian spaces, to use the rigidity and massiveness of the stone to fix the breathtaking, hypnotic flash of the charismatic leader in order to represent a passionate and fused alliance of the Führer and the "racial people":

> But I found Hitler's excitement rising whenever I could show him that at least in size we had "beaten" the other great build-

ings of history. To be sure, he never gave vent to these heady feelings. He was sparing in his use of high-sounding words to me. Possibly at such moments he actually felt a certain awe; but it was directed toward himself and toward his own greatness, which he himself had willed and projected into eternity.[41]

This combination of grandeur and permanence tended to create an absolute retention of *charisma*, as if it was a matter of putting them into store, in the words of Canetti; or even a sort of crystallization of enthusiasm, a "symbol of a [mass] that cannot crumble."[42] To support this hypothesis, we can turn to the idea that Hitler had of his relationship to his eventual successors. Devoid of any charisma, they would fall back into bureaucratic domination. However, by virtue of its retention of charisma, Nazi monumentality would confer upon them something of the charismatic aura of its founder. Although Canetti does not appeal to the Weberian notion of charismatic authority, his work is useful because of the notion of the retention of *charisma* that he develops in his analysis of the interaction of grandeur and permanence:

> The [masses] through whose arousal he came to power are to be rearoused, over and over again, *even when he is no longer here*. Since his successors will not be able to achieve that end in his fashion, for he is unique, he leaves behind the best kinds of assistance, well-prepared places of any kind that serve in the tradition of crowd arousal. The fact that they are his buildings gives them a special aura. . . . The memory of his very own [masses], whom he has aroused himself, shall aid his weaker successors. . . . The power he has acquired through his [masses] will thereby survive.[43]

In other words, the characteristics of Third Reich architecture reflect more on the status than on the style that would be considered the "Hitlerian solution" to the aporia of charismatic authority. With this in mind, we can begin a critical reflection on the Hitlerian definition of architecture as "words of stone," a definition that strangely implies combining the volatility of speech and the fossilization of words in the building material, which tends to mix the ephemerality of "the extraordinary" with its inscription in and for eternity. It is as if eternalization (which should not be confused with the political desire for immortality) had what we might call an "Egyptian" way to salvage, to retain something of the "extraordinary" quality of the image of the charismatic leader (in the sense of that which breaks the ordinary course of things).

Paradoxical as it may seem, a relationship that would otherwise not be considered is established in architecture between the ephemeral, the "exceptional," speed and the choice of eternity—at the same time a denial of finitude and a retention of charisma—under the form of a millennial empire. In this sense, the question of the stone, and the time of dualisms that accompanies it, is revealed to be an essential question for an analysis of architecture and totalitarian regimes.

c. Totalitarian Logic, Architecture and Space

Like all political regimes, totalitarianism aims to institute a singular experience of space based on a conception of the proper place of the locus of power.

THE DEPOLITICIZATION AND AESTHETICIZATION OF THE POLITICAL: MONUMENTAL ART

What seems to be ignored in most of the vulgar interpretations of totalitarianism is that this form of regime (to the extent it can be called a regime) is paradoxical: it is a regime whose logic is to suppress politics but claims to save it, because it is traversed by the illusory desire to bring about a reconciled society that has overcome social division and its effects. Thus, according to a theory that is too often repeated, totalitarianism is described as an *overpoliticization* of all spheres of existence. These analyses correspond without a doubt to the all-consuming penetration of the society by the State—to society's near absorption—which tends to reduce the plurality of the social field to a unified ensemble of norms, values, and rules so as to produce a nearly homogenous social universe. The unique party and a network of militant organizations—the Movement—is the omnipresent agent of this incessant march towards unification. But, because of the inappropriate term "overpoliticization," this homogenizing, totalitarian logic confuses a process of the organization and mobilization of the masses that tends towards a non-State with one that institutes a public and political space allowing for action to manifest itself.[44]

The result is the "innocent" countermeaning of Krier and others who dare to invoke the Arendtian notion of public space to "salvage" Nazi monumentality. It is also the result of Ernest Jünger's theorization of the ascendency of party or "Movement," the order of "total mobilization," which is based on a forgetting of politics, or, to be more precise, a conscious denial of politics, perhaps even a hatred of it. This denial of politics appears at many levels: the disappearance of political thinking as such, the erosion of different limits instituted by the law, or, most importantly, the effacement of the very idea of limit and especially the foreclosure of the political field as a space of liberty where, through speech and action—the faculties of political beginnings—the people (the *all ones*) can realize the human condition of plurality and allow it to create meaning.

Architecture, as a constitutive element of a totalitarian regime—the one through which it displays its *archē*, its order—institutes a space where nothing is public, nothing is political. Far from permitting the coexistence of humans through the institution of an agonistic space of speech and action, a differentiated space of appearance that is necessary for action to occur, the totalitarian regime rather aims to constitute and mobilize a mass that is submissive in every sense of the word to a multifaceted experience. This experience is the "discharge" in Canetti's sense of the term, the experience of a fused homogeneity corresponding to the laws of history, in unity with the movement of the race and its biological links, and finally of the command-obedience relationship.

Since it is a question of space and of Arendt, we should not forget that Arendt aptly describes what happens in a mass society where, in some way, we are falling on top of one another:

> What makes mass society so difficult to bear is not the number of people involved, or at least not primarily, but the fact that the world between them has lost its power to gather them together, to relate and to separate them. The weirdness of this situation resembles a spiritualistic séance where a number of people gathered around a table might suddenly, through some magic trick, see the table vanish from their midst, so that two persons sitting opposite each other were no longer separated but also would be entirely unrelated to each other by anything tangible.[45]

In this description of mass society, the deliberate reference to magic and spiritualism—and not to the Greek solution, the *polis*—must be retained to determine the specific character of the space that institutes totalitarianism. Only by acknowledging such mystical overtones can we figure out how to recognize in Nazi monumentality not a new public space, "the beautiful facade of the regime," but rather the very conditions of mass slavery cut off from all political experience. In the totalitarian Nazi universe, what is important is exactly the opposite of public and political space—it is about the very destruction of such space in order to replace it with the space of absolute cohesion, under the dominion of a command that is equally absolute. To see this, we only need to turn to an article by Speer written in 1937, "Les infrastructures du Tempelhofer Feld pour le 1ᵉʳ mai 1933 à Berlin" [The Facilities of Tempelhofer Field in Berlin for May 1, 1933].

In the new festivals of the regime, the people are no longer represented as a political subject, but instead as a support, as material that has overcome all separation:

> The form given to public festivities was known during those days as a fundamental transformation. The idea of the machinery of State was filled out through a new life that had recently burst forth from the people and as a consequence had become intimately bound in the most profound way with their way of life. *The people had become the living support of the State.* These festivals were for this reason "popular festivals" in the most profound sense of the term. They uphold at all points the [State's] typical character. While in the past the armed forces paraded alongside the wall of a curious and detached crowd, the masses of awakened people march today in the millions.[46]

Nazi monumentality, with a gigantism of the mass (the "human walls") to match the gigantism of the buildings, is far from creating a "public." Instead its massive and "compact" product searches for an absolute cohesion:

> The stadium, with its human walls, which are elevated and encircle it, communicated to all the participants a lively notion of the power of a demonstration that is both a huge event and one *permeated by the feeling of absolute cohesion.* Tempelhofer Field, with its gigantic surface, could only give an inadequate understanding of the personal experience shared by the masses marching in the millions. There was the danger that—without the use of artificial modes of power—each person who took part was only incompletely and insufficiently aware of the total size of such an event.[47]

The work on space occurs but it is concentrated on a central point where visibility was privileged and that coincided with the locus of power. Speer's description aptly shows that this structure is directly opposed to a geometric form such as a circle that allows for *l'entre-connaissance* [mutual understanding] or even isonomy. Rather, the structure aimed to, in this case, raise the masses, to direct them towards a central point and through this raising to make them congeal, as if they could not form a bond until they had reached this point:

> *The gigantic dimensions of the Field made all spatial delimitation appear inadequate and rudimentary.* For this reason we could try to create a central point of visibility which would form the core impression of the gathering. It was necessary that the symbolic optical center of the event and the expression of the will of the masses who took part in the marches was so large and so powerful that one could feel the same efficacy and importance at the farthest point of the Field. We built a one-hundred meter long platform for flags, which rose above the terrace to a height of ten meters. More than a thousand flags and banners, many of them representing the marching groups, were placed there, clearly in view. The Reich government, with guests of honour, stood in the middle of the platform of flags. . . . The event was intentionally staged at the beginning of dusk, *which reinforced the effect of concentrating on this central point* because the illumination of the mountain of flags through multiple spotlights gave them a red color which strongly contrasted against the blue of the sky. This contrast continued to build as night descended, while the construction accessories and debris disappeared in the penumbra of the evening.[48]

The architect Speer aptly recognized the expression of the project of domination, the animating force of the Third Reich, in its architecture:

> We looked to produce a collective mentality which had to take megalomania as a norm. . . . Architectural remodeling of German cities at the same time gave the gigantic monuments, *which were destined above all to tell the isolated person of their insignificance*, a propaganda framework for the manifestations of the mass in the marches . . . though the remodeling was already in itself a gesture of propaganda. *The submission of the individual will and the renouncement of it to the collective one as statist objects expressed itself in the architecture.*[49]

Besides its gigantic and megalomaniacal character, this space has several specific characteristics whose addition or reunion only increases the exercise of domination or mass mobilization. It is a sacred space, a magical space that used different forms of animation of the masses to abolish all resistance, all critical spirit on the part of the spectators. Moreover, this is a real hypnotic space where we see again the same focus as that described by Speer earlier. But in this case, the center has become the person of the leader. As Roger Caillois wrote in 1951 in an essay on "Le Pouvoir Charismatique: Adolf Hitler comme idole" [Charismatic Power: Adolf Hitler as an Idol],

> The converging fires of the projectors make the Leader the only clear point in the theatre. We know that this is a classic procedure for provoking hypnosis. It does not take long to reduce to gratefulness a public put deliberately on edge by an endless wait.[50]

Sound preparation, staging, and the use of emotional triggers (flags, music, etc.) work together to produce a quasi-ecstatic state or a mystical union: "I exist in you and you exist in me," declares the Führer, as cited by Caillois.[51]

It is therefore in the paths opened by Neumann, Caillois, and Canetti that we can begin to acquire a better understanding of the relationship of totalitarian architecture to the implementation of very particular types of animation of the masses. But we are also on the side of Arendt, provided that one does not read in the wrong direction. She poses with sufficient clarity, it seems, the contrast between a political space that at the same time binds and separates, and a totalitarian space that locks us in shackles, like a circle of iron, abolishing the space between humans where political freedom and a common world may arise.

Where and how do we situate the contribution of these architectures to the constitution of the *space of political mobilization* and not that of overpoliticization? We recognize again here the problem of the threshold with the question of the monumental and the exaltation of giganticness. At what point can a given architecture be considered as aiding the constitution of the totalitarian enterprise? The sign that announces that this threshold has been reached is the relationship between the monumental and depoliticization and the effacement of action. According to Walter Benjamin, fascism organizes the masses without undermining the fundamentals of the domination that they at the same time are subjected to and tend to reject;

capturing their energy and expression without granting them autonomy or concrete satisfaction, the aestheticization of political life offers the masses *objects or scenes of substitution*, war or monumental art. This aestheticization of politics, this substitution of an aesthetic scene for a concrete practice of transforming social relations, shows through in the monumental character of fascist art. Fascist art aims to perpetuate the domination of a "so-called elite," preventing, through the effects of monumental shaping, the multitude from having any autonomy, such as the idea that it has the power to turn itself into the subject of a revolutionary action. The monumental creates the illusion of the eternal and the immutable. Moreover, it gives rise to a real aesthetic dogmatism, where the producer does not recognize the product as the result of his own productive activity. According to Benjamin, mass spectacles—huge celebrations, monstrous meetings—keep the masses under a "spell" of a new type: they are giving a show to themselves, the masses, through this very gigantism. And far from recognizing this as a sign of their power, they experience the spectacle as a radical heteronomy. Taken as "human material," the crowd constitutes itself as a bloc, dissolving the very notion of a human subject and, a fortiori, the idea of a political actor—in sum, the fascist spectacle destroys all possibility of a process of subjectivization.

The regular association of the mass with architecture—Speer often speaks of "human walls"—suggests, then, a characteristic of the totalitarian oeuvre that is shared in its attitude towards the mass and architecture, namely, compactness. And compactness, the elimination of all in-between space and therefore also all political space for creating the new, would oppose the *porous* or *porosity* that, thanks to an incomplete fabric, would open up spaces of liberty, or rather spaces celebrating the marriage of liberty and play. Using the city of Naples, in 1928 Walter Benjamin and Asja Lacis drew up a counterportrait to totalitarian architecture. It was refined to the point of considering the temporal dimension, which they depicted as a refusal of the definitive and the choice of the unpredictable:

> As porous as this stone is the architecture. Building and action interpenetrate in the courtyards, arcades, and stairways. In everything they preserve the scope to become a theatre of new, unforeseen constellations. The stamp of the definitive is avoided. No situation appears intended forever, no figure asserts its "thus and not otherwise."[52]

INCLUSION/EXCLUSION: THE CATHEDRAL OF LIGHT/NIGHT AND FOG

Following the strategy of disjunction, we could logically make a distinction between Nazi monumentality and the concentration camps, or between reactionary culturalism (neoclassicism) and the industrial and centralist *Sturm und Drang*. Indeed, Krier writes about this regime: "[Hitler's] barbaric crimes were, after all, not perpetrated in a monumental environment but in degrading industrial sheds and camps."[53]

Does the strategy of disjunction again apply here? Can a study of architecture and totalitarian regimes accept, without qualifications, this division between the majestic monumental environment and the squalid industrial barracks? With this separation, would we not be guilty of the same blindness as that of Speer, a blindness that could be attributed to that which Arendt so aptly calls, writing about Eichmann, *nonthinking*?[54] Must the study rather, in addressing the question of the *total* institution of space, look for the secret but undeniable relationship between the "civilizing facade" of majestic monumentality and the squalid inhumanity of the camps where death was "administered" en masse? After all, the blocks of granite used by Speer to construct "great Berlin," capital of a new world empire, were polished in the concentration camps. More precisely, it is the attention focused on the logic of totalitarian regimes that led to the discovery of the sinister edge that depends—in spite of apparent opposition, but very symptomatic—on "the cathedral of light" that has been called the world of "Night and Fog."[55] Like the two sides of a coin, there is a visible, luminous, mystical part that is exhibited and a nocturnal part that is hidden. In order to better preserve the peace of his soul, the architect Speer was never invited to visit the nocturnal part.

Indeed, the logic of a totalitarian regime aims to promote unity—the unity of the *all One* under the double image of the One-people and the One-power—and to erase signs of social division. It erases the division between the State and the society, the line that separates political power from administrative power, and especially the internal division of the social through the self-proclamation of a reconciled society. From there, it implements a joint logic of inclusion and exclusion: the very project of negating the internal division of the social (the project of inclusion) contains a dismissal, a projection of division to the outside of the society—the project of exclusion. This double logic institutes a differentiated space, but one in which the two parts are inseparable from one another: the "glorious" space of the One-people requires the immediate production of an outside space, a residual and squalid space, the industrial barracks to which one deports the Other, the enemy—where one decides to put to death, to exterminate. In the process of identifying and constituting the One-people, the definition of the enemy is key, as Claude Lefort recognizes: "The constitution of the People-as-One requires the incessant production of enemies."[56]

According to the fine analysis of Lefort, at the symbolic level the totalitarian institution of the social is distinguished by a radical mutation, the production of a new image of the social body. Unlike the society of the Old Regime, democracy involves the dissolution of the social body and the disincorporation of the individuals; conversely, because of democracy and against it, the totalitarian regime endeavors to "reveal a new image of the social body," to reincorporate the social.[57]

> An impossible swallowing up of the body in the head begins to take place, as does an impossible swallowing up of the head in the body. The attraction of the whole is no longer dissociated from the attraction of the parts. Once the old organic constitution disappears, the death instinct is unleashed into the closed, uniform, imaginary space of totalitarianism.[58]

Totalitarianism provides a new image of the body that takes into account the duplication of space: it is at once *glorious* space, where architecture contributes to reincorporate the social; and *residual* space, where one rejects the "parasites," the "waste" that it is best to eliminate because they may damage the integrity of the body. In this regard, these analyses remind that it is best to measure the effects of the totalitarian regime both at the level of the institution of social space and by determining the contributions that the architecture is likely to bring. The denial of division, the love of unity, the will to make the body, or rather to remake the body, are translated into an obsession with grandeur and an obsession with the monumental. The monumental appears then as that form of art capable of staging the unity of reconciled society, beyond internal division, the appearance of a new "we" that is exalted in a compulsion to megalomania. This can be seen in the very precisely totalitarian text of Paul Nizan, "Du Problème de la monumentalité" [The Problem of Monumentality], on the Soviet Union:

> Western man is struck at every step by the feel of a particular aspiration that could be called the aspiration to greatness. . . . History

does not know of a society where similar aspirations rule to those of Soviet society.... The Soviet Union finds itself facing the problem of greatness. The aim is to create an art expressing the power of the collectivity with a force at least as great as that of the art of ancient Greece. Bourgeois art has lost the sense of the monumental. A civilization deeply torn by contradictions is no longer able to lead the collective membership.... In the USSR, civilization is such that each can say: *our* Academy, *our* University, just as one says *our* factory, *our* Kolkhose. A capitalist monumental architecture expresses the desegregation of a society, whereas a socialist monumental architecture would express the profound unity of the masses. The former is the sign of domination, the latter that of community. A capitalist public edifice is that sign of desegregation; a socialist public edifice that of unification. One feels this will in the project of the Palace of the Soviets. The demands expressed about the buildings of the socialist epoch invest the architecture with a colossal responsibility.[59]

By retaining Nizan's formula and applying it to all totalitarian regimes, in spite of their differences, we can recover the question of the status of architecture: architecture in such regimes is, in essence, invested with a colossal responsibility. The significance of architecture deserves to be interrogated more in interpretations of totalitarianism, as it incorporates a sensitivity to the symbolic dimension of the institution of the social—it insists on the fundamental mutation of space, on *the labor on space* that happens in totalitarian regimes, as the interpreters of totalitarianism have taught us. Thus Arendt, in a different way than Lefort but similarly privileging the question of space, allows us to think together the joint logic of inclusion and exclusion, and to discern the hidden link between architecture and terror. In opposition to the constitutional regimes that create "the vital space of liberty" in developing, thanks to positive law, a space between people (*inter-esse*), totalitarian regimes, according to Arendt, "by pressing men against each other," destroy all space between them, and reduce that which remains to a desert of tyranny. "It substitutes for the boundaries and channels of communication between individual men a band of iron which holds them so tightly together that it is as though their plurality has disappeared into One Man of gigantic dimensions."[60] The "band of iron" institutes a solid, compact, and enclosed space, which folds back in on itself. The space between people is therefore destroyed, communication is therefore controlled, and what emerges instead is a mass experience of *desolation* that abolishes the community between people to unleash a collective movement of self-destruction through the body of the Führer.

To what extent is architecture responsible for this? It is also to and from this situation that architecture must respond. What remains to be determined is the contribution of architecture to the shaping of a society that is damaged by the spell of the *all One*.

Given the displacement performed at all levels of architecture, from its style to its status, we cannot fail to be struck by the reciprocal actions between architecture and totalitarianism:

- On the one hand, the strange attraction of totalitarian regimes to architecture, as if totalitarianism seeks to find in it the terrain for the selection of its element, its *archē* or commandment.

- On the other hand, the particular explanation of architecture's role in the totalitarian influence (as such, it differs from cooking!) lies in the very relationship between the totalitarian logic, mobilization, the animation of the mass, and the constitution of apolitical or even anti-political spaces. This relation is so unambiguous that it leads us to go a step further and ask ourselves about the "Egyptian" nature and the compactness of an architecture exposed to this logic.

This is where we return to our initial question and the accepted point of observation, namely, the political institution of the social bond, or if one prefers, the form of community.

The peculiarity of totalitarian regimes is not so much the execution of violence against a problematic human essence, nor even the displacement of human limits, but rather their ability to undermine human connection, to destroy relationships and the intersubjective order. The refusal of plurality, the denial of division; the refusal of temporality, the denial of finitude: what is at issue here is the social bond and the political bond between people. What complex and paradoxical connections does architecture maintain with the establishment of a bond under the sign of unbinding—the isolation of the political sphere, desolation in the sphere of intersubjective relations? How is architecture a part of this form of community that prevents friendship in order to bear in itself the destruction of all community? How do architecture and the "remodeling of cities" express this destruction of community?

It is a form of community that finishes by springing the "safety catch" of self-preservation, the ground zero of instrumental political reason, to devour the entire society in an abyssal movement towards collective self-destruction, towards death. The contradiction is provided by Hobbes: in totalitarian spaces the fear of death is by far overcome. It is enough to reread the sentences cited by Caillois emphasizing the "charm of the name of One":

> When all appears lost, we believe again in him. When all despair, we put our hopes in him. Adolf Hitler, your name is our faith. This faith in you allows us to pass through all countries, the standard which became the symbol of German immortality. Take our life, Führer, take all of us, take our bodies, take our souls. In your hands we place our destiny.[61]

"What is this monster of vice?" The thing without a name. The thing that defies naming. The unnameable.

Part III
Critical-Utopian Political Philosophy

Chapter 7

Hannah Arendt against Political Philosophy?
(2001; republished 2009)

The question, insofar as it is framed as a question, might come across as surprising. Isn't Hannah Arendt quasi-unanimously praised for having developed one of the great political philosophies of our time? Before an answer is given, it might be useful to examine the reception of her work.

About thirty years ago, as the analysis of the political was under the influence of either Marxism or functionalism, or of some indigestible mixture of the two, Arendt's work shined as a beacon of resistance: it could be read as a political philosophy that made it possible to resist the scientization and the sociologization of the political. Even if Arendt's idiosyncrasies could not be ignored—especially her peculiar relation to Machiavelli—she could effortlessly be identified with political philosophy and its tradition. It could even happen that "for the needs of war" she be strategically lumped together with Leo Strauss, as if an agreement existed between the two authors regarding the proper way to approach the political and as if the divergences separating them only boiled down to political choices narrowly defined. Strauss, for instance, contrary to Arendt, never wrote a book on revolution. The connection, however, overlooked a little too quickly the fact that Straussians denied Arendt the status of philosopher and accused her of

---

Translated by Olivier Ruchet. Originally published as "Hannah Arendt contre la philosophie politique?," in *Hannah Arendt: L'humaine condition politique*, ed. Étienne Tassin (Paris: L'Harmattan, 2001), 11–46. Translated from "Hannah Arendt contre la philosophie politique?," in *Pour une philosophie politique critique* (Paris: Sens & Tonka, 2009), 231–63.

writing what amounted to a kind of journalism that at best displayed philosophical leanings. Such identification has not disappeared. Some continue to write books on Arendt's political philosophy, while others regard her as Aristotelian or neo-Aristotelian.

The intellectual landscape has noticeably changed to the point that we can no longer hold on to our initial perception of Arendt and that persisting in reproducing it unchanged could lead dramatically astray. The conjuncture has a revealing quality, not unlike photographic material. The current situation, at least on the French scene, may be described as a return to political philosophy that, truth be told, really is a return to political philosophy as an academic discipline that entails the classical symptoms attached to that kind of phenomena (creation of associations, of journals, organization of conferences, and so on). It would seem that Leo Strauss's lesson, that political philosophy is not the concern of university professors but rather of the man on the street, had been lost.

In that movement, it is important to distinguish as starkly as possible between the return of political things and the answers given to that return. Political things are back. It is no longer *homo academicus* choosing to revive a discourse that had momentarily been left aside, but it is political things irrupting into the present, interrupting the neglect in which they were left, struggling to ensure that an end be put to that neglect and that the many questions they inevitably raise be answered. As totalitarianisms are breaking up, that is, enterprises that aspired to put an end to the political, it is the political that is staging a comeback. Yet the permanence of the political, far from working as an incentive to follow once again the well-trodden course of tradition, demands rather that we open new ways, as its very expression raises all the more questions because it is characterized by a great fragility.

In short, we are here in the presence of two intellectual orientations, and it would be mistaken to confuse them or to think they are headed in the same direction or share a similar destination. It is not the case, despite the efforts of some who actively try to muddy the waters. On the one hand, we can observe the restoration of an academic discourse that, naively or not, begins anew, restarts as if nothing had happened and as if a succession of unprecedented and inhumane ordeals had not irremediably broken our tradition in the twentieth century. On the other hand, we experience the expression of a need of humanity: the rediscovery of the political after totalitarian domination tried to cancel or to erase forever this constitutive dimension of the human condition.

With regard to this historical and philosophical ambiguity, how should we situate Arendt? Should we, as we were tempted to do thirty years ago, place her on the side of the renewal of political philosophy, where testaments are piling up upon testaments, thereby also counting her work as another testament? Or should we place her on the side of a return of political things and to thinkers who, by denouncing totalitarian domination, have facilitated that return—that would be the side of those who have championed and who still champion that return by recognizing and enunciating the essential alternative: politics or totalitarianism? The answer seems obvious. Arendt's body of work is doubly revealing. On the one hand, reading Arendt allows us to clearly distinguish between these two movements and to avoid succumbing to the ambiguity of the present. Better yet, her work allows us to realize that the current return to political philosophy has the paradoxical effect of distracting us from political things to the point that they become obscured and that their potentially untimely content is sidelined. In short, Arendt's work powerfully reveals the significance of the movement in favor of a restoration of political philosophy. On the other hand, her position, her very critical gesture, the lucidity it elicits in her readers reveals the singularity of Arendt. She was that rare thinker who helped rediscover political action, precisely insofar as she never ceased to struggle against the tradition of political philosophy, its weightiness, its artificial constructs, and its blind spots. From that situation a new perception of her work emerges, so that it is no longer possible, nor legitimate, to identify that work with political philosophy, even if only strategically. A figure of resistance, then: Arendt was doubly so, evidently against the scientization of the political that ever threatens; wasn't an appeal recently launched in favor of a renewal of sociology in the shape of a "scientific political philosophy"? But Arendt was also and above all a figure of resistance against the restoration of political philosophy and its overshadowing of political things. Arendt's resistance was even more vigorous in that she criticized the object itself more than simply the restoration of it. Upon closer inspection, indeed, it appears that Arendt's work was from the very beginning developed in opposition to political philosophy.

Arendt against political philosophy? Both the question and the answer certainly display a deliberate air of provocation. But the provocation comes from Arendt herself, when she invites us to meditate the sentence from René Char: "Our heritage was left to us without a testament."

We are then reminded of her well-known statements, pronounced on the occasion of the famous TV interview with Günther Gaus in 1964.[1] Arendt claims she is not a philosopher and states that her work should rather be described as political theory. To the question "I should like to hear from you more precisely what the difference is between political philosophy and your work as a professor of political theory," she responds:

> The expression "political philosophy," which I avoid, is extremely burdened by tradition. When I talk about these things, academically or nonacademically, I always mention that there is a vital tension between philosophy and politics. That is, between man as a thinking being and man as an acting being, there is a tension that does not exist in natural philosophy, for example. . . . But he (the philosopher) cannot be objective or neutral with regard to politics. Not since Plato! . . . There is a kind of enmity against all politics in most philosophers, with very few exceptions. Kant is an exception. This enmity is extremely important for the whole problem, because it is not a personal question. It lies in the nature of the subject itself. . . . I want no part in this enmity. . . . I want to look at politics, so to speak, with eyes unclouded by philosophy.[2]

These few lines express the core of Arendt's position on the matter.

First, there is an insistence on the illegitimacy of uniting the terms philosophy—which points to the approach and process—and politics—which points to the object itself. In the eyes of Arendt, the expression is unacceptable because it is misleading: the idea of political philosophy suggests an essential affinity, a consubstantial relationship between philosophy and politics, whereas in reality they entail two distinct activities, or to be more precise, two forms of life between which there exists not a proximity but a tension that might even take the form of an open antagonism. It is thus suitable to abandon the term "political philosophy," which works as a veil to obscure things and can even prove deceitful. This situation is due to the attitude of philosophers as members of a corporate body; starting with the Platonic institution of political philosophy, they have imposed a hierarchy between the *vita contemplativa* and the *vita activa* to the point of deprecating *praxis* and *bios politikos*. Regarding the political question, philosophers have thus according to Arendt neglected the demands of universalism that were specific to them in order instead to give pride of place to their corporate interests and to remain at bay from city affairs. Instead of recognizing an elective affinity between philosophy and politics, we must hence notice a hostility that is not incidental but rather essential between the two activities. It is due to philosophy itself, underscores Arendt. It is the reason why she adopted the singular position of "political theorist," inviting us to convert our gaze, to stop observing political affairs through the lenses of philosophy. "As a kind of phenomenologist," Arendt summons phenomenology against philosophy by calling forth a kind of epoché, not to free oneself from psychologism or sociologism, but, indeed, from philosophy. Only by bracketing philosophy could one truly gain access to political affairs, and consider them with "eyes unclouded by philosophy," undisturbed by the profoundly anti-political concerns of philosophy. Far from being the expression of a passing irritation, this hostility towards philosophy returns as a leitmotiv in several of Arendt's texts. These texts must be taken seriously, and one could propose a maximalist, if not emphatic, reading of them. Are not these well-known texts to a certain extent often misread? Doesn't the knowledge of these themes dear to Arendt go hand in hand with a certain misunderstanding in the guise of a resistance, as if we were to grant that, indeed, Arendt criticized political philosophy, "yes, but still," she remained a philosopher of politics, she practiced the trade of political philosophy.

Taking these texts seriously entails overcoming that resistance and taking note of the gap between Arendt and political philosophy, grasping that gap to be able to explore its depths, exploring it so that it may produce its effects. "The curious and difficult problem of the relation between politics and philosophy," or the strange attitude of philosophers towards the political domain: these recurring questions never ceased to torment Arendt. But one may not be content to simply shed light on the gap; doing so would hardly be adequate, since it is not Arendt's purpose to return, in the name of her hostility towards political philosophy, to an analytical-empirical science of political phenomena.

Therefore, a somewhat more adventurous question is sooner or later bound to spring up, in consonance with the tonality of Arendt's body of work: What is the intellectual space opened by Arendt's gap? What is the *terra incognita* that she sought to discover or rediscover in opposition to tradition? What is the new thinking of politics she was aiming for, under names that sound as little satisfactory as "new political philosophy" or "authentic political philosophy"? Do the stakes in the debate merely boil down to a question of authenticity?

I. Philosophers and the Denial of Action

To summarize the bone of contention between Arendt and political philosophy in a relatively blunt manner, one could start with the quote from Robert

Cumming she cites in her lecture on Kant and with which she visibly agrees, as the simplicity of Cumming's appraisal seems to correspond to what she tried to demonstrate with more complex arguments. According to Cumming: "The subject-matter of modern political philosophy . . . is not the polis or its politics, but the relation between philosophy and politics."[3] And Arendt immediately adds that the remark applies to the entire tradition of political philosophy, especially its Platonic beginnings in Athens. To elucidate this "curious and difficult problem," Arendt always turns to the same guide, Pascal, in particular to his *Pensées*, paragraph 331. It would be hard to overstate how important that short text was to Arendt: it is almost an obsession of hers, and she returned to it every time she sought to define the relationship between philosophy and politics in the tradition and to draw attention to the hostility that defined the relationship between the two phenomena. In her body of work, the reference occurs at least four times: (1) in the 1954 text "Concern with Politics in Recent European Philosophical Thought";[4] (2) in the *Lectures on Kant's Political Philosophy*; (3) in *The Life of the Mind*, vol. 1, p. 152;[5] (4) in the 1969 lecture "What Is Political Philosophy?"[6]

Let us read Pascal's *Pensées*, paragraph 331, once again: "We always picture Plato and Aristotle wearing long academic gowns, but they were ordinary decent people like anyone else, who enjoyed a laugh with their friends. And when they amused themselves by composing their *Laws* and *Politics* they did it for fun. It was the least philosophical and least serious part of their lives: the most philosophical part was living simply and without fuss. If they wrote about politics it was as if to lay down rules for a madhouse. And if they pretended to treat it as something really important it was because they knew that the madmen they were talking to believed themselves to be kings and emperors. They humored these beliefs in order to calm down their madness with as little harm as possible."[7]

Set against a relatively neutral definition, according to which classical political philosophy focused on the *polis* and modern political philosophy on the state, this fierce and insolent text is iconoclastic. Its unmasking strength, coming from a form of socialite pessimism unrelated to the tradition of cynicism, consists in destroying the favorable imaginary representations surrounding Plato, Aristotle, and their works dedicated to politics. What we tend to locate on the side of seriousness, what we even take as the epitome of seriousness, as if political philosophy were the crowning of philosophical work, should, in fact, be classified as entertainment and games. It amounted to a playful exercise, aiming at introducing some rule in an unruly and anomic universe. Thence the displacement of object: "If they wrote about politics it was as if to lay down rules for a madhouse." To better destroy the majestic reputation of these foundational works, Pascal suggests that their appearance of seriousness was only a philosophical trick, a sort of indirect course—the *via obliqua*—deployed to be heard by the insane who, occupying the seat of power, take themselves seriously. However, for Arendt, despite his insolence, or maybe thanks to his Christian moralist insolence, that text by Pascal tells the truth about political philosophy and about its real motivations. It unveils the constitutive intention—the disdain for human affairs—the preventive and curative character of that philosophical intervention. It would be important to remedy that lack of wisdom, or to remedy human folly, knowing that the theater of that madness is the city.

This is the reason why, in her indictment of political philosophy, Arendt doubly cites Pascal, both as writer and as witness for the prosecution, who by his own admission revealed the unthought of political philosophy. At first, Arendt does not immediately indict political philosophy as such, but rather the attitudes of the philosophers who wrote political philosophy. And she is careful to distinguish between two different institutions, Socrates's, on the one hand, often likened to Solon's, and Plato's, on the other. As much as the former institution was able to integrate political things and to debate them from the perspective of the *polis*, the latter seemed to institute political philosophy against the realm of human affairs. A fundamental shift can be observed between the two: while the former remained concentrated on the *polis* and on political action, the latter apparently only retained the relationship between the philosopher and the city. Arendt repeatedly attributes the original trauma that opened the gap between philosophy and politics to the trial of Socrates and to his conviction. "Our tradition of political thought began," she wrote in "Philosophy and Politics," "when the death of Socrates made Plato despair of polis life and, at the same time, doubt certain fundamentals of Socrates' teaching."[8] That major shift had multiple effects: besides Plato's radical mistrust of the *polis*, it led him to question Socrates's teachings, notably regarding the value of *doxa* and the possibility of elevating oneself from *doxa* to truth. First and foremost, however, a new question arises from the event: How may the philosopher protect himself or how may the group of philosophers protect themselves from the agitation of the multitude, how may they free themselves from having to care for human affairs? In the same way, the question of the best regime was transformed. It was no longer from the perspective of the polis and in its interest that an answer to the question had to be found, but from the perspective of philosophy and to ensure its necessary protection. The new formula became: "What is the best regime form, that is, which regime form may grant the philosopher the greatest degree of security and allow him to carry on with his work sheltered from the frenzy of the polis and from the madness of the multitude?" This prevalence of the philosopher's perspective, this new way of framing the political question, goes hand in hand with a tendency to prioritize values other than the values of the polis, such as the quest for permanence and stability. That change of perspective, at the same time as it deprecates political things, tends to obscure them to the point that it veils their nature and diverts the political from a situation of coexistence and to the necessity of an organization that would allow a harmonious balance of the whole.

However, far from being content with the mere denunciation of the self-protective attitudes of philosophers, of their *esprit de corps*, Arendt strikes a blow that is both more profound and more audacious. In a sense, her gesture could be compared to Heidegger's when he criticizes traditional metaphysics for being built on the forgetfulness of being and when he invites a critical reading of tradition, under the hold of the forgetting that should not be reduced to a purely negative phenomenon. In Arendt's case, it means denouncing the Platonic institution of political philosophy that, in its hostility towards the polis, is said to have led to a forgetting of action, of acting politically. Such forgetting weighed so much on tradition that nowadays the essence of politics may be "innocently" defined as relations of command and obedience, or more simply as the exercise of domination. Therefore, besides an invitation to dismantle the tradition under the influence of the primary institution, one may perceive in Arendt's writings a call to turn to "political writers"—Machiavelli, Montesquieu, Tocqueville—who in her view had the precious merit of approaching politics "with eyes unclouded by philosophy," or, at least, of standing outside the Platonic institution and its effects. Or perhaps more covertly, we may discern a call to pay attention to those moments in history when, in the interval between two different political forms, action reemerges, the gaps where action "appears different from *archē* and *princeps-principium*."[9] Such is the admirable "deconstruction of the political fields" carried out by Arendt, according to Reiner Schürmann.[10] From that point a complex set of movements follows, either with Arendt calling for a return to a first beginning that would precede the Platonic institution (Homer, Socrates) and that would be a repetition rather than a return and with which the point would not so much be about imitating, about perpetuating, as it would be about reactivating. Or, acknowledging "the end of political philosophy," the end of tradition under the blows of Marx, Kierkegaard, and Nietzsche, Arendt contemplates, with an element of risk and ambiguity, a new beginning. A new "task of thinking"[11] such that we may rediscover action and the political by lifting the doubt that prevents, according to Arendt, philosophy from grasping political affairs in their irreducible specificity, even if the new beginning eventually acquires the name of "authentic political philosophy." Indeed, the field of ruins of contemporary culture is certainly deplorable, but it also implicitly comprises "the great chance to look upon the past with eyes undistracted by any tradition, with a directness which has disappeared from Occidental reading and hearing ever since Roman civilization submitted to the authority of Greek thought."[12]

"Eyes undistracted by any tradition." It is thus fitting to return to Arendt's anti-Platonism to fully measure how much her critique of the Platonic institution of political philosophy is perpetually on the lookout to identify founding schemes that would have the effect of forgetting politics and excluding action. *Brevatis causa*, after reading that criticism we can identify four schemes that both found political philosophy and destroy political acting:

1. The folding of the polis into the home or the household, *oikos*, with the concurrent erasing of the differences between a space of freedom where action is its own end and a space of necessity oriented towards the reproduction of life under the despotic authority of the head of the family.

2. The dissociation of the couple *archein/prattein* (to begin and to act) that defines the exercise of politics in the city to the point that it substitutes another distinction to it, the distinction between to command and to execute. At the same time, action and all its distinguishing features—fragility, unpredictability, irreversibility—is evacuated and replaced by a new identification of politics with government. Action as action in concert, between equals, is itself replaced by the division between the rulers and the ruled.

3. In the name of the desire for robustness, a rejection of action, whose fragility is denounced as a shortcoming. From there ensues a new way of thinking the political along the model

of work, *poiésis*. Politics is henceforth thought within a means-ends framework; it is thus exposed to a promotion of violence, as expressed in the famous saying "the end justifies the means." Seeking models that would either be utopian or theoretical, it then falls upon political activity to apply, to transfer these models to the real, with the real no longer thought of as the network of relations generated by action but reduced to a set of existing conditions.

4. Finally, the denial of the ontological condition of plurality, which particularly in Plato brings forth a limitless valorization of unity such that it exercises violence against the very nature of the city and reveals a tropism towards tyranny in the philosopher's work, as the denial of plurality leads to the acceptance of the tyrant.

Such are the typical characteristics of political philosophy, *nolens volens*, reproduced by most philosophers that have claimed to be representatives of that tradition, according to Arendt and her study of these schemes. Pascal's text thus indeed acquires the value of an admission, or rather Arendt seizes Pascal's sentences and transforms them into an admission, as if, through Pascal's derision, it was possible to bring political philosophy to admit what it really is. Thus Pascal, who was hostile to political affairs because of his Augustinism, was nevertheless able to recognize by affinity and sympathy, so to say, another hostility, whose origin was admittedly different, but which was nonetheless real, among the founding fathers of tradition. The admission is double, since besides revealing the identity of political philosophy, Pascal's sarcasms underscore the divorce between philosophy and politics and what partly founds it, that is, the supposed abyss between the wise and the insane. Far from simply registering that admission, Arendt attempts to transform it into a genuine unveiling of the unthought of classical political philosophy, of its tradition, and into an invitation to dismantle that tradition by identifying the blind spots that determine it and that have given it a specific shape. Hence, Arendt in no way participated in this hostility of philosophers towards political affairs, nor did she endorse Pascal's position. Against the latter, she was like a judge in the presence of a witness for the prosecution who will turn the testimony against tradition and thereby found the legitimacy of the trial against classical political philosophy, in particular Platonic, in order to get to the paradoxical verdict according to which the greatest works of the tradition rest on a mistrust of politics on the part of philosophy and on a forgetting of action. Of that struggle, two elements must be noted:

- She attacked the entirety of political gestures that constitute the tradition with its system of inclusion and exclusion, for instance, the division between the wise and the insane. In *The Promise of Politics*, she attempted to better define her anti-Platonism: "Plato," she wrote, "the father of political philosophy in the West, attempted in various ways to oppose the polis and what it understood by freedom by positing a political theory in which political standards were derived not from politics but from philosophy."[13]

- She no less attacked the Platonic institution of political philosophy, insofar as Plato allegedly transposed the freedom of the *polis* onto another stage, namely, the Academy, as if by that institution he had wanted to struggle against the polis while nevertheless maintaining in a constricted space something of his experience of political freedom. Arendt was therefore truly parricidal.

At that point, as we observed, an alternative opens: either the repetition of an original beginning, or the quest for a new beginning in order to be able to approach politics "with eyes unclouded by philosophy." But is this really Arendt's project? If she is determined to distinguish as neatly as possible between two forms of experience—political and philosophical—can we thereby conclude that in order to grasp politics she dismisses philosophy for good? Doesn't she, indeed, conserve from philosophy an essential moment: the moment of astonishment or wonder? And isn't that wonder susceptible to reveal the ontological condition of plurality as well as the condition of natality? Isn't the same wonder alone able to open to a new beginning? Towards the end of the essay "Philosophy and Politics," she precisely contemplates, under the mark of that wonder, a new possible conjunction between philosophy and politics. "Philosophy, political philosophy like all its other branches, will never be able to deny its origin in *thaumadzein*, in the wonder at that which is as it is. If philosophers, despite their necessary estrangement from the everyday life of human affairs, were ever to arrive at a true political philosophy they would have to make the plurality of man, out of which arises the whole realm of human affairs—in its grandeur and misery—the object of their *thaumadzein*."[14]

II. The Connection of Philosophy to Death and the Political Question

Arendt's critical contribution thus consists in identifying the tradition's blind spots and then highlighting them, in order to drive a wedge between philosophy and politics, the two activities responding to radically different orientations. One of her most fruitful hypotheses is that there exists a relationship, still in need of unpacking, between philosophy's relation to death and the way politics is received and grasped. A certain relationship to death would lead to a certain political thought. In the course of her critical inquiry, Arendt does not so much pay attention to doctrines as to attitudes, or rather to the philosophers' attitudes resulting from their doctrines.

Despite the diversity of philosophical systems, is there a specifically philosophical attitude regarding death? And wouldn't *Phaedo* be at the origin of that attitude shared by most philosophers?

Insisting on transmission, Arendt is less interested in elaborating a new interpretation of *Phaedo* than in presenting in some way an accessible version according to which "to study philosophy is to learn to die" to better appreciate how the tradition unfolded, even if it is at the cost of a simplification that borders on misinterpretation. Indeed, in Plato's famous sentences according to which philosophers are "men studying to live as nearly as they can in a state of death" or "the true philosophers . . . are always occupied in the practice of dying,"[15] the point is not so much about dying as it is, as Monique Dixsaut puts it, "to manage to purify thought of everything that comes from the body, rather than to learn how to die or to prepare oneself for a dignified death."[16]

For Arendt, the philosopher would thus be enamored with death, because in death he would be able to access the separation between the body and the soul, since in death, thanks to death, the soul would free itself from the body and from all the demands that hinder its quest and its pursuit of the truth. According to Arendt, this association with death represents a quasi-structural attitude on the part of philosophers: appearing in Ionia, it has manifested itself throughout the history of philosophy, all the way to Heidegger. "Throughout the history of philosophy a very curious notion has persisted of an affinity between death and philosophy. Philosophy for many centuries was supposed to teach men how to die."[17] Whoever converts to philosophy would immediately develop a peculiar relation to death, as if death unlocked the paradigm of the emancipation of the soul from the body-burden. And Arendt insists on the tremendous influence of

Phaedo on the origin of an ancient spiritualist tradition spanning centuries; after Plato, the philosophers' predilection for death became a *topos* of philosophical discourse. Beyond the circle of philosophers, that predilection has fed standard representations of philosophical activity. However, for Arendt, that very predilection, that elective affinity between death and philosophy is problematic. Beyond the fact that such affinity does not go without saying, it almost automatically generates a form of suspicion towards life that goes all the way to depreciating the domain of human affairs, of politics and of everything that is connected to them.

In the 1969 lecture "Philosophy and Politics," Arendt insists again on the overwhelming weight exercised by *Phaedo* on the tradition of philosophy and pushes her criticism beyond the simple assessment or regret, showing how the choice of philosophy distracts from the city and its values. Indeed, according to Plato, doesn't the body inhabit the city, and isn't political virtue located on the side of the body? If this is the case, to free oneself from the body-burden leads to an exit from the civic abode to an untying of the bonds that fasten to the city, to a distancing from the virtues upheld in the city, namely, glory and the quest for immortality. "The true votaries of philosophy abstain from all fleshly lusts, and hold out against them and refuse to give themselves up to them—not because they fear poverty or the ruin of their families, like the lovers of money, and the world in general; nor like the lovers of power and honour, because they dread the dishonour or disgrace of evil deeds."[18] Up to a certain point, Arendt's critique echoes Nicole Loraux's criticism of *Phaedo*. According to Loraux, the famous dialogue that inaugurates the Western history of the soul initiated an extraordinary operation aiming to substitute the immortality of the soul for civic immortality, at the expense, of course, of the city. *Phaedo* is thus "an enterprise serving a reappropriation of values governing the city. By irreducibly separating the soul from the body, Plato forever severs the idea of the immortality of civic glory to which it was attached."[19] Substitution, as the great feat of *Phaedo*, "consists in replacing one immortality by another, in replacing the word of glory by the survival of the soul."[20]

If both criticisms underscore a turning point in the deprecation of the political in the West, their respective reasonings differ. For Arendt, everything is a matter of course. She first needs to explain what in the philosophers' orientation distracts them from the city in order to, in a second moment, discover the other orientation that may chart a new course for politics, and may showcase and restore the dignity and the greatness of political affairs. On the first course, the purification sought by philosophy by way of the separation from the body triggers a form of unbinding, while on the second course politics endeavors to establish a new bond. In order to reach its full potential this double orientation needs to be referred to the analysis of the human condition and thus to the opposition between its two constitutive dimensions: natality and mortality. "If we think in terms of the human condition"—writes Arendt in her 1969 lecture "Philosophy and Politics"—"among the most basic conditions under which life has been given to man is the simple fact that it arrives through birth and that it departs through death, natality and mortality."[21] In doing so, Arendt not only shows that the orientation of philosophy towards death immediately triggers a deprecation of human affairs: she takes the critique further. With the reference to the human condition, she projects in a way two different series, depending on whether the analysis favors natality or mortality. These two ontologically grounded orientations lead to the crossings of two entirely different landscapes.

On the one hand, the insistence on mortality necessarily leads one to take some distance from the city. From there arises a promotion of the unbinding that very soon becomes the promotion of solitude, as is experienced in thought. As we already saw with Loraux, there ensues a substitution of the immortality of the soul for the immortality offered by civic glory.

Conversely, the accent put on natality leads to political affairs, to understand their substance and to determine their conditions of possibility. The very fact of being born is already an experience of plurality, of the ontological condition of plurality, without which political action would not have seen the light of day. We come into being, we are born of the union of a woman and a man, we are born among other human beings. Our birth inscribes us within a family, a people, a political community. It is thus indeed through the fact of birth that we discover the condition of plurality, the fact that humans inhabit the earth, and beyond all that the political domain. It is in natality that both the experience of plurality and the possibility of politics are contained. "Natality," writes Arendt, "is indeed among the basic conditions of all political life, and of all change. Mortality is the opposite—we come and join, we go and leave. And when we leave, we leave precisely this world, i.e., we go alone, by ourselves."[22]

This orientation towards natality is doubly an orientation towards politics, as the fact of being born is an experience of beginning. We appear among other human beings as newcomers, susceptible to beginning, of introducing something new. Birth, an event itself, is pregnant with future events. In that sense a tenuous but precious thread links birth to beginning (not so much biological birth as the repetition of that birth with the appearance on the public stage) and beginning to freedom. It is as beings of the beginning, "beginners," that we can bring an experience of freedom to life, that we are beings-for-freedom. It is not without reason that Arendt ends her great book on totalitarianism by a reminder of that eminently political faculty. "Beginning, before it becomes a historical event, is the supreme capacity of man; politically, it is identical with man's freedom. *Initium ut esset homo creatus est*—'that a beginning be made man was created' said Augustine. This beginning is guaranteed by each new birth; it is indeed every man."[23] Isn't the political domain the domain *par excellence* where the experience of birth and the experience of beginning may intertwine? Doesn't the sudden appearance on the public stage—the accomplishment of great deeds and the utterance of great words—have the value of a second birth, that is, the taking up and the confirmation in the political realm of the brute fact of birth? This birth to politics is always the birth of a beginning; at the same time, there is the beginning of a possibility and the possibility of that beginning. In short, it is the interruption of a process thanks to a word or a deed that, suddenly, evading any predictability, itself becomes an event.

At the end of this journey, it is not sufficient for Arendt to have unveiled the relations that exist between natality and politics and between mortality and unlinking, leading to an enfolding of the soul onto itself. It leads to a true crossroads with the underscoring of a qualitative difference between two possible modes of being: politics, on one side, and philosophy, on the other. To better underscore that qualitative difference, Arendt turns to Heidegger, summoning him more as a witness confirming the irresistible attraction of philosophy for death than as an authority. She quotes from section 53 of *Being and Time*—the existential project of an authentic being for death. From the perspective of modes of existence, thought can be described as an anticipation of death in the sense that it includes mortality as one of the fundamental characters of human existence. This allows the *Dasein* to save its authenticity from loss and dilution in the regime of the "They" [*das Man*]. It represents the most specific possibility of the *Dasein*, its signal possibility. As if in thought the *Dasein* had an anticipating experience of the collecting onto oneself. Thus the quality of mortal would be the eternal source of the mode of existence that philosophy incarnates, and the quality of "native," or of being-for-birth, the source of that other mode of existence that is politics. Arendt concludes on the contrast between the two orientations by arguing: "Speaking in terms of existential modes, the difference between or opposition of Politics and Philosophy is identical with the difference between or opposition of Birth and Death, or conceptually speaking: Natality and Mortality. Natality is the basic condition of all living together, and hence of all politics; Mortality is the basic condition of thought in the sense that thinking relates to something 'unrelational' to something that is as it is in and by itself."[24]

Arendt's work in unveiling that blind spot of tradition leads, in the face of a given body of thought, to the enunciation of a critical question: What is the force under the hold of which that body of thought was constituted? Is it a force oriented towards mortality, towards a contempt for the body and the deprecation of politics? Or is it a force oriented towards natality, the experience of plurality and political action?

Is it possible, for instance as Spinoza did, to reorient philosophy by wrenching it from a relation to death, that is to say by defining the free man as a man whose "wisdom is a meditation of life, not of death" (*Ethics 4*, proposition 67). Doesn't Spinoza, to whom Arendt came late, at the same time as he invites a reflection on what a body can achieve, also have the particularity of having turned, in great emancipatory texts, and especially in his *Theologico-Political Treatise*, towards politics and towards a reflection on the conditions of freedom?

Or is philosophy assigned, since Plato and the *coup d'éclat* of *Phaedo*, to an inexorable destiny in which orientation towards mortality and disinterest in political affairs endlessly combine? If the difference between philosophy and politics is indeed a difference between two modes of existence, how can we solve or pretend to overcome the tension between the man who philosophizes in solitude, or at least standing back, and the man who, within plurality, acts in concert? Doesn't the very idea of political philosophy turn out to be inconceivable, and therefore illegitimate?

III. The Kantian Reversal and the Question of Equality

On that point, Arendt's approach sensibly diverges from the approach followed thus far. Identifying a blind spot of political philosophy—the relationship of the philosopher to mortality—she unpacks the profoundly anti-political effects of that relationship, such as the deprecation of political life and of action. Even if the goal here remains identical and therefore consists in criticizing tradition, she proceeds differently. She first underscores the Kantian innovation with regard to equality, in order to reveal the limits of tradition, or more exactly the inegalitarian presupposition on which it rested. From there a new path can be opened, aiming both at breaking with tradition and at offering a passage beyond political philosophy. To fully measure what is at stake with this question, let us return to what Leo Strauss confesses regarding "the stronghold of the classical position" in his article on Rousseau. "The basic premise of classical political philosophy may be said to be the view that the natural inequality of intellectual powers is, or ought to be, of decisive political importance. Hence the unlimited rule of the wise, in no way answerable to the subjects, appears to be the absolutely best solution to the political problem."[25] Things are evidently different outside the realm of the absolutely best. According to Strauss, the disproportion between the exigencies of science and those of society or of the city transforms the image of the best regime, and, in a sense, renders it more accommodating. "The true or natural order (the absolute rule of the wise over the unwise) must be replaced by its political counterpart or imitation, which is the rule, under law, of the gentlemen over those who are not gentlemen."[26] However, that basic premise of classical political philosophy logically leads to the devices that Arendt never ceased to denounce in tradition. To wit, the conception of politics as an organization drawn up by those who "know" in order to regulate and to control the lives of those who "do not know"; in short, to borrow Pascal's terms, politics as laying down rules for a lunatic asylum. In addition, the idea that the first object of political philosophy is not politics—action, political life—but the difficult, sometimes perilous, relations between the philosopher and the city, between the group of philosophers and the community of citizens. In the inegalitarian perspective, the best regime is the regime that places the wise out of reach of the insane, of their lapses and their acts of madness. It is thought, defined in the interest of philosophers, secluded from the city, if not against the city.

It is precisely the basic premise of classical political philosophy—the division between the wise and the insane—that Kant tears to pieces, and, examining the matter closely, he does so in a much more radical way than Rousseau had done. According to Arendt, even if Kant considered life to be a temporal ordeal, he could only reject a philosophy for which true knowledge is only accessible to a separated soul, unobstructed by senses. According to Kant, indeed, the act of knowing results from the meeting between understanding and sensibility to such a point that the *Critique of Pure Reason* has been interpreted as "a justification, if not a glorification, of human sensibility."[27] What is more, even in his youth when he manifested Platonic tendencies, Kant never considered that the body and the senses were sources of error. From that essential orientation of Kant's philosophy, Arendt draws two consequences:

1. Far from having access to such freedoms that would separate him from other men, away from common consciousness, the philosopher, in Kant's eyes, receives a relatively modest role, all things considered: his task is to shed light on common consciousness about itself, to reveal its own knowledge to it. "For Kant, the philosopher remains a man like you and me, living among his fellow men, not among his fellow philosophers."[28]

2. Likewise, any ordinary man, and not only the philosopher, is able to appreciate the pleasure and pains of life.

Such is the profoundly egalitarian dimension of Kant's philosophy. Didn't the author of the *Critiques* contemplate as possible an encounter between philosophy and opinion? In his eyes, to profess a philosophy of which the common people would not be able to understand any proposition would be tantamount to professing an inhuman philosophy. It is thus in a resolutely egalitarian perspective that Arendt interprets Kant's innovation. "These two consequences," she writes, "in turn, are obviously but two sides of the same coin, and the name of the coin is Equality."[29] To support her interpretation, she cites the famous passage in Kant where he relates how he was awakened from his moral slumber by Rousseau. Reading Rousseau transformed his view of other men, his relations to other men. "I myself am a researcher by inclination. I feel the entire thirst for cognition and the eager restlessness to proceed further in it, as well as the satisfaction at every acquisition. There was a time when I believed this alone could constitute the honor of mankind, and I despised the rabble who knows nothing. Rousseau has set me right. This blinding prejudice vanishes, I learn to honor human beings."[30] Thus what Kant's novel approach reveals and underscores is not only the inegalitarian structure of classical political philosophy: the critique reaches much further. Indeed, the author of the *Critiques* shows how the shape, the orientations, the very substance of political philosophy were directly dependent upon the inegalitarian premise, under the sway of the division between those who know and those who do not know. With the denial of the premise, along with the illusion of superiority that accompanies it, the tradition collapses, and, to put an end to it, it is not at all necessary to propose a political philosophy that would have egalitarian tendencies—wouldn't such a project be contradictory?—but to operate a strange reversal that directly strikes at the very idea of political philosophy and at what is inseparable from it, for instance, the hierarchy of modes of existence. "With the disappearance of this age-old distinction, however," Arendt argues, "something curious happens. The philosopher's preoccupation with politics disappears; he no longer has any special interest in politics; there is no self-interest and hence no claim to either power or to a constitution that would protect the philosopher against the many."[31]

The Kantian exception in the history of political philosophy thus manifests itself. Kant's distinctive character is that he never wrote political philosophy as such. And yet that negative character, that deficit that represents an exception in the tradition, that lacuna, is the sign of its strength, and demonstrates the reversal that took place. Awakened from his political slumber by the exhilarating experience of the French Revolution, Kant managed to avoid the pitfalls of political philosophy, he managed not to reproduce its shortcomings and in particular its mistrust of politics. The idea never crossed his mind that to safeguard philosophy, it would be suitable to restrain and to control the community of citizens. In a positive and inventive fashion, thanks to that "lacuna," Kant, following in the footsteps of Socrates, was able to establish politics as an object for philosophy, on the same level as history. The distance from political philosophy is palpable: while the latter takes the relations between philosophy and politics as its objects, Kant's thought returns, so to speak, to politics itself, which is very different.

On that point, Arendt concurs with Éric Weil's interpretation in his book *Problèmes kantiens*. According to Weil, "politics ceases, with Kant, to be a preoccupation reserved to philosophers; it becomes, concurrently with history, a philosophical problem."[32] Thus the philosophical question regarding the meaning of politics, or of history, replaces the question of the best regime that will be able to offer the best guarantees to philosophers as a corporate body separate from the rest of the city. "What matters is no longer to arrange history and politics, it is to understand their shared meaning, the meaning that must govern an arrangement."[33]

As a result, unless one chooses the path of the restoration of classical political philosophy and therefore the path of a resumption of the inegalitarian premise—that is, the path taken by Strauss and his disciples—one must follow in the wake of the Kantian reversal. Truth be told, Arendt, by choosing the latter option, opens an intellectual space by struggling on two fronts. First, against Hegel and the dissolution of the thought of politics in a philosophy of history. If there is indeed in Hegel, in the eyes of Arendt, a rehabilitation of politics in the wake of the Kantian reversal, it is clear that what Hegel manages to find, he immediately loses again by transforming it into a philosophy of history that leads to a dissolution of politics. Thus, doesn't the model of the cunning of reason lead to the negation of action? Then, for sure, against Strauss and his students, who, in their return to classical political philosophy, *nolens volens*, reproduce the blind spots already identified and denounced.

In a sense, Arendt endeavors to open a third path: if it is true that modernity, thanks to the Kantian reversal (without mentioning Machiavelli) strikes a blow at classical political philosophy, it needs to be thought not only under the aegis of loss and decline, because it also bears another conception of politics that breaks with the blind spots of tradition. It also prevents this new political philosophy—this "true political philosophy"—from being exposed and left to dissolve and lose itself in a philosophy of history.

Conclusion

"A true political philosophy": Doesn't this program, maybe unknowingly, express the limits of Arendt's criticism? Doesn't the formula suggest that beyond classical political philosophy and its "vices," it would be possible to access another political philosophy that, freed from those shortcomings, could reach political philosophy in its very truth and authenticity? But can we conceive of a truth of political philosophy, is it legitimate to work towards the coming of a "true political philosophy," or, under the guise of such a demand, would it only be about reproducing and reinforcing an illusion consubstantial with the very project of political philosophy? For Jacques Rancière, whose radical critique in *Disagreement* sometimes bears Arendtian accents—the truth of political philosophy would be its falseness. There would be no point in entertaining the dream of an authentic political philosophy, since it is the very idea of political philosophy—or of a politics of philosophers, inseparable from a principled opposition to the antecedence of a politics of the *demos*—that would need to be rejected uncompromisingly, rather than only such or such historical manifestation.[34] The truth is, Arendt is no stranger to that radicality; it is because she fears falling back in the bad old ways of the politics of philosophers that she so obstinately and so forcefully refuses the title of "philosopher" and more modestly situates herself on the side of political writers.

Therefore, arriving at the conclusion of this route, we are now maybe in a position to better explain the need to approach politics "with eyes unclouded by philosophy." The expression entails, first, not to approach politics from the point of view of philosophy, the corporate interest of philosophers, and then not to submit political action to the distinction and hierarchy between two modes of being, the philosophical and the political, with the first rank granted to contemplative life, and finally not to reproduce the knots of tradition, fear of action, bent towards mortality with its unavoidable consequences, the inegalitarian premise. It is only after that complex preliminary exercise that Arendt, "as a kind of phenomenologist," in her own words, considers she is able to return to action itself, to tackle its irreducible specificity, away from work and labor, to awaken sleeping or forgotten meanings. Of philosophy, as has already been observed, she only intends to keep, in order not to fall into either positivism or empiricism, the feeling of wonder in the face of the ontological condition of plurality. But rather than defining that "true political philosophy" in its substance, assuming there is such a thing as true political philosophy, which would in a sense boil down to describing the entire body of work of Arendt, it seems suitable to modify the angle of approach and to pay attention, to lend an ear to the *tone* of that philosophy, its own tonality. Isn't it in this tonality that we encounter both the resumption of the opposition to political philosophy and the attempt to go beyond it, by untying, in a way, the knots of tradition? Isn't it this tonality that, far from being a simple superstructure, would orient the fundamental choices of that political philosophy to allow it to devise new positions, to reply to tradition's anti-political positions?

Once the question is thus shifted and reframed, it appears that *Arendt professes a heroic conception of politics insofar as she partakes of a political conception of heroism*. It is by treading that path, thanks to that heroic tone, that she endeavors to respond, in an inventive fashion, to counter the three blind spots of tradition and to counteract the heaviness and prevalence of inherited thought.

Let us immediately clarify, to lift any ambiguity, that Arendt's heroic conception of politics is of a particular quality. We are not unmindful of the dangers of such valorization of heroic tonality. The twentieth century has experienced forms of totalitarian heroism, either in the exaltation of the soldier in the throes of total mobilization, or in the glorification of the new man. There is certainly no dearth of "good souls" who, once that door has been opened, try to bring Arendt's heroic tonality closer to Heidegger's, to the point that they claim to identify a typically antiheroic heroism, erected against the city. Without embarking on a confrontation between Arendtian and Heideggerian heroisms—such a confrontation should follow in Jacques Taminiaux's footsteps, who took great care to show in *La fille de Thrace et le penseur professionnel* how much Arendt thought in critical response to Heidegger—we may first clarify that Arendt professes a conception of heroism that is surprisingly sober. Inspired by Homer, she first defines the hero as a free man who, in the company of other men, fought in front of Troy. At the same time, she eliminates post-Homeric conceptions that have tended to situate the hero in an indeterminate space between gods and men, with the hero becoming a half-god or a deified man. Better yet, the hero, according to Arendt, does not possess heroic qualities, nor does he manifest a supernature that would tell him apart from other men, his peers.[35] It is enough that he is endowed with the political quality *par excellence*, courage, a quality that was rediscovered by Machiavelli against the Christian embrace of humility. Courage is what makes it possible to respond "Present!" in a critical situation or in a situation in which the liberty of men is at stake. "The notion that only he is free who is prepared to risk his life has never vanished entirely from our consciousness. . . . Courage is the earliest of all political virtues, and even today it is still one of the few cardinal virtues of politics."[36] It is because the political actor overcomes his fear of death that he can leave the domestic realm dedicated to reproduction and to the protection of life to lay himself open to multiple risks present in the public realm, from ostracism to death. As we can see, the categories with which Arendt invites us to think about politics relate to heroism. It is so with the transition from the obscurity characteristic of the private realm to the light of the public realm. It is not so much a progression as a leap that, in its suddenness, wrenches from the shelter of the private realm and exposes to the perils of public life. It is the same with regard to the no less sudden transformation of the name, when the political actor reveals to others and to himself a problematic identity, the identity of the *Who*, the patronymic, the name of the father steps aside from the repetitive series of generations to shine with a new brilliance. Under the condition that great deeds and words allow him to access civic immortality. In Arendt's case, this heroic conception of politics is pre-Platonic, in the sense that it deliberately returns prior to the Platonic institution of political philosophy (in particular prior to *Phaedo*) to go back to Homer, as if she wished to designate Homer as the great teacher of politics and refused, contra Plato, the magisterium of Socrates, or at least of Plato's Socrates. Doesn't she reemphasize the indelible link between the *polis*, the experience of freedom, and Homeric adventures?

In *The Promise of Politics*, what does she retain from the Homeric epic, if not the prefiguration of "the magnificent experience of life's possibilities among one's equals"?[37]

Such are Arendt's retorts to the three blind spots of classical political philosophy.

If political philosophy, or the politics of philosophers, is characterized by the fear of action, fear of the action of citizens that might come and disturb the serenity of philosophical life, on the contrary a heroic conception of politics favors action to the point that it ensures its precedence over any possible form of theorization, since, according to Arendt, who wrenches the hero from the myth, the hero is the acting man in the highest sense. It is, closely following Greek linguistic custom, exactly the term she uses to describe him in *The Life of the Mind*.[38] That, it should be noted, does not only apply to the hero of the Greek city or of the Roman republic: it also applies to the modern revolutionary hero, inasmuch as he remains a political actor until the very end. Doesn't Arendt explicitly advise to turn to modern revolutions, and to study them, if one really wants to grasp the characters of action?[39] We could thus expect from a heroic conception of politics, in the sense meant by Arendt, that it overcomes the fear of action and leaves far behind the limited and overly cautious point of view of philosophers.

As we saw, in her study of political philosophy, Arendt brought out two series of determinants in order to reflect on the relation to politics: natality, on the one hand, and mortality, on the other. As much as mortality, contemptuous of the body as it is, distracts from the city and from political life, natality is linked to the ontological condition of plurality and directs to politics. The hero, however, in Arendt's conception, establishes an essential relation to natality. Political actor *par excellence*, he is the being of beginning, the "commencer," the one who may interrupt, by acting in concert, a process, and in the gap may allow an event to unfold, or the beginning of the possibility. His sudden arrival in the public realm has the value of a second birth, which, as such, repeats and metamorphoses the brute fact of biological birth. It is within that political reinscription in the condition of natality that the hero is ready to confront the risk of death. It is as if the being-for-birth, who in the beginning experiences his powers for the first time, necessarily preceded the being-for-death. Because even if the hero is born to himself and to others by taking upon himself the risk of death and the chance of civic immortality, he nonetheless remains a being-for-birth, since that relation to death is placed under the sign of natality, of a second birth, in the light of the city. Didn't Maurice Blanchot write: "In dying the hero does not die, he is born; he becomes glorious, he accedes to presence and establishes himself in memory, a secular survival"?[40]

As for the inegalitarian premise, wouldn't we first be tempted to think that the hero sensibly reinforces it by adding to it what Nietzsche calls "the pathos of distance," which would mark a separation between himself and other men? But it would be forgetting that in the case of Arendt, the heroic conception of politics is resolutely linked to a political conception of heroism. What does this mean? It is not enough, indeed, to underscore that Arendt professes a sober conception of heroism, one must also add that that political character of heroism is the condition of possibility of that sobriety. One must understand "political character of heroism" in the strongest meaning of the term; it means negatively that it is not about a metaphysical conception, the hero devoting himself to the adventures of negativity, choosing the path of a supernature in order to better negate the human condition, nor is it about an aesthetic conception, with the hero striving to make his life a work of art. The insistence on the political character of heroism means that that heroism unfolds and manifests itself in the limits of the human condition: Isn't it precisely the relation to politics that must allow such a hero to struggle against the *hubris* of heroic adventure and to resist the bewitching calls of a supernature, whatever its name? But what is more, that heroism crops up in the midst, at the heart of a specific political experience, of an experience of freedom that bears the name of the city. It is in the framework of the *polis* and *for-the-polis* that the hero reveals himself to himself and to the other beings as the political actor *par excellence*, the acting being in the highest possible meaning. Instead of setting himself up as *upsipolis*, *above the city*, and eventually necessarily against it, the hero as Arendt conceives of him is all the more anxious to fit within the city because it is that political character, in the strong meaning, *for-the-polis*, that preserves him from turning into a wild beast against other men and prevents the ever-threatening slip from heroism to tyranny. In a way, the political quality of that heroism is what serves as safeguard and introduces in that inordinate course something like some measure. What is more, that heroism is devoted to politics because it manifests itself, as Jacques Taminiaux has shown, within action in concert, undertaken with others, an experience *in actu* of the human condition of plurality, diametrically opposed to the pathos of distance and of the will to separate.

Maybe could it be the heroism of great modern revolutions, in particular that of 1848 or of the Commune of 1871—that could allow us to come closest to Arendtian heroism? A heroism of the gap, such that the hero after a remarkable feat consents, as a republican citizen, to fall back into line, and a heroism of a new kind that, contrary to classical heroism, would tend towards that paradoxical form that would be the heroism of those who have no name. As was remarked by contemporaries and by historians after them, who knows these heroes of 1848 or 1871, who took the initiative of an assault or resisted to their death on the barricades, in the face of the forces of repression?

These three retorts springing from a heroic conception of politics no doubt sketch a global design. They point to a conception of politics that, if it conserves a relation to philosophical wonder, resolutely situates itself outside of political philosophy, not at its edges, nor at its margins, but in its exteriority. There is in Arendt, following Giambattista Vico, a "heroism of the mind" that allows her to conquer that position of exteriority, as if the heroic tone paved the way to a new approach of action. Thus instead of making of "true political philosophy" a new avatar of the politics of philosophers that would aspire to finally grasp politics in its truth, above the unpredictability of action, we could get a sense of its critical and ironic extent thanks to a Pascalian (Pascal, again) formula that would be: "True political philosophy does not care about political philosophy." Does not care about tradition, does not care about inherited thought, does not care about current and burdensome undertakings of restoration. This formula, that does not erase nor weaken Arendt's opposition to political philosophy, perhaps circumscribes a place from which we can read the author of *The Human Condition*. We could, indeed, without much risk of erring, presume that the reading of Arendt will differ whether that struggle against tradition is taken into account or not. As if we minimize it, or more exactly, if we do not take it seriously by reducing it to the expression of some contingent idiosyncrasy, if we strive to make of Arendt one of the greatest political philosophers of our time, we will soon have a canonical Arendt, mummified, petrified, which before long will function as an authority to legitimize existing conservatisms, whether they pertain to education or to the republic. Numerous are the "Arendtians" who prefer to silence that opposition to political philosophy.

Conversely, if we lend our full attention to this essential orientation, to this irony, if we welcome its disturbing force, don't we notice that this exteriority is an obligatory pathway to access what for Arendt is unclassifiable, or even "scandalous" and in no way participates in an enterprise of canonization? In short, we thus increase the chances of finding the *enfant terrible* whose thought, by one of its sides, points to a left-libertarian notion of politics. It is enough to recall her positions on Israel in the major text written in 1944, "Zionism Reconsidered,"[41] her critique of the nation-state, her critique of sovereignty, of political parties, her interest in civil disobedience, her relation to Rosa Luxemburg, her choice of the republic of councils.

Before we explore these avenues, let us recognize in Arendt a gadfly, a torpedo fish, a modern Socrates who, like a spoilsport, throws sand into the wheels of young people who rush to libraries to "do" political philosophy and asks them the preliminary question, most embarrassing of all: But, *what is political philosophy?*

Chapter 8

For a Critical Political Philosophy?
(2002; republished 2009)

What living relationship can we form today with critical theory? This is a more generous and certainly more fruitful question than "What is living and what is dead in critical theory?" Whoever puts the question in that form would be like a surgeon palpating a body in order to determine what is worth saving. In contrast, the question we propose comes from within ourselves, from our interests, from our current relation with emancipation. In fact, to the extent that we persist in making the problem of emancipation our own, we will at the same time be establishing a link with critical theory.

But how do we apprehend the current time? Is it sufficient to understand it as a renewal of political philosophy? And if that is in fact the case, what relation ought we to form with critical theory in such a climate? It would also be necessary to know what kind of renewal is at stake. Are we in the midst of a return to political philosophy, that is to say to an academic discipline or, to what is quite a different thing, to political things themselves? For those who hold the first position, it is a movement internal to the history of philosophy, even if they modestly bear or believe they bear "circumstances" in mind. The somewhat enigmatic eclipse of political philosophy would call for a return to this neglected discipline, more or less

---

Translated by Asher Horowitz. Originally published as "Pour une philosophie politique critique?," *Tumultes*, no. 17–18 (2002): 207–58. Translated from "Pour une philosophie politique critique?," in *Pour une philosophie politique critique* (Paris: Sens & Tonka, 2009), 265–318.

in parallel with a restoration of legal and moral philosophy. The return of political things is completely different. In the moment totalitarian domination breaks apart, political things make a return. No longer is it the interpreter who chooses to return to a discourse temporarily left aside in order to revive it, political things themselves irrupt into the present and interrupt the oblivion that affected them, or bring an end to the attempts to make them disappear. Two entirely different situations that one must all the more guard against confusing, since it should not be denied that the return of political philosophy could have the paradoxical effect of diverting political things to the point of blocking them off. In 1842 Ludwig Feuerbach, in *The Necessity for a Reform of Philosophy*, already suggested distinguishing two types of reform: either a philosophy that arises from the same historical sources as those that preceded it, or a philosophy that would arise from a new era in human history. "There is a fundamental distinction involved between a philosophy that owes its existence to a philosophical need . . . and one that corresponds to a need of mankind."[1] So we should also learn to distinguish, under the term *renewal of political philosophy*, between the mere reawakening of an academic discipline that sets off again as though nothing had happened and a post-totalitarian appearance of the need for politics. Let us understand: the rediscovery of political things after totalitarian domination attempted forever to destroy the political dimension of the human condition, in short, the offspring of a need of humanity. And if one should ask us to name a political thing that is returning, can we not reply by way of the political question itself, or the resurgence of the distinction between a free political regime and despotism, or else Spinoza's question, taken up from La Boétie: "Why is it that people fight for their servitude as though it were their salvation?"

If one weighs the consequences well, this distinction with respect to the import of the renewal of political philosophy is not immaterial. It would appear, at the very least, that if it indicates only the restoration of an academic discipline, its renewal would involve at a minimum a disinterest in critical theory, if not plain opposition. As a matter of fact, is it not a question, for these "new philosophers" of politics, of supplanting critical theory insofar as in their eyes it is partly linked with the *hermeneutics of suspicion* (the infernal trio of Marx, Nietzsche, Freud), and so, as a critique of domination—as everyone knows—ought to be ousted because it renders us blind to the specificity of the political? On the contrary, if this renewal is received as the return of political things, the theoretical situation appears quite different: for, to the extent that the political question is not reduced to the nonconflictual administration of the established order, but opens up a reformulation of the question of emancipation *hic et nunc*, a link to critical theory, as a critique of domination, becomes imperative inasmuch as the route of emancipation passes necessarily, if not exclusively by way of that critique. Better, it is precisely because one acknowledges an irreducible difference between politics and domination that one cannot ignore those phenomena revealed by the critique of domination and that are held legitimate to examine precisely in order to devise a perhaps original link between critical theory and political philosophy. Can critical theory be considered to be in any way political philosophy? Is it not exactly along this path that one might initiate a critical political philosophy that, far from diverting us from political things, from the resurgence of the political question, would lead us back to it all the more surely, since the orientation to emancipation would allow us to avoid two equally fatal dangers: on the one hand, a forgetting of the phenomenon of domination, and on the other, a blindness to the difference between domination and politics?

The exploration of what could be a critical political philosophy, a possible joining of critical theory and political philosophy, requires a complex procedure.

To begin with, it is necessary to try to respond to a preliminary question one ought not put off. Can critical theory be considered to be in any way a political philosophy or, *a minima*, are there affinities between critical theory and political philosophy? It goes without saying that an absolute difference between the two would make the construction of a critical political philosophy more difficult, if not impossible. A joining may be conceived only in the case of a relative proximity of the two, even if it could be undertaken only at the cost of significant changes. The task then falls to us to determine whether critical theory, concerning which Max Horkheimer, one of its founders, declared, "authority is . . . a central category for history,"[2] explicitly or implicitly contains a political philosophy.

But to establish that there is an orientation towards political philosophy in critical theory would not be sufficient to immediately confirm the possibility and legitimacy of a critical political philosophy. Such an orientation is without doubt necessary, but in no way amounts to a sufficient condition. One of the most valuable qualities of critical theory is to take on the historicity of the labor of the concept. What this means for us is that we need once more to take into account the inseparable historical and philosophical dimensions of the problem. If we believe the newness of the epoch is tied to the removal of totalitarian domination understood as the destruction of politics, and so to the rediscovery of the political, we find ourselves with the following choice: alternatives or a joining.

As an *alternative* between two paradigms, the critique of domination that defines critical theory, and the thought of the political as different from domination, we would find ourselves in the presence of two camps: on the one hand, a critique of domination that would untiringly continue to investigate the manifestations of the division between master and slave; on the other, those who, while responsive to the dawn of the political, splendidly ignore the shadows in this picture, that is to say, the persistence of domination.

For a joining of the two, but one foreign to a facile eclecticism, the daunting task of thinking them together would resolve into a conflictual coexistence, the critique of domination and the thinking of the political, the existence of the one not barring the route to the other. Would it be suitable to propose again a hinge between the two?

Bearing our title in mind, it is clear that the hypothesis of alternatives will not detain us inasmuch as it has an unfortunate tendency to become caught up in the one-sided logics of opposing camps and wallows in the clash of paradigms. It seems to us that the only path worth trying, that of a *critical political philosophy*, would at least have the merit of keeping apart two easy choices that all too easily become a slippery slope, that is irenicism or catastrophism.

Critical Theory as Political Philosophy?

A difficult question to resolve, since in order to produce a satisfactory answer one must first be in possession of a definition, or better, a conception of political philosophy that would render possible a judgment of the adequacy or inadequacy of such an identification. This difficulty appears as soon as one turns to the responses that have been given, be they positive or negative.

Thus George Friedman, in *The Political Philosophy of the Frankfurt School*,[3] replies in the affirmative. Without making use of a preliminary definition, that author perceives a political philosophy in the collective work of the Frankfurt School insofar as critical theory elaborates a critique of modernity and aims to intervene in its crisis. For the Frankfurt theorists, the essential object of critique would be the modern paradox, meaning the arrival with modernity of an irrational rationality, a reason that does not fulfill its promise and gives birth to a world in which unreason triumphs.

A paradox that requires a response to the initial question of *The Dialectic of Enlightenment*: Why does humankind, instead of having arrived at a truly human condition, find itself foundering in a new barbarism? According to him, the problem of the philosophers of the Enlightenment is the point of departure for the political philosophy of critical theory,[4] as long as one relies upon the beginning passage of the chapter "The Concept of Enlightenment," in *Dialectic of Enlightenment*: "Enlightenment, understood in the widest sense as the advance of thought, has always aimed at liberating human beings from fear and installing them as masters. Yet the wholly enlightened earth is radiant with triumphant calamity."[5] If the program of the Enlighteners consists in liberating the human world from the grip of myth, the question becomes: Through what internal process does reason arrive at its own self-destruction, that is, revert to a new mythology? The fundamental thesis of Theodor W. Adorno and Max Horkheimer is the efficacy of the internal movement of self-destructive reason.[6] The destructive mythology of reason emerges from the heart of reason itself, in no way from archaic survivals or planned manipulation. Far from holding a reassuring view of a reason divergent from myth, critical theory reveals their proximity, or worse, their affinity. Even awakened reason engenders monsters. Would critical theory be the contrary of the classical problematic of the Enlighteners, who made reason the declared enemy of myth? According to Horkheimer and Adorno, there would be a secret complicity between reason and myth. As for the motor of inversion, would it not consist in the joining of the liberation from fear with the assumption of sovereignty? It is in that junction, in that identification that the secret complicity of reason and myth takes hold. On the part of critical theory, it is not so much a matter of taking leave of reason; on the contrary, for its part, there is a will to salvage it.

To follow the analysis of George Friedman, the attack by critical theory against bourgeois philistinism, but also against orthodox Marxism, is inscribed in an aesthetic turn, as though the political question had abandoned the economy in order to turn to art and the promise of happiness it announces. A question is missing here: Is this critique of modernity, so complex and paradoxical, sufficient to constitute a political philosophy? Nevertheless, the work's conclusion does raise some doubts about its status as political philosophy. Would not the valorization of Eros, notably in the work of Herbert Marcuse, have the effect of turning people away from the problems of the city? Would not a typically modern excess engender ignorance concerning the question of justice? Finally, how to conceive an emancipated society: Would it still retain a political dimension or would it be placed beyond politics, as though emancipation meant being liberated from politics? Yet in spite of expressing these doubts, the author does not feel prevented from retaining his chosen outlook and continues to see in the critique of modern reason the elements of a possible political philosophy.

From the opposite direction, Leszek Kolakowski, in the harsh pages he gave to the Frankfurt School, concludes in the negative. Drawing inspiration from a liberal position and holding on to a rather taxonomic definition of political philosophy drawing from its most classical subjects, he denies this status to critical theory and consigns it variously to ideology, utopia, or social critique. But this relegation of critical theory outside of political philosophy is also not without problems.

Critical theory is certainly not a political philosophy in the academic sense, all the less so since its practitioners hold themselves at a distance from that which Arthur Schopenhauer called "university philosophy," only to reject it. But having said that, it is important to add that within the field of modern philosophy critical theory is distinguished by a particularly acute sensitivity to the political question or to the question of emancipation. A philosophy for dark times, one might say. Returning briefly to the Young Hegelian problematic as laid out by Ludwig Feuerbach in terms of the opposition between philosophy and nonphilosophy, would not the political question belong to the exterior of philosophy as the nonphilosophy that does not cease to disturb the false stable identity of philosophy? Does not politics, as practice, bring back into a philosophy that forms itself on the basis of the negation of space and time precisely that space and time that are the primary criteria of practice? According to Herbert Marcuse in *Reason and Revolution*, is Hegel's philosophy not unique in having made possible the transition to social theory? And having done so, does Marcuse in chapter 6 of the first part, not describe what occurred in Hegel's political philosophy and so to political philosophy in general, since the Hegelian oeuvre is central to modernity? "His basic philosophical ideas had fulfilled themselves in the specific historical form that state and society had assumed, and the latter became central to a new theoretical interest. Philosophy had in this way devolved upon social theory."[7] At this point two paths open up: either State and civil society remain internal to the system, philosophy turns into administrative science with Lorenz von Stein and the dialectic of sociology, or the question of the State and civil society turns into the question of their abolition, that is, into the question of revolution, which is by definition exterior to the system. A displacement of political philosophy thus takes place to the extent that the political question is henceforth in some way beside itself. This passage of the political outside itself, this exit of the political into another element, implies a translation of philosophy, but above all that the language of the political be translated into the more general language of emancipation. "The transition from Hegel to Marx is, in all respects, a transition to an essentially different order of truth, not to be interpreted in terms of philosophy. We shall see that all the philosophical concepts of Marxian theory are social and economic categories, whereas Hegel's social and economic categories are all philosophical concepts. Even Marx's early writings are not philosophical. They express the negation of philosophy, though they do so in philosophical language."[8] In addition, whereas in Hegel's system all the categories employed concern the existing order exclusively, Marx's categories refer to the negation of that order. They look forward to a new form of society and are directed at a truth that would appear with the abolition of civil society. "Marx's theory is a 'critique' in the sense that all concepts are an indictment of the existing order."[9] To this is added the fact that the critique of society becomes the work not of philosophy, but a sociohistorical emancipatory practice.

In order, then, to judge the nature of the political philosophy of critical theory, we ought to take into account the two self-extrications—that of philosophy and that of politics—that constitute it; extrications that in no way signify an abandonment of these matters, but their displacement into another element, that is to say, the economic element, and the pursuit in a different manner of the ends of philosophy and politics. It follows that critical theory, rather than being the abandonment of political philosophy, or its negation pure and simple, is its translation into the language of emancipation or that of revolution. A translation that results in the paradoxical situation within which critical theory is a rupture with political philosophy, yet only to better take it up again and continue it, briefly, to rescue it by other means, in a different element and with other routes. In a word, critical theory is conceived by its founders as a salvage by transplant of political philosophy. There is no doubt that here the model elaborated by Karl Korsch, in his opus *Marxism and Philosophy*, is at work.[10]

With this in mind, one will grasp the extent to which the negative response to the question that concerns us bypasses the issue, having not considered and understood the displacement and the salvage by transplant of political philosophy, and just how much that response proves unacceptable.

The political question, even translated into another language, is present in the texture of critical theory. It has the status of a constitutive dimension. From the dedication to *Minima Moralia*, Adorno evokes, not without melancholy, the bonds between philosophy and politics and recalls that the task of philosophy had been the teaching of the "good life." But the "melancholy knowledge" that Adorno offers us is not that of resignation; if it is necessary "to scrutinize its [life's] estranged form, the objective powers that determine individual existence even in its most hidden recesses,"[11] it is not at all in order to renounce the quest for the good life, for that which the classics sought out in the search for the best regime in words. And even if there is an undeniable shift between the beginning and the conclusion of *Minima Moralia*, the final insistence on Redemption is not foreign to this quest.

Thus critical theory puts us in the midst of a group of philosophers who did not consider it a failing to write about modern society and contemporary forms of domination. In place of reducing critical theory to a theory of knowledge, as its reception in France is often tempted to do, it would be without a doubt more fruitful to recognize in it a critique of modernity in its most varied manifestations, a critique oriented towards emancipation, and so an "old mole" ready to excavate its most divergent subterranean corridors so as to better subvert bourgeois society. Out of that, an impressive body of works that are just as much contributions to a critique of politics. Let us remember, from Max Horkheimer et alii, "Authority and the Family," "Egoism and Freedom Movements: On the Anthropology of the Bourgeois Era,"[12] "The End of Reason,"[13] "The Authoritarian State,"[14] *Eclipse of Reason*.[15] And in collaboration with Theodor W. Adorno, *Dialectic of Enlightenment: Philosophical Fragments*; the direction of *Studies in Prejudice*, notably the major work where the collaboration with Adorno dedicated to the authoritarian personality was decisive.[16] From Leo Lowenthal and Norbert Guterman, *Prophets of Deceit: A Study of the Technique of the American Agitator*.[17] From Leo Lowenthal, the study of parties, *False Prophets: Studies on Authoritarianism*.[18] From Herbert Marcuse, "The Struggle against Liberalism in the Totalitarian View of the State,"[19] "Some Social Implications of Modern Technology,"[20] "State and Individual under National Socialism,"[21] without mentioning his better known works. Adorno's articles on Fascist propaganda, on belief in astrology, *The Stars down to Earth and Other Essays on the Irrational in Culture*,[22] the critique of the culture industry. If one turns to the minor works of the Frankfurt School, the recent research of William E. Scheuerman demonstrated that, with Franz Neumann—author of the major work on Nazism, *Behemoth: The Structure and Practice of National Socialism, 1933–1944*[23]—and Otto Kirchheimer, there was an original reflection upon the fate of law in modern society, as well as the elements of a critical theory of democracy, notably in the opposition to the Nazi jurist Carl Schmitt.[24] Finally, one should mention the work of Friedrich Pollock on *The Economic and Social Consequences of Automation*[25] and "State Capitalism: Its Possibilities and Limitations."[26]

This critique of politics could not have come about on the part of critical theory without a theoretical distance taken in relation to Marx. The latter, in 1843, at the moment, according to the traditional interpretations, he moved from the critique of politics to the critique of political economy, wrote in a letter to Ruge: "domination and exploitation are one and the same concept." There follows, *brevitas causa*, the tendency to derive the political from the economic taken as a determining instance. But critical theory, notably its founding theoreticians, reject that identification, which amounts in their eyes to a confusion of domination with exploitation; they reject this diminution of politics in relation to economics that leads necessarily to the inclusion of the critique of politics within political economy. For Horkheimer, and this from 1930 in his work concerning the bourgeois philosophy of history, the history of human societies is constituted in and by the division between dominating and dominated groups, domination permitting the appropriation of alienated labor. It is no accident that in the chapter devoted to Machiavelli Horkheimer declares: "But society is not just based on the domination of nature in the narrower sense, nor merely on the invention of new methods of production or the construction of machines, nor on the maintenance of a certain standard of health[;] it is equally based on the domination of human beings by other human beings."[27] And it is in that text that Horkheimer explicitly and without reserve determines politics under the sign of domination: "The aggregate of the paths that lead to this condition, and of the measures which serve to maintain this domination, goes under the name of politics."[28]

But it is necessary to turn to Adorno and *Negative Dialectics* to find the most profound attempt to differentiate domination from exploitation, in linking it to a source that has nothing to do with the economy. It is under the heading of "Contingency and Antagonism" that he poses the question of whether antagonism, "a piece of natural history prolonged," perhaps appeared one day unfolding from the survival needs of the species or, in a contingent manner "from arbitrary, archaic acts aimed at seizing power." Posing in this way a contingent catastrophe at the origins of human history, and distancing himself at the same time from the *topos* of a golden age, he engages himself in overthrowing "Reason in history," the very idea of historical necessity whether it is thought in Hegel's terms or those of Marx and Engels. Yet it is in no sense a question of posing, in the form of the contingency of antagonism, a new reification that would bring a halt to every project of historical intervention in prophesying for domination "an infinite future, for as long as any organized society exists." Adorno's move is as critical as it is complex: it is not sufficient for him to offer a distinction between exploitation and domination, to challenge the preeminence of the one over the other, it is necessary to envisage a domination that is not the result of economics, that is alien to that field. In relation to Marx, whom he criticizes on this point, Adorno writes, "Economics is said to come before dominion, which must not be deduced other than economically." This implies that the contingency of antagonism results from the existence of a domination that is as indeterminate as it is contingent, and is destined to remain so. It is in no way a matter of substituting an anthropological or psychological necessity for an economic necessity. According to Adorno there was at the heart of the atheism of Marx and Engels a veritable deification of history, the primacy of the economic having the effect of securing, offering guarantees to *praxis*. In fact, if the economy has primacy in domination and, as a supplementary and essential condition, domination is considered as unfolding from the economy, the transformation of the economy would automatically bring in its train the disappearance of domination. "The primacy of economics," writes Adorno, "is to yield historically stringent reasons why the happy end is immanent in history. The economic process, we hear, produces the conditions of political rule and keeps overturning them until the inevitable deliverance from the compulsion of economics." Inversely, the primacy of domination and the hypothesis of an indeterminate domination allow for considering that the transformation of the economy may leave the reign of domination unchanged. Is it not one of the possible definitions of the failure of revolution that domination continues beyond the transformation of the economy? A failure to which Marx and Engels were not entirely strangers inasmuch as, wanting to distance themselves from the anarchists, they left open the question of the end of domination. "The revolution desired by him and Marx was one of economic conditions in society as a whole, in the basic stratum of its self-preservation; it was not revolution as a change in society's political form, in the rules of the game of dominion."[29] The hypothesis of an irrational catastrophe in the beginning as much as the vertigo of the present catastrophe knock down the idea of a historical totality composed as though endowed with an economic necessity that is calculable and therefore controllable. Hence the exigency of a new thinking of domination, exterior to the economy, that would neither arrive as a fetishization of politics nor as a tendency to think of domination as eternal or as coextensive with human history. On the contrary, it is putting into question the inevitable character of totality that originates and permanently strengthens the will to change the world. "Today the thwarted possibility of something other has shrunk to that of averting catastrophe in spite of everything."[30]

With Max Horkheimer, the attention given to the question of domination gives rise to the theorization of authority thought as welcomed, or, even more, interiorized. In examining large social formations and the dynamic of their development, Horkheimer states that the direction and the rhythm of their processes are in the last instance determined by laws internal to the economic apparatus of society. However, as he had already remarked in the inaugural lecture for the Institute for Social Research in 1931, the behavior of people in a given era "cannot be explained solely by economic events which have transpired in the immediate past."[31] From this stage of the proceedings on, Horkheimer insists on the character of people, on their psychic dispositions that should be considered in relation to the relatively stable institutions of a given society. The economy can therefore not act. "The whole culture, therefore, is caught up in the dynamism of history,"[32] but only reimmersed in a plurality of factors. In brief, a thinking of overdetermination is emerging. But rather than invoking culture to explain the psychic disposition of individuals, Horkheimer deliberately turns to the power of the State. "The decisive factor (within the framework of economic possibility, of course) is rather the State's ability to govern, the organization of its powers, and, ultimately, its physical force."[33] Horkheimer's insistence upon the political division, not the division between exploiters and exploited, but that between those who command and those who carry things out is another further distance he takes with regard to the economy. "In the histories of all developed societies the knowledge and capabilities of men and the corresponding material apparatus of production have been such that only through a characteristic division of men into leaders and followers could the social life process go on."[34] To account for a given social unit, which is proper to invoke: a spiritual cement, that is to say a dynamic conception of culture, or rather "the extremely concrete form of executive power"?[35] Is this latter hypothesis identified as a call to well-founded realism? Is the psychic apparatus of members of class society not the interiorization or at least the rationalization and complement of physical force? Having arrived at this point, Horkheimer has recourse to the dark hypothesis of Nietzsche in *The Genealogy of Morals*, according to which the transformation of man, "forgetting incarnate," into an animal capable of memory, of promising, an animal with foresight and therefore social, is the outcome of a history in the grip of terror. Horkheimer cites the famous passages of section 3 of the second part: a hidden link, but no less real, forever persisting, binding, that one calls "conscience," customary morality or even sociality to this first, originary terror. "One might even say that wherever on earth solemnity, seriousness, mystery, and gloomy coloring still distinguish the life of man and a people, something of the terror that formerly attended all promises, pledges, and vows on earth is *still* effective. . . . Man could never do without blood, torture, and sacrifices when he felt the need to create a memory for himself."[36] Following upon this passage by Nietzsche, one of those who inspire the Frankfurt School's thinking on domination, Horkheimer recognized without reservation the place of violence in the history of civilization: "The role of coercion, which marks not only the origin but also the development of all States, can indeed be hardly overestimated when we try to explain social life in history up to the present."[37] By violence one should also understand punishment for and the threat of punishment for those vulnerable to hunger. However, for Horkheimer the question persists as strongly as ever: "Why the subject classes have born the yoke so long."[38] In responding to this question, we must of course take into account violence, yet Horkheimer does not attribute everything to the concrete acts of an executive power. Once he has, with Nietzsche's help, recalled the dark background of culture, he considers it necessary to take into account the whole of culture, understood as a specific factor in the social dynamic. "In any case, the preservation of outmoded forms of society, for example, cannot be immediately ascribed to an exercise of naked power or to a deception of the masses concerning their material interests."[39] Violence therefore does not suffice to explain the division of dominators and dominated, and even less the acceptance of this division, the acceptance of domination. In order to understand the interiorization that produces this acceptance, it is proper to call upon the whole of culture, spiritual cement or rather the complex interplay taking place between culture, stable institutions, and the psychic or interior apparatus. Neither the economy in isolation, nor violence alone, but an overdetermination that puts in play within this dynamic whole that is culture the other dynamic element, which is the psychic apparatus, so important since the beginning for critical theory. "The fact that both of these occur, as well as the manner in which they occur, are themselves conditioned by the dispositions of men."[40] Out of the whole extensive work of Horkheimer's on authority, let us hold on to three important points:

- The bringing to light of acceptance on the part of the dominated: "simple coercion alone does not maintain such a state of affairs and that men have learned to approve of it."[41]

- The clearest recognition of the omnipresence within history of the phenomenon of domination, which constitutes, according to Horkheimer, the framework for the vital progress of society. "The majority of men have always worked under the leadership and command of a minority, and this dependence has always found expression in a more wretched kind of material existence for them."[42] As for human types, they present, despite their diversity, one feature in common: "their essential characteristics are determined by the power-relationships proper to society at any given time."[43]

- In contradistinction to the quietism of a Norbert Elias and his theory of the development of civilization, Horkheimer's insistence on the interweaving of relations of domination with those of culture, an interweaving such that, in the last resort authority can be defined as a condition of accepted subordination, or as a state of interiorized subordination. One can perceive here the link between this first reflection on authority and the subsequent research into the authoritarian personality. "One function of the entire cultural apparatus at any given period has been to internalize in men of subordinate position the idea of a necessary domination of some men over others, as determined by the course of history down to the present time. As a result, and as a continually renewed condition of this cultural apparatus, the belief in authority is one of the driving forces, sometimes productive, sometimes obstructive, of human history."[44]

The negative response to our initial question is unacceptable, to the extent of being an extreme oversimplification. Having failed to perceive a salvage by transplant of political philosophy on the part of critical theory, it claims to find itself in the presence of a discourse that would have nothing in common with political philosophy or its object, even though numerous elements in critical theory, transformed to be sure, hold together a relation with the major orientations of political philosophy, for example, the research on freedom and the project of building society according to the requirements of reason.

But the positive response—that critical theory is a political philosophy—cannot be upheld, because in order to be sensitive to the political dimension of critical theory, to the critique of politics that it contains, that response minimizes and at the same time masks the displacements and transformations to which critical theory subjected political philosophy. Without inquiring here and now into the nature of political philosophy, let us be satisfied with isolating one or two of the nuclei that are constitutive of that philosophy. At least two requisites appear to be necessary:

- an affirmation of the substantiality of the political, that is to say, a specificity of political things that renders them irreducible and heterogeneous to other phenomena with which they tend to be conflated, social or socio-historical phenomena;
- an insistence upon a distinction between a free political regime and despotism, or in more contemporary terms, between politics and totalitarian domination.

In spite of the elements of a critique of politics that we have shown to be at the heart of critical theory, can we nonetheless announce that we are in the presence of a political philosophy? One can justifiably doubt it. Horkheimer himself shows reservations with respect to the idea of political philosophy and visibly tries to establish a distance from a project of this type. Actually, in a 1938 article, "La philosophie de la concentration absolue,"[45] a merciless critique of a contemporary work by Siegfried Marck, *Le nouvel humanisme en tant que philosophie politique*, published in Zurich, Horkheimer shows his reservations three times over with regard to a philosophy that presents itself as political. At first a suspicion: If one judged according to the attitudes of post-1919 socialists, would political philosophy not be a term that masks an absence of freedom or the failure of *praxis*? Then a question: What remains of political philosophy if one considers that its fate remains tightly bound to that of the declining democracies of the period? Finally, a reminder. Contrary to Marck's positions, Horkheimer underlines that political philosophy has for a long time been the object of an essential transformation and lets it be understood that to invoke it in isolation is a sign of a regression to a state prior to that transformation. "It remains true," writes Horkheimer, "that we think of the philosophy that qualifies as political as having for a long time changed into the critique of political economy."[46] The "for a long time" indicates that the metamorphosis of political philosophy is in all likelihood referred back to the critical labors of Marx, who in the 1840s effected an exit from philosophy in order to transport its subject into the critique of politics and then into that of political economy. According to Horkheimer, this metamorphosis places political philosophy before an alternative: either it consents to this transformation and retains its critical force in unmasking the historical situation; or else it clings to its identity and in that case becomes an ornamental discourse, without a grasp of the real. "In that case, it falls to the epigones who are beautiful souls."[47]

One can also hold that critical theory, far from identifying itself with political philosophy, rather distanced itself from it and that it would be thanks to this distancing, according to Horkheimer, that it would succeed in remaining faithful to its critical vocation. We can note at least two tangible deviations between critical theory and the idea of political philosophy.

In the first place, it is not sufficient to propose a critique of domination, no matter how complex, nor to envisage the existence of a domination not necessarily deriving from the economic, in order to succeed at creating a political philosophy. For, without falling into a radical discrediting of the political domain, as, for example, did Moses Hess when he identified it with domination in "The Philosophy of the Act,"[48] politics would not be reduced to a relation of domination, to the existence of a structure determined as a schism between a dominant minority and a dominated multitude. Spinoza in the *Tractatus Theologico-Politicus* already affirmed this: it is beyond domination that the State is or ought to be established, to the degree that it is an institution for freedom. "It very clearly follows from the fundamental principles of the state which I explained above that its ultimate purpose is not to dominate or control people by fear or subject them to the authority of another. On the contrary, its aim is to free everyone from fear so that they may live in security so far as possible, that is, so that they may retain, to the highest possible degree, their natural right to live and to act without harm to themselves or to others. It is not, I contend, the purpose of the state to turn people from rational beings into beasts or automata, but rather to allow their minds and bodies to develop in their own ways in security and enjoy the free use of reason, and not to participate in conflicts based on hatred, anger or deceit or in malicious disputes with each other. Therefore, the true purpose of the state is in fact freedom."[49] To be sure, critical theory does not limit itself to the critique of domination or, to be more exact, the critique of domination with which it proceeds is inseparable from the aim of emancipation. It is the domination-emancipation couple that supports the peculiarity of the concepts of critical theory, well outlined by Marcuse in the important 1937 text "Philosophy and Critical Theory." "If critical theory, amidst today's desperation, indicates the reality it intends must comprise the freedom and happiness of individuals, it is only following the direction given by its economic concepts. They are constructive concepts, which comprehend not only the given reality but, simultaneously, its abolition and the new reality which is to follow. In the theoretical reconstruction of the social process, the critique of current conditions and the analysis of their tendencies necessarily include future-oriented components."[50] There is thus no doubt that the exit from domination aiming at emancipation does contain, under the name of a rational society, the ideas of freedom and happiness. But there is an obstacle in that critical theory suffers a curious silence concerning the reign of freedom. Implicit in this lacuna would be "It goes without saying." At the basis of this silence there would be more than the ban on representation, but the serious error that, within the couple domination-emancipation, chooses to refer, to situate politics on the side of domination—inasmuch as it is an ensemble of means allowing the establishment and maintenance of domination—and not at all on the side of emancipation or freedom. As though emancipation consisted not in the establishment of a free political community but in the liberation from politics, that is, in transcending an organization of society resting upon domination.

But politics opens up, beyond an undeniable domination, the possibility of a bond—and of a space—specific in multiple forms, because it can, far from privileging unity, be established as the bond of division, as Nicole Loraux showed with respect to the Greek city. The political bond, be it in the form of assembling or of division, establishes a being-together, a singular mode of human coexistence or, in addition, an acting together under the sign of freedom. Even Jacques Rancière, who we know refuses all projects of political philosophy, even as critique, distinguishes two modes or two logics of human being-together, politics and the police, which, in other terms, imply the difference between politics and domination. "Spectacular or otherwise, political activity is always a mode of expression that undoes the perceptible divisions of the police order by implementing a basically heterogeneous assumption, that of a part of those who have no part."[51] One might surmise that he is moving in the direction of a critical political philosophy, since he calls for thinking together the heterogeneity of the political in connection with domination or the police. "We should not forget either that if politics implements a logic entirely heterogeneous to that of the police, it is always bound up with the latter."⁵² Yet it is true that he holds himself firmly distant from any notion of political philosophy; he is not afraid to write, in an apparently contradictory manner, that politics has no unique subjects or questions. It is to the extent that there is a political institution of the social, to use the terms of Claude Lefort, or the constitution of a political bond in action undertaken in common that domination can recede, even give way, the aim of politics being the institution of a bond beyond the division between the governing and the governed, beyond the command-obedience relationship. If one follows the analyses of Hannah Arendt in *The Human Condition*, the political is thought as having emerged from the experience of freedom that took place at the heart of the Greek *polis*—but equally during the great modern revolutions—and in opposition to the experience of domination that, under the hold of necessity dwelt in the interior of the household, the *oikos*. In this case, identifying the political with domination amounts to confounding two distinct orders of the real, opposing logics of being-together and cutting the umbilical cord that ties the political to that which is its living source, that is to say, freedom. Freedom is, in effect, the proper question of politics, one could say, in the strong sense, its element. Such is the specificity of the political according to Arendt in her study "What Is Freedom?" "The field where freedom has always been known, not as a problem, to be sure, but as a fact of everyday life, is the political realm. . . . We can hardly touch a single political issue without, implicitly or explicitly, touching upon an issue of man's liberty. . . . Freedom, which only seldom in times of crisis or revolution becomes the direct aim of political action, is actually the reason that men live together in political organization at all. Without it, political life as such would be meaningless. The *raison d'être* of politics is freedom, and its field of experience is action."⁵³

A first deviation, then, in relation to political philosophy by virtue of which one could consider that critical theory, whether as a whole or not, urgently and by necessity, needing a critique of domination for its epoch, missed the specificity and irreducibility of political being-together by having mistakenly lodged politics on the side of domination and its instruments. The privilege accorded to the critique of domination in order to escape the weaknesses of the political philosophy with which it was contemporaneous led critical theory to do without reflections about the persistence and dignity of political things, even though the idea of freedom was for it evidently of the essence.

A second difference. The anti-totalitarian orientations of critical theory are indisputable and are as much evident in Horkheimer's 1942 essay "The Authoritarian State" as in *Behemoth* the major work of Franz Neumann focusing on Nazism, not to mention numerous articles by T. W. Adorno. These orientations deserve considerably more of our attention, being that they are close to an anti-totalitarian critique often ignored in France, which is to say that of the German left, Karl Korsch, Otto Ruhle, and others, published under the title *La contre-révolution bureaucratique*.[54] Thus the question of the authoritarian State or of totalitarian domination was the subject of a correspondence between Horkheimer and Karl Korsch.[55] In this sense there exists an apparent proximity between critical theory and certain strains of political philosophy that are distinguished by associating a political critique of totalitarianism with a rediscovery of political things. With careful attention, these same critiques, even though they describe an opposition of democracy to totalitarianism, are nevertheless constructed upon the opposition of the political to total domination. Under various headings, they consider that totalitarianism, far from being a monstrous excrescence of politics, rather pursues its destruction, to the point of bringing to an end the political condition of humans. In spite of the differences that exist between the work of Claude Lefort and that of Hannah Arendt, these two interpretations indicate, in the departure from the ordeal of totalitarianism, a bringing back to light of that which was destroyed, or a coming into being of the knowledge of the political domain, the domain of human affairs.

The reader of "The Authoritarian State" cannot help being struck by the similarities of analysis. Horkheimer compares Nazism to "integral statism," that is to say, the USSR, and perceives two types of a new form of domination as immediate and open domination. To integral statism he opposes attempts to establish true freedom, forms of a classless democracy that could "prevent the elevation of the administrative sector to positions of power."[56] At many times in this text a call is issued for a revolution against the authoritarian state so that one day people could regulate their own affairs in solidarity. A revolution that Horkheimer puts in the care, not of a party or a vanguard, but separated individuals, recalling that, historically, humanity was not betrayed by the intemperate efforts of revolutionaries but by the opportunistic wisdom of realists. In a discourse on state capitalism as a contemporary possibility, Horkheimer, attacking it with vehemence, criticizes that form of thought that "recognizes only the dimension of the cycle of progress and regression" and ignores "the active intervention of men."[57] In conclusion he declares: "As long as world history follows its logical course, it fails to fulfill its human destiny."[58] Yet, despite such proximity, there is a peculiarity of critical theory that holds it at a distance from that constellation of political philosophy that manifests itself as the critique of total domination. At many turns in Horkheimer's texts the continuity between the authoritarian state and liberalism is affirmed, as though the new form of state that destroyed liberalism nevertheless was its heir. Thus, in "La philosophie de la concentration absolue," Horkheimer deems that "the authoritarian state characterizes that part of European society that takes the place of liberalism. The task of controlling the masses separated from the means of production and preparing the people for the struggle over the world market . . . was the result of liberalism."[59] This thesis of continuity is opposed, just as much in the analyses of Hannah Arendt as of Claude Lefort, by one of radical discontinuity. For the author of *The Origins of Totalitarianism*, total domination is the innovation of our century; it constitutes its heart, better yet, is, quite precisely, the "without precedent." In this fashion, it should not be confused with other forms of authoritarian domination known historically, despotism or tyranny. And it is in order to meet the challenge of the unprecedented that there is a will for analysis multiplied ten times over by an appeal to the imagination on the part of the partisans of discontinuity, which would not be the case for a theoretician who seeks to locate the authoritarian state within the horizon of the already known. There remains a certain stridency in Horkheimer's essay "The Authoritarian State," inasmuch as the author tries to understand the regimes of Stalin and Hitler and appeals for a new resistance, that of isolated individuals. To be noted equally in this essay, the metaphysics of history is dismissed, that is to say, Hegel's thought, but also that of Marx. Horkheimer criticizes the Hegelian representation of the development of world Spirit manifesting itself in a succession of stages according to a logical necessity. According to him, Marx made the mistake of remaining faithful to Hegel on this point. "History," he writes, "is represented [by Marx] as an indivisible development. The new cannot begin before its time. However, the fatalism of both philosophers refers to the past only. Their metaphysical error, namely that history obeys a defined law, is cancelled by their historical error, namely that such a law was fulfilled at its appointed time. The present and past are not subject to the same law."[60]

If the Marxist metaphysics of history is rejected, Marxism as an instrument of analysis is preserved. The authoritarian state is inferred from the economy or from the ensemble of the socioeconomic structure grasped in the dynamic of culture. The economic field is the source for the intelligibility of the new form of domination, because it is a political-economic logic, the passage with state capitalism from market to planning, that is capable of explaining the authoritarian state. On this point, the interpretations of totalitarianism we have mentioned differentiate themselves from critical theory. For Arendt as for Lefort, it is fitting to resort to a political logic if one wants to understand the genesis and constitution of total domination. Doing so, they grant a title of nobility to a political comprehension of history that tends to restore its place and efficacy to the domain of politics. On this point, it is fitting to differentiate by shades, because, if one considers the whole of critical theory, one can see that the genesis of totalitarianism is taken up by two nonexclusive logics, a logic of the socioeconomic structure, state capitalism, and a logic of modern reason. It is in fact in the development of reason, its subjectification and consequent instrumentalization, or indeed in the complicity of reason with myth, reason inverting into a new mythology, wherein reside the possible sources of a new form of domination.

Responsive to the unprecedented in total domination, political philosophy strained to offer an original interpretation of this new form of regime that is in a sense a nonregime; an interpretation one might well judge in either case to be of phenomenological inspiration, Arendt insisting on the movement that carries totalitarianism along, Lefort on the image of the body that in totalitarian society releases a vertiginous course towards identity in the grip of the spell of the name of the One. There is nothing like this in critical theory, at least with Horkheimer or Marcuse. Approaching the authoritarian state from the direction of a socioeconomic logic, Horkheimer only reaches a rather empirical description of the phenomenon. Even though occasional recourse to the hypothesis of the bureaucratization of the world confers the force of a critique of the political to his analysis. However, Franz Neumann in his book *Behemoth* (1942), well received by Adorno and Marcuse, had the merit of presenting an original thesis according to which the totalitarian State would actually be a non-State and in this sense a break with the European tradition from Plato to Hegel. A non-State, because *Behemoth* gave rise to a regime and a situation of nonlaw and of an absence of juridical status; a non-State, because *Behemoth* suffers the lack of a unified State apparatus by way of the proliferation of bureaucracies of all sorts; finally, a non-State, because under the guise of order there reigned only the charismatic power of the leader. One can presume that reading Neumann did not leave Arendt indifferent. The latter proceeds in the same direction as the author of *Behemoth* in proposing that the totalitarian regime had the layered structure of an onion. Can one not perceive a thread that joins the thesis of a non-State with Arendt, for whom total domination meant the destruction of the political?

A double deviation, then, in relation to the political philosophy that chose to rethink the political by the test of totalitarianism, critical theory, in order to remain faithful to the critique of political economy in the sense it understood that, did not succeed, in spite of epochal changes, in truly accounting for the historically novel, without having conceived of a political logic, even though its opposition to the new regime ceded nothing as to being radical; even though it was resolutely anti-totalitarian to the point of inquiring into the political forms capable of overthrowing this form of domination, namely, in its case, council democracy.

At the end of this examination, one can conclude with the transformation of the initial question. Henceforth the correct question would not be "Is critical theory a political philosophy?" but rather a more dynamic, open-ended, movable question that would be formulated as follows: Does critical theory have the capacity to contribute to the elaboration of a critical political philosophy oriented to emancipation? One of the required changes would be, within the couple domination-emancipation, to lodge politics not on the side of domination, but on the side of emancipation.

The Articulation of the Two Paradigms or the Creation of a Critical Political Philosophy

From this preliminary examination we emerge with a doubly negative proposition, quite in the style of the Frankfurt School: critical theory is neither a political philosophy nor a pure and simple negation of political philosophy. In an affirmative mode, critical theory is a salvage by transplant of political philosophy, that is to say it transfers the questions belonging to the latter into another element, the problematic of domination and emancipation. Where the shoe pinches, at least with Horkheimer, is the fact of having placed domination on the side of politics, as though the ideas of freedom, happiness, social solidarity, autonomy, and rationality—the fabric of emancipation—had nothing to do with the political.

Having covered that issue, we can return to our initial inquiry: What living relation can we establish today with critical theory in face of the renewal of political philosophy? From the start, it appeared to us that, given the nature of this renewal, different possibilities were on offer. If the renewal signifies a return to an academic discipline, appearing as a transformation into the history of political philosophy, and thus an occultation of the political stakes in the present to the benefit of the management of the established order, we end up with a choice, critical theory or political philosophy. Which, in the end, leads to the choice of political philosophy against critical theory. Just as we were able to read *Why We Are Not Nietzscheans*,[61] we could read in the same vein "Why We Are Not Critical Theorists"? And the French intellectual scene has observed philosophers pass from one interest, to be sure mitigated for critical theory—Luc Ferry and Alain Renaut were, once upon a time, the authors of a preface to Horkheimer's *Critical Theory*—to an attachment, without reservations, to political philosophy conceived as an irrevocable eviction of critical theory and anything that remotely touches upon a critique of domination.[62]

If, on the contrary, this renewal signifies the return of political things after the collapse of totalitarian domination, the situation is quite different. It is no longer a matter of choosing one over the other but of attempting an articulation of the critique of domination, a recovery of the Frankfurt School, and a rediscovery of the political, of political things in their irreducible heterogeneity, in their substantiality and dignity, in the sense that they are not subject to being exchanged.

There are thus two paradigms, the paradigm of the critique of domination issuing from critical theory and the political paradigm. How to join one to the other? What living relation to form with critical theory in the face of a coexistence of paradigms? How could a living relationship be established by a possible conjunction of paradigms? After a succinct presentation of the two paradigms, it will be our task to examine under what terms a conception of a possible joining is advisable.

Could one not search out this articulation by invoking the name of Spinoza? In the *Political Treatise*, the latter actually tried to open a road not traveled, distanced from the two paths he describes and criticizes. First the moralists, who mock or grieve over human affections, which leads to conceiving a chimerical doctrine of politics. Then the practitioners of politics, who reduce the latter to a collection of stratagems aimed at dominating people. To the contrary, Spinoza searches for another route, a philosophical path that guards as much against turning human actions into objects of ridicule as reducing them simply to tactics. Neither to laugh nor to cry, moreover not to manipulate but to comprehend and to try to think a politics in the direction indicated by Reason, a very difficult path by Spinoza's own admission. Following Spinoza, it is incumbent on us to explore a path other than that opened by either of the two paradigms that strives to bring together a critique of domination with a thinking of the political, or the inverse. In order better to understand why this is necessary, one need only observe that, taken alone, each of these two paradigms knows a symptomatic drift.

Irenicism, on the part of the political paradigm, that is, a representation of politics as an activity that is called to take place in a smooth space, without harshness, cleavage, or conflict, oriented towards a pacific and problem-free intersubjectivity. Catastrophism, on the part of the paradigm of the critique of domination, that is, the attitude that believes that everything is a relation of domination, without exception, without the possibility of opening a space or a time of freedom that would escape the scission between dominators and dominated. Whether it is a matter of politics, justice, or the media, or any other activity that touches the coexistence of people, the intellect must choose between an irenic vision and a catastrophic one, as though it were not possible to escape from the "merchants of sleep" of each of these camps, as though it were not possible to perceive that which would complicate and disturb the systematic application of each of these paradigms.

The Paradigm of the Critique of Domination

A few preliminary remarks. The thought concerning domination in critical theory is of great complexity. It contains, in effect, a number of levels that are tangled together, but that one ought not to conflate. One can distinguish at least three levels that are all pertinent to the critique of politics: each one of them contributes to domination in the political arena in some measure.

The first and essential level, since it is clearly recognized as having a power of determination without equal, is that of the domination of nature, that which opens a path to a critique of reason, since, to return to the estimation of Guy Petitdemange, "the dialectic so described between reason and nature is the most fruitful advance of the Frankfurt School."[63] For, having established a *conjunction* between liberation from fear and the pursuit of sovereignty, reason ends by "considering the world as prey" and thus in denying every otherness. It is as though it abdicated its rational quality and made itself into nature. "The subjugation of nature will revert to subjugation of man, and vice versa, as long as man does not understand his own reason and the basic process by which he has created and is maintaining the antagonism that is about to destroy him."[64] The chance for redemption comes by way of a self-reflection of reason capable of discerning in itself this movement towards domination that translates itself into an orientation towards self-preservation and the nefarious effects this engenders. If human history is in some manner enframed by the domination of nature, it comes back to the philosopher to rethink this history in terms of this form of domination and its effects. "A philosophical interpretation of world history," write Horkheimer and Adorno, "would have to show how, despite all detours and resistances, the systematic domination over nature has been asserted more and more decisively and has integrated all internal human characteristics. Economic, political, and cultural forms would have to be derived from this position."[65] The episode of Ulysses and the sirens, at the heart of which Ulysses succeeds in neutralizing the sirens' enchantment, as much for his sailors whose ears he stuffed with wax as for himself bound to the mast, already displays the separation between compulsory manual labor and the enjoyment of art. A scission in line with the constraint the domination of nature implies. Beyond this originary situation, the domination of nature refers to technique and, for example, to the ambition of a Bacon to allow human understanding to dominate a demystified nature. "What human beings seek to learn from nature is how to use it to dominate wholly both it and human beings. Nothing else counts."[66] Once more, it would be necessary to mention the plurality of conceptions of technique that runs through the Frankfurt School, that of Herbert Marcuse in a 1941 text, which in a sense reappears in *One-Dimensional Man*, or that of Walter Benjamin, who, thanks to the contrast between two techniques, endeavors to conceive of another shape of technique, closer to play than to toil and capable in that way of substituting the liberation of nature for its domination.

Since man is a part of nature, the domination of the latter necessarily brings in its train the domination of man by man. "At the moment that human beings cut themselves off from the consciousness of themselves as nature, all the purposes for which they keep themselves alive . . . become void."[67] One of the essential mediations between the two forms of domination is clearly human labor. An activity transforming nature, labor is exercised within a division of intellectual and manual labor, between the function of direction and the function of execution. There would thus be a continuity of domination in history. "The social forms that are known to us were founded essentially on the basis of an organization that allowed only a relatively small portion of the population full enjoyment of the respective culture, while the great masses were forced to continually renounce their instincts. The form of society dictated by material conditions up to this point was separation of management and labor, of ruler and ruled."[68] This domination of man by man had, according to Horkheimer and Adorno, a privileged object, that is to say, the body. From there, a double history of Europe, the well-known official one that relates the development of civilization, the other subterranean, obscured, that concerns the destiny of the instincts and human passions, denatured by civilization. "Most mutilated of all is the relationship to the body," as they observe in *The Dialectic of Enlightenment*.[69] Finally, the domination of internal nature. Each subject must place in subjection nature within him. The principle of domination, after the reign of brute force, became the object of a development of spiritualization and interiorization. It is through this latter route that Horkheimer approaches the hypothesis of voluntary servitude. Does he not write: "Domination becomes 'internalized' for domination's sake."[70]

If we turn to the formation of the paradigm of domination, we distinguish three essential components.

To begin with, domination is thought along with Hegel, and, more precisely, the dialectic of master and slave as it is presented in *The Phenomenology of Spirit*. Taking his point of departure from Hegel's celebrated sentence "Self-consciousness achieves its satisfaction only in another self-consciousness,"[71] Marcuse reveals its principal scansions, be it in his dissertation or in *Reason and Revolution*:[72] (1) the immediate form of a confrontation of two individuals in a struggle to the death; (2) as a result of working over things, passage to a mode of the mediation of consciousnesses that takes the form of a division between he who appropriates the labor of others—the master—and he who works for another—the slave—and who lives in a situation of unfreedom; (3) beyond this "one-sided and unequal" recognition, the transformation of the slave through work, the worker becoming autonomous in and through the object of his labor. Transforming nature, the worker transforms himself, while the master, within enjoyment, is given to the consumption of things. It is via this imbalance between that which persists and that which vanishes that the slave breaks up the power of the master; (4) if the relation of master and slave aims at reciprocal recognition, it is clear that this agreement cannot be accomplished and remains affected by a determining inequality. But if the Hegelian dramaturgy is present in critical theory, one can ask oneself if it is not made worse through being taken up in the story of Ulysses. In fact, Horkheimer and Adorno indeed cite Hegel, and notably the passage in which the master is relegated to enjoyment, while the slave emerges from unfreedom thanks to his making and fashioning of things. But it would appear that for the critical theorists, there would be an obstruction to the slave's transformation and at the same time of the relation as a whole. If at first they read the history of Ulysses through Hegel—they write: "[Ulysses] is represented in the sphere of work.

Just as he cannot give way to the lure of self-abandonment, as owner he also forfeits participation in work and finally even in control over it, while his companions, despite their closeness to things, cannot enjoy their work because it is performed under compulsion, in despair, with their senses forcibly stopped." Their conclusion is distanced from the Hegelian development. The slave would not see any transformation, and the master only regression. They continue: "The servant is subjugated in body and soul, the master regresses."[73] The result would be permanent domination, its regular repetition in history, a dereliction there to be seen in the fate of power. "No system of domination has so far been able to escape this price, and the circularity of history in its progress is explained in part by this debilitation, which is the concomitant of power."[74] Should one see in the particularity of the situation of Ulysses and his bondsmen the explication of a deviation from the Hegelian schema? Ulysses, the traditional figure of a commander, of domination, does not simply appropriate the labor of another—it is even specified that he renounces steering—but, through the measures he took to neutralize the sirens, he also protects his slaves. Their senses sealed and therefore their relation with the external world disturbed, the latter remain in the embrace of this protection, beneath the liberatory transformation that the Hegelian scenario would proclaim. Does not Horkheimer, in "The End of Reason," write: "Protection is the archetype of domination"? As though one could observe in the condition of protection a qualitative leap in domination, to the extent that for the appropriation of the labor of another there would be substituted a form of relation even more alienating, the harmony of the protector with his dependents, with no possible opening for mutual recognition, each of the protagonists remaining prisoner of the fixed role given to him. "Procurers, condottieri, manorial lords and guilds have always protected and at the same time exploited their clients."[75] In their domain they take care for the reproduction of life.

Perhaps we encounter in the distance in relation to the Hegelian schema one of the reasons for the distance from Marx. If one recognizes in the latter the dialectic of master and slave in the form of the couple domination-servitude, as we have seen already, the work of critical theory consists in dissociating domination from exploitation while substituting for the idea of a necessary antagonism that of a contingent antagonism referred back to possibly arbitrary acts of power. This being the case—with access to an autonomous history of domination—from the slingshot to the atom bomb according to Adorno—there is a push to depart from Marxist quietism and to think the history of humanity under the sign of an insurmountable restlessness to the point of ceaselessly nourishing the enigma of a history not to be resolved, but remaining so.

An exit from quietism that is strengthened by the second element, the resort to Nietzsche. With this choice, it is not simply a matter of "making the reified categories of Marxism dance," but of penetrating the nocturnal sphere of history from which the philosophers classically turned away in order to privilege the relatively transparent history of the last two millennia. To the contrary, the psychologist in the Nietzschean sense, in search of the anterior history of the human soul, strives to recover, on the hither side of the birth of reason or of civilization, the primitive text, "the terrible basic text of *homo natura*."[76] As though this text held in its grip that which tends to escape, as though human history, the history of the human herd, had to struggle endlessly with the return of the archaic, especially the return of the division between a majority of subjects and a minority of masters. Thus the invocation of *The Genealogy of Morals*, and its orientation towards the prehistoric and subterranean history of humans, to the torture, pain, and punishment that contributed to making the natural man, "forgetting incarnate," a predictable animal, calculable, because capable of promising, of becoming a responsible being, and therefore social. This very ancient problem, Nietzsche insists, was not resolved with great tenderness: "perhaps indeed there was nothing more fearful and uncanny in the whole prehistory of man than his *mnemotechnics*."[77] Cruel pages in the prehistory of humans in which humans discovered that pain was the most efficient adjuvant for the inculcation of memory. "Ah, reason," writes Nietzsche, "seriousness, master over the affects, the whole somber thing called reflection, all these prerogatives and showpieces of man: how dearly they have been bought! How much blood and cruelty lie at the bottom of all 'good things.'"[78] This primal terror has never deserted human history, to the point where there is barbarism beneath every monument of culture, according to Walter Benjamin. The critical theorists are to a certain extent Nietzscheans because they understood that behind "the enormous, distant, and so well hidden land of morality," is a land even more secret, that of power. Is it not an arbitrary act of power that section 17 (second essay) of *The Genealogy of Morals* describes, when Nietzsche gives an account of the birth of the state, the fruit of "acts of violence" on the part of "some pack of blond beasts of prey, a conqueror and master race": "The oldest state thus appeared as a fearful tyranny, as an oppressive and remorseless machine, and went on working until this raw material of people and semi-animals was at last not only thoroughly kneaded and pliant but also *formed*."[79] And did not this novel machine of oppression cause to disappear "a tremendous quantity of freedom," a hypothesis retained without doubt by critical theory in order to explain the domination of internal nature?

Pertaining to this, it would be correct to add, at least in the case of Horkheimer, a brief and entirely standard reading of Machiavelli. In the first chapter of his work *Beginnings of the Bourgeois Philosophy of History*, he presents the author of the *Prince* and the *Discourses* as the founder of a new science of politics that, in imitation of the scientists and physicists of his era, would search for a uniform principle permitting the extrication of laws proper to human history. But this science, according to Horkheimer, would have had for its principal subject matter the fact of domination, the division of human societies into dominating and dominated. The political scientist whose laboratory would in some way be the past, would search in the reading of Livy or the writers of antiquity for "the eternal laws of domination," based upon the hypothesis of the invariability of human nature. Would Machiavelli's novelty not consist in two modulations? To the pragmatic and traditional knowledge of domination, Machiavelli would like to add the dimension of consciousness and thus of reflection; further, he would reorient the practice of domination in assigning as its supreme end the constitution of a strong state, as the condition for the development of the individual and society.

Even though Horkheimer does not forget Machiavelli's insistence on the importance of division, even if he perceives in the author a sympathy for democracy, even though he relates the extraordinary discourse of the leader of the Ciompi, he fails to surpass the perspective of domination and to conceive how Machiavelli, in order to think political freedom, succeeds in articulating domination with its opposite, the will to live in freedom. Every human city, according to Machiavelli, is constructed in the confrontation of two desires, that of the great, to dominate and that of the people, to not be dominated. But it would seem, in reading Horkheimer, that only the desire of the great exists, as though the political scene would be entirely overrun by the *libido dominandi*, as though this *libido* proper to the great did not run afoul of the opposition of the people, of the desire for freedom that moves it. Does Machiavelli not recognize in the people a quality of guarding its liberty more than other classes of citizen? Thus Horkheimer's one-dimensional reading; since, having privileged domination without having taken account of its contrary, the desire for freedom, he fails to see in Machiavelli a thinker of political freedom. A failure that recalls a more general question: Does the thinking on domination produce the means to think freedom, or does it remain there unconscious and permanently without access?

The Political Paradigm

The central proposition of the political paradigm, that which founds it, could be Rousseau's declaration in *The Confessions* according to which "everything depends radically on politics." This in no way signifies what beautiful souls are eager to declare, that "everything is political," thus confusing the reality of "depending on" and the matter of "being." "Depending on," "touching on" indicate a link between two different instances and not an identity or a homogenization abolishing differences. It would be right to understand in Rousseau's proposition that all the manifestations of a given society, be it the relationship with nature, the relations among people, the relation to self and other, are to be seen by way of diverse mediations with the political mode of being of this society, with the regime in the expanded sense of the term. The deliberately indeterminate character of this formulation means that the different dimensions of a specific society are dependent upon the political institution of this society.

This dependence with regard to the political system granted, it follows from the status of the political—second constitutive element of the political paradigm—that politics ought to be thought as nonderived, better, as underivable from any instance whatever, be it the economic, the social, the military, the religious, and so on. For example, democracy, although certain of its historical forms are contemporaneous with the capitalist system, cannot be derived from the latter. The logic of democracy may intersect at times with that of capitalism; and yet it cannot be identified with the latter. In relation to the capitalist system, democracy retains an irreducible remainder, which only a political approach is capable of rendering comprehensible. Thus in the text "Sur la democratie: Le politique et l'institution du social," Claude Lefort and Marcel Gauchet declare that "what remains is the leap to the conclusion that the status of politics in general is that of a phenomenon which is essentially derived. . . . An impossible leap. Such care to show that one does not set up a fully real last instance and so not to restrain secondary instances to pure appearances . . . the folding back of the political onto the economic conceals the proper foundation found in the social institution of a system of power."[80]

Is this to say, as that formula might allow one to believe, that the social is the foundation of politics? Not at all. Politics is no more derivable from the social than from the economic or any other instance. We should understand instead that the social and the political form an indissoluble couple, inasmuch as the political, as the "leading framework" of a mode of human coexistence, is a response, a position-taking in relation to the originary division of the social, a division that is of the very being of the social. "The logic that organizes a political regime," write Lefort and Gauchet, "is a response joined to the open question by the advent, and in the advent of the social as such."[81] The social, from the moment of its appearance, its coming into being, far from being a solid, substantial, homogeneous, and stable reality, is immediately haunted by the possibility of its disappearance and its division, as though its arrival brought within it the question "Why is there a society rather than nothing?" and at the same time the threat of nothing or of loss of self. Considered from this perspective, it would seem that Kant's unsocial-sociability had been transposed from a sociopsychological level to an ontological one. The social can no more be the foundation of politics in the sense of a determining principle than one can have society without the political institution, even though this institution is not found working save in relation to the originary division of the social, of the self-examination constitutive of the advent of the social. Every other conception would end in the absurdity consisting of "putting society before society." For the political paradigm, if one follows for now the reasoning of Claude Lefort, this is the mode of the establishment of the social, of the generative principles of human coexistence, and further, the leading framework "governing both the temporal and spatial configuration of society."[82]

Without any doubt, there is a link binding this singularity of the political institution of the social to the idea of the irreducibility of political things. The latter could even be one of its possible expressions. Whatever the definition offered, a third element of the political paradigm consists, in part against materialism, but not only against that, in affirming the heterogeneous character of political things, and thus the character of political things being not susceptible to reduction to any other order of reality. Whether it is a matter of the political institution of the social, the articulation of practices to opinions through assessments, or the appearance of action whose end is freedom, the stakes for the partisans of the political paradigm are to make appear, even to reconquer, the texture of political things, their consistency. At the same time, such partisans must prevent the reductive operations that could be expressed in the form of "politics is nothing but . . ." as well as the no less nefarious identifications. The political paradigm is constituted by the affirmation of the specificity of political things and in the determination to consider reality within the space of the political, by eventually dissociating it from every other dimension that could make it leave its orbit to the point of turning against and disturbing the logic that is proper to it. Thus the lengthy effort in modernity to separate the political from the theological, to put an end to the theologico-political *nexus*.

But one of the effects of the political paradigm, and not the least, is to refuse, thanks to bringing to light the specificity of political things, the reduction of politics to domination or the identification of the one with the other. More positively, it is a matter for the political paradigm of radically affirming the difference in the substance of the political in such a manner that it cannot be confused with the fact of domination, breaking with a much time-honored belief that considers politics as the ensemble of stratagems and means that aim at permitting some to dominate the multitude, as though this belief had not been affected, even destroyed, by the revolution in the Greek polis or by the great modern revolutions. From this point of view, it is probably with Hannah Arendt that one encounters the most explicit differentiation, and thus the most revealing of the tendencies of the political paradigm. Arendt, inspired by the Greek idea of politics, assigns to each of two phenomena a space, a scene, a distinct order of reality; she situates the fact of domination on the side of the *oikos* and political matters on the side of the city, thus opening an abyss between the two, reproducing at the same time the qualitative leap that existed between these two spheres in the ancient city. The logic of domination, of the scission between dominant and dominated, is that which rules the household or the *oikos*, the father of the family ruling there as a despot on the members who compose it, women, children, and slaves. As Arendt underlines, the words *dominus* (from which we derive domination) and *pater familias* were synonyms. And, as she recalls in a note, according to Fustel de Coulanges, "all Greek and Latin words which express some rulership over others, such as *rex, pater, anax, basileus*, refer originally to household relationships and were names the slaves gave to their master."[83] In order to satisfy the exigencies of the reproduction of life, the *oikos* lives under the imperative of necessity within relations of domination-servitude. It is only through leaving the *oikos*, in surpassing the boundaries that circumscribe the *agora*, that the citizen enters the political space, all of whose members are equals in the sense of *isonomia*, reaches the political, that is to say, the possibility of common action undertaken in concert and whose reason for being is freedom. In this constellation, freedom is situated at the antipode of domination, because it signifies a position exterior with respect to the relations of command and obedience—"It meant neither to rule nor to be ruled"[84]—and positively putting to work the condition of plurality through action and speech. Even if this experience of freedom disappeared with the establishment of empires, Roman emperors having taken the title of *dominus*, it is no less the case that the mutation that appeared with the Greek polis remained the generative experience of the political that arose again in diverse forms throughout the discontinuous history of freedom. According to Arendt, as soon as we have the word politics in our mouths, we form a relation, whether we know it or not, with the Greek city, the *polis*. "The idea that politics and freedom are bound together, making tyranny the worst of political governments and indeed antipolitical, threads its way through the thinking and action of European culture down to recent times."[85] From the union of politics and freedom it necessarily follows that the fact of domination, in spite of the opinion that believes it recognizes there the essence of politics, has nothing to do with the political, is even situated as its exact opposite, or, again, represents its destructive element par excellence.

In La Boétie's terms, the opposition of the two phenomena can best be described by the contrast between the *all One* (*Tous-Un*), the situation where the relation between people comes undone in order to make room for the figure of the master, and the *all ones* (*Tous-uns*), the situation where the connection among people, mutual understanding, friendship give birth to a whole (the all) of a particular type, inasmuch as, although being a whole, it does not deny the ontological condition of plurality but allows for its expansion (the ones in the plural) to the point of permitting to arise a specific political bond, oriented to freedom and constituted in the continued rejection of the domination-servitude relation. A distinction not ignored by Marx when the latter wrote in his 1843 critique of Hegel, "the one has truth only as many one's."[86]

It bears noting, such is the pregnancy of the political paradigm that, with Arendt, Machiavelli receives a completely special place. Far from being, as with Horkheimer, the typical philosopher of politics, in the sense of a collection of the means of domination, he appears for Arendt as the modern philosopher who, beyond the Middle Ages, knew how to rediscover the grandeur of politics, at a distance from domination, rather as the experience of freedom and courage. "What remains surprising," declares Arendt, "is that the only postclassical political theorist who, in an extraordinary effort to restore its old dignity to politics, perceived the gulf [between the *polis* and the *oikos*] and understood something of the courage needed to cross it was Machiavelli."[87]

One can then see that at the heart of the political paradigm two relations in antithesis are held, which can be formulated as follows: where there is politics, that is to say, the experience of freedom, domination tends to disappear; inversely, where domination reigns, the political is effaced from human experience and becomes the object of a project of destruction.

The possibility of two unilateralisms arise from the explanation and confrontation of the two paradigms, each belonging to its own paradigm and capable of giving birth to two derivatives, catastrophism for the paradigm of the critique of domination, irenicism for the political paradigm.

On the side of the paradigm of the critique of domination, the unilateralism would consist, in the name of focusing on the fact of domination, in ignoring not only the specificity of the substance of the political, whatever definition one gives it, but also in the consubstantial link between politics and freedom, as though politics were reduced to domination to the point of being identified with it, as though politics did not occur precisely in a permanent struggle, unceasingly, between political freedom and domination. In an even more serious manner, the paradigm of the critique of domination would ignore not only the essential relation of politics to freedom, but also the question of the political bond, or politics establishing a Connection among people, a specific connection inasmuch as it allows plurality to appear, to be revealed in the form of a relation that in particular is not so much to unify as it is to bind and separate at once. The binding separation of the *all ones*. However, the question of the political bond, once transferred into the problematic of domination and emancipation, seriously threatens to come back in some way mutilated, amputated. If politics is reduced to domination, emancipation is logically conceived as an exit from domination. But this emancipation, exit from domination, is it thought of as an entry to the political field, in an experience of freedom? Or rather, because of the identification of politics and domination, is this emancipation rather more conceived as an exit from politics, as though freedom in this case meant freedom from politics? Is it sufficient to evoke freedom and happiness to define an emancipated society? Rather, is it not necessary to grant an equivalence between emancipation and the occurrence of the political question, emancipation no longer represented as the disappearance of politics, but its advent as a question, as a persistent enigma, and not amenable to a solution?

The representation of politics unilaterally through the prism of domination can without doubt lead to catastrophism. In thinking history under the sign of the repetition of domination, and the domination of repetition, history represents itself to the interpreter as endless catastrophe.

By the same token, the latter remains blind to breakthroughs of freedom, or even to founding moments of freedom. Moments that in their succession can be read as a discontinuous history of freedom whose strongest occasions are Greek democracy, the Roman republic, the Italian republics, and the great modern revolutions, where the feelings for revolt and the desire for freedom mixed to reinforce each other.

Finally, is it not necessary to see in this paradigm a tendency to think totalitarianism simply as an extension of domination, albeit monstrous, which is one of the unfortunate effects of the paradigm of the critique of domination? Those who take it up would remain, in effect, insensitive to the "without precedent" of total domination and its most disturbing characteristic, that is to say, the destruction of the political sphere, and, beyond that, of the human political condition.

It is true that critical theory, which takes up the paradigm of the critique of domination, is vulnerable to these objections. While simultaneously making two reservations: (1) The critical theorists are sufficiently aware of the nonidentical to reject thinking history under the sign of any identity whatsoever, even that of domination. Thus Walter Benjamin, sensitive to the critique of the ideology of progress into which Auguste Blanqui proceeded, nonetheless perceived in *Eternity by the Stars* (1871) the production of a new phantasmagoria. Did the revolutionary not engage in thinking history under the sign of a transhistorical identity of disaster? (2) It bears taking into account the ensemble of critical theory, that is, also those who are not content to refer to freedom and happiness but who attempted (F. Neumann and O. Kirchheimer) to think the difference between a democratic state, an authoritarian state, and totalitarianism, in brief, those who worked to think emancipation in the form of the advent of the political question and not its disappearance.

As for the political paradigm, it suffers or could suffer from a different form of unilateralism. The legitimate desire to think the political in its substance and specificity could be satisfied in some with a forgetting, or more, an occultation of the fact of domination, as though the advent of the political question takes place henceforth in a smooth, homogeneous space without harshness or conflict. Among some, we should take care to specify. Because at the present time the political paradigm seemingly knows a double orientation: there would be a neo-Kantian orientation that would insist on giving priority to intersubjectivity, to a mild intersubjectivity without drama or detour, that would have a tendency to reduce politics with its acrimony to the latter, as though politics could be thought exclusively by way of freedom of thought and the freedom of communication it implies. Do we not remember Kant's famous phrases in "What Does It Mean to Orient Oneself in Thinking?": "Yet how much and how correctly would we *think* if we did not think as it were in community with others to whom we *communicate* our thoughts, and who communicate theirs to us!"[88] If it is true that freedom of thought cannot be dissociated from freedom of communication, may one for all that accept restricting the political question to these two, certainly essential, freedoms? This, without taking into account action and its logic as it was described by Hannah Arendt in *The Human Condition*, or without taking into consideration the political institution of society always, according to Claude Lefort, in a relation with the originary division of the social.

From this propensity to think the political question at a distance from the fact of domination—as though political space once instituted could be held supremely exterior to all the phenomena that tend to disturb or abolish it—results the drift to irenicism. One may certainly rejoice in the rediscovery of the political after totalitarian domination attempted to destroy the experience of the political and even the political condition of humanity. One may no less applaud the determination to think the political as underived or underivable. But this rediscovery, this determination, ought they to be conceived in a reconciled universe, pacified to the point where sources of conflict and situations of domination had disappeared as though by magic? That there would be antithetical relations at the conceptual level between politics and domination would not result in the magical disappearance of the entanglement, at the sociohistorical level, of the political question or the fact of domination. Does not the confusion of these two levels have as a consequence the tendency of contemporary political philosophy to have its renewal accompanied by a denial and occultation of political questions, of rudely political questions? At its terminus this tendency can go as far as the ejection of the place of entanglement and enclose political philosophy within itself, inviting it to return to its internal history and in the interior of this history eventually to effect syntheses between this or that author, in conscious disregard or not for the exterior. And perhaps one cannot save the entanglement of politics and the fact of domination. Is not the *all ones* permanently exposed to degradation into the *all One*, power *with* others into power *over* others? In brief, the rediscovery of the political is not a guarantee of the essence of politics, as though politics, having once reappeared would be assured of persisting forever in its essence. If, after Martha Nussbaum's great book *The Fragility of Goodness*, the theme of fragility had not been overused or banalized, we would be tempted to speak of the fragility of political things. One of the most evident manifestations of irenicism is the predominance of consensus, of the consensualist model, which cannot measure up except by excluding the fact of domination, susceptible as such of being reintroduced into the political sphere of conflict. It is clear that the Machiavellian inspiration cannot fall victim to the same criticisms. It is constituted precisely in the conflict between the grandees and the people, in the affirmation of the permanence of conflict, and in the hypothesis that conflict—thus of domination and the struggle against domination—is the cradle of political freedom.

The Option of Articulation

With the two unilateralisms brought to light, the solution by alternative can only be rejected, because it would come back to preferring one unilateralism to the detriment of the other, and without a solid reason for holding on to this preference. There thus remains the choice of a joining of the political question to the fact of domination, leading us down the road to a critical political philosophy. With a careful look, this critical political philosophy already exists. If one considers two thinkers among the most important of the political paradigm, Hannah Arendt and Claude Lefort, one must recognize in their work manifestations of this project, without for the moment taking into account Arendt's opposition to the very idea of a political philosophy. Do not the one and the other in fact think the fact of domination and politics together? Is the recovery of politics not accompanied, better, instigated, by the critique of totalitarian domination? It is by all means a case of politics and domination being thought together, since we observe the same process over two times: first the critique of totalitarian domination presented as that "without precedent" of the twentieth century, then, on the basis of that critique, the rediscovery or affirmation of politics conceived as the very antithesis of the totalitarian system, and that could take the form of democracy or a republic, or a system of councils for Arendt. To be sure, in the case of both the one and the other, no "Chinese wall" separates politics—democracy or republic—from total domination. Each of the two political forms is threatened with a fall into total domination. Yet the two antithetical poles remain in a relation of exteriority. Totalitarian domination is thought as the other of politics.

Would it not, however, be advisable in the wake of this process to think the articulation of the fact of domination and the political in an internal sense, that is to say, tied up with, taking place in the midst of politics? Under this hypothesis it would be necessary to understand that the political form—democracy or republic—could be threatened in its interior by the resurgence of domination, not necessarily totalitarian. In order to envisage this hypothesis in all its fullness, it is necessary to add on a supplementary hypothesis, that of the always possible, always threatening degeneration of political forms. Democracy or republic, as forms of the political, are not stable forms or irreversible forms. The return of the fact of domination threatens them internally, to the point of risking their destruction, of ruining them and having them lose their meaning. One of the weaknesses of the political paradigm is thinking that the arrival of a political form would create a condition of not-returning, guaranteeing forever the persistence of this form. But this weakness of the political paradigm results in the exclusion of the fact of domination or the relegation of this fact to the exterior of the political form. Thus the irenic vision of the political scene, which would also be sheltered by one knows not what miracle from the return of domination. It is true that it is not a matter of fate and that the Machiavellian version of the political paradigm is not exposed in principle to irenicism, because by virtue of containing the antagonistic pair of the grandees and the people there is a joining of politics and domination, inasmuch as it conceives freedom as being permanently born from the struggle against domination. "Political freedom," writes Lefort, "is understood through its opposite; it is the affirmation of a mode of coexistence, within certain borders, such that no one has authority to decide the affairs of all, that is to say, to occupy the site of power."[89] But of this version one might ask whether it always succeeds in sticking to this point of articulation? Does it not sometimes have the tendency to abandon it without inquiring into the "corruption" of democracy or the republic? Is it not, in effect, necessary to approach the matter in an inverse way to the irenic question and consider that it is the struggle against domination from which the political form, democracy or republic, draws its principle? As though in some way the fact of domination, recurring historically, were the motor that through struggle—that of the people against the grandees—engenders the continuous institution of the political. In this case, it is not a matter of turning away from the thought that has as its object the fact of domination, insofar as it does not eternalize that fact and envisages its cancellation. Which happens to be the position of critical theory. Likewise, the alternative passage from critical theory to contemporary political philosophy is inauspicious.

Let us now turn to a thinker of emancipation, Giambattista Vico, to whom Horkheimer devotes a chapter of *Beginnings of the Bourgeois Philosophy of History*. According to Vico, emancipation is at the heart of human history, in a double movement, ascending and descending. "Men for Vico," writes George Navet, "form and transform their civic world up to arriving at liberty and equality in popular republics. The problem is that they display an incapacity to maintain and retain it, to have it enduringly persist, *a fortiori*, to have it progress."[90] As we see, Vico calls for thinking emancipation and its contrary together, that is, its always possible degeneration. Having done so, not only does he come to join the political principle with the fact of domination, but he moreover supplies a hypothesis that would aid in thinking this articulation. It is, in effect, through the hypothesis of degeneration—apparently ignored in the political paradigm—that we ought to be able to engage thinking on the path of articulation, that is, in the direction of a critical political philosophy. But towards what does this degeneration go? A hypothesis of a different order, not foreign to critical theory, permits a response to this question. Rather than remaining enclosed in the oppositional couple democracy-totalitarianism, it would be proper to have a third intervening term, that of the authoritarian state, which would allow for thinking the degeneration of democracy or republic, without, however, dispensing with the method from the side of totalitarianism. The articulation of the critique of domination to the thinking of the political is conceivable because either democracy or republic are permanently exposed to being corrupted, that is, degenerating into the authoritarian state. Which implies not confusing the latter notion with that of the totalitarian state or totalitarianism. This is quite exactly what one critical theorist, Franz Neumann, had the virtue of making possible; his thought is, in effect, arranged around three poles, the democratic state, the authoritarian state, and the totalitarian state or totalitarianism. Following his analysis devoted to Nazism in *Behemoth*, the totalitarian state, analyzed in chapter 1 of the first part, has the peculiarity of being a non-State, to the extent that this form of domination is exercised without recourse to the rule of law, in a State of nonlaw. There would be direct domination by dominant groups over the rest of the population "without the mediation of that rational though coercive apparatus hitherto known as the [S]tate."[91] That is what distinguishes totalitarianism from the authoritarian State, where domination is exercised via recourse to the State apparatus.

It seems the major outlines of the articulation appear more distinctly. It is proper to think the political principle and the critique of domination together because each manifestation of the political principle, democracy or republic, is threatened by degeneration into one form that despite its distance from democracy or republic remains under state control, that is, the authoritarian state. In fact, we are within the framework of an opposition internal to a democracy or a republic. In this case, the articulation is no longer between the critique of totalitarian domination and the thought of the political, but between the critique of authoritarian domination and the political principle. We should specify that in this case it is not so much a matter of thinking an articulation in the form of a theoretical synthesis of two antithetical paradigms. Instead, we must learn to view the political scene as the theater of a struggle, without respite or relief, between the fact of domination and the institution of politics, precisely because of the possible degeneration of this institution. If democracy is that form of society characterized by the welcome reception of conflict, is not the major conflict, first and above all, that which bears upon its very existence and its terms?

Conclusion

Let us return to the initial question: What living relationship can we establish with critical theory in face of the renewal of political philosophy? Returning to this question in order to answer it signifies that we refuse the option of alternatives notably in its present form. In other words, we refuse what presents itself as an unproblematic transition from critical theory to political philosophy in the same way as the uncontested predominance of the political paradigm that rests clearly on the eviction of the critique of domination. This eviction would presuppose that, in the political sphere, this form of critique was surpassed to the extent that the political domain is conceived as a smoothed-out place where all forms of domination have disappeared, or as a place where an unproblematic intersubjectivity could be given free rein, an intersubjectivity that is called by some nonviolent communication.

A living relation with critical theory can therefore take the route of a joining of the two paradigms. Does not critical theory have an inclination towards such an articulation, with regard to two of its elements that favor it? At no time—which is not the case with all critiques of domination—is domination thought as an ineluctable fate. Solicitous of the nonidentical, critical theory would not give way to the pathos of domination running like a black thread through universal history. Domination is rather thought as a complex dimension, historically specific, historically recurrent in the life of human beings, but that can be transformed, that ought to be transformed by them. In that respect, it is decisive to state that the concepts of critical theory have a double aspect: critical of domination, they carry in their very texture the idea of its cancellation. This is the reason the political question is not absent in critical theory, but most often remains "in the depths," so to speak. It is also necessary to learn to distinguish among the members of the Frankfurt School, who do not all speak with one voice. If Horkheimer has a propensity to reduce politics to domination, Adorno on the contrary distinguishes them, because he is interested in dissociating them and making a link between emancipation and politics. "An emancipated society, on the other hand, would not be a unitary state, but the realization of universality in the reconciliation of differences."[92] That the interest in emancipation can be an interest in the political is certainly the conviction of Franz Neumann and Otto Kirchheimer, exceptional up to a point in critical theory, when they attempted to elaborate a critical theory of democracy.

One of the conditions of the relation maintained with critical theory, in putting the articulation to work, would be to start from the political paradigm. Why this privilege? Can one not conceive the articulation simply as the opening of each paradigm to the other, moving now from domination to politics, now from politics to domination? But in truth, are the two movements symmetrical? Would not the paradigm of the critique of domination, even in the case of critical theory, have a difficult time producing a fully developed thinking of the political, fettered as it is from the start by the identification of politics and domination? There would be a difficulty in ascending from a critique of domination to a thinking of the political, because the contrast with the political is not thought. There cannot be such a joining unless there is a prior recognition of the specificity and heterogeneity of political things. By contrast, for the political paradigm, it is only necessary to admit that, in the actuality of political existence, phenomena of domination can come to oppose politics, to corrupt it, and even to destroy it. The rediscovery of politics does not authorize one to ignore the fact of domination. It is therefore in according priority to the political paradigm, but in refusing to absolutize it, that one may establish a relationship with critical theory. It is also necessary that thinkers of the political are sufficiently alerted to its fragility, its inconstancy, and know that each form of freedom is exposed to being corrupted, to degenerating, for example, into an authoritarian state. Difficulties, to be sure, remain. We should, in reality, be aware of the difficulty of this articulation, knowing the philosophical presuppositions upon which such a step rests. Looking at it more fully, questions arise about the possible relations between phenomenology, on the part of political thought, and Marxism, on the part of the critique of domination.

Be that as it may, "For a critical political philosophy" implies holding oneself as much at a distance from irenicism as from catastrophism, the Grand Hotel Abyss. Responding to the return of political things, by a joining of the two paradigms, requires making the element of disquiet our abode.

Part IV

Utopia, Democracy, and Emancipation

Chapter 9

E. P. Thompson's Passion

(1988; republished 2012)

> There is a secret agreement between past generations and the present one. . . . Like every generation that preceded us, we have been endowed with a *weak* Messianic power, a power to which the past has a claim. . . . Nothing that has ever happened should be regarded as lost for history.
>
> —Walter Benjamin[1]

The Making of the English Working Class was first published in London in November 1963. Without dwelling on the tribulations of this classic, which is preceded by a mythic aura on this side of the Channel, we can suggest that this book-event, already known, commented upon, and criticized in other European countries as well as in the United States, ran up against resistance from the scribes in France. Breaches of this silence were rare: an introductory article by Patrick Fridenson in *Le Débat*, reflections by Cornelius Castoriadis and Maximilien Rubel.[2]

Is this due to the scale of the work? Provincialism? A concern to protect a revolutionary monopoly, or the legend beloved by French liberalism according to which England is the land of reform and France that

---

Translated by James D. Ingram. Originally published as and translated from "Présentation: La passion d'Edward P. Thompson," in *La formation de la classe ouvrière anglaise* (Paris: Seuil-Gallimard, 1988), xxvii–xlviii.

171

of revolution? Lack of interest in the social question in the 1970s? Many elements could account for this silence. Now that the translation has appeared, we can foresee two main forms of resistance: either attempts at ideological appropriation or academic isolation within the history of the workers' movement.

To prevent such a reception, we should turn first of all to Edward P. Thompson, an unusual intellectual figure in the contemporary French universe—which shows how the tradition of Michelet and Quinet has faded here. Who is E. P. Thompson? Historian, radical sociologist, Marxist with workerist inclinations, "New Left" polemicist, socialist thinker?

Let us rather say political writer. Let us understand by this a thinker who does not separate the writing of history from the political question here and now—convinced, moreover, that knowledge of the political, at the same time that it allows us to get beyond the economism of some and the empiricism of others, enables us to grasp political being, the *acting in common within time* of social groups that form and appear on the scene of history at a determinate moment as classes. This political writer does not separate the interpretation of history from the question of its expression—whence the importance he attaches to "literary sources," innumerable half-erased traces on the edge of anonymity that relate the experience of the event. From this comes a combative writing that mixes the mordancy of the great English satirists with modes of perception taken from the Romantic tradition. It is a thinking that, alert to the adventures of emancipation in modernity, all the same does not declare the age of freedom over. This nonresignation, a "toughening" for emancipation, draws on the crossing of multiple traditions, on listening to the barely audible voices of the vanquished—Jacobin voices, radical voices, Luddite voices, millenarian voices, utopian voices—in order directly to relaunch them into an endless interrogation on the forms of freedom to come.[3]

In following Thompson's trajectory, a guiding thread soon appears, a recurring struggle against what he calls "exterminism," be it in the form of fascism or nuclear proliferation.

A communist since the middle of the Second World War—not long after, in 1947, he joined partisans building a railroad in Yugoslavia—after the war Thompson was an activist in the peace movement and devoted himself, among other things, to adult education ("extra-mural studies") in literature and history. At the same time, he learned to "make history" within the group of historians of the Communist Party. He had a passion for the archives and, thanks to a climate of debate and exchange, found a series of controversial questions at the intersection of his work as a historian and the elaboration of his political positions. In 1951, following a first joyously admiring reading of William Morris (contrary to legend, Morris was neither a sentimental socialist nor a socializing aesthete), he took on, without really being aware of the scope of the task, a major rehabilitation of the socialist thinker. Morris thereby finally attained his true stature as an original thinker who managed to transform the Romantic opposition to industrialism into revolutionary social criticism, a political writer (especially in his essays on art and socialism)[4] who, opposing both the Fabians and Engels, the founder of Marxism, had the audacity to open up new paths to utopia, inventing novel questions (if not, indeed, a new mode of questioning) within the socialist tradition. Thompson's work *William Morris: Romantic to Revolutionary* [1955][5] marks a point of no return in Morris criticism.

A curious aspect of Morris's proximity to Thompson: if the 1955 interpretation, as enthusiastic as it was, still bore traces of Stalinist "piety," there can be no doubt that Morris's thought, political sensibility, passionate imagination, and utopian élan accompanied Thompson through his continuous dissidence each time he had to breach the "river of fire."

Thus, in 1956, after the Khrushchev report, Thompson became critical but remained within the party, and launched the *Reasoner*. After the Hungarian Revolution was crushed by the Soviet bureaucracy, at the same time that he quit the Communist Party he published the *New Reasoner* with John Saville, inaugurating the New Left in England. Until 1963 this current, principally led by Thompson, undertook a critique of Stalinism (rejecting its base-superstructure model, monistic determinism, and anti-humanism) by trying to elaborate a socialist humanism—or, better, an ethical communism that drew on many sources: plebeian radicalism, the Romantic critique of utilitarianism, Blake, Morris, and the young Marx. While the first New Left turned toward indigenous, specifically British traditions and made efforts to build bridges with the workers' movement, the second New Left, with Perry Anderson and Tom Nairn, chose, on the contrary, the path of continental Marxism, privileging sophisticated theory far from worker "false consciousness" and aligning itself first with Gramsci, then with Althusser.

It is within this internal rupture of the New Left that we should situate, without reducing it to it, *The Making of the English Working Class*. As its tumultuous, irreverent writing shows, the work confronts in an indirect but no less resolute way the questions that were then in dispute. Which revolutionary traditions to claim? How to think the phenomenon of class? Can a dominated class resist the hegemony of the dominant class, and if so, how? What is the relation between social struggle and the struggle for freedom and justice? What vision of socialism should be proposed? Which revolution sought? Must human emancipation and democracy be thought together?[6]

The greatness of Thompson, who was indissolubly both a historian and a political writer, is to set himself up in the irreducible tension between Marx and Morris, able to transform the "silences" of each thinker into fuses, elements of a creative dialogue without any possible closure:

> The injury which advanced industrial capitalism did, and which the market society did, was to define human relations as being primarily economic. Marx engaged with orthodox political economy, and proposed revolutionary economic man as the answer to exploited economic man. But it is also implicit, particularly in the early Marx, that the injury is in defining man as "economic" at all. This kind of critique of industrial capitalism is found in Blake and Wordsworth very explicitly, and is still present in Morris, and it is wholly complementary, not in any sense at odds with, the Marxist tradition. That again is where I am now working.[7]

This book is made up of several ones. The chapter on Luddism, "An Army of Redressers," constitutes a small work in itself.

What makes this book an event? We can discern three poles.

I. According to almost unanimous opinion, no historian exerted as deep an influence on working-class history and Marxist theory as E. P. Thompson. His work transformed the theoretical context in which the concept of class and the question of class consciousness were put to work. This should be no surprise. *The Making of the English Working Class* was born of a polemic on two fronts. On one side, it was directed against the long-standing disciplinary closure of economic history, which, established with Adam Smith and classical political economy, has accompanied the history of capitalism. This tradition was deeply infected by capitalist ideology and positivism, on Thompson's judgment, and had to be unsparingly criticized. On the other side, there was a struggle against economistic tendencies within Marxism, which led Thompson to reject an outrageously simplified notion of the working class according to which it was born in "the more-or-less spontaneous generation of the new productive forces and relations."[8]

It was necessary to attack the equation made by certain Marxists, though not only by them, steam engine + cotton spinning = new working class, and, beyond this, any automatic, direct correlation between the Industrial Revolution and the dynamics of social life and culture, as if the working class, in its social being, was nothing but a reaction, the effect of a determining economic process:

> The making of the working class is a fact of political and cultural, as much as of economic, history. It was not the spontaneous generation of the factory-system. Nor should we think of an external force—the "industrial revolution"—working upon some nondescript undifferentiated raw material of humanity, and turning it out at the other end as a "fresh race of beings."[9]

Was Thompson's project not to contribute a better understanding of the phenomenon of class, one that, contra economism and theoreticist structuralism, would insist on what Claude Lefort in a pioneering article had much earlier called the "proletarian experience"?

> Who is not aware that [the proletariat] has not only *reacted* in history to external, economically defined factors—the extent of exploitation, the standard of living, the mode of concentration—but that it has really *acted*, intervening in revolutionary ways not according to a schema prepared by an objective situation, but as a function of its total cumulative *experience*.[10]

On this basis, consider the opening attack in Thompson's work on the very idea of making: "*Making*, because it is a study in an active process, which owes as much to agency as to conditioning. The working class did not rise like the sun at an appointed time. It was present at its own making."[11]

"Class is defined by men as they live their own history, and, in the end, this is its only definition."[12] How did Thompson give this apparently simple formulation its full meaning? Let us try to deploy it as he himself did later:[13]

- Class is a historical category: it comes from observing a social process that extends over a given period of time and manifests constants in analogous situations. At a certain stage of maturity, the creation of class institutions and culture can be observed.

- If understanding class requires taking into account objective determinations—historical facticity—we must avoid reifying class, grasping it as a thing on the basis of a group of quantitative determinations, since this leads to a static mode of perception that can lead, from a practical perspective, to substitutionism.

- Fundamentally, class is a conflictual historical relation. The notion of class cannot be separated from that of class struggle, to which Thompson gave both priority and universality. Classes do not struggle because they exist; they come to exist because they struggle.

If in this way Thompson rediscovered Marx's idea that the working class is "the greatest productive power,"[14] he made up for the latter's silence when it comes to the internal process by which a class-in-itself becomes a class-for-itself. This is to emphasize that he was determined to trace the total, plural experience through which the class constitutes itself and to describe concretely the movement by which it accedes, through and thanks to time, to consciousness. This insistence on class consciousness does not, however, lead Thompson to conceive of class as a cultural formation. Beginning his analysis by studying objective determinations but not limiting himself to them, he strives in this "biography of the working class" to narrate its "crystallization" into a class as it occurred when class consciousness emerged out of a multiplicity of common experiences.

Not to soften the conflict between Thompson and Perry Anderson but rather to complicate it and above all to formulate it in other terms, could we not consider Thompson's insistence on culture, values, ethical-political conduct, and class ethos, far from leading to "culturalism," as an insistence *on the political*? For Thompson, culture, ethics, and modes of sociability and solidarity could not be dissociated from the *political resistance* the working class put up against other classes. Even more, at the heart of this *action-in-common within time* against exploitation and domination there takes shape an orientation towards another way of living together, another form of community. In this sense, if we legitimately distinguish between utopia and ideology, was not one of Thompson's most innovative contributions to have dared to explore the function of utopia in the making of class consciousness? It is as if the social being of the working class, its access to its for-itself, came out of a flight beyond the present—the conditions contained in the present—towards another community, as if its specific identity as a historical subject appeared with the utopian turn to a "completely other" social. We can then recognize in Owenism "one of the gigantic, but ephemeral, impulses which caught the enthusiasm of the masses, presenting the vision of a quite different structure" from that of industrial capitalism.[15] This presents us with another face of the working class. It is no longer the proletariat as understood by the young Marx that greets us: "The question is *what the proletariat is*, and what, consequent on that *being*, it will be compelled to do."[16] On page after page we see, on the contrary, a working class described in all its often-ambiguous concreteness, as if on this point Thompson wrongfooted Marx. Indeed, for Thompson, it is a matter not only of describing what the whole proletariat represents to itself at a given moment as its goal—the final chapter on "class consciousness"—but moreover of doing justice to the living individuals who make it up, of "saving" their struggles and aspirations. Whence the importance of names and testimonies. This is another face of the working class, a face with many, complex facets—not the "average" worker of the cotton mills, but the reality of the small trades, the multiplicity of experiences. It is an enigmatic face whose features do not for all that fade into indistinction but instead, on the basis of this diversity, in the end make up an identity. This frequently admirable analysis takes us back to a question that is always open: What is a historical subject?

II. It is a return to a classic, and thus catastrophic, vision of the Industrial Revolution. An observer, R. M. Martin, testifying in 1834 before the committee of handloom weavers, describes the physical and spiritual deterioration of the English people as follows: "I have observed it not only in the manufacturing but also in agricultural communities in this country; they seem to have lost their animation, their vivacity, their field games and their village sports; they have become a sordid, discontented, miserable, anxious, struggling people, without health, or gaiety, or happiness."[17]

On what does Thompson base this return to the older, cataclysmic version of the Industrial Revolution? He argues first of all against the school of historical and empirical sociologists: for them, if one compares the situation of the industrial worker in 1840 with that of the domestic worker of 1790, one sees a clear improvement, so that the Industrial Revolution would be a period not of catastrophe, but of progress. As for the undeniable traces of suffering, they can be attributed to an incomplete "modernization" whose basic orientation is good. For Thompson it is not a matter of choosing a camp or dogmatically affirming a previously held thesis. Careful to take into account the findings of the works he criticizes, he exposes and refutes their interpretative presuppositions. At this point in the process, we cannot fail to note the recurring presence of William Morris, as if Thompson were returning to modes of perception forged by reading him. It is in fact the perspective opened by the Romantic criticism of industrialism, Morris's criterion of the "quality of daily life," that determines where Thompson can legitimately oppose the new anti-catastrophic orthodoxy.

The empiricists lost the sense of the totality, the sense of the global process. The Industrial Revolution constituted a *total social phenomenon* that, according to Thompson, was situated at the intersection of three dimensions: unprecedented demographic growth, the technological effects of the Industrial Revolution, and political counterrevolution from 1792 to 1832. The result of these multiple logics was a veritable state of political and social *apartheid*, above all during the Napoleonic Wars, a condition generated as much by political counterrevolution as the steam engine:

> We can now see something of the truly catastrophic nature of the Industrial Revolution. . . . The people were subjected simultaneously to an intensification of two intolerable forms of relationship: those of economic exploitation and of political oppression. . . . For most working people the crucial experience of the Industrial Revolution was felt in terms of changes in the nature and intensity of exploitation.[18]

"This violence was done to *human* nature."[19] Far from the acritical respect for the quantitative common to empiricism and utilitarian industrialism, Thompson constantly strives to reintroduce the qualitative point of view the better to do justice to the experience, feelings, and aspirations of those who suffered the painful effects of industrialization and opposed it in one way or another. He thus insists on what he sees as the fundamental distinction between standard-of-life and way-of-life. While the former only takes into account quantitative elements (wages and consumer goods), the latter refers to a qualitative whole (kinds of satisfaction). One cannot be deduced from the other, since assessing the latter requires evaluation, considering the representation of the social at stake and having recourse to "literary" documents that express how conflicts were felt in ways irreducible to statistical measures. We must allow for separate trajectories:

> It is quite possible for statistical averages and human experiences to run in opposite directions. A per capita increase in quantitative factors may take place at the same time as a great qualitative disturbance in people's way of life, traditional relationships, and sanctions. People may consume more goods and become less happy or less free at the same time.[20]

The conclusion:

> Thus it is perfectly possible to maintain two propositions which, on a casual view, appear to be contradictory. Over the period 1790–1840 there was a slight improvement in average material standards. Over the same period there was intensified exploitation, greater insecurity, and increasing human misery. By 1840 most people were "better off" than their forerunners had been fifty years before, but they had suffered and continued to suffer this slight improvement as a catastrophic experience.[21]

Exploitation always happens in a determinate historical context, assuming specific forms depending on property relations and forms of state power. Taking place in a counterrevolutionary climate, the process of industrialization was exceptionally violent in Great Britain. Let us add to this the complex imposition of new work discipline under the conjoined influence of utilitarianism and Methodism. There was an effort of general domestication, a "moralization" of the "inferior classes" put to work in the most diverse domains (the factory, Sunday school, leisure, sexuality, etc.). There was, despite all the acts of resistance, the systematic creation of a way of life inherent to industrial capitalism, and with it the formation of new work habits and the establishment of new temporal discipline. Wary of the coolness of certain twentieth-century analysts, Thompson, for whom child labor remained one of the most shameful pages in the history of industrialization, denounces at the heart of this exceptional violence the violence proper to capitalism itself, but even more the brutal technological differentiation between work and life: "It is neither poverty nor disease but work itself which casts the blackest shadow over the years of the Industrial Revolution."[22]

It is indeed a denunciation—Thompson does not shy away from value judgments. On the contrary, for him writing history requires us to confront these measures of happiness and social change that were shared by those who experienced the Industrial Revolution. Attentive to the Romantic critique of utilitarianism and thousands of acts of anonymous resistance, it is possible to acknowledge our implication in this history even as we hold it at a distance. For what is announced in this resistance is another conception of the social bond; what is sought is a "new moral world," different forms of community, other possibilities for instituting modern society. Traversing these "dead ends," evoking these "lost causes" gives us independence from the sanction of history:

> Our only criterion of judgement should not be whether or not a man's actions are justified in the light of subsequent evolution. After all, we are not at the end of social evolution ourselves. In some of the lost causes of the people of the Industrial Revolution we may discover insights into social evils which we have yet to cure.[23]

Here the historian meets the political writer. What does this in-depth reconstruction of work habits teach us about ourselves, what we have become, and what we have lost? No doubt an interrogation of our present, of the possibility of freeing ourselves from the Puritan conception of time, of our freedom to come, as Thompson provides in his analysis entitled "Time, Work-Discipline, and Industrial Capitalism." Thus the question:

> If we are to have enlarged leisure, in an automated future, the problem is not "how are men going to be able to consume all these additional time-units of leisure?" but "what will be the capacity for experience of the men who have this undirected time to live?"[24]

※

III. Let us return to one of Thompson's essential theses, the potentials of which have perhaps still not been exhausted nor the true significance appreciated. In one of the great metropoles of modern capitalism this social formation was built in a counterrevolutionary political context. More precisely, the "imposition" of capitalism coincided with an aborted revolution, or with the "presence-absence" of a latent revolution that never managed to arrive. From this came a counterrevolutionary mobilization in which work discipline was mixed up with the great law of hierarchy and subordination:

> It is in this insight—that the revolution which did *not* happen in England was fully as devastating, and in some features more divisive, than that which did happen in France—that we find a clue to the truly catastrophic nature of the period. . . . Had events taken their "natural" course we might expect there to have been some show-down long before 1832, between the oligarchy of land and commerce and the manufacturers and petty gentry, with working people in the tail of the middle-class agitation.[25]

Throughout the "Passages" of the nineteenth century the revolutions that reversed into a new form of domination under the grip of repetition should be explored, but also societies established in fear, under the spell of revolution and bearing its indelible stigmata. Here perhaps we can find a key for the analysis of certain modern societies—societies sick from a revolution that never came. One thinks of Melville's *Billy Budd* and the fear of the Great Mutiny that leads Captain Vere, convinced of the handsome sailor's innocence, to maintain order at any price. It is on the basis of this thesis that Thompson revives the question of English Jacobinism. At a time when booklets are being cranked out on "Jacobin totalitarianism" and the Vendée genocide, it is salutary to read these analyses of an oppositional Jacobinism, *outside* power, and to rediscover the complexity of the Jacobin phenomenon in Europe. Jacobinism at its dawn, a Jacobinism that fights for freedom of the press, freedom of conscience, that hates tyranny, monarchy, social hierarchy, and relations of dependence, a Jacobinism that dreams of equality and tolerance. In short, despite a certain doctrinaire narrowness, a Jacobinism that retains its freshness and its anti-authoritarian pugnacity.

Thompson seizes on three concerns in particular in his portrait of popular radicalism:

- An insistence on its English rootedness and the importance of indigenous traditions (the challenge of the Levelers, Dissenters, free-born English struggling against the "Norman yoke," etc.) in the constitution of Jacobinism in the 1790s. Thompson, seeking to tear down the Chinese wall that divides the eighteenth and nineteenth centuries, takes care to understand two things:

the continuity of traditions and changes in their contexts. At the same time that he strives to emphasize the intensity and extraordinary scope of the agitation of the 1790s (from 1792 to 1796), he refuses to see it as a mere epiphenomenon of the taking of the Bastille. Political practices as much as traditions and founding texts bear witness to an English agitation that aimed to create an English democracy, keen to recognize the "birthright" of the poorest man. According to Thompson, Bunyan's *Pilgrim's Progress*, along with the *Rights of Man*, was the basic text of the English workers' movement. Starting in 1792, the rising wave was reinforced by Thomas Paine. Far from being episodic, this complex agitation—between the Revolution of the Saints and the Declaration of the Rights of Man—is a true act of birth: it transforms the infrapolitical attitudes of the people, determines class cleavages, and inaugurates traditions that continue to our day.

- A will to defend English Jacobinism against the accusation of totalitarianism (without pronouncing on its validity for French Jacobinism). Thus the definition of radical thinker John Thelwall, who had the merit of restoring the Jacobin phenomenon within the framework of political conflicts of the day: "I adopt the term Jacobinism without hesitation. . . . I use the term Jacobinism simply to indicate *a large and comprehensive system of reform, not professing to be built upon the authorities and principles of the Gothic customary*."[26]

Hostile to "French ferocity" but struggling against the weight of ancient authorities, the English Jacobins did not preach the extermination of their adversaries. They were partisans of internationalism, of replacing war with arbitration, of tolerating dissidents and free thinkers, and struggled to integrate all those who had been cut off from humanity. Thomas Paine, the "beacon" of English Jacobinism, placed all his confidence in the free play of public opinion within a human society that dared to break with its state of minority: " 'mankind are not now to be told they shall not think, or they shall not read.' [It was] Paine also who saw that in the constitutional debates of the eighteenth century 'the Nation was always left out of the question.' By bringing the nation *into* the question, he was bound to set in motion forces which he could neither control nor foresee. That is what democracy is about."[27]

- The assertion of a hidden tradition connecting the Jacobins of the 1790s to the movements of 1816–1820. Starting from this initial democratic enthusiasm, an underground movement continued, enabling a "plebeian millennium" to rise along with the syndicalist current towards 1811 in the form of a new popular radicalism, borne by hatred of the English "white terror" and a series of new experiments.

The development of the Jacobin presence shattered the placatory vision of English politics, that is to say, a political community divided between a dominant class enlightened enough to ease up when necessary and a dominated class (or classes) reasonable enough to limit its aspirations to reform. And yet, as it emerges from *The Making of the English Working Class*, this history is also tumultuous, violent, roiling, and bitterly conflictual. Perhaps we should reverse the image, recall the revolutionary origins of this society, and rather distinguish between a dominant class permanently mobilized against the threat, sometimes subterranean, sometimes open, of the reign of the rights of man and the coming of the man of the Commonwealth. At the end of the beautiful chapter on "Planting the Liberty Tree," Thompson returns once again to the revolution that has not taken place and to the break that, repressed, it brought in its wake, as if to definitively ruin the myth of the English counter-model:

> In the 1790s something like an "English Revolution" took place, of profound importance in shaping the consciousness of the post-war working class. It is true that the revolutionary impulse was strangled in its infancy; and the first consequence was that of bitterness and despair. The counter-revolutionary panic of the ruling classes expressed itself in every part of social life. . . . In the decades after 1795 there was a profound alienation between classes in Britain. . . . England differed from other European nations in this, that the flood-tide of counter-revolutionary feeling and discipline coincided with the flood-tide of the Industrial Revolution. . . . The 'natural' alliance between an impatient radically-minded industrial bourgeoisie and a formative proletariat was broken as soon as it was formed. . . . If there was no revolution in England in the 1790s it was not because of Methodism but because the only alliance strong enough to effect it fell apart; after 1792 there were no Girondins to open the doors through which the Jacobins might come.[28]

The balance sheet was not only failure and frustration; out of this ferment several traditions came into being that belong to the history of modern democracy.

∽

Almost a quarter century has gone by since the appearance of *The Making of the English Working Class*. In what respect is this book, through its remoteness in time, still an event for us?

We can without difficulty imagine the welcome the author would have received around 1968, what kind of investment would have been made in him. It is enough to reread the closing sentences:

> Such men met Utilitarianism in their daily lives, and they sought to throw it back, not blindly, but with intelligence and moral passion. They fought, not the machine, but the exploitive and Oppressive relationships intrinsic to industrial capitalism. In these same years, the great Romantic criticism of Utilitarianism was running its parallel but altogether separate course. After William Blake, no mind was at home in both cultures, nor had the genius to interpret the two traditions to each other. It was a muddled Mr. Owen who offered to disclose the "new moral world," while Wordsworth and Coleridge had withdrawn behind their own ramparts of disenchantment. Hence these years appear at times to display, not a revolutionary challenge, but a resistance movement in which both the Romantics and the Radical craftsmen opposed the annunciation of Acquisitive Man. In the failure of the two traditions to come to a point of junction, something was lost. How much we cannot be sure, for we are among the losers.
>
> Yet the working people should not be seen only as the lost myriads of eternity. They had also nourished, for fifty years, and with incomparable fortitude, the Liberty Tree. We may thank them for these years of heroic culture.[29]

It was a negative event, we could say. It is as if, in its untimeliness, reading Thompson's book irresistibly gave rise, without our being aware of it, to a melancholic meditation on what we have become. Is what remains of this history that recounts through the odyssey of the working class the *new* of the nineteenth century not simply the suffering of past generations, the oppressive feeling of the world's pain, suspended, suddenly relieved by the beating wings of utopian breakthroughs? Can we not find here an invitation patiently to rethink the social question—that is, beyond the blind outbursts of ideology, be it constitutive or reactive? We now know the share of illusion spread by the idea of a "chosen" class that, as the point at which all alienations are concentrated, is transformed into the opposite image, an agent of total, irreversible emancipation, the source of a solution to the riddle of history. But does the legitimate criticism of this illusion authorize us to consider the social question, the question of emancipation, settled, behind us, and from this point forward without an object? To be sure, we can locate the mechanisms for managing the social question in our societies, but can the social question be settled? It makes sense to dispel an illusion, or perhaps from the criticized illusion arises an irreducible "remainder." Our question then becomes how to think this "remainder" that continues to shape our present. By what name do we recognize it here and now, what status do we give it? Already in reading Thompson we can perceive as a warning the strange mode of operation peculiar to our societies that consists of declaring that a question that has not been settled and continues to haunt our present in incontestably new forms at the same time becomes a question that has been overcome and is therefore of no further interest. In short, under the pretext of criticizing an illusion, as if the illusion had nothing to teach us, there is a flight into oblivion. We simply turn our backs, forgetting that oblivion is reification.

A few trails can be outlined:

- For Walter Benjamin, the question of emancipation could not do without conjuring the nineteenth century: it necessarily passes through criticism of the myths that surround it. What new paths for this task are opened by Thompson's book, a magisterial study of another nineteenth century? What critique does London, metropole of modern capitalism and site of the 1851 Great Exposition, capital of phantasmagorias, require of us?

- Thompson's initial project was to write a work on the politics of the working class from 1790 to 1921, of which this volume would be only the first part. It is hardly surprising, then, that, as part of an interrogation of the political particularity of the working class, with this book Thompson made an essential contribution to the study of the "plebeian public sphere." In his typology of public spheres, Jürgen Habermas traced the latter's appearance to the French Revolution and described it as "stripped of its literary garb": "its subject was no longer the 'educated strata' but the uneducated 'people.'"[30] Reading Thompson, who corrects and modulates this notion of the "uneducated people"—in fact it is a matter of another culture—we better make out one of the essential moments in the constitution of this plebeian sphere, the popular radicalism of the 1790s. Experiencing a resurgence in 1815, the radical movement opened the period of struggle that led to 1832, and later to Chartism. But above all, we see more clearly the specific character of this plebeian sphere:

- First of all, its place or space of manifestation: cafés, taverns, dissident churches, and large rallies where the composite character of the movement appeared, bringing together austere, puritanical "saints" and hedonistic, unruly rowdies.

- The practical critique of the constitutional tradition, which operated as a shackle on the rise of democratic thought, nevertheless going hand in hand with an ongoing struggle for the recognition of their "birthright."

- At least in the British case, the importance of the religious origins of plebeian democracy. The world of Dissent, despite its complexity and ambiguities, with its attachment to principles of self-administration and local autonomy almost to the point of anarchy, was one of the cradles of anti-authoritarian practices.

- An egalitarian ethos of fraternity that could very quickly take the form of institutions where the worker experience of solidarity and mutuality took shape.

- Finally, and Thompson returns to this repeatedly, the declaration of principle announced by the London Corresponding Society: "That the number of our Members be unlimited." Is this an echo of the Levellers' fight to separate political rights from property rights? Certainly, but beyond this, it was an essential contribution of the plebeian public sphere to modern democracy—"one of the hinges upon which history turns," Thompson pronounces it.[31] It is the end of exclusivity, of politics considered as the exclusive domain of an elite or a group of professionals, as if English Jacobinism, by mixing with dissenting religious traditions, dismissed the model of revolution from above in order to transplant modes of action and organization tested in the religious field into the political field, thus affirming the people's will to self-determination. "Unlimited in number" included not only a call for universal suffrage or an invitation to autonomy, but also a more secret call, harder to perceive, to multiplication, to multiplicity. Democracy is thought or aimed to the reign of the multiple, as the search for diversity—even more, for the kaleidoscopic: it is established in the refusal of any homogenizing unification.

It is easy to imagine how Hannah Arendt, for whom the workers' movement wrote in the political field "one of the most glorious and probably the most promising chapter of recent history,"[32] would have found in the work one of the "pearls" that belongs to the lost treasure of modern revolutions. And if we can delight in the tenacious effort in recent years to think the specificity of modern democracy, does this book not give us a happy occasion for renewed reflection? To rediscover the modern democratic revolution, should we content ourselves with Constant and Tocqueville, even if, when it comes to the latter, there are some very bold readings?

What would our thinking of democracy be, what would our interpretation become, if *The Making of the English Working Class* were able to turn our attention also to the tumultuous world of plebeian practices, to what Claude Lefort calls the "libertarian idea of democracy," drawing on a reexamination of French coal mining, the republican movement, the clubs and ferment of 1848, the Paris Commune, and, beyond that, the "chimeras" that, according to Jacques Rancière, haunted the "nights of labor"? It would also be necessary to see clearly that this plebeian public sphere does not rest on a strict separation of the political and the social. Its actors saw places of production as one of the places for expressing the political. Thus John Thelwall: "A sort of Socratic spirit will necessarily grow up, wherever large bodies of men assemble. . . . Every large workshop and manufactory is a sort of political society, which no act of parliament can silence, and no magistrate disperse."[33]

- Finally, *The Making of the English Working Class*, which tells the story of the constitution of workers' communities, raises a crucial question for us: How to think together the demands of democratic community and being-in-the-world?

∽

And if *The Making of the English Working Class* were a great Morrisian book? Did not Thompson, who in 1977 published a revised edition of *William Morris: Romantic to Revolutionary*, in a clarification happily avow the importance of his relation to Morris? For Thompson, it was not a matter of bringing the author of *News from Nowhere* closer to himself; to the contrary, the relationship worked in the other direction:

> Morris, by 1955, had claimed me. My book was then, I suppose, already a work of muffled "revisionism." The Morris/Marx argument has worked inside me ever since. When, in 1956, my disagreements with orthodox Marxism became fully articulate, I fell back on modes of perception which I had learned in those years of close company with Morris, and I found, perhaps, the will to go on arguing from the pressure of Morris behind me. To say that Morris claimed me, and that I have tried to acknowledge that claim, gives me no right to claim him. I have no licence to act as his interpreter. But at least I can now say that this is what I have been trying, for twenty years, to do.[34]

A great Morrisian book? It is as if, by awakening these names snatched from the night of oblivion, by "fanning the spark of hope in the past," Thompson tirelessly pursued a reasoned meditation on Morris's lines from *A Dream of John Ball*, a sort of condensation of his vision of history:

> Men fight and lose the battle, and the thing that they fought for comes about in spite of their defeat, and when it comes turns out not to be what they meant, and other men have to fight for what they meant under another name.[35]

Chapter 10

The New Utopian Spirit
(1991; republished 2013)

What would be different has not begun as yet.

—Theodor W. Adorno, *Negative Dialectics*[1]

What about utopia today?

After the rediscovery of utopia in France during the years 1960–1970, which manifested itself through the reissue of great utopian texts and publication of texts reclaiming the concept of utopia, we have seen the waning of certain taboos. We have seen the waning of conservative or liberal taboos; we have also seen the waning of Marxist taboos, which on the matter of utopia are just another form of conservatism. We could also note—following the thesis of a sociologist—that there was a complex relationship, which is to say not merely negative, between the May 1968 movement and utopia.

But we have seen for a number of years a contrary movement towards the elimination of utopian discourse and discourse on utopia. It is as if the rediscovery of the political—a development we can celebrate—had the effect of relegating utopia to a prepolitical naiveté, or worse, associating it with illusions that deny the political. In short, utopia was ridiculed or portrayed as an obstacle to modern liberty. One of the platitudes of the new *doxa* is found in this contention: the idea that democracy must reject utopia

---

Translated by Devin Penner. Originally published as "Le nouvel esprit utopique," *Cahiers Bernard Lazare*, no. 128 (1991): 132–63. Translated from "Le nouvel esprit utopique," in *Utopiques II: L'homme est un animal utopique* (Paris: Sens & Tonka, 2013), 191–226.

and, conversely, that utopia veers away from democracy. Quite frankly, this hypothetical contradiction between political thought and utopian thought shows little regard for the tradition of modern political philosophy.

To illustrate the problem, we can use Paul Benichou's remarkable work, *Le temps des prophètes*.[2] Benichou's work criticizes the grand utopians of the nineteenth century but has the merit of recognizing in them an unusual quality: the heroism of the spirit, a notion borrowed from Vico and taken up by Michelet. Benichou's book tries to recover part of our philosophical tradition that has been hidden or obscured by Marxist or progressive criticism—the tradition of political liberalism, which has long been confused with that of economic liberalism. Political liberalism, as it appeared in France at the beginning of the nineteenth century, was one of the sites on which our political culture was formed, and provides an indispensable contribution to modern ideas of emancipation. Moreover, the rediscovery of political liberalism emerged through the criticism of two dogmatisms: on the one hand, Catholic or neo-Catholic dogmatism; on the other, the socialist dogmatism of the nineteenth century, which, in the name of a science of society and a science of history, or of a theory of social organization, would go against the current of modern liberty and engage history in authoritarian and regressive ways. In contrast, Benichou claims that socialist dissidents—Pierre Leroux for example—are interesting because they are ultimately more liberal than socialist. While we do not have to agree with all of the theses of this work, let us retain Benichou's invitation to pose the question of utopia as a relationship of three terms: utopia, emancipation, and modernity. Modern emancipation requires challenging all the authority figures: Homer in realm of literature, Aristotle in the realm of philosophy, Jesus in the realm of religion, the monarch in the realm of politics (where the modern principle of *libertas facit legem* was invented). We find this definition of emancipation as much in Pierre Leroux as in the young Marx, who links the concepts of political emancipation and human emancipation in *On the Jewish Question* and *Critique of Hegel's Philosophy of Right*.

At this point in history, is it paradoxical to propose a reflection that associates the idea of utopia with the idea of emancipation? Have not the totalitarian experiences of our century linked utopia to the reversal of emancipation? If this is the case, continuing to embrace utopia would demonstrate a perseverance that, while honorable, also shows a regrettable blindness and a will to maintain a belief despite the denials of reality. To speak like Rousseau, which "student of the law" does not know,[3] which archbishop does not say, that utopia leads to totalitarianism?

But we cannot content ourselves with what students of law dogmatically repeat. Thus we will stay an equal distance from two dogmatisms: at a distance from the dogmatism favorable to utopia, which envisions a benevolent kind of state that is oriented essentially towards liberty and emancipation; but also at a distance from the dogmatism hostile to utopia, which asserts that it inevitably results in tyranny. The proper path seems to be to reject the opposition between resignation about the end of utopia and its uncritical valorization.

This is why I will orient myself with two propositions. First proposition: utopia cannot be voluntaristically dissociated from the question of totalitarianism. This is not to validate the hyperbolic proposition that "utopia is the gulag." The denunciation of utopia as totalitarian ideology is as one-sided and erroneous as the uncritical apology for utopia. A serious investigation of utopia first raises a historical question: How were utopias related to totalitarian systems and ideologies? For example, Baczko highlights that utopias were at one point an instrument in the struggle against bureaucratization.[4] But there is an equally important theoretical questions. The question is not "is utopia totalitarian?" but rather: Does the image or myth of the reconciled society, of a social world in full harmony with itself—an image that can be found in the genealogy of totalitarianism—*necessarily* permeate the utopian tradition? As soon as this question is posed, it appears at least problematic to present the utopian tradition as unitary and homogenous. To build a modern utopian tradition—and this is perhaps our most urgent task—we must ensure that utopia does not turn into a theory of full reconciliation.

My second proposition is that it is no better to reduce utopia to totalitarianism than it is to confine it to a genealogy of totalitarian adventures. It is as unfair and incorrect to consider utopia as necessarily totalitarian as it is to consider democracy as necessarily "bourgeois."

Just as modern democracy cannot be reduced to "bourgeois" forms, utopia cannot be reduced to its potential totalitarian consequences. If we grant that utopia always carries within it a surplus element, are not potential totalitarian effects an excess that should be attributed to the ideologization of utopia rather than to utopia itself? That these effects result from the gap between utopian discourse and discourse about utopia? Somewhere between the two lies the neutralization of the *vis utopica*, the reduction of the "absolute gap" that, according to Fourier, defines utopia. The process of ideologization, the transformation of utopia into ideology, occurs through this erasure of the gap between utopian discourse and discourse about utopia. To judge, we must refer to the utopian theory that emerged during the pinnacle for utopias in the nineteenth century. These show that utopia is first and foremost a form of writing or a spiritual experience—a commitment to distance or the examination of distance—which prevents those who are aware of it from engaging in a directly "realist" mode of reading.[5]

Using these two propositions, I will try to resolve the contradiction between emancipatory and potentially totalitarian utopias, drawing inspiration from the diagnosis and recommendation of Adorno's *Negative Dialectics*: "Philosophy, which once seemed obsolete, lives on because the moment to realize it was missed."[6] However, the historical failures of practice paradoxically free up space for thought, and it would be a mistake not to use it. We can use this space to carve out a path for self-reflection, to question *the blind spots of emancipation*—which, in this case, means questioning the blind spots of utopia. Accordingly, utopian thinking must integrate what is right and relevant from the critique of utopia and, secondly, use this criticism as an antidote against an uncritical mythologization of utopia that leads to its ruin. Then, a simple question should be sufficient to invalidate the thesis that utopia and revolution necessarily lead to totalitarianism: What would the social world be, what would society look like, without utopia and without revolution? Does not one of the possible definitions of totalitarianism precisely correspond to the regime of a society that, positing or proclaiming itself to be the good society, transparent to itself, could dismiss both the utopian gap and the very idea of revolution? It is as if the full coincidence of this society and its *topos* with itself leaves no place for revolution, but only for evolution. Thus it is important to avoid confusing the necessary critique of utopia with rather suspect and reactive proclamations of the end of utopia.

My approach to theorizing utopia proceeds through successive displacements, which allow me to reach, or at least try to reach, a new understanding of utopia. The first displacement is to turn away from any globalizing discourse on utopia, as these often rely on the idea of "eternal utopia"—consider, for example, the hasty declarations of Alexander Zinoviev or Leszek Kolakowski. Instead, we must examine the often-conflicting plurality of utopian traditions in modernity. In an article published in 1973–1974, "The History of Utopia and the Destiny of Its Critique," I tried to distinguish three main utopian traditions: (a) utopian socialism, which asks the question "What is utopian socialism?" without presenting a pre-determined answer; (b) neo-utopianism; and, finally, (c) a new category, the "new utopian spirit."[7]

At this first level, the new utopian spirit was polemically directed against the Marxist machinery of exclusion when it emerged in the 1970s. However, as this stage of the controversy passed, it became a question of bringing to light another socialist tradition and a lost dimension of socialism. Two main tendencies were involved: the new utopian spirit as an autonomous tendency, and the new utopian spirit in a complex relationship with Marx. These can both be seen in a work that is little known in France: William Morris's *News from Nowhere*.[8]

The second displacement: to address the question of utopia today, we cannot just invoke the plurality of traditions, reveal another constellation, or formally describe it in opposition to other types of utopias. This is especially true because such approaches can be mixed with the dangerous fantasy of having found the "correct" tradition. Still, we must give philosophical consistency to the constellation that we have chosen to highlight if we are going to fully capture its autonomy. The philosophical meaning of the new utopia is found in a critical relation to the modern dialectic of emancipation. We take this concept from Walter Benjamin's *On the Concept of History* and Theodor Adorno and Max Horkheimer's *Dialectic of Enlightenment*. The dialectic of emancipation is a paradoxical movement through which modern emancipation turns into its opposite, giving rise to new forms of domination and oppression—to barbarism. And it does this even though the original intention was indeed emancipatory. The dialectical approach provides an interpretation of modernity that is completely different from the quietist one that is content to see it only as an unfinished process. By following this approach, we are able to open up a new space of confrontation between three terms: dialectic of emancipation, utopia, and modernity.

The Plurality of Utopian Traditions

We return to the first displacement, the plurality of utopian traditions and the new utopian spirit. I used the term "new utopian spirit" to designate and also constitute a particular constellation of works that aim to overcome their specificity in and by a change in the form of utopia. To put it another way, it refers to a utopian constellation of the nineteenth century that is irreducible to what we traditionally call utopian socialism because it establishes a critical distance from grand utopian visions. It emerges from dissident figures such as Pierre Leroux, dissident of Saint-Simonism, and Joseph Déjacque, dissident of Fourierism and author of a utopian text titled "L'humanisphère."[9] In 1973–1974, I thought it was important to show that because of their changed form these utopias escaped the death sentence pronounced by Marxism, knowing full well that it is necessary to distinguish between the criticism made by Engels in his famous 1880 pamphlet and Marx's much more complex criticism, which cannot be reduced to a pure and simple rejection of utopia. Of course, my purpose in designating this particular constellation as the "new utopian spirit" was partly polemical. My target was not Gaston Bachelard, author of *The Right to Dream*, as he can help us to imaginatively read utopias, especially the Morrisian utopia; rather, my target was his Marxist disciples, which is to say Louis Althusser and his group. After all, they were in the process of renewing and perfecting, with the help of Bachelard's concepts—epistemological break, for instance—the rather crude machine assembled by Engels in *Socialism: Utopian and Scientific*. Departing from the "new *scientific* spirit" practiced and presented by this form of Marxism, the aim was to sketch not the continent, but rather the somewhat unknown island of the new utopian spirit. I had multiple aims: the first was to question the utopia-science opposition, which serves as a dominant theme and true instrument of exclusion—it tries to control all competing ideas—in Engel's text and interpretations of it. We know the main contours of this view: utopia and the great figures of utopia from the beginning of the nineteenth century are introduced, but utopia is dismissed immediately afterward. Utopia is returned to a state of precocity—of immaturity or infancy—in the name of the seriousness of adulthood and maturity. Like the alchemy/chemistry opposition, utopia is assigned to the side of the ludicrous—it is portrayed as a barrier to insurrection. What is more disturbing about this dismissive homage to utopia is that it functions not just as an instrument of exclusion, but also as an instrument of integration. In other words, utopia is *excluded* as an *autonomous* process, but "surpassed-preserved" as an historical moment in the genesis of a higher form of social theory. Thus, utopia has no value on its own; rather, its value has an external source, which is the science of Marx. In preparation for this science, utopia is only of temporary interest: it is "progressive" until the advent of Marx's thought, but it becomes reactionary afterwards. So Marxism emerges in the position of a higher body that holds the key to reading and interpreting utopias, or which decides what is "dead" and what is "living" in utopias. This hypothesis is so pervasive that it also affects a thinker as undogmatic as Lucien Goldmann, who, in in *The Human Sciences and Philosophy*, writes, "Marx allows us to take the measure of Saint-Simon, but conversely the thought of Saint-Simon does not allow us to take the measure of Marx."[10]

I will form a suspicion that also serves as a hypothesis: the Marxist machinery of exclusion-integration for utopias functions on the model of the Hegelian theory of religion. The utopia/science opposition unwittingly reproduces itself as the Hegelian opposition between Judaism and Christianity—Judaism, the inferior form of religion, is overcome-subsumed, "elevated" in Christianity, which is the superior form of religion *par excellence*, the very essence of religion. Let us briefly recall how Hegel founds these assertions: in its valorization of exile (the figure of Abraham), the sublime religion of Judaism is wrong to maintain the separation between man and God, while Christianity is able to surmount the division between the human and the divine through the mediation of Christ. In this sense, Christianity is an absolute religion, with Judaism relegated to the rank of an outdated and obsolete figment of the spirit. Hence the Hegelian blindness to the continuity of Judaism, to its persistent appearance within nations, which is appraised by Hegel as "Jewish madness." Utopia is to Marxist science what, from a Hegelian perspective, Judaism is to Christianity.

From this point of view, it is interesting to observe that Marx is defined by a double aspect: he claims to put an end to the Jewish question—not to Jewish existence, as Adorno emphasizes in his *Essay on Wagner*—and he also claims to unite utopia with "science," or, more precisely, with the generic predictions of communist critique. So, if we follow my suspicion, should we not make utopia the "Jewish idea" in the field of social theory. Like Judaism, which resisted being absorbed by Christianity by the affirmation of its irreducible otherness, does utopia not persist through the assertion of its unalterable difference? Utopia or the "stiff-necked" idea.

Multiple liberating effects arise from this mode of questioning:

- We should first of all note that the utopia/science pairing is not originally Marxist. It was first used in the controversy between Auguste Comte and the Saint-Simonians, which saw the father of positivism invoke the authority of science to discredit the fantasy of utopia. The subsequent appearance of this pairing in Marxist literature is merely a sign of the penetration of positivism into a current of thought that was originally revolutionary.

- After reopening the Marxist case against utopia, we can legitimately interrogate the distinction made between the *Marxist* critique of utopia—that of Engels, which was foundational to Marxism, as Maximilien Rubel showed—and *Marxian* criticism, that of Marx. If we follow the progression of the latter form of critique, we see that it has not been carried out in the name of science—unless we interpret the concept of science in a Hegelian sense as the name of Marx's 1843 opposition between the "partial revolution" and the "radical" or total revolution. As Karl Korsch understood well, the core of the Marxist critique is not to censor the *excess* of utopia in order to assign limits to it, in the name of "realism," but rather to reveal its failure. In the "total revolution," utopia is *at fault* because, far from breaking with the existing order, it turns out to be only "the shadow cast" upon it (for example, Proudhon). Moreover, from the point of view of "critical communism"—and not the point of view of scientific socialism—Marx judges utopian socialism to be "in many respects, revolutionary."[11] A new question immediately arises: If we focus on the *form* of utopias rather than their *content*, what should be the relation between utopias and critical communism? In other words, what relation do we see between the *novum* of utopias and the generic predictions of communism?

- But even if Marx recognizes utopian socialism as the "imaginative expression of a new world,"[12] this form of socialism is nonetheless subject to a movement of integration, of a dialectical going beyond that has unquestionably destructive effects.

This is where we start to see that the interest in the new utopian spirit is not merely polemical, but also inventive and philosophical. Let us return to the suspicion stated above: just as Judaism persisted, developed and enriched *after* the rise of Christianity—and not only as a witness to the truth of Christianity, but also as a sign of its limits—giving rise to an autonomous history, we can consider that there is a history of utopia—of its form and specific practice—to be rediscovered *after* Marx. In this regard, the new utopian spirit is about radically contesting the exorbitant claim of Marx and Engel's revolutionary theory to be the superior form or completion of socialism, and therefore the highest tribunal of social emancipation. For instance, we see this claim in Marx's 1877 letter to Sorge: "It is natural that utopian theories, which *before* the era of materialist critical socialism contained the rudiments of the latter within itself, can now, coming belatedly, only be silly, stale, and basically reactionary."[13]

Through the hypothesis of the new utopian spirit, we can see a persistence or, better yet, a renewal of utopia after 1848, which factually shows that it was not "silly, stale or basically reactionary." Utopia does not end in 1848. This essential moment in the history of emancipation inaugurates an extremely complex history between the utopian current and the communalist movement.[14] From 1848 to 1871, an expanding social movement critically assessed itself, including a reflection on the failure of 1848, a critique of Jacobin traditions, and a critique of the utopian movement. It is in this sense that the Paris Commune represents a pivot in the history of utopia: looking backward, it casts a powerful light on the extraordinary utopian fermentation that preceded the third revolution of the nineteenth century; looking forward, it shows the real utopian transfiguration of this revolution. Around the time of the Commune we see a series of works that escape the sovereign discourse of Marx. It will suffice here to mention the birth of revolutionary Fourierism with Coeurderoy and Déjacque—"L'humanisphère," by the latter (1858–1859), but also *La grève de Samarez* (1857), by Pierre Leroux; *L'instruction pour une prise d'armes* (1864), by Auguste Blanqui; *Paris en l'an 2000*, by Tony Moilin (who was shot by the Versaillais); *L'éternité par les astres* (1872), again by Blanqui; and *The Pilgrims of Hope* (1886) and *News from Nowhere* (1889–1890), by William Morris.

With this constellation, it appears that the new utopian spirit does not fall under the sovereign judgment of the supreme theory, but rather sketches its limits. It highlights that which the revolutionary theory of Marx ignores, that which it censors (for example, the transformation of work into play), that which it obscures, and that which it wrongly considers to be resolved (such as the question of repetition in history).

We can distinguish two main currents in this constellation. One emerges from inside the utopian tradition, particularly in the wake of Fourierism. It is expressed in the break with the belief in self-sufficiency and the supremacy of a single consciousness. It works to free utopia from its pretention to scientificity, to rediscover the relationship of utopia and desire—that which Déjacque called "multiple passionality"—and bring about a critique of substitutionism or utopian pedagogy "from above." Thus it involves the passage from a monological to a dialogic form that, instead of invoking the objectivity of social science, aims to set in motion the intersubjectivity of utopian desires, in search of a utopia that is not valued as a model but rather as an inspiration to the utopian approach. The other current is constituted in a complex relationship to the thinking of Marx. It mainly consists of the work of William Morris (1834–1896), which was rediscovered by the great historian of the English working class, E. P. Thompson. Morris is peculiar in that he "converted" at the age of forty to the thought of Marx, but he nonetheless wrote a gem of utopian literature, *News from Nowhere*, after this conversion. So we can suppose that if Morris "takes over" the Marxian critique of utopias, it is to bend it in a revolutionary direction, not a conservative or reformist one.

The Morrisian oeuvre presents an ambiguity. Would we say, following an important English critic, John Middleton Murry, that Morris struggles in his time against an already degraded Marxism and rediscovers, through the detour of utopia, a radical Marx? Or, from a non-Marxist perspective that draws on the utopian tradition, is it a question of working at the frontiers of Marx's thought, of trying to use a utopian "lift-off" to explore its limits, of introducing "lines of flight" contra the illusion of a solved riddle, likely to restore to history its full enigmatic charge and to human emancipation its problematic character?

The hypothesis of the new utopian spirit brings utopia back to life today (see, for example, surrealism, Walter Benjamin, Ernst Bloch), and also opens a plural space of confrontation that challenges the validity of all universal discourses on utopias, including neoliberal and Marxist discourses.

The Dialectic of Emancipation and Utopia

I now proceed to the second displacement: the new utopian spirit and the dialectic of emancipation.

The new utopian spirit could be described as the presence within utopian culture of a movement that is suspicious of utopia. It is a movement of self-reflection, as if it had integrated the argument of the enemies of utopia in its approach, without renouncing its primary goal or being resigned to proclaim the end of utopia. What is at stake here is the project of continuing the utopian movement, either through the creation of new figures or by the elaboration of new speculative practices that give rise to another utopia, that allow us to think of utopia otherwise. We are invited to explore this constellation and, in the process, reach a new understanding of utopia. There is a challenge here: force utopia to measure itself against the hypotheses that are the most unfavorable to it, against quintessentially anti-utopian hypotheses. In the terms of Walter Benjamin, the task is to stare at Medusa's head without being paralyzed by it. In this case, this means taking seriously the hypothesis of repetition in history, the hypothesis of catastrophe or, if we prefer, of the repetition of the catastrophe or the catastrophe of repetition. The spirit of this new understanding of utopia can be captured in the following proposition: only utopian thinking that does violence to itself, which includes within it the critique of utopia, has the resilience necessary to destroy the myths that undermine utopia.[15] Paraphrasing Levinas's reflection on freedom, we could call this "difficult utopia."

We can add a supplementary hypothesis to develop this first description: the new utopian spirit gets its substance and philosophical meaning through its relationship with the dialectic of emancipation—the paradoxical movement through which modern emancipation becomes inverted into its opposite. Does not this inversion, this reversal of emancipation, constitute the very experience of repetition? The work of the new utopian spirit and difficult utopia—secondary, reflexive, or dissident utopia—consists of an intervention of a new type against the dialectic of emancipation, one that disrupts the circle of repetition.

We can break down this intervention as follows:

- We can start with a more or less perceptive awareness of this idea of the reversal of modern emancipation in the form of the dialectic of reason.

- It aims to identify the blind spots of emancipation, or the centers or nodes in which this reversal takes place and the repetition begins.

- These centers give rise to the work of deconstruction and critique, which opens a new path to utopia, giving it a new direction by revealing what Adorno calls "lines of flight."[16]

In short, the task of the new utopian spirit, as it deploys the dialectic of emancipation, consists of "purging" utopia of the mythology that endangers it, doing so not to proclaim the end of utopia but rather to preserve utopia from the seeds of regression that threaten it. The autonomy of the new utopian spirit transcends both the thought of Marx—there is neither the end of utopia, nor the affirmation that the riddle of history is finally resolved—and the great dogmatic utopias. By tracing this double distance, we give back to utopia its ability to play with this riddle of history, so that it either discovers that something remains unexplainable, or it decides to sojourn within the riddle. Demythologization is another way for utopia to be the "Jewish idea."

Adorno and Horkheimer's dialectic of reason is an appropriate starting point for thinking about the dialectic of emancipation. The initial question they ask, formulated between 1942 and 1944, is: Why does a humanity seeking emancipation fall back into a new barbarism instead of committing itself to truly human conditions? Why this reversal of emancipation, which leads to the self-destruction of humanity? Why, in Levinas's terms, do we see a "reversal of reasonable projects"?[17] This question was stated, as Habermas pointed out, under the inspiration of nocturnal writers of the "bourgeoisie." In fact, Nietzsche's *Human, All Too Human* is a wonderful account of the inversion of modern freedom: how emancipatory socialism leads *nolens volens* to an unprecedented strengthening of state structures. "Socialism is the fanciful younger brother of the almost expired despotism whose heir it wants to be; its endeavors are thus in the profoundest sense reactionary. For it desires an abundance of state power such as only despotism has ever had; indeed it outbids all the despotisms of the past inasmuch as it expressly aspires to the annihilation of the individual. . . . On account of its close relationship to them it always appears in the proximity of all excessive deployments of power."[18] The strategy of critical theory, which is sensitive to the nocturnal face of history, is to wrestle arguments against progress away from the enemies of progress, so that they can be put in service of progress.

The model is thus that of the dialectic of reason: Which process internal to reason leads to its self-destruction, to its inversion as a new mythology? This is a radically different question from the one Georg Lukács asks in *The Destruction of Reason*, which strives to keep intact the "purity" of reason in its search for external causes of this destruction.[19] Indeed, Adorno and Horkheimer's fundamental thesis with regard to this regression of reason into mythology is the efficiency of the internal movement of self-destructing reason: "the cause of enlightenment's relapse into mythology is to be sought not so much in the nationalist, pagan, or other modern mythologies concocted specifically to cause such a relapse as in the fear of truth which petrifies enlightenment itself."[20] So the mythology destructive of reason emerges from the bosom of reason, and has nothing to do with ancient remnants or concerted manipulations. Far from keeping reason at a safe distance from myth, critical theory, anxious and unsettled, reveals their proximity, or worse, their affinity. The "impurity" of reason is clearly reflected in this internal movement of self-destruction. When awakened, reason breeds monsters. Critical theory also takes the opposite approach of the classical Enlightenment problematic that makes reason—enlightened thinking—a declared opponent of myth, a force of demythologization that is opposed as such to the return of mythology. According to Adorno and Horkheimer, there is, on the contrary, a secret complicity between reason and myth, because there is a rational kernel of myth and a mythological kernel of reason: "Myth is already enlightenment, and enlightenment reverts to mythology."[21]

In fact, does the myth behind the narrative of origins not anticipate reason? This very story claims to represent, confirm, explain, and thus announce a form of objectifying thought. Meanwhile, the Enlightenment becomes more and more "entangled" in mythology. Of course, reason desires demythologization, but is not the work of deconstructing myths carried out in a typically mythical form, that of reprisals? The provocation of critical theory goes so far as to call into question the idea of law. It asks: Is not the recurrence or regularity of the connection between the phenomena on which it is based the reemergence of the repetition specific to the mythical universe? Moreover, does not an "arid wisdom," which professes there is "nothing new under the sun,"[22] subject reason to a fate that is nothing more than self-preservation?

To better understand the mechanism of this reversal, let us pause briefly on the opening line of *Dialectic of Enlightenment*, which presents a theme that recurs throughout the work: "Enlightenment, understood in the widest sense as the advance of thought, has always aimed at liberating human beings from fear and installing them as masters."[23] The relation between these two propositions very precisely defines the dialectic of enlightenment: the legitimate project of liberation from fear gives rise to an inversion when it inscribes itself under the sign of sovereignty, when it confuses liberation from fear with sovereign will. *The proximity or secret complicity of reason and myth lies in this recognition.* Because liberation from fear is tied to sovereignty—that is to say, to the domination of either nature or man—reason is not freed from mythical fear but rather internalizes it, or even discharges it by transforming it into, for instance, the appropriation of nature. Adorno and Horkheimer write: "The modest hunting ground [of the civilized man] shrinks to the unified cosmos, in which nothing exists but prey."[24] It is as if the confusion of liberation from fear and sovereignty pushes mankind to hunt down and tame the unknown with all its force. There is, indeed, an internalization or radicalization of mythic fear. What is repeated in this movement is the fear of the outside, the heterogeneous—the fear of an otherness that compels reason to privilege identity over the outside or other: "Nothing is allowed to remain outside, since the mere idea of the 'outside' is the real source of fear."[25] Is this an illusion of reason? Reason cannot pretend to be more than nature unless it first becomes aware of that which is "natural" in itself, namely, the tendency towards domination. At the same time the critique identifies one of the focal points of inversion or, in other words, the general motor of the dialectic of reason: the critique points towards another aspect of reason that would free men from fear while renouncing sovereignty and welcoming both exteriority and otherness. Thus begins a complex process that, on the one hand, pursues a relentless deconstruction of the Enlightenment, and, on the other, does not dismiss reason but rather affirms a desire to save it. This process is carried out in two directions. If we look at Adorno's *Hegel: Three Studies*, there are two parts to the self-reflection of reason that is capable of leading to a "truly human society": it is about finding "a healing awareness of the marks of unreason in its own reason, and the traces of the rational in the irrational as well."[26] This suggests two orientations: the more conventional approach is that of a critical-cathartic work, which aims to purify reason from the elements of unreason that it contains; the less conventional approach is a hermeneutic one, which refuses to reify reason and instead treats it as fluid in order to extract its "truth content" and therefore detect blind spots of reason, which might appear as symptoms of the wanderings of unreason. Thus we see the principle already stated: "Not least among the tasks now confronting thought is that of placing all reactionary arguments against Western culture in the service of progressive enlightenment."[27]

In one case we see an undertaking with a well-established path that is critical of reason; in the other case, we see a more adventurous and risky project that seeks to expand reason by interpreting, transforming, and integrating traces of unreason. I propose to build a dialectic of emancipation on the foundation of this complex model of the dialectic of reason, a model that can account for the failures of reason without falling into resignation or defeatism. If we pursue the parallel to the end, the highly questionable program of modern emancipation could be defined in these terms: "The purpose of emancipation was to free men from servitude and suffering, and make them sovereign." We can easily see the essential components of this dialectic:

- First, it highlights an internal causality that inverts modern emancipation into its opposite.

This implies that we stop attributing the reversal to historical circumstances—war, scarcity, being surrounded, and so on—or to incompleteness. There is an "impurity" to the project of modern emancipation—this project is not totally uniform in its sense of freedom, which prevents us from importing it as it is, unchanged, into new historical conditions, or deciding to bring it purely and simply to completion. More to the point, the hypothesis suggests that the desire for sovereignty diverts the legitimate search for autonomy into a new form of heteronomy. Thus the obligation for emancipation to self-reflect ensures that the same causes do not produce the same effects:

- This means that internal causality searches for sources that instigate the inversion of emancipation, despite and against the will of historical actors. There are multiple sources. If we admit that utopia is closely tied to political reason, one source could be the effect of internal mythologies on reason. Another source of the inversion could be the denial of a dimension whose support complicates, but does not cancel, the project of human emancipation. We see this in, for example, the theory of voluntary servitude, because it is not true that, as Marx asserts, the secret of servitude is fully located in the workshop. We also see this in the way the legitimate project of autonomy degenerates into the desire for sovereignty and then for domination, because if we fail to subject the idea of sovereignty to criticism we fail to set limits on it by recognizing that there is always something already there, there is always a given.

- This self-reflection engages thinking on emancipation either in the sense of a cathartic critique or in the sense of an expansion and complication of the project of emancipation. The project is willing to confront that which reinforces its problematic character.

This transposition of the dialectic of reason to emancipation is all the more valid because enlightened thinking's orientation towards emancipation—the decision for emancipation—allows us to consider that any dialectic of reason to a certain extent already contains a dialectic of emancipation within it.

And utopia? Contrary to appearances, we have not forgotten about it. Indeed, the new utopian spirit, the new wave of utopian thinking, is the resurgence of the *vis utopica*: in the face of an already perceptible dialectic of emancipation, the nature of the new constellation is to establish a new thinking—a new form or new speculative practices—that pushes utopia, an active force, to ensure each node of inversion finds its purpose in the *novum* and therefore eludes the hold of historical repetition. Once awakened, two directions are available to utopia: one is the critique of utopian reason; the other is the expansion of utopian reason, a radicalization of utopian "lift-off." Giving free rein to fantasy, the latter displaces questions of tradition, opens passages towards an unexplored other place, or else it launches an assault on that which is most contrary to it, as if the principal maxim of this new endeavor is "the truth of utopia is found in its excess."

Adorno and Horkheimer themselves practiced this transposition in showing how reification and the eternalization of necessity produce a socialist dialectic by reducing the relationship between freedom and necessity to a purely quantitative one, so that freedom forever collides with nature as an alien and irreconcilable power.[28]

The New Utopian Spirit and the Issue of Repetition

But it is through Walter Benjamin, who on various occasions attempted a new understanding of utopia, that we encounter the most perceptive thought of a dialectic of emancipation related to utopias.

Benjamin is a superb starting point for thinking differently about utopias. His renewed vision of the nineteenth century, a period when phantasmagoria and luxuriance alternate, leads to the rehabilitation of utopia. While considered a primitive theory in modernity, Benjamin takes utopia seriously, considering it in itself rather than in relation to another form of social theory. But Benjamin is also, in the words of Victor Hugo, a "sentry of dreams," who, rather than being dazzled by the imaginative flight of great utopias, remains vigilant and ensures that the new of utopia does not mean the return of the same.

In his "Exposé of 1935," Benjamin proposes a theory of utopia that offers a valuable contribution to the new utopian spirit. Following a phrase he borrows from Michelet—"each epoch dreams the one to follow"—Benjamin aims to distinguish two very distinct strata in each utopian constellation. This duality evokes the double composition of Beauty, which, according to Baudelaire, is made up of an eternal element and a relative, circumstantial element. In the collective consciousness of an era, the emergence of a new means of production—it is the enlightened Marxist speaking here—corresponds with idealistic images in which one sees an interpenetration of the old and the new. This is the historical stratum. Through these images, Benjamin writes, "the collective seeks both to overcome and to transfigure the immaturity of the social product and the inadequacies in the social organization of production."[29] Thus the ambivalence of utopia, the new Janus, which presents at once a critical face, the going beyond, and a mythological face, the transfiguration. Because of this ambivalence, this composite character, utopias take part, in spite of their revolutionary orientation, in the phantasmagoria of the nineteenth century.

A second, ahistorical stratum represents, in a way, the invariability of utopia, the "eternal" element that reappears in every utopia. The interpenetration of the old and the new itself turns out to be a composite. It returns to the former means of production, but it also points towards an even older past, a prehistory. It is as if the movement towards the recent past immediately puts it at a distance, because the need to distinguish it gives rise to a movement towards a much more distant past. As Benjamin writes, "These tendencies [of overcoming and transfiguration] deflect the imagination [which is given impetus by the new] back upon the primal past. In the dream in which each epoch entertains images of its successor, the latter appears wedded to elements of primal history [*Urgeschichte*]—that is, to elements of a classless society."[30]

In the encounter between the old—experiences of classless society stored in the collective unconscious—and the new, utopia is born. This is how the Fourierist utopia can be read: on the one hand, it finds its first impulse in the introduction of machines—which historically provides a real machinery of passions—and, on the other hand, it responds to the land of Cockaigne, "the very old symbol of fulfilled desires." We see here the work that must be done by the "sentry of dreams" to decipher utopias. Aware of this double composition, he must practice a critical hermeneutics on a given utopian work, which means separating it from myth to unleash the emancipatory potential of utopia, and doing this without fragmenting the work. This protects the reader against univocal judgements, favorable or unfavorable.

But what is the meaning of this separation of utopia and myth? Adorno's critique of Benjamin's project in an August 2, 1935, letter provides elements of a response.[31] His basic answer is twofold. Adorno does not contest Benjamin's thesis of the double composition of utopia, but he objects to Benjamin's quietist conception of the relationship between the old and the new, which takes the form of a utopian resurgence of classless society—a thesis inspired by Marxism—to oppose it with a far more troubling interpretation: "The category in which the archaic fuses with the modern seems to me more like a catastrophe than a Golden Age."[32] Utopias are not illuminated by the golden age's rays of sun, but rather the dark of night, which reemerges to obscure human history.

What we see here is the reemergence "of an irrational catastrophe in the beginning"[33]—a prolonged piece of natural history—that is to say, the contingency of the antagonism that should be thought of, according to Adorno, as a manifestation of domination and not as a derivative of economic necessity, a notion that accounts for the totality of its development. We see a radical anti-Hegelianism, but also an anti-Marxism that wonders: Shouldn't the Spirit of the world be defined as a permanent catastrophe? With a touch of dark humor, Adorno writes, "No universal history leads from savagery to humanitarianism, but there is one leading from the slingshot to the megaton bomb."[34] The catastrophe is constituted not only by the contingency of the antagonism and the suffering it entails, but also by the very repetition of the catastrophe—"its progress toward hell," the "eternal recurrence of damnation,"[35] in short, never-ending terror. Adorno strongly emphasizes the nocturnal face of history, suggesting that we cannot accept the *topos* of the golden age as it is. Unless we return to the category of the mythico-archaic, unless we give in to the allure of the mythical image, the interpreter must reveal the ambivalence of the golden age. The golden age is both Arcadia and Hell—that is to say, an underworld, a world of subterranean power, a world of mythical terror. Asserting the ambivalence of the golden age requires dialectizing it, transforming mythical images into dialectical images. Just as the rule of the commodity is not purely and simply Hell, the golden age is not simply Arcadia.

Moved by Adorno's objection, Benjamin pushes his critique further, resulting in a maximal degree of suspicion. Indeed, he recognizes the merits of Adorno's critical reflections on the golden age. However, on an essential point he resists and argues that utopia as a dialectical image cannot reproduce the dream on its own. Benjamin appeals to another category that is neglected by Adorno, that of awakening, to highlight "a connection [that] still needs to be developed," the connection between image and awakening.[36] If the dream can reproduce the mythological image, the awakening, the task of the present, can define itself as the breaking of the mythological image and the construction of the dialectical image—it is through awakening that utopia is liberated from its mythological shell. A complex approach with maximal suspicion: thinking on emancipation cannot be detached from utopia, but at the same time it must accept utopia with extreme caution, because utopia is inherently ambivalent. An active force against the dialectic of emancipation, utopia at the same time takes part in it insofar as its double composition results in two focal points of mythologization: the transfiguration of the existing social order—in Marxian terms, the cast shadow of present society—and the grip of the archaic—the world of terror—over the new. It is no longer enough to say, following Georges Henein, "The Mona Lisa of utopia isn't guaranteed to prevail, but can cast a new smile and return to men the Promethean spark through which their recovered freedom can be realized."[37]

Promethean spark? Isn't this a blind spot of utopia? Thus we would rather say that interpreters of utopia must relentlessly practice a critical hermeneutics whose task is to free utopia from the myths that surround it so that it can redeploy its liberating energy.

Separating utopia from myth therefore entails isolating the centers of mythologization to stop both the work of transfiguration and the return of the archaic under the veil of the new. It is not so much about a more vigilant critique as about a real change of perspective in Benjamin, which is apparent if one compares the "Exposé of 1939" to that of 1935. We could say that he produces a crystallization that combines Adorno's critique—the golden age must be considered in relation to hell—and an encounter with Blanqui, the infernal vision of *L'enfermé*.[38] We can compile the signs of this change in perspective: the disappearance of Michelet's contentious famous phrase, and, additionally, the disappearance of the section devoted to utopia and thus the abandonment of the theory of the two strata in his 1939 project. And yet, at no point does Benjamin's vital interest in utopia and its relationship to emancipation weaken (see sec. 2). Rather, utopia is present—obstinately present—and its turn towards emancipation is now seen, in Adorno's terms, from the point of view of "hell." But, in Adorno's terms, is this right? In the "Exposé of 1939," one is struck by the new importance of Blanqui, who occupies an exceptional place in that he literally frames the text, from the introduction to the conclusion. Indeed, Benjamin's change in perspective is epitomized by the substitution of Blanqui for Michelet.

At the end of 1936 and beginning of 1937, Benjamin discovers Gustave Geffroy's extraordinary book, *L'enfermé* (1897), which is devoted to Blanqui. Much more than a biography, it is in the eyes of Benjamin an "exemplary . . . monograph,"[39] which uses Blanqui's story to try to convey the terrifying essence of the nineteenth century. But, a year later, at the end of 1937, the true encounter takes place: an irrepressible and irreversible shock when Benjamin reads *L'éternité par les astres*,[40] an 1872 text written by Blanqui when he was locked up in Fort du Taureau after the third defeat of the French proletariat and the demise of the Paris Commune. Blanqui starts with Laplace's system, using it to develop a serious cosmological speculation. The book sketches out a fantastic theory about the duplication of planets—including the duplication of planet Earth—which leads to the affirmation—or the hallucination, according to Benjamin—of the eternal return of the same. We should recognize here that in Benjamin's journey Blanqui is not simply a representative of permanent revolution or radical communism; rather, Blanqui stands out on the horizon of the nineteenth century as an unusual, enigmatic revolutionary figure, who mysteriously associates the idea of revolution with an infernal vision of repetition. In a January 6, 1938, letter to Horkheimer, Benjamin writes, "If hell is a theological subject, this speculation may be defined as theological. While deriving his data from mechanistic natural science, the worldview that Blanqui outlines is in fact an infernal view."[41] In this infernal view, the century that Fichte and Saint-Simon inaugurated with the joint announcement that "the golden age is not behind us, but ahead of us" turns out to instead be a *time of repetition*. It is not that the old wins out over the new, but that the very experience of the new is informed by the old. Blanqui provides a diagnosis of the nineteenth century but also a judgment on history: the fabric of history is repetition, just as the fabric of the cosmos is duplication. It is as if the existential and political proof of repetition—the containment and recurring defeat of the social revolution—contaminates Blanqui's vision, which in turn experiences an incredible expansion. It is as if the event of repetition that is at the heart of a modern age dominated by phantasmagoria, "the errant negotiators of old and new,"[42] had, through the force of Blanqui's astronomical theory, won over the entire cosmos. Thus the theory of repetition transposed to the stars deals a fatal blow to the illusion of novelty and opens up a cosmic abyss. Benjamin writes, "Blanqui's vision has the entire universe entering the modernity of which Baudelaire's seven old men are the heralds."[43] The object of repetition is the catastrophe, or, in Adornian terms, the "contingency of antagonism"—a new violence, a new defeat inflicted on the oppressed, which once more ruins any chance of an alternative order, any possibility of leaving prehistory. In sum, "humanity figures . . . as damned" in Blanqui's work: "Everything new it could hope for turns out to be a reality that has always been present; and this newness will be as little capable of furnishing it with a liberating solution as a new fashion is capable of rejuvenating society. Blanqui's cosmic speculation conveys this lesson: that humanity will be prey to a mythic anguish so long as phantasmagoria occupies a place in it."[44]

Do we need to unequivocally insist that Blanqui's cautionary lesson destroys all belief in progress, since it maintains that progress is an illusion under which the specter of repetition advances? Despite its shimmers, shouldn't we classify utopia itself alongside phantasmagoria?

Or should we instead ask, how do we tear utopia from the world of phantasmagoria? For Benjamin, it is as if Blanqui, who becomes the essential hub for reorganizing his project, repeats Adorno's gloomy warning that the grip of the old over the new does not manifest itself as a revival of the golden age—the Arcadia of classless society—but rather manifests as a return of catastrophe, the resurrection of the world of terror or Hell. At the intersection of Blanqui's "flash of lightening"[45] and Adorno's warning is a new conception of emancipation, which goes beyond vigilant criticism, beyond a change in perspective—it is nearly a revolution. For what does it mean to think about emancipation, to persist in thinking about emancipation in light of a vision of Hell and the theory of permanent catastrophe or the repetition of catastrophe? Does such thinking not demand a revolution that is precisely constitutive of the new utopian spirit, resisting any impulse towards resignation?

Rather than reject utopia in the realm of phantasmagoria, Benjamin regards Blanqui's theory as one of the last phantasmagorias of the nineteenth century. Sensitive to the highly obsessive nature of this idea, Benjamin tries to show that Blanqui's theory, despite its critical intentions, ultimately takes on a mythological tone. It is as though Blanqui himself falls under the influence of the repetition of the myth, the resurrection of primitive history that appears in the nineteenth century. Indeed, the theory of repetition has outrun its critical impact by becoming the exact inverse of the doctrine of progress and submitting in turn to the logic of identity. Departing from the critical terrain, it has become dogmatized and ontologized; it has passed from a proposition with the status of an "as if"—act as if the catastrophe was a permanent threat—to a conclusive judgment about the existence of the catastrophe. Benjamin's work consists of restoring critical force to this hypothesis of repetition, and thus it contributes to the "organization of pessimism" without falling into the enchanted circle of the eternal return, without contributing—*nolens volens*—to the closure of history. The lesson we should remember from Blanqui is that any real thought of emancipation must be measured against the terror of repetition. This is perhaps the source of a higher calling: snatch humanity away from the catastrophe that constantly threatens. It is also important, as we have already observed, that the one who has the audacity to fix the head of Medusa does not allow themself to be fascinated by it. To remain a dialectical image, the image of *Eternity by the Stars* must be transformed into a negative utopia, one in which the catastrophe ceases. For his part, Adorno writes, "Today the thwarted possibility of something other has shrunk to that of averting catastrophe in spite of everything."[46] Benjamin contributes two formulations to this new thinking on emancipation: "The concept of progress must be based on the idea of catastrophe" and "The salvaging clings on to the little crack in the permanent catastrophe."[47] These are the paths that the new utopian spirit must take to bring maximal suspicion to the very heart of utopia. The dialectical apparatus of emancipation and utopia—or rather, utopia against the dialectic of emancipation—is elaborated with the most evidence and rigor in "Theses on the Concept of History" (written 1939–1940). In it, Benjamin identifies three foci from which the inversion of emancipation takes place and that are targets for the onslaught of utopia: the valorization of work, the belief in continuous progress, and the orientation towards the happiness of future generations.

Let us first recall that this text, a truly spiritual exercise at the edge of the abyss, struggles to develop a new concept of history and also a new project of emancipation, a new conception of utopia. As Benjamin writes about his reflections, it is a question of "delivering the brave citizens from the nets in which these politicians [of the left] have ensnared them."[48] Or, in another version: it is about "freeing the brave citizens from the magical charm under which a politics conceived under the sign of progress holds them." I want to succinctly retrace the *movement* of this text in order to appreciate the way another conception of history also produces another conception of utopia, or opens new pathways to utopia.

History is what constitutes the representation of liberation as the struggle for the happiness of future generations. In it, Benjamin perceives, in addition to the erasure of the names of Blanqui and Marx, the loss of the passions proper to the avenging class, hatred and the will to sacrifice. The result is an immediate weakening of revolutionary energy. But does not Benjamin's proposed change of direction—substituting the redemption of enslaved ancestors, the historically defeated, for the happiness of future generations—lead to a different attitude towards liberation? It is no longer a question of appropriating the world as new owners who are intoxicated with their legitimacy, but rather one of rectifying the suffering of defeated generations. Does not the "completely other" social leave ineffaceable traces of suffering, which is to say there is an acute sense of fragility because the suffering of the past permanently threatens access to otherness? Is there not a growing distrust of the yearning for fullness, as if the memory of the defeated surrounds the new society with a persistent aura of nostalgia?

There is no need to return to the devastating effects of the belief in progress, except to emphasize that, beyond the three faults Benjamin identifies—the unitary conception of progress, indefinite perfectibility, continuity—he primarily denounces the representation that supports this belief, namely, the idea of homogenous and empty time. Countering this representation, Benjamin reintroduces the category of the "leap" or "jump" to a conception of history that tries to construct the present as a time in which it is possible to rupture the *continuum* of domination. And to avoid giving the illusion of progress, he reminds us that the persistence of barbarism in history always jeopardizes the reality and possibility of progress.

Now, to those who like to "swim with the current" and exalt work and technological development as the sources of all wealth and all culture: Is this not a secularized form of the return or repetition of the old Protestant work ethic? Is not the exaltation of work, the savior of the new era, based on the blind decoupling of progress in the domination of nature and social regression? Worse yet, does not such a conception of emancipation reveal the control of a mode of production that promotes the exploitation of nature without recognizing that such a "victory" holds within it the possibility of the domination of humans over humans? Against such a reversal of emancipation, Benjamin turns to utopias that, in and because of their extravagance seek a different relation to nature, one that is capable of freeing their potentiality. As Benjamin writes, "Fourier's fantasies, which have so often been ridiculed, prove to be surprisingly sound. According to Fourier, as a result of efficient co-operative labor, four moons would illuminate the earthly night, the ice would recede from the poles, sea water would no longer taste salty, and beasts of prey would do man's bidding. All this illustrates a kind of labor which, far from exploiting nature, is capable of delivering her of the creations which lie dormant in her womb as potentials."[49]

In the "two days after dialectic," utopia must face the problem of the "alienation of the very work of disalienation." To transform itself or confront that which brings it the cruelest denials—repetition—utopia must discover the way that leads, in its very fragility, to "the strait gate through which the Messiah might enter."[50]

It is true that the interest in utopia has seriously waned. But, with the proposed displacements, perhaps we have progressed slightly down the initially envisaged path—a narrow, difficult path, which avoids the pitfalls of both acritical evaluation (naivete) and systematic vilification (disillusionment or, worse, the fatigue of reason). It is a path that is worth taking, however. The work of utopia reflecting on itself or the encounter of critical philosophy and utopia should not be neglected.

Consider for a moment the supposedly insurmountable opposition of utopia and democracy. Can this opposition be reconciled through the new utopian spirit? Pierre Leroux, for one, interprets the modern utopia and the welcome news it brings—earthly rule will take the form of association—as fundamentally tending in the direction of democracy. Indeed, by privileging the law of attraction over the law of domination, does modern utopia not aim at the disappearance of the rulers/ruled division, at the erasure of relations of command and obedience? This democratic inspiration was apparent in the utopian movement from the start, but hasn't it permeated and won the movement in its entirety? In this regard, we could mention the critique of substitutionism and the demand for plurality, two central features of the new utopian spirit. More profoundly, the utopian movement stresses a radical indeterminacy, which is at the heart of the democratic experience in relation to the disincorporation of the social, the dissolution of all fundamentalism, and the transformation of symbolic markers. The result is the birth of open utopias, which avoid proposing a particular utopian content, but rather provide an invitation or incitement to utopia. These open utopias call for the always latent desire for utopia to awaken and flourish. They seek to have utopias, in their diversity and extravagance, become an integral part of democratic debate, bringing back the question of social otherness in a thousand different forms.

Conversely, if the real utopian element is the human bond—intersubjective relations and the relation to humanity, an invisible society that doubles as the visible—how could democracy break free from utopia? How could democracy, insofar as it is authentic and not a veneer intended to disguise damaged goods, cut itself off from utopia and, in the process, from the quest for a new form of human community? This would be a nonfusional community that, through the experience of democratic division, can invent a new form of bond. Without this new bond, we would not see the disincorporation of the social, but rather its disintegration until the "war of all against all" resurfaces. Would this not be a repetition of the catastrophe?

Utopia is ultimately the beyond of politics—a beyond that is tirelessly sought by modern politics with the aim of reaching its proper consistency. The term and the idea of the political beyond—which are not to be confused with political spiritualization—are frightening. Indeed, is the political beyond not one of the paths leading to the denial of the political by suggesting an illusory horizon in which politics is surpassed? And are not many modern utopias inhabited by the fantasy of the end of politics, by the idea of a society that, after reaching a stage of full development, could do without the political dimension? Paradox of utopia and ambivalence of the political beyond. But once we reaffirm the ineffaceable character of the political—of the political divisions inherent to democracy—and reject the illusion of a reconciled society, is not utopia the necessary beyond that both gives substance to the political and reveals the path towards democratic institutions? Doesn't utopia reveal the metapolitical meaning that is working to politically institute the human bond?

Perhaps the arduous path I have sketched out will calm the hasty people who reactively craft obituaries and bid "goodbye" to utopia, mistakenly believing we have finally discovered a place where there is no exteriority to the social. Before we let the "wing of imbecility"[51] prevail, let us instead wager on the indestructible link between humanity and utopia, patiently meditating on this sentence from Levinas: "As if humanity were a genus allowing within its logical space (its extension) an absolute break; as if in going toward the other man we transcended the human, toward utopia."[52]

Chapter 11

The Utopian Conversion
Utopia and Awakening
(2013)

Who can say why such and such a person would spend their whole life, or almost, writing on utopia? Or why the desire to think utopia is the aim of their work? Who can account for this persistence in exploring, no doubt discontinuously, the vast realm of utopias? How should we try to explain the lure, or better, the attraction utopia can exert, where some have wanted to see the sign of a law of attraction? It is as if here stood an essential object whose inexhaustible content at once revealed and concealed itself. Utopia is a kind of enigma.

As for its persistence, it seems to follow from a sustained revolt against the hatred of utopia. All the world's prosecutors denounce "impossible and guilty utopias," utopias that are guilty because they are impossible. Auguste Blanqui rightly pointed to this linguistic struggle around the term utopia. For those who uphold the existing order, it is important to reject utopia as impossible and thus liquidate its will to alterity. Blanqui's intervention is all the more precious because it very exactly defines the moment in which the hatred of utopia is born in modernity, namely, the 1840s. This hatred culminates and becomes murderous in the bloody repression of the workers' insurrection of June 1848, as the critics of utopia put down the pen and

---

Translated by James D. Ingram. Originally published as and translated from "La conversion utopique: L'utopie et l'éveil," in *Utopiques II: L'homme est un animal utopique* (Paris: Sens & Tonka, 2013), 13–60.

take up the gun. Now, in our day this hatred of utopia is much reinforced insofar as commentators, historians, and philosophers do not hesitate to make utopia the cradle of totalitarian domination. Here we will recognize a characteristic gesture of our age: discrediting any phenomenon of rupture—1793, revolution, utopia—by immediately accusing it of prefiguring or preparing for totalitarianism. So we commonly read the expression "totalitarian utopia," as if all of a sudden utopia and total domination had become synonyms. To these accusers, rushed and little bothered with exactitude, it suffices to recall that the spread of totalitarianism began by liquidating everything near and far that had a whiff of utopia. Totalitarianism, far from being the child of utopia, could only rise from its corpse.

Why the utopian conversion? This expression should not lead to illusions. It has nothing to do with "conversion" in a religious sense, taking up the interpretation of the Catholic editor of Thomas More's *Utopia*. Judging that the essential function of More's book is maieutic, André Prévost seeks to show that *Utopia* is the instrument of a true *metanoia*, a metamorphosis of the soul turning away from the world and the earthly city and turning towards God. He writes:

> Once again, More's construction shows itself to be, not a paradigmatic example to imitate in a literal manner, but an instrument of internal rebirth. The dialectical movement it follows leads less to reforms or revolutions than to a *conversion*, a *return*, a natural communion with other men, an acceptance of fundamental principles that foregrounds responsibility to God.[1]

If it is a conversion, this movement can only be a *conversion to utopia*. The utopian conversion signifies and can only signify the conversion to utopia itself and not to its themes or contents, to a complex of drives, attitudes, and even postures proper to utopia. A manifestation of "the heroism of the human spirit" in Vico's sense, utopia is this disposition that, thanks to an exercise of the imagination, does not fear within a given society to transcend its limits and conceive of what is different, the completely other social. Even with the system of untouchability, one of the most rigid social structures there is, almost inevitable in the eyes of its members, all the same, according to James C. Scott's analysis in *Domination and the Arts of Resistance*, the untouchables can nevertheless imagine an upside-down world—better still, they can go beyond "this simple negation" and conceive of a world without untouchables or Brahmins.[2] Is not this departure from the system of untouchability the fruit of a utopian conversion? What's more, the utopian conversion opens the way to man as a utopian animal. In truth, there are many ways there.

As we can tell from the text "The Utopia of Books,"[3] Emmanuel Levinas opened another path towards man the utopian animal, or rather what he calls "the utopian human." Starting from an emphatic reading of the Aristotelian formula "man is a linguistic being" (*zoon logon ekhon*), he proceeds to a first extension by pushing the gift of language to the book: the being given language would be not a bookish animal, but a literary one. The presence of the book allows Levinas to make a second extension, from literary animal to prophetic animal, since the book interpreted gives free rein to inspiration, be it prophesy or utopia. Even if Levinas invents this double extension starting from language, is it really around the book, always threatened by closure, that man as a utopian animal must be sought? Is it not rather around a completely other storyline, one foreign to understanding, to the knowledge given to intentionality—a storyline that comes from proximity, from the fact of the neighbor, of meeting—that the birthplace of the utopian human must be discerned? To tell the truth, the utopia of books and the utopia of the human are indissociable, situated at an intertwining such that the nonintentional vivacity of the utopian human constantly introduces a tension into the utopia of books to the point of causing a reduction from the said to the saying, thereby suddenly giving rise to the utopian human or the utopia of the human. In Levinas's wake, we could do the same with the other Aristotelian proposition, that man is a political animal (*zoon politikon*), a being capable of constructing a *polis*, a self-sufficient community whose end is not to guarantee its members' survival but to allow them to lead a happy life. It is to recognize that politicalness, the faculty of establishing a *polis*—distinct from gregarious gatherings—contains the demand to live well (*eu zen*) and, at the same time, the search for a form of political community that can guarantee living well, another possible name of utopia. This search for the "true city," as well as reflecting the Aristotelian critique of Plato's *Republic*, implies resisting the "rage for the One" and respecting the specificity of this political community. "A city, by its nature, is some sort of plurality. If it becomes more of a unit, it will first become a household instead of a city, and then an individual instead of a household."[4] Following Levinas's example, it is legitimate to proceed to a new extension of this other Aristotelian affirmation and to make, subject to certain conditions, a passage from man the political animal to man the utopian animal.

Another path would consist in taking up Ernst Cassirer's analyses in the *Essay on Man*. According to this text, man would have discovered a new way of adapting to his environment. In the human world an intermediate stage would be established between a stimulus and the action that responds to it. Unlike animals, the human response to an external stimulus is never direct and immediate, since it is always the object of a *detour*, so that the human reply is differentiated, which is to say indirect or mediated. It is in this sense that Cassirer claims that man lives in a new dimension of reality, the symbolic dimension made up by language, myth, art, and religion. This detour, established like a supplementary dimension in relation to reality, counts just as much from a theoretical point of view as from a practical one insofar as human action occurs within imaginary emotions, fears and hopes, illusions and disillusions, fantasies and dreams. Moreover, without ever falling into irrationalism, Cassirer proposes enlarging reason by replacing the *rational animal* with the *symbolic animal*, or rather superimposing expressions of the former with those of the latter in such a way that these distinct figures, far from being opposed, would be in a relation of exchange and reciprocity.

Now, is not utopia, which maintains complex relations with myth, one of the obvious figures of the symbolic dimension? The question is all the more legitimate insofar as utopia, since it was conceived by Thomas More, is constituted through a detour in relation to historicity and its levels of possibility, through a differentiated action in relation to the social-historical. If we agree to see in *Utopia* a rhetorical invention that, grappling with an existing order, abandons frontal attacks and to the contrary practices an "indirect approach" (*ductus obliquus*) to better overcome the poles of opposition, we will easily recognize in this slanted approach, this obliqueness that runs through the detour and the deferred approach, a clear expression of the symbolic field.[5] And is the effect of highlighting the symbolic dimension not to reveal social-historical man as a utopian animal, allowing us to make out one of the faces of the *animal symbolicum*?

Let us return to the utopian conversion. Why have we chosen the term conversion? Whether it has to do with philosophy or utopia, it has the merit of drawing attention to a movement (with respect to utopia it occurs to me to speak of a displacement), a dynamic process—in the case of utopia, the movement by which man or the collective turns away from the existing order so as to turn towards a new world, "the imaginative expression of a new world," in Marx's words when he expressed his admiration for Charles Fourier and Robert Owen. Now, this movement, this displacement from one pole to another, from *topos* to utopia to take up Gustav Landauer's hypothesis in *Revolution*, immediately brings about a turn that is expressed by a disaffection from the existing order and the appearance of a new investment in the different community to come, a disaffection for order immediately followed by investment in a new form of bond among men, the human bond. One has only to read Fourier and the "Preliminary Discourse" of the *Theory of the Four Movements and of the General Destinies* to grasp the conversion's tempo. It takes place in two tightly linked stages: first, a philosophical movement takes up Cartesian doubt, "partial doubt," and radically extends it to the point of giving rise to an *absolute Doubt* applied to Civilization, its necessity, its excellence, and its permanence. "I decided to apply doubt to all opinions without exception, even regarding with suspicion arrangements which had universal agreement." Then there is the properly utopian moment, which unfolds in the form of a movement of *Absolute Distance* [*Écart Absolu*]. "My assumption was that the surest way of arriving at useful discoveries was to stand aloof in all ways from the paths followed by the inexact sciences, none of which has made any discovery remotely useful to the social body."[6] Whence comes a change of terrain and a resounding break with the philosophers that consists in replacing the question of industrial and domestic measures with the ultraclassical one of throne and alter. To follow the meditation of Pierre Leroux, who ceaselessly interrogated the specificity of utopia, beyond this turn from disaffection to new investment the utopian or "dreamer" turns into the *homo novus* who, in the grip of an unprecedented Revelation, breaking with all inventoried theories and practices, undergoes an uncoupling, or, better, a true takeoff.

The idea of utopian conversion also appears to be in a better position than any other to answer the question, How does man become a utopian animal? How is "the utopian human" born, how does it arise? Can we content ourselves with Levinas's answer, even if we salute its anti-Hegelian boldness? "In the presence of certain acts of resistance and martyrdom dared in our world in the name of the pure human—the utopian human—against the efficacy of power, this ethics affirms its objective status, its display of *Wirklichkeit*, effective reality, no longer lets itself be pushed back among the powerlessness of 'beautiful souls' or 'unhappy consciousness.'"[7] Is the birth of the utopian animal limited to acts of resistance and martyrdom? If we pose the question of how, are we not rather led to explore a complex constellation of gestures, attitudes, and philosophical elaborations that goes well beyond resistance and martyrdom in that it constitutes itself, upon close examination and even within distinct problematics, under the sign of awakening.

It would seem that in a first step, despite Fourier's attacks on the corporation of philosophers, philosophy and utopia go hand in hand. Do Saint-Simon and Fichte not both proclaim, against Rousseau, that the golden age is not behind but ahead of us? Fourier, when he invites us to practice absolute Doubt and Distance, invites us to denounce a target of the Enlightenment: the magma of prejudices that make up settled opinions represent the danger par excellence. Fichte and Fourier meet when the one deems it necessary to apply Cartesian doubt to the political field, to the whole of moral and political ideas, while the other demands that we extend Descartes's doubt to Civilization so as to be suspicious of its legitimacy. Does not philosophy, namely, that of Fichte, make explicit a party of movement that provokes a utopian separation and thus the possibility of conversion? Taking up the idea that we were children before being men, Fichte calls on us to question our daily life and all the presuppositions on which it is based, unbeknownst to us, without any critical examination:

> Based on the reputation of our fathers or teachers, we accept without evidence principles as basic principles, which are not. . . . We step into the world and find our basic principles in all human beings with whom we become acquainted, because they, too, accepted the same [basic principles] based on their parents' or teachers' reputation. . . . Our faith in the reputation of our teachers is complimented by the faith in the general consensus. . . . This is the origin of the general opinion-systems of peoples, the results of which are commonly passed off as expressions of common sense.[8]

Whence comes the call for criticism and to reject what is taken for historical wisdom. This wisdom, this supposed wisdom claimed by the enemies of the French Revolution, Burke, Rehberg, claims to be founded on past experience. For the latter, "history is the lighthouse of all tides and times," "the master teacher of peoples, the unerring herald of the future."[9] Fichte immediately explains that this privilege granted to history has the disastrous consequence of reducing the future to the past and the possible to the real. What is implicit in this thinking of history mobilized to deny the difference of the future is that everything should remain as it currently is. This is why the question of right, of what should be, of what could be otherwise, never emerges from the tribunal of history. Against this privilege of history and also of experience, the philosopher sets about revealing and promotes an "originary form" that is nothing other than freedom. With freedom thus established and a philosophy of freedom being constructed, two strictly opposed orientations are revealed. On the side of historical wisdom and its partisans, it is important to valorize the imitation and reproduction of what was and what is. On the side of the philosophy of freedom resounds the invitation to create what should be otherwise. It is here that Fichte is close to Saint-Just when the latter declares that now, according to the creative dynamic of the Revolution, heroism—the heroism of freedom—has absolutely no models. This crisis of imitation will lead to a theory of genius that, like the hero, will repudiate the models of the past all the more as he claims to create one for the future. This conflict between imitation and creation, far from being limited to historical or aesthetic stakes, assumes a political and, even more, an existential dimension:

> The radical conflict Fichte detects at the root of existence is reflected especially in the opposition of creation and imitation: the choice of subjectivity for freedom that is accomplished in the creation of the self and in the idealism based on the autonomy of the I is opposed to the choice of heteronomy, of servitude to the not-I and the reduction of subjective freedom to the power of reflecting things.[10]

From this choice between freedom and servitude follows an alternative that is decisive for the utopian conversion: man will be either hope or memory. Only a free subjectivity will be up to conceiving a "principle of hope" that can prompt a utopian conversion. No sooner is the traditional objection to the divorce between theory and practice raised than the philosopher interpreting the French Revolution shows that the objection collapses as men abandon the proposition that "everything must remain as it currently is."

How can we account for the extraordinary utopian flowering of the nineteenth century if not by recalling the "miraculous" character of the French Revolution, which gave free rein to what could be otherwise to overturn the borders of the possible and the impossible? Let us listen to Edgar Quinet: "The tremor the Revolution gave the earth, and so many extraordinary things were seen . . . that no social miracle seemed impossible. . . . What was obvious to all was that the French Revolution brought faith in the impossible back to the earth." At the same time a new destiny was opened to utopia, its status having been transformed. "What was once called a trick, utopia, was now called theory."[11] A new relationship was thus invented between theory and praxis.

Infinitely more fearsome than parents and masters, even if through their "wisdom" they are part of it and reinforce it, is a quasi-absolute master, one that seems (wrongly) to share with death inevitability. The existing order, or rather the established order, that in its illusory objectivity seems like the reign of things, is this master of a crushing force that imposes itself on us with the power of what is as it is, and not otherwise. There is no doubt that this grip, at once ordinary and permanent, makes subjectivities more inclined to acceptance and servitude than to revolt and the passion for freedom. No doubt that behind this "establishment" is hidden a subterranean history, that of the domestication of the body, "the fate of the human instincts and passions repressed and distorted by civilization."[12] Did not Nietzsche in *The Genealogy of Morality* unveil the role of terror and barbarism in the genesis of civilization, so that "with the aid of the morality of mores and the social straitjacket, man was actually *made* calculable"?[13] Is it not here that the provenance of these repeated appeals to realism, to realistic politics, a kind of hypnotizing *idée fixe* that always ushers in what is called a return to normal? This grip with an indiscernible face comes with what could be called a practical, even "ontological" dogmatism that pervades our days and nights, surrounds our daily life, enclosing it within bounds that appear impassable, an escaping that seems inconceivable. Caught in this established order or establishment by bounds that are all the more invisible for being confused with being itself, the idea of leaving it appears unthinkable, if not by acts immediately accused of "madness" or "crime." To try to measure this incommensurable force that is more serious and destructive than the dogmatism of orthodoxy because it is more deeply rooted, we must return to the Greek etymology of "dogma." *Dogma* signifies first and essentially what appears good, what is appropriate and thus what goes without saying, so much without saying that it escapes all interrogation, all questioning, examination, *a fortiori* all critique, since order as it is settles, is situated, is produced and reproduced below all problematicity—what Levinas calls "the resting-within-itself of the Real which refers to itself in identification."[14] The problem, if it is a problem, is that this order does not constitute a problem. Within this order, one is not afraid to invoke freedom; it is obviously only conceivable within the bounds of this order and signaling towards an exterior. But what is an experience of freedom that accepts being deployed only within preestablished bounds?

Now, does not pointing to this cold dogmatism of the established order that is as it is and not otherwise at the same time indicate on what the utopian conversion must work? Let us take up Gustav Landauer's terms in *Revolution* in order to better explicate them. The utopian conversion turns away from a *topos*, from an establishment with all that connotes, a determinate conjunction of space and time, in order to turn towards *utopia*, a place of nowhere and a time of no time, indeterminate. It is as if the movement of this *metanoia* managed to disentangle itself from the attachment to a given established order, an establishment, and invest not in a new order, but, thanks to the *suspension of time and space*—an epoch of rest, according to William Morris, humanity's vacation—attempt the open experimentation of a new being-in-the-world and a new being-together in a world that, far from fearing separations, passages, or leaps into the beyond, inaugurates a "new disorder," a "fraternal disorder," to take up the lovely expression of the insurgents of the Year III, that allows inventions, dreams, and fantasies to flower until the heroic spawning of a *vita nuova*. Let us listen to Michelet, who finds in the 1790 Fête de la Fédération all the traits of a utopian conversion in revolutionary times, like a marriage of utopia and revolution: "Time and space, the two material conditions to which life is subject, perished. A strange *vita nuova*, eminently spiritual, was beginning for France, making her whole Revolution a sort of dream, at one time delightful, at another terrible. It knew neither time nor space."[15] *Brevitatis causa* we cannot revisit Marc Richir's acute phenomenological reading of Michelet's description. Let us retain from this analysis only this possible moment of utopian conversion, contemporary with the revolutionary event, the collapse of the symbolic landmarks that had been constitutive elements of the established order of the Ancien Régime. "All the symbolic landmarks that *symbolically instituted* the country as a network of places, positions, and social roles, all these landmarks faded or tottered; they were subject, after the upheaval, to a true phenomenological epoché. . . . They proved to be ineffective, coming from a past era, suspended by the passing abeyance of the festival."[16] In the suspension of the revolutionary festival, the parenthesis of a centuries-old order of domination, a new experience of humanity was born. Whereas under the Ancien Régime men, taken according to the differences of a society of orders, met and measured each other first of all as superiors and inferiors, in the space-time instituted by the Revolution, a society of citizens, like learned to recognize like. Where there had been order appeared the bond, "the bond of the human species," according to Michelet. Let us rather say, the human bond.

∽

Utopia's weapons are diverse: obviously, the revolution that, in its tumults and its opening, suddenly reactivates the dreams of the collective that people the sleep of the dominated and exploited; equally, the practices of small groups—the laboratories of utopia, according to Ronald Creagh[17]—that, within diversely organized communities, work to revive the social bond behind the State's back, replacing relations of domination with reciprocal connections. We can also note practices that are at once material and symbolic like clothing, for instance, the famous Saint-Simonian vest that buttons at the back, requiring each day the assistance of the other and so reminding those tempted to forget human solidarity. As for the utopia of books, that written in books, it has at its disposal an arsenal of means that are distributed differently according to the text: obliqueness in Thomas More or the *ductus obliquus*; carnivalesque inversion, with the large in the place of the small and the small in the place of the large; satirical depreciation, with gold used for bedpans and everything unclean; laughter in Fourier, so that the corporation of philosophers who take everything literally understand nothing of their utopian speculations; "romance," or utopia written in a romantic mode in William Morris.

It is much more important to inquire into the *how* of the utopian conversion, to try to determine the method or rather the forms by which this conversion can take place, the double movement of detaching from a given order, an establishment, the search for a new being-in-the-world immediately through the arrival in a new world. What are the paths of this conversion? How can we account for this metamorphosis, this near "alchemy," this complex movement that each time aims to leave a "dogmatic slumber" and finally to experience awakening? For my part, I distinguish between two such paths: the phenomenological epoché and the dialectical image by means of which Walter Benjamin thought utopia.

Let us pause a moment on Levinas's essential formula as it suddenly uncovers a passage or, better, a rapprochement between the phenomenological epoché and utopia. In effect, Levinas asks, "Does not the visible face of this *ontological interruption*—of this *epoché*—coincide with the movement 'for a better society'?"[18] Make no mistake, the relation posited between the epoché and utopia is not one-way. Let us understand that if, on the one hand, utopia makes the ontological interruption perceptible and manifest, on the other hand and conversely, the phenomenological epoché allows the internal movement of utopia—in short, the utopian conversion—to be understood. In other words, if we understand that the *visible* face of the ontological interruption, the epoché, is the movement for a better society, utopia, can we then not argue that the *intelligible* face of the movement for a better society, utopia, is the ontological interruption, the epoché?

On the one hand, when we go from the epoché to utopia, we uncover how the epoché manifests itself, how it appears; on the other hand, when we go from utopia to the epoché, we perceive how utopia functions as the *how* of the utopian conversion. In one case, we have the ontological interruption, the interruption of being that tends to persevere in its being, the *conatus*, but also the ontological interruption of an established order that seems to be confused with being itself, makes possible an exit from being, an escape, an otherwise than being, and at the same time disinterestedness and the advent of the for-the-other, responsibility for the other, of what according to Levinas animates and feeds the *vis utopica*. In the other case, through the confrontation with the epoché, we come to understand directly how utopia is set in motion and set to work, in a sense its principle. Utopia runs or can run on the epoché: it is by the interruption or suspension it carries out and that constitutes it that it can transcend what seems to go without saying but does not go without saying, that it can rise above the so-called real and master it, to the point of letting what is different occur. In truth, can we conceive of a utopia without an epoché?

Is something like the phenomenological epoché not at the heart of the utopian conversion, or, more exactly, in order to reach it, is it not necessary to practice something like the epoché? Is it not legitimate to see in the utopian conversion and its bracketing of the established order a gesture close to that of phenomenology suspending the "thesis of the world"? Are we then not justified up to a certain point in describing the utopian conversion in terms of the epoché, if not to speak of a utopian epoché? Indeed, insofar as the utopian conversion proceeds to a suspension of the established order as it is, even a suspension of time and space, it approximates the phenomenological epoché, as if utopia, despite its specificity, in its turn invented a form of reduction that would be its own. It is therefore hardly surprising that this suspension of the established order engenders comparable effects, up to a certain point, to those of the phenomenological reduction as described by Levinas in a very beautiful text, "Philosophy and

Wakefulness." Here he highlights the radicality of the Husserlian gesture. It has to do, according to him, with providing a response to the degeneration of meaning, the petrification of knowledge with respect to living thought. And Levinas insists on the revolutionary character of the reduction by having recourse, not without intent, to a political vocabulary. In its radicality, does not Husserl's gesture, like that of the revolutionaries, aim to give life to silenced voices, suppressed by the world's knowledge?

> This is the revolution of the Phenomenological Reduction, a permanent revolution. The Reduction will reanimate or reactivate that life, forgotten or become anemic in knowledge. . . . Beneath the resting-within-itself of the Real which refers to itself in identification, beneath its presence, the Reduction raises up a life against which thematized being, in its sufficiency, has already kicked, and which it has repressed by its appearing. Drowsy intentions awakened to life will reopen vanished horizons, ever new, disturbing the theme in its identity *qua* result, awakening subjectivity from the identity in which it rests in its experience.[19]

Is not the aim of the utopian reduction, among others, to reactivate the dreams of the vanquished, to give life to the utopian drives that led them to revolt? Is its object not to revive in its turn the demand for equality that traverses the centuries and to reject the intolerable division between "master and slave"? Against historical wisdom, the petrified knowledge of nations that claims to rule humanity and keep it in its place, does not the utopian epoché also work to "awaken dulled intentions," to "reopen lost horizons" against the impossible horizons the dominant classes constantly point to in order to better disarm the dominated. This conversion, part of the heroism of the human spirit, does it not seek to awaken subjectivities that have so incorporated and internalized the constitutive elements and constraints of the established order that, if they manage to conceive utopian dreams, immediately suppress them in the name of the supposed ineluctability of the human order? When the reduction becomes intersubjective, it is not content to deny or reject; it can reveal a barely glimpsed set of human relations, as if sidelining Hobbes's "odious hypothesis"—the war of all against all—encrusted within the wisdom of nations made way for the appearance of another figure of the human, opposed to the world's self-evidences. What is more, the reduction must perform a leap in the permanent revolution, open itself to a new modality of awakening, in short, to conceive within the break with the philosophical tradition a thought that would not be knowledge, but that would be other than knowledge. Now, as much as we wrest utopia from understanding and return it to the I-Thou relation, on the side of meeting, born of proximity, of the fact of the neighbor, does it not meet the intersubjective reduction to the point of merging with it, inasmuch as it undergoes an analogous movement as well as the renunciation of the primacy of the I and its hegemonic will. Born of proximity, utopia, far from being an intentional project, is a nonintentional test of the for-the-other, a test that is redoubled since utopia as the future of utopia is dedicated to the other. "The very relationship with the other is the relationship with the future."[20] Levinas warns that the nothingness of utopia is not the nothingness of death. While the latter, beyond annihilation, is the impossibility of having a project, the impossibility of possibility, the nothingness of utopia, the hope of realizing what is not yet, manifests its negation in the form of a bracketing of interest, a game of *conatus essendi* and the excessive activity that comes out of it. In order to achieve the possibility of other possibilities, of uncovering a becoming-otherwise, the nonidentical or the completely other social. Thinking otherwise than knowledge, utopia, tested in the context of a philosophy of escape, will accede to a radical practice of the epoché. It will no longer be a matter of leaving the being that has become, but of leaving being qua being towards an otherwise than being. Under the sign of disinterestedness, utopia is the work of the subjectivity of a subject that does not amount to a tension over itself, or to the concern for being—a subjectivity that is like a dedication to a world to come."[21]

We could thus wish that this description of the epoché opens a path to the intelligibility of the utopian conversion and, beyond this, through the transformation of subjectivity, interrogates the birth of man as a utopian animal. We see that utopia thought under the sign of the phenomenological epoché aims to wrest us from dogmatic slumber in its different forms and especially to wrest us from the dogmatic slumber of the established order that is as it is. It also matters to it, thanks to the suspension of the course of things, to provoke an awakening, the awakening of another figure of subjectivity unburdened of everything that, under the hold of the established order, it has incorporated and internalized. Thus Levinas speaks of the awakening of sleeping significations that can open unknown horizons and let the pure or "utopian human" appear. Far from being limited to mere intentions, in his work he takes on Hobbes, the anti-utopian thinker par excellence, going so far as to conceive a veritable *Counter-Hobbes*, a counter-model to the *Leviathan*. To the war of all against all he opposes another hypothesis, that of proximity and its precedence. Rather than affirm peace or sociability, he radically shifts the terrain by asking the question, What, within the economy of being, does the domain of interhuman relations, so little known and little explored, signify? More precisely, does not the relation to the other person signify an interruption of the game of being or perseverance in being, *conatus*? Levinas also replaces the self-evidences of common sense, often close to the petrified bourgeois knowledge of Hobbes, the thinker of possessive individualism, the revelation of a more ancient, originary, anarchic intrigue, that of the proximity that the philosopher reaches when practicing the phenomenological reduction. This gesture allows unknown landscapes to arise, awakens significations hidden by the world's knowledge to the point of coming up with an extravagant hypothesis when it comes to the State according to which the latter would not be born of a limitation of violence, but a limitation of the infinity of the for-the-other.

Let us now turn towards another thought, that of Walter Benjamin, who likewise associates utopia with awakening, all the while thinking the trajectory the exit from sleep, or from the dream, would have to take. Without taking up here Benjamin's general problematic, let us try, in order to prepare the confrontation with the epoché, to take ourselves to the point of its completion that is the dialectical image interwoven with the question of awakening. Thought under the sign of brilliance, the dialectical image is the energy that suddenly polarizes the field of the dream, wresting the dreamer from sleep and launching towards awakening. "The sentry of dreams," to take up Victor Hugo's expression, has to be able to hold the two ends of the chain, the image and the awakening, together. The dialectical image has the value of an interpretation and does not simply reproduce the dream. This interpretive construction is not foreign, with Benjamin, to a materialist inspiration: in fact, he conceives a genetic relation between the conditions of life and their expression. In Benjamin's eyes, utopia is "a precipitate of the dreams of the collective." Thus, "the collective, from the first, expresses the conditions of its life. These find their expression in the dream and their interpretation in the awakening."²² Again, to fully grasp how Benjamin understands the dialectical image, it will be necessary to retrace the essential steps of his path.

One part of Benjamin's originality comes from his having practiced a utopian conversion, a conversion to utopia of enormous scope. He is all the more carried to take utopias seriously because he judges that, in order to take stock of an epoch, one must pay the closest attention "to the dream consciousness of the collective," to its dreams as embodied in the *Passagenwerk* or in utopias. He is also determined to explore the hitherto neglected, even ignored, zones of history; his utopian conversion is also without precedent. "It is not only that the forms of appearance taken by the dream collective in the nineteenth century cannot be thought away; and not only that these forms characterize this collective much more decisively than any other—they are also, rightly interpreted, of the highest practical import."[23] But if Benjamin's gaze turned towards utopias, "the dreams of the collective," and beyond that to the dreamlike expressions of the nineteenth century, he was not captivated by them. This is why he recommends advancing into this virgin forest "with the whetted axe of reason" in order to clear the expressions of the dream of "the undergrowth of delusion and myth."[24] This clearing is of the highest practical importance, Benjamin judges, because it is about emancipation. Understand that his crossing of the nineteenth century pursues an obviously critical end. He treats the nineteenth century as "the dream we must wake up from; it is a nightmare that will weigh on the present as long as its spell remains unbroken."[25] It is essential to ward off the hexes that are so many obstacles to a new dawn of freedom. "We have to wake up from the existence of our parents."[26] In truth, Benjamin's aim is more cathartic-redemptive than merely critical, or rather the criticism is subordinated to a cathartic work that seeks not to reject utopias in the name of a supposedly higher authority, for instance, science, but to rescue them. How to do this in order to save utopias and satisfy their profoundly emancipatory impetus? Now this redemption of utopias passes precisely through a transformation of utopia or the dream-image into a dialectical image. If we believe Pierre Klossowski, at the end of his life Benjamin would have invented an esoteric doctrine, a sort of mashup of Fourier and Marx, as if it were a matter of duly noting Marx's "critical communism" without losing anything of Fourier's *vis utopica*—a plural conversion to utopia, then, which should not be surprising since in his youth Benjamin, like many writers of his generation, had prized Ernst Bloch's *Spirit of Utopia* to the point of devoting a review to it, unfortunately lost.

Another part of Benjamin's originality came from the double movement that defines his approach as a sentry of dreams: first of all, the boldness that consists, in spite of the criticisms of Marxism and positivism, of looking to the collective dreams of the nineteenth century at the same time as calling no less boldly to resist the harmful fascination that these dreams are still capable of exerting over us. It follows in Benjamin's case that the conversion to utopia would not suffice; it must undergo a complication, *and this in the interest of utopia*, inasmuch as the exercise of suspicion, owing to the ambiguity that inhabits utopia, must result in its redemption in the form of a metamorphosis of the utopian image into a dialectical image in the form of an awakening. How should we understand the ambiguity of utopias? It is multiple. Many utopias fall into the grip of the phantasmagorias of the nineteenth century, which, as illusions, effect a transformation followed by an effect of distraction in the Pascalian sense. Worse still, Benjamin notes a process of exchange between phantasmagoria and utopias so that phantasmagorias express a utopian tonality while conversely the utopias take on phantasmagorical characteristics. On this point, we can consider more closely the utopias of the arcades that exert a baleful, even deadly charm over the inhabitants of the modern metropolis, a charm born of the somnolence of nineteenth-century capitalism. But the expression and growth of ambiguity depends above all on the entanglement within the dream of the utopian and the mythic image, as if these two images pulled in opposite directions, according to opposite orientations. One, the mythic image, reactivates the dream of the origin, "the persistence of fate in the historical world."[27] The other, the utopian image, takes flight, or tries to, towards a becoming-other that would break with the world of myth. Following Benjamin's emancipatory critique, it would seem that there are dream-images in which, owing to myth, "death seizes life," in which fate or the violence of the gods returns. This is why myth, as a reactivation of originary powers, the return of the archaic, blocks utopia's awakening force, paralyzing and destroying it by spreading a new sleep. For those who want to restore utopia's power of wakefulness, it follows that they must neutralize the mythic image, reduce its enchanting power to zero. In his first notes, Benjamin, determined to struggle against myth and its enchantment, split from the surrealists, who in his view remained in the realm of the dream. To the contrary, for him we must dissolve "'mythology' into the space of history." Against the author of *Paris Peasant*, he declares: "whereas Aragon persists within the realm of dream, here the concern is to find the constellation of awakening."[28]

One will not be surprised that Benjamin has emphasized the ambiguity of utopia to the extent that in the "Exposé of 1935" he proposes an original theory of utopia according to which the latter would always include two indissociable strata: one historical that would correspond to a critique but also a transfiguration of the latest mode of production, the other ahistorical, beneath history. It is to recognize first of all that utopia is a mixed, composite, dreamlike expression whose very dynamic rests on the co-penetration of the Ancient and the New, all the more complex in that the Ancient is split between a recent Ancient and a distant Ancient. Utopia can thus only be ambiguous; better, only ambiguity can be its element. How could utopia not be ambiguous when in his theory of two strata Benjamin presents it as necessarily composed of different, even strictly contradictory elements. This situation or penchant for ambiguity can only be exacerbated when we consider the second stratum, which returns to prehistory. Rather than accept Michelet's progressive schema—each epoch dreams the next—Benjamin shows that the distance taken with respect to the latest mode of production can only be achieved if the plastic imagination orients itself towards the most ancient past, as if evoking the most ancient would allow it to separate, to take its leave of the most recent. "In the dream," he writes, "in which each epoch entertains images of its successor, the latter appears wedded to elements of primal history (*Urgeschichte*)—*that is*, to elements of a classless society."[29] Following Benjamin, it would be very exactly the co-penetration of the New and experiences related to a classless society, "stored in the unconscious of the collective," that would give birth to utopia, underlining once again the composite character of utopia insofar as it would include both images that come from the most distant past and images that want to belong to the New. For example, according to Benjamin the Fourierist utopia would hold its historical sphere of appearance of machines on the basis on which it imagined a true machinery of passions and its ahistorical sphere of the Land of Cockaigne, "the primeval wish symbol that Fourier's utopia has filled with new life."[30] Yet this insistence on Benjamin's part—that whether it is in the form of the Land of Cockaigne or of a rediscovered classless society on the basis of a reading of Bachofen, it leads to a major ambiguity, that of the Golden Age—became the object of a controversy with Adorno over the course of the summer of 1935. Without returning here to the controversy, let us recall that Adorno continually reminded Benjamin that the Golden Age—the Land of Cockaigne or classless society—would be ambiguity par excellence because it would be at once Arcadia and Hell, a mixture of dream images and mythic-archaic images. According to Adorno, Benjamin would have uncritically accepted the category of the Golden Age and, by his dualist hypothesis of the strata of utopia, opened the door to a mythic image to which he remained, in spite of himself, a prisoner. In short, Benjamin, for want of having denounced the transfiguration of the Golden Age, its ambiguity, allowed himself to fall back into a massively mythic thought.

We can see that Adorno's criticism is especially severe—all the more severe because, failing to take into account Benjamin's work of interpretation, it is unjust and unfounded. Beyond the fact that Benjamin did not need Adorno to remind him of the double nature of the Golden Age, he was in no way unaware that the co-penetration of the Ancient and the New can produce fantastic, bewitching forms. Adorno is still less justified in his accusation since Benjamin, far from giving in to a crude realism, carefully holds back from taking up the symbol of a Golden Age as such. How did Adorno fail to see that Benjamin rejects the progressive vision of Michelet and conceives the wish-images of the nineteenth century as already in ruins. It no longer has to do with the residue of a dreamworld. This is why the dream he follows within the sleep induced by capitalism is the presence of a universe at once attractive and repellant, an infernal bric-a-brac made of bits and fragments from which subjects must free themselves if they want finally to be able to awaken. Adorno is thus mistaken about Benjamin's work: the latter has not taken the category of the Golden Age as the comforting guarantee of access to a harmonious age in the near future; in a climate of unrest sparked by looming catastrophe he submits the dream material, the dream images of the nineteenth century, to a work of interpretation and construction. According to an image that was dear to Benjamin, the subject of the dream must "stretch a bow between sleep and wakefulness." How could Adorno have ignored the correction Benjamin makes to Michelet's formula when he writes towards the end of the Exposé of 1935: "Every epoch, in fact, not only dreams the one to follow but, in dreaming, precipitates its awakening." How could Adorno not have seen that Benjamin holds himself on the threshold of the dialectical image when he declares in the same Exposé: "The realization of dream elements, in the course of waking up, is the paradigm of dialectical thinking. Thus, dialectical thinking is the organ of historical awakening."[31]

There are numerous passages in *The Arcades Project* in which Benjamin, a painter in search of his subject, discovers a dialectical image and accentuates it the better to bring out its features. In any case, when Benjamin develops the notion of the dialectical image, he presents and conceives it above all as a technique of historical awakening. In doing so he makes an essential contribution to the question before us, that of utopia and awakening. But how shall we describe Benjamin's movement? Shall we be satisfied with the relation already given between dialectical thinking and awakening? Does this reply not pose more questions than it answers? Indeed, is it sufficient to define the dialectical image to see in it the authority that manages suddenly to disentangle the mythic-archaic image from the dream image? A correct but formal definition, it cannot account for the complex functioning of the dialectical image and fails to answer the question of how. What dialectical thinking is involved? How does it manage to pull us out of sleep? The Benjaminian notion of the dialectical image does not fail to astonish. Does not an image as such defy contradiction and consequently escape the dialectic, to which it is fundamentally foreign? In truth, this first objection is quickly surpassed, for, as Benjamin repeats on several occasions, in the field of images the dialectic is described under the sign of ambiguity. In the "Exposé of 1935," he goes further when he states: "Ambiguity is the manifest imaging of dialectic, the law of dialectics at a standstill."[32] Let us take three orientations from this essential passage: first, the relation between ambiguity and the dialectic in the sphere of the image, as if ambiguity were the manifestation of possible contradictions; next, the determination of a specific form of dialectical thinking, the dialectic at a standstill; finally, the reversal of ambiguity. Indeed, as soon as we turn to the dialectical image, the status of ambiguity appears to change. The appearance of utopia in the form of the entwinement of the dream image and the mythic image, the Land of Cockaigne or the Golden Age, apt to fetter utopia's emancipatory force, remains a confession of utopia's weakness. In this context, ambiguity is suddenly revealed as the path that will allow utopia to shake off myth insofar as it opens the way to the dialectic and thus to awakening. The dialectical image is thus an image that is at first ambiguous and that at the moment of the standstill abruptly becomes dialectical, giving free rein to the contradictions and at the time freeing the *vis utopica* proper to the dream image. What is more, ambiguity introduces a new figure of the dialectic, dialectic at a stillstand, that is more complex than that we classically associate with the dialectic. If we follow Benjamin, the dialectic is not only the deployment of internal contradictions of a set of phenomena and thus movement; it can also be immobilization, a standstill, the meeting of a nonidentical, nonintegrable phenomenon with a movement of totalization, for example, suffering would interrupt the play of contradictions as well as the sublation destined to overcome them. This immobilization of the dialectic is one of the birthplaces and one of the definitions of the dialectical image in Benjamin's corpus. "Where thinking comes to a standstill in a constellation saturated with tensions—there the dialectical image appears."[33]

To this new figure of dialectician thus returns the task of constructing the dialectical image, which is to say the place where the tension between contradictions is the most intense—a standstill on the image, we could say. At a standstill, indeed, ambiguity is crystalized, creating a place where the contradictions explode, freeing the emancipatory, even revolutionary virtuality of the image. Moreover, the construction of a constellation saturated with tensions by immobilization is not a contemplative suspension but a practical cessation and thus a wrenching out of history, out of the continuum of domination—in short, a rescue. So it is with Fourier's utopia and its composite character. On the one hand, it suffers on one side from Modern Style; on the other, it manifests a playful dimension, presenting a play space that relates to what Benjamin calls a second technology that envisages a relation of nondomination with nature. Benjamin's gesture provokes the metamorphosis of the dream image into a dialectical image. At the moment of danger, facing the returning catastrophe, it is essential to seize Fourier's utopia, to make it explode the better to dissolve its ambiguity and liberate its redemptive force and truth content.

Let us return to the immobilization of the dialectic and its two faces. "This standstill is utopia," Benjamin declares. Let us understand that this cessation of the dialectic, for as much as it is a tearing away, a rescue, is utopia in the sense of an upsurge of what is different, the advent of a radical alterity, as if this immobilization of the dialectic abruptly gives free rein to escape, to exit, the nonplace of utopia suddenly expanding the possibility of another place. Conversely, utopia is cessation, which means that utopia, instead of designating the projection of a better world towards the future, is first of all formed in a cessation *hic et nunc*, an immobilization such that contradictions explode and at the same time the imperative of rescue appears. There is at least one great utopia, William Morris's *News from Nowhere*, that integrates this suspension of time into its constitution. Was its subtitle not, as we have seen, *An Epoch of Rest*? This suspension of the historical continuum, "the faculty to hold oneself for a time *outside history*" (Nietzsche), is the soil out of which utopia blossoms, informed that there can be no happiness, large or small, without the possibility of forgetting, a forgetting that is not reification.

More essential still is that this immobilization of the dialectic gives rise to constructions in several senses, but that all share an orientation towards awakening. First of all, it is an interpretive construction that refutes Adorno's criticism of Benjamin for "locating the dialectical image in consciousness as 'dream,'"[34] as if the dialectical image were the double of the dream and only of the dream. Such a criticism amounts quite simply to ignoring Benjamin's work of interpretation, which can be legitimately compared to psychoanalytical practice. In effect, for Benjamin, as for the analyst, it is not enough to record the dreams or unconscious manifestations of the patient; they must still be interpreted as symptoms in order eventually, thanks to this interpretation, to transform the neurotic structure and put an end to the phenomena of repetition. What else do the dialectical construction and the dialectical image it produces do? Should they not be taken as interpretation, and does not this interpretation in its turn produce "curative" effects, what Benjamin calls rousing oneself from slumber and awakening? When he constructs a dialectical image, for Benjamin it has nothing to do with presenting an image that would be the double or the copy of the dream, but, completely opposite to that, with elaborating a distantiated image that works to deconstruct the dream, to undo it, if not to break the dreamlike and mythic *nexus* and at the same time support historical awakening. Adorno tends to confuse Benjamin with Jung or Klages, who valorize mythic images, enchantment, and abandoning oneself to sleep. And we can understand without difficulty Benjamin's barely contained anger when he wrote to Gretel Adorno: "The dialectical image does not replicate the dream—it was never my intention to make that claim."[35] This confusion of the dialectical image with the dream is all the less tolerable because, according to Benjamin, the image contains within itself the possibility of awakening, "the instances, the ingresses of waking consciousness," insofar as it only produces its figure on the basis of these places, as if the end it pursues, historical awakening, served as an irrefutable compass. From that, Benjamin's reaffirmation: "Here too, then, a connection still needs to be developed, a dialectic conquered: that between the image and awakening."[36]

The demand Benjamin formulates also shows how the immobilization of the dialectic, its suspension—the dialectic at a standstill—has the effect of immediately constructing a constellation saturated with tensions, a dialectical scene, better, of clearing the place where the contradictions prove to be more explosive. It is thanks to the ensuing conflagration—the dialectical image is a dazzling image, Benjamin promises—that the dialectical image frees the dream image from the enchantment in whose grip the mythico-archaic images often "squint" towards nothingness and death. We have already seen that it is precisely to immobilization that Benjamin relates the dialectical image and thus historical awakening:

> To thinking belongs the movement as well as the arrest of thoughts. Where thinking comes to a standstill in a constellation saturated with tensions—there the dialectical image appears. It is the caesura in the movement of thought. Its position is naturally not an arbitrary one. It is to be found, in a word, where the tension between dialectical opposites is greatest. Hence, the object constructed in the materialist presentation of history is itself the dialectical image. The latter is identical with the historical object; it justifies its violent expulsion from the continuum of historical process.[37]

The brilliance of the dialectical image, the rescue it effects, can even be compared to the Benjaminian image of the revolution. In it, we recognize the same moments and the same effects: "But in the final analysis, only the revolution creates an open space for the city. Fresh air doctrine of revolutions. Revolution disenchants the city."[38] The revolution as historical awakening.

The project Benjamin often reiterates in *The Arcades Project* is to develop "an experiment in the technique of awakening."[39] The task of the sentry of dreams is thus to become a technician of awakening, able to find or rather construct the constellation of waking. All the same, unlike the surrealists, the sentry of dreams stays awake in order to avoid becoming enchanted or fascinated by the allure of myths drawing inexorably towards nothingness while neither rejecting nor neglecting those forms of dream, the collective's dreamlike visions in which the relation to death can be overcome. This is to say that it is no longer sufficient for the sentry of dreams to reveal the false currency of nineteenth-century dreams; he must further take note of the collective's dreams, grant them a degree of reality, pay attention to them—better, in a sense, take care of them because under certain conditions they open a possible path to historical awakening. To Benjamin's mind, there is a close correlation between the dream and the awakening. Indeed, if the collective expresses its life conditions in the dream and produces the interpretation of it in waking, this means that dream and awakening are closely connected. The dream is the condition of possibility of awakening, since only its interpretation can give access to it. Here we measure the complex status of the dream. To be sure, a dream does not necessarily lead to an interpretation; it can sink into enchantment and be heavy with sleep. But if this is not the case, it can also turn towards waking up.

Sleeping without dreaming does not allow for an interpretation, it therefore cannot lead to an awakening. Benjamin explicitly gives the dream the chance to bring about awakening, perhaps by a ruse. "The dream," he writes, "waits secretly for the awakening; the sleeper surrenders himself to death only provisionally, waits for the second when he will cunningly wrest himself from its clutches. So, too, the dreaming collective, whose children provide the happy occasion for its own awakening."[40] Utopia, as a precipitate of the collective's dreams, can under certain conditions open the way to revolution. Thus, while Benjamin summons the dream technician to make a connection between sleep and waking up, this implies, among other missions, concentrating attention as, if necessary, his intervention of the dreamlike forms, the dream images, of the collective. Does not Benjamin, not without irony, conceive of a dream ruse? Does he not go so far as to give a dialectical image, which is also a dream image, the quality of being "the wooden horse of the Greeks in the Troy of dreams"?

Being assigned the mission of dream technician brings for the sentry of dreams a redefinition of his role. He is first of all invited to a cathartic-redemptive hermeneutic with respect to utopia: far from dispelling or dissolving utopia, instead, by the very laborious separation from mythico-archaic images, he strives finally to liberate their emancipatory virtualities by guaranteeing their rescue. Because he has to learn to build a connection between sleep and waking up, he likewise has to learn to consider dream images otherwise, that is, to give up the reassuring image of a dreamlike voyage towards the near future and replace it with the idea of a difficult labor with uncertain result, to manage to wrest himself from the state where, under seductive masks, death roams. The sentry of dreams must proceed to a *dramatization* of the situation, the bent bow referring to a brutal alternative, waking or nothingness. Moreover, the sentry of dreams becomes a dream technician to the extent that he makes himself into a dialectician, that he practices dialectical thinking, "the organ of historical awakening." This is to recognize that in his work as interpreter he must privilege the ambiguity that all the more easily acquires a philosophical significance, as ambiguity is the law of the dialectic at a standstill. He must give himself over to a veritable hunt for ambiguity: thus, concerning the two strata of utopia, he must replace the idea of complementarity with that of tension and thus, thanks to this interpretation to construct, as we have seen, constellations saturated with tension. He seeks to construct a dialectical image as the place where the tension between dialectical opposites is the strongest, the most intense. It is this explosive charge that the dialectical image contains, to which it owes its brilliance, that suddenly polarizes the field of the dream and tears the dreamer out of sleep and throws him towards awakening. The moment the dream's ambiguity is resolved, the explosion occurs that dissolves the mythico-archaic part that enchanted the collective. This is the double face of awakening: it rejects the share of myth that threatens utopia and at the same time liberates the dialectical image within utopia. Whence the proposition: dream figure + awakening = dialectical image. *Where the dream image was, there is now the dialectical image.* The dialectician becomes the sentry of dreams in several respects inasmuch as Benjamin comes to conceive of the dream differently. The dream, held between two opposing impulses, sleep and waking, in a moment is transformed into an agonistic scene. The image of the bow to be stretched between sleep and waking makes clear that on the field of the dream a veritable battle unfolds. The dream, far from being a peaceful haven that would guarantee, in Michelet's formula, a soft transition to the near future, must now be thought as a conflictual, agonistic moment and place where the collective is torn between the drive to sink into an even deeper sleep and the drive to rip itself out of this deadly sleep, to experience awakening. If it is true that the dream secretly awaits awakening, it is no less true that, from its first manifestations, it resists it. "The first tremors of awakening serve to deepen sleep," Benjamin warns.[41] Also, contrary to our oversimplified earlier proposal, the dialectical image is not only a dream image affected by waking, to which awakening would be added, but a dream image penetrated, warped by the struggle for awakening between adverse tendencies. It is akin to the psychoanalytic situation where the first signs of untying a pathological structure can immediately elicit increased resistance, as separation from the symptom at first proves to be painful.

Finally, last but not least, developing "an experiment in the technique of awakening" is the object of a true Copernican revolution when it comes to the thinking of history. If for the classical historian "what has been" would constitute the fixed point around which the present needed to be turned in order to gain the best possible knowledge of that "what has been," for the sentry of dreams-cum-dialectician this is no longer the case. Here the Copernican revolution signifies that the present now becomes the fixed point around which gravitates "what has been" until a "tiger's leap," to use Blanqui's expression, from the present seizes "what has been" and fixes it by dialectical immobilization by bringing out contradictions and simultaneously dissolving ambiguity. It is in the caesura that results from immobilization that, as we know, the dialectical image appears. It is indeed in this brutal rupture that the awakening is produced that wrests the collective from the hypnotic slumber that keeps it in the vicinity of death. This dialectic specific to recollection, focused on "what has been," appears in the tiger's leap, since, oriented towards emancipation, it watches for the small rift, the breach through which the fragile chances of freedom can be seized and the catastrophe of repetition escaped. This is the case with Benjamin's relation to Fourier, from whom he takes the idea of play to develop his esoteric doctrine under the sign of reconciliation with nature. It is a Copernican revolution again in that it does not have to do with a change of historical epistemology, but a passage, or better a turn, from history to politics. The historian is free to conceive his present relation to what has been as a stroll through the gardens of history, borne by a desire for knowledge, but the dialectician must abandon this contemplative point of view. For him the stakes are political; he must let be born from the thus immobilized present, from the urgency of a moment of danger, the utopian summation that will give the sentry of dreams a lynx's gaze so that he can surely make out in what has been the point of intervention where the shell breaks and opens the way to the future. "To approach, in this way, 'what has been' means to treat it not historiographically, as heretofore, but politically, in political categories."[42]

We have two answers to the question of how the utopian conversion works: either a conversion to utopia on the model of the phenomenological epoché to envisage the possibility of a utopian epoché, or a conversion to utopia in the form of the dialectical image, the latter coming from a transformation of the dream image. On first view, these two modalities of utopian conversion do not lack common, or apparently common, traits: bracketing, immobilization. Whether it is the epoché or the dialectical image, both know the suspension of a process or the immobilization of thought. For example, according to Marc Richir, the suspension of the revolutionary festival, which was not foreign to utopia, in its arrest of ordinary time, the time of daily life, can be compared to the phenomenological epoché to the extent that this arrest allows the manifestation of other phenomena than those authorized by everyday life. Is bracketing not cessation, the suspension of the natural approach of the world posed as an object and set apart from all systems of explanation (psychology, sociology) permitting, thanks to the setting aside of abstract constructions, the return to things themselves. It is in this sense that we can interpret the utopian conversion in terms of the epoché, utopia in its double movement of doubt and absolute separation proceeding to the bracketing of the world as it is, the suspension of the course of things and, at the same time, the suspension of the knowledge of the world in order to allow the appearance of what is different. Following Levinas's conception of the epoché, the return to things themselves need not be limited to knowledge: what matters to him is the intersubjective reduction, the ultimate stage of the epoché, allowing the advent of manifestations of life outside of knowledge and as such hidden and repressed. As we have seen, Levinas does not hesitate to highlight the revolutionary dimension of the Husserlian gesture: he throws a bridge between the phenomenological reduction and the permanent revolution. As if both had the constant task of awakening life from its thematization—the instituting against the instituted—of reanimating slumbering intentions, of awakening subjectivity trapped in its identity, of opening or reopening lost or unexpected horizons. As for the dialectical image related to utopia as dream image, it is, as we have insisted, the fruit of an immobilization of thinking required to construct constellations saturated with tensions. More precisely, it is fruit of the particular form of dialectical thinking that is the dialectic at a standstill—what will allow Benjamin to write the initially enigmatic sentence: "Standstill is utopia."

Beyond this the scenography appears similar. In both cases it is a question of a struggle between a particular form of sleep and awakening. Against a petrified knowledge, Levinas expects the epoché will be able to give life to silenced voices, to ascend to a psyche other than that of knowledge. This is why he makes it his aim to awaken complex slumbering intentions that can open lost horizons. But for Levinas the insistence on the intersubjective reduction gives rise to a specific modality of awakening, one born on the basis of the Other, on the basis of proximity, of the neighbor. This is a true upheaval and break from Husserl, for whom mind remains knowledge, since Levinas, such is his greatness, conceives the possibility of a thinking otherwise than knowledge, a non-gnoseological event. The relation with the other tears the I from its hegemonic will. It awakens subjectivity from "egology," from egoism and egotism. Meeting the face of the Other, an exceptional intrigue, a veritable trauma, awakens the I from its dogmatic slumber, from its sovereignty folded into itself and its satisfied quietude. The exit from sleep is introduced by wakefulness, not as a state but as vigilance, even more as insomnia. For the encounter with the Other, at the same time that it is a fission of the subject—"the derangement of the self by the Other"—is a continual sobering, without respite, so that the I can be exceeded. Although it is a question of the same antithetical couple for Benjamin, sleep/awakening, we are far from Levinas, if not from a formal point of view. Indeed, for the author of *The Arcades Project* it is a matter of pulling ourselves out of a hypnotic sleep, from the spells of the nineteenth century that hold us in the vicinity of death—in short, of interrupting a nightmare in a way that will finally push us to historical awakening. In "clearing" utopia of myth, thanks to the immobilization of thinking, it is important to tear the mythical envelope that encloses the contradictions of history, neutralizing and annulling them. The awakening will be the event that suddenly makes possible the manifestation of contradictions as such, giving them free rein in history and opening to their revolutionary effects. Whereas for Levinas meeting the Other and the upheaval it provokes situates awakening on an ethical register, even on the side of "ethical madness," for his part Benjamin lights a battle that is above all political, occurring on the field of the political, including all the practices, representations, and symbolic points of reference of the institution of the social. Benjamin also takes care to distinguish between the historian and the technician of awakening: the former is borne by an interest in knowledge, the latter by an interest in emancipation and by an impetus to rescue. Because the tiger's leap by which the Now, the present, extracts from what once was a utopian chance that forestalls, with the same enthusiasm, the imminent catastrophe. If the dialectical image dazzles, it is because the awakening it manages is at the same time an explosive intervention into an extreme situation, a last-minute rescue. "The rescue that is carried out by these means—and only by these—can operate solely for the sake of what in the next moment is already irretrievably lost."[43] With regard to this definition of rescue, we understand that Benjamin was able to declare that the hero is the true subject of modernity. It is his task of perceiving in a flash the breach or small fissure through which to save the world and to use it to bring to a brutal halt the catastrophe on the brink of breaking out. This conception is curiously close to that of Levinas, for whom "the hero is the one who always glimpses a last chance" and seizes it before death.[44] It nevertheless remains that despite scenarios that play out in both cases between sleep and awakening, the differences between the two approaches and two utopian conversions appears all the more easily in that one comes from phenomenology and the other from Benjamin's highly particular Marxism.

A phenomenologist, Levinas seeks movements of thought, philosophical gestures that will let him elucidate the *eidos* of utopia to the point of managing to think utopia otherwise. It is a thinking of utopia all the richer in that it is nourished by the meeting with Martin Buber and especially with Ernst Bloch, not only welcomed as the thinker of the principle of hope, but also an anti-Heidegger when it comes to relations with death and time. Is it not in the awakening to the other, the awakening to the for-the-other that Levinas will encounter the concrete situation on the basis of which to think utopia, in its dimension of the to-come, as dedicated to the other. Indeed, as we have seen, for Levinas the modality of the awakening is first of all ethical; it depends on the relation to the Other, or rather to a specific Other insofar as it overthrows the economy of the I. "Ethics," Levinas declares, "is when I not only do not thematize another; it is when another *obsesses* me or puts me in question. This putting in question does not expect that I respond; it is not a question of giving a response, but of finding oneself responsible. . . . [In being-in-question] subjectivity keeps nothing of its *identity* of a being, of its *for-oneself*, of its sub-stance, of its *situation*."[45] The analysis of a situation that Levinas shares with Ernst Bloch is particularly revealing. "The hunger of another awakens men from their well-fed slumber and their self-sufficiency."[46] This is how the description of awakening is refined in Levinas's text. According to Levinas, we should distinguish between awakening—"the non-quietude that is the agitation of the Self by the Other"—and the notion of the spiritual or the reasonable relating to conscience that takes care of something. Now, beyond this opening of conscience, there is another opening, "an opening that is prior to intentionality, a primordial opening that is an impossibility of hiding; one that is an assignation . . . an *insomnia*."[47] This is how awakening becomes more than wakefulness; it metamorphoses into insomnia: "Insomnia is disquiet at the heart of its formal equality by the Other who cores out all that which, within insomnia, makes up a core in resting, in presence, in sleep—all that which is identified. Insomnia is the tearing of that resting within the identical."[48] Taking up the criticism according to which in Husserl the very spirituality of spirit is still knowledge, Levinas's whole movement in the text "De la conscience à la veille" will consist, by invoking this primordial opening, prior to consciousness in arriving at an awakening irreducible to knowledge, prior to intentionality, an awakening that rules out "the presence that is satisfied with its place."[49] This awakening within awakening is that which signifies the defection of identity and which the awakening at the heart of awakening brings about a still deeper sobering, a "more vigilant insomnia."[50] Now, it is this modality of awakening caught in an endless deepening, an outdoing aroused by the aversion to any possible falling back into sleep and the identity of presence, that leads to utopia.

In line with awakening, the awakening within awakening, Levinas's first speculative gesture is to emigrate utopia from the places where it has wandered and to return it to its first element, the field of interhuman relations, the human bond—a concern where it rediscovers contemporary philosophy's concern to free man from categories derived from things. "Before all else it is a matter of finding a place wherein human beings cease to concern us in terms of the horizon of being, a place wherein they cease to offer themselves to our powers."[51] A rupture with the ontological order, which makes it clear that utopia belongs neither to the order of understanding nor to that of knowledge—laws of history or laws of society—but to the register of the encounter. Utopia that comes from proximity is a form of thinking otherwise than knowledge, meeting the other man as such in his incomparable unicity and not with the other as part of the world. Utopia as meeting, invocation, is to take up the categories of Martin Buber on the side of the I-Thou relation by specifying immediately that, where Buber sees a symmetry, Levinas insists on the asymmetry of the relation. Akin to awakening, utopia is incontestably of the ethical order inasmuch as it comes to the encounter and thus belongs to the fact of the ethical par excellence. This assigning of utopia to its proper register, the human bond, removes it from the discourse of philosophical self-evidence that introduces a teleological system within totality and teaches the orientation of history. Moreover, the register of utopia is to be confused neither with that of science nor with that of a morphological prediction (Marx). Animated by awakening, moreover shaped by "nostalgia of the just,"[52] utopia opens towards the placeless place from which history can be judged. Its *unreality*, which comes from a philosophy of escape and is inseparable from its effectiveness, turns out to be the place where criteria are forged to judge the self-evidences of realism and kindle resistance to the course of history that drives events, opposing it in the name of "the utopia of the human."

Levinas warns: "The nothingness of Utopia is not the nothingness of death."[53] I can only discuss a few elements of this difficult but essential formula here. First of all, the nothingness of utopia is not thinkable within death, nor in the angst that is the experience of nothingness. It is thus a matter of dissociating the nothingness of utopia as well as death as well as angst. Turning to the thinker of utopia, Ernst Bloch, Levinas demonstrates the legitimacy of this dissociation: "For Bloch, it is not death that opens the authentic future; on the contrary, it is in the authentic future that death must be understood."[54] It is as if death found itself taken up, enveloped in another dimension that would take away its relation to angst and its primacy. If utopia maintains a relation with nothingness, it is therefore with another nothingness than that of death, the nothingness of the "not yet," accessible not in angst but in hope "the hope of realizing what is not yet."[55] Awakening, vigilance to what is not yet, manifests itself in two negations. Perceiving in Bloch a separation between a human subject that is still foreign to itself, "a pure fact of being, the pure fact that he is, the facticity of man in the historical world," and a historical subject separated from the world in its facticity, "at a distance from the site where he would be able to be."[56] Now, according to Levinas the nothingness of utopia works to abolish this separation by giving birth to another subjectivity than the Heideggerian subjectivity for whom, in its being, it is a matter of his very being, another subjectivity in that it is constituted by the care for what is not yet, that is like "dedication to a world to come."[57] Far from feeling an idyllic vision, Bloch's thought poses the existence of an obscure core of subjectivity in its singularity such that the work of man is not commensurate with utopia. "There is failure in every life, and the melancholy of this failure is its way of abiding in unfinished being."[58] The nothingness of utopia returns to another negation to attain "not yet being," the negation of the *conatus essendi*, of subjectivity as perseverance in being. It is thanks to this negation that another subjectivity can be born in the care for the Other, the care for a world to come that presents itself as disinterestedness. This negation that can take the form of an epoché that suspends the *conatus*, being's tendency to persevere in its being, and turns towards another region, that of interhuman relations, of proximity, unveils not a being otherwise, another organization of the *conatus*, but a being otherwise than being as disinterestedness, evasion, exit from being qua being, such that, contrary to all self-evidences and the wisdom of the world, there appears the pure human, the utopian human or the utopia of the human.

~

From his first texts, notably in *Time and the Other*, Levinas associated, as we have seen, the future, orientation to the future, with the other. Turning towards the future is turning towards the other and vice versa. Thus awakening in its ethical modality, born from the relation to the other, from care for the other human, necessarily orients one to the future and in so doing uncovers a new path for transformation into utopia. It is in this passage of awakening to utopia that the latter wins its autonomy, its specificity, by separating from the self-evidences of philosophical discourse. In fact, utopia, far from being a march towards a predetermined end of history, is a movement towards the future, hope. In this way the movement towards the future proper to the awakening in its ethical modality makes itself a meeting with utopia. "The drive toward the future is a relation with *utopia*,"[59] Levinas declares, at the same time highlighting a double assignation, that of utopia to time and that of time to utopia. As much as the former is well known to every observer of modernity, the latter arises from a rupture with Heidegger and opens unknown horizons when it comes to thinking of time. It is what I will later call the Blochian revolution to which Levinas gives his approval. Assigning time to utopia introduces a new thinking of time, since now temporality is no longer defined by the relationship with nothingness. Assigning time to utopia is now to assign it to hope. "Time is pure hope," Levinas writes. "It is even the birthplace of hope. This is hope for a completed world in which man and his labor shall not be merchandise. A hope and a utopia without which the activity that fulfills being—that is, humanity—could neither begin nor continue in the long patience of its science and effort."[60] This new conception of utopia on the side of hope and not founded on the necessity of history carries within itself another thinking of temporality. According to Levinas, Bloch managed to detach time from the idea of nothingness in order to attach it to the achievement of utopia. "Time, here, is not pure destruction—quite the contrary."[61] Utopia makes use of the separation, the potential difference between the unfinished world and hope, the anticipation of a fulfilled world. This utopia short-circuits time and this short-circuiting of time proves to be the condition of the revolutionary consciousness. Levinas the reader of Bloch goes so far as to think that the utopia of hope is a temporalization of time, the source of its movement of temporalization. It is when we have arrived at this point that we can best sense the size of the philosophical revolution that consists in thinking death on the basis of time, enframed, reoriented by the perspective, the hope of a fulfilled world. Once again we find the most overwhelming assignation, that of time with utopia. "Time, as the hope of utopia, is no longer the time that is thought of on the basis of death. Here, the first ecstasis is utopia, not death."[62]

Benjamin, even if he maintained a relationship with Bloch's thought on utopia, was situated completely differently than Levinas. He belongs to what Paul Ricoeur calls the school of suspicion (Marx, Nietzsche, Freud). Anchored in an anthropological materialism, he tries to give a genetic interpretation of utopia or dream images by referring them to the collective's conditions of existence while maintaining their dreamlike expressive quality against the theory of reflection. Unlike Levinas, whose phenomenology prevents him from having recourse to dialectical thinking, Benjamin conceives of awakening as the potentially explosive moment that resolves the dialectical tensions that traverse the ambiguous dreams of the collective, where mythical-archaic images and dream images crisscross and mix together. Awakening has the task of disentangling utopia from myth and allowing the dazzling emergence of the dialectical image. Still, it should be noted that Benjamin has recourse to a practice of suspicion that is "well tempered." He does not reduce the truth content of a given utopia to the conditions of its appearance: in doing so, he appreciates a specificity, an irreducible "remainder," of utopia by going so far as to invoke the inalienable character of dream images. Proclaiming in *The Arcades Project*, "This standstill is utopia," he adds, not without provocation, "and the dialectical image, therefore, dream image."[63] It is as if, despite the metamorphosis it provokes, the dialectical image nonetheless remains a dream image, as if the relations between the two types of images are situated within an indeterminate space between discontinuity and continuity. This declaration is somewhat surprising. Can the dialectical image be legitimately identified with the dream image? A great Benjamin interpreter, Susan Buck-Morss, rightly takes care to distinguish between these two images: "a dream image is not yet a dialectical image, and desire is not yet knowledge."[64] Does appearing to confuse them not confirm Adorno's accusation that Benjamin has transferred the dialectical image to consciousness in the form of the dream? But does this surprise not arise from failing to distinguish between analytical reason and dialectical reason? Does it not forget that it is within a dialectics at a standstill that the dialectical image can be both at once? For the complement of the contentious declaration of *The Arcades Project*—"the dialectical image [is the] dream image"—is the vigorous clarification given in the August 16, 1935, letter to Gretel Adorno: "The dialectical image does not replicate the dream—it was never my intention to make that claim." It is to recognize that the dialectical image, despite the transformation it imparts to the dream image, is nonetheless inscribed in either the symbolic or the dreamlike expression of the nineteenth century. That is where it in a sense finds its support, the ground from which it takes flight towards the places where awakening will irrupt, as if the dream image were the dialectical image's indispensable springboard. Indeed, to a certain point the latter belongs to the world of the dream. Dialectically, it remains an image, just as the psychoanalyst's reading of a patient's dream belongs to the dreamlike dimension, whose reality it cannot ignore, even if it separates itself from it through the work of interpretation. Let us say between discontinuity and continuity, since the dialectical image retains something of the dream image, all the more so to the extent that the latter, in its ambiguity, presents two sides, one pulling it towards the mythical-archaic image, the other calling it towards the dialectical image. It follows from this that the dialectical image cannot do without the dream. Only a dialectical reason that is sensitive to the tensed bow, to the dialectic between the image and awakening, can think Benjamin's two propositions together. Benjamin's statements only make sense within the totality of the bow that underlies them, not remaining analytically frozen in one of the process's moments, closed up in itself. Let us add to this that, contra Adorno, Benjamin recognizes an objectivity in dream images. Dreamlike figures are inalienable, he affirms as clearly as possible. We can neither get rid of them by denying their existence nor confuse them with other figures. If Benjamin holds onto the existence of these dream figures despite their ambiguity, it is because he has already posited the existence of a collective symbolic space so that these dreamlike images would be inalienable without taking up the totality of the scene. In fact, we can no more ignore dream images than the places in which awakening bursts in.

Benjamin walks a razer's edge and opens a narrow path: neither negating the dream image nor simply accepting it nor simply recording it, but an interpretive construction in anticipation of the emergence of the dialectical image, in anticipation of waking. This is how Benjamin occupies an original situation within Marxism: without pronouncing on the Marxian critique of utopia, he participates in the new utopian spirit.

If we draw a border from utopia and the utopian conversion, Levinas and Benjamin, despite their differences, the ethical modality of waking for one and politics for the other, are to be found on the same side. Both belong to the small group of philosophers who cannot hate utopia since they know that philosophy and utopia maintain close, unbreakable ties. Can there be a philosophy without any utopian dimension that has broken with utopia? Can we conceive of a utopia at a distance from all philosophy, even if it takes a nonphilosophical form or, as in Thomas More, of another philosophy, "alert to the world's stage," unlike the dominant philosophy? Does not precisely awakening, irrespective of its modalities, offer a fragile walkway between philosophy and utopia, all the more because philosophy and utopia owe their existence to a conversion, a *metanoia* that in each case demands resolve, even obstinacy in the practice of doubt and separation or in that of wonder, and that cannot be content, like the tyrant of Syracuse, with simulation or pretending. Through this relation to awakening, Benjamin and Levinas belong to the group of philosophers who scorn those who profess the hatred of utopia, the "sleep merchants" of the day who, stuck in a hypnotic, deadly sleep find or think they find in their imprisonment something to justify their aversion to utopia. Even if their philosophical works follow different paths to rediscover utopia or dream image, they share the virtue of revealing the intellectual poverty and sterility of the prosecutors of utopia, exacerbated by the lack of any conceptual elaboration being made up for by an ideological discourse of denunciation. The very connection between utopia and philosophy, between utopia and awakening, should force these prosecutors at least to scan these philosophical trajectories before launching into semi-anonymous diatribes. Truth be told, they really do not care much that they employ the term utopia in a vulgar sense.

To be sure, in the case of Levinas and Benjamin, the inquiry could and should be extended, because they share having developed, in different ways, an essential, inventive relation to Ernst Bloch, the thinker of utopia. Bloch, Benjamin, and Levinas is a still more fertile trio to the extent that here utopia and awakening spread and crisscross through two philosophical enterprises that have not always avoided confrontation: phenomenology and Marxism.

To conclude, let us turn to Thomas More, the author of *Utopia*. Is he not already, in a different historical and philosophical context, a technician of awakening? Did he not, in effect, invent a technique of waking that is closer to materialism insofar as it concerns transformations in living conditions? Did he not at the same time elaborate a technique of continual awakening to the extent that he drew a new way of keeping the utopian disposition or the happy meeting of waking and utopia alive and active? We could, to be sure, interrogate the relations between the creation of insularity and the epoché. Does not the break with the continent mean bracketing, suspension? But beyond this, does not reading *Utopia* carry the good news that the inhabitants of Utopia enjoyed, what was then, a considerable reduction of the working day to six hours? This is how the technique of waking concerning time devoted to daily work is described: "Of the twenty-four equal hours into which they divide the day and the night, the Utopians devote only six to work. They work three hours before noon, when they go to lunch. After lunch, they rest for two hours, then go to work for another three hours."[65] Still more remarkable is the care More takes to keep the Utopians awake, to maintain and constantly reactivate among them what we could call the utopian disposition or affective tonality (*Stimmung*) that sets the tone, determines a style and way of being. It is indeed extraordinary in his writing, for this magnificent disposition is the object of an "anti-climax" as its sublimity is laid out in prosaic rather than sublime terms, with a sobriety such that it goes almost unnoticed to the point that many critics take up the old refrain of *Utopia*'s stasis. "Once stimulated by learning, the minds of the Utopians are wonderfully quick to seek out those various skills which make life more agreeable."[66] There is immediately mention of the two arts necessary for literary study, printing and paper-making. A utopia of books?

It is thus that the technique of maintaining wakefulness, the culture of letters, is connected to the technique of waking—the reduction of the working day—one obviously being the other's condition of possibility. What do the Utopians do during their hours of leisure? Most of them study. They are studious Utopians:

> The other hours of the day, when they are not working, eating or sleeping, are left to each person's individual discretion, provided that free time is not wasted in roistering or sloth but used properly in some chosen occupation. Generally these intervals are devoted to intellectual activity. For they have an established custom of giving daily public lectures before dawn; attendance at these lectures is required only of those who have been specifically chosen to devote themselves to learning, but a great many other people of all kinds, both men and women, gather to hear them. Depending on their interests, some go to one lecture, some to another.[67]

In this way, More, with his interest in material living conditions, resonates with what Maximilien Rubel calls "Marx's utopian socialism" when the latter describes, at the end of his *magnum opus*, *Capital*, the reign of freedom: "Beyond (the realm of necessity) begins that development of human energy which is an end in itself, the true realm of freedom, which, however, can blossom forth only with this realm of necessity as its basis. The shortening of the working-day is its basic prerequisite."[68]

The utopian conversion, the conversion to utopia, thus invests in the question of temporality and gives itself more precisely the object of an inversion of working time and leisure time, the latter carrying it as the reign of freedom over labor, the armature of the reign of necessity. But to remember Ernst Bloch's revolution when it comes to the relations between time and death, does it not seem that this conversion, with its investment in temporality, is called to show itself still more boldly? Did not Bloch, the author of *The Spirit of Utopia*, invite us to think death on the basis of time, an effectively revolutionary gesture inasmuch as it dethrones death from its position of absolute master and at the same time reaches the economy of the human condition? Could we not, with the help of Levinas, reader of Bloch, push boldness a step further by imagining that under the effect of such a reversal, *Dasein*, beset by its care for being—"in its being it is a matter of this being itself"—makes way for being human in its relation to the other being, animated by the care for the other man, by "one-for-the-other," the other qua other opens the figures of a "future of utopia." Levinas writes, "time does not go back to being-toward-death. That time, in its very to-come, does not go back to finitude stretched toward being-toward-death but rather might have another signification, and that there might be another eventuality in the analysis of death."[69] Another signification? *Dasein*, being-toward-death, would be replaced by the utopian human, human as a utopian animal, the being for utopia. As if utopia, the future of utopia, suddenly offered to the human being—to human beings—its own-most, its most emblematic possibility: the utopian conversion.

Chapter 12

Letter from a "Revoltist" to Marcel Gauchet, Convert to "Normal Politics"

(2004; republished 2008)

In your most recent work, *La condition historique*, a book of interviews with François Azouvi and Sylvain Piron published by Stock in 2003, you accused me of "revoltism."[1] Now it is up to you, in the process of making a name for yourself (to use an expression that dots your discourse), to allocate praise and blame, so you risk a neologism to call me nothing less than a revoltist. But what is this revoltism, clearly forged on the model of revolutionism?

In each case, let there be no mistake, the suffix "ism," itself pejorative enough, aims to highlight and denounce an ideologization of the phenomenon in question. It is as if the patient, by dint of having carried revolt or revolution to the extreme, suffered an insurmountable spasm, fixation, or cramp of revolt, falling victim to the logic of an idea that cannot, for want of flexibility, embrace the new social-historical order. Perhaps you could have better elucidated the stakes of the matter for the reader. To be sure, four pages before delivering your diagnosis you mention that I happened to be in charge of a book series at Payot. Why not be a bit more explicit and explain to the reader that it is the "Critique de la politique" collection? That would have let them discover, were they the least bit curious, that

---

Translated by James D. Ingram. Originally published as "Lettre d'un 'révoltiste' à Marcel Gauchet converti à la 'politique normale,'" *Réfractions*, no. 12 (2004). Translated from *Lettre d'un "révoltiste" à Marcel Gauchet converti à la "politique normale"* (Paris: Sens & Tonka, 2008).

you were not afraid to associate your pen with that of a "revoltist"—but perhaps you yourself were afflicted with this infantile disorder?—when in 1976 we cosigned an introduction to La Boétie, *Les leçons de la servitude et leur destin*.[2] We would have parted ways in exemplary fashion, you laboring to think power with freedom, me forever arrested in the "great refusal" that makes me think freedom against power.

So revoltism it is! More than a spasm, it would be a combination, from your perspective indigestible, of democratism and hypercriticism—indigestible because, according to you, "In the end, the philosophy of democracy and the imaginary of subversive radicalism do not mix."[3] In short, to express myself in your inimitable style, the "good girl" democracy does not like ultraradical positions. Is she therefore destined for a grey, passionless moderation? Let us understand that this thing, revoltism, is formed in two moments: first a divestment from revolution that is then immediately offset by an engagement in revolt. The break with revolution would arise from the choice of democracy. If democracy is seen and accepted as "an unsurpassable framework," a distance from revolution necessarily follows, since what is specific to the latter, as we know, is its intolerance of any horizon, still less an unsurpassable framework. Death to all unsurpassables! Such is revolution's first joyful cry. Revoltism, a complex, sophisticated ailment, would consist in resigning oneself to the existence of democracy, a resignation all the stronger in that it has to do with framework-democracy, as one used to speak of framework-laws, all the better to reinvest in revolt, collective invention, under the triple sign of radical demands, utopia, and protest from the margins. To be sure, I have long known that you do not like the margins, still less the small—what philosophy from Plato to Hegel rejects as "negligible quantities." For everything that has a whiff of anti-Hegelianism awakens in you a "formidable" (an adjective you so like) Fouquier-Tinville of the concept.

I would on your account have theorized this vision "in the tradition of Lefort" under the sign of savage democracy, in a sense the height of revoltism. You do me a great honor. Let us be clear: it is unquestionably to Claude Lefort that we owe the concept of savage democracy, and it is no use slyly trying to enlist me in your settling of accounts with him. That is not my affair. All I tried to do in the text " 'Savage Democracy' and 'Principle of Anarchy' " is explicate Lefort's concept as best I could by comparing it to Reiner Schürmann's principle of anarchy, as if this detour could reveal what the enigmatic, unsettling term "savage democracy" held in reserve.[4] I was moved by a double motivation: to suspend Lefort's discretion concerning what he himself calls "the libertarian idea of democracy" and above all by means of this idea to head off minimalist interpretations that reduce savage democracy to a mere site of permanent contestation without seeing that it is a question of the "dissolution of the markers of certainty" to the point of bringing about an indetermination of the foundations of power, law, and knowledge. You consider this a "highly dubious" concept, as if it were a spoiled dish it might not be wise to consume. One suspects that your response would be negative: outfitting your remarks with some supplementary courtesies—"aesthetics of intransigence," "cult of rupture"—you accuse the partisans of savage democracy of irresponsibility and resignation, or rather you run the old ethics of conviction/ethics of responsibility play on them. Even if, good prince, you grant it a few agreeable traits—the refusal of power, the possible effects of social transformation—you nonetheless conclude that this rigid attachment to an ethics of conviction, to an irresponsible radicalism, can only lead to a corruption of democracy. The revoltist would be the beautiful soul of our day. Let us leave savage democracy there. All things considered, for my part, I prefer the idea of insurgent democracy. I will return to it. But let us instead examine the presuppositions on which your indictment is based, on which you rest your diagnosis.

First of all, what authorizes you to separate revolution from democracy in such a peremptory, rigid way? Can we accept without further ado your assertion that there is a contradiction between revolution, which struggles against unsurpassables, and democracy, now assigned the status of unsurpassable framework? Reading you, if one is a democrat, which is to say attached to something that would have the value of a simple framework, one immediately ceases to be a revolutionary; conversely, if one chooses revolution, one turns one's back on democracy. All this seems quite arbitrary—rather abstract to a revoltist like me. Revolution is not an immutable entity with determinate characteristics like those of a stone or a tree. A revolution is a historical event; there is a plurality of possible revolutions and a plurality of revolutionary traditions. There are at least two, according to Oskar Anweiler: Jacobin and Communalist.[5] It seems safe to assume that the question of the relation to democracy does not arise in the same way with the two conceptions. So why hammer on with such generalities?

Behind your arguments what does one find if not a singular weakening of democracy, one furthermore reduced to an anti-revolutionary framework? But what then do you do with the democratic revolution with which you were once aligned? Is there not something of an uprising in this alliance of revolution and democracy you expected in the fall of totalitarian domination? In *La Démocratie contre elle-même*, you write, "The democratic revolution replaces this representation of a foundation lodged above with the representation of a foundation situated below."[6] Do you want to say that once the democratic revolution has occurred, democracy is nothing more than a framework, a form that is immediately transformed into an anti-revolutionary, even counterrevolutionary, rampart? But what is a democracy, born of revolution, that aims to bar the way to revolution by declaring that the revolution is over? In this respect, is the democratic revolution ever over? Does it come to an end, for example, by replacing a foundation situated above with one lodged beneath? In its interminable course, does the democratic revolution not take on the very idea of a foundation, making the crisis of foundations its own, thanks to which it is able to find a new face? If we agree to see in democracy something other than a political regime—but do you still agree after identifying democracy with a framework?—if we can recognize it as a specific political institution of the social that welcomes conflict instead of concealing it, that multiplies the sites of collective invention, that circulates the will to autonomy in all social spheres, that triggers a series of experiments in political freedom, if we agree to see its true face, then the democratic revolution, far from being frozen in its result, a form, is to be understood as a process, an endless breakthrough, adventurous, not established in a universe of certainties or guarantees but immersed in uncertainty, plagued by fear of failure or regression. Finally, since when would making a revolution necessarily be antidemocratic? Do you discount the revolution of 1848, Rosa Luxemburg's opposition to Bolshevism, the council revolutions, the action committees of 1968?

Really, as you unapologetically avow, you have "veered right." We are not surprised to note through the interviews your proximity to François Furet, may he rest in peace. One day a critical mind will have to assess the Furet effect—institutional, intellectual, political—on the French intelligentsia in the last part of the twentieth century. We will then perceive the harm to historians, philosophers (it was in Furet's seminar that Alain Renaut claims to have discovered Rawls!), and more broadly the educated public, readers of periodicals. We will be shocked to see how independent, creative minds, more inclined to heresy than orthodoxy, could take an interest in the work of an author who tirelessly constructed a new middle way, a mixture of 1789, Thermidor, Doctrinaire thought, Orleanism (ah, the reign of the "qualified"), Third Republic–style centrist republicanism, and Aronism. It is as if Furet's works, which ward off utopia as much as revolution, had served as a smiling, skeptical, even cynical refuge for penitents of all kinds. But why the devil do those with nothing to repent, who roundly denounced

Stalinism when Furet was still a Stalinist, approach him? A mystery! Is it a symptom of the weariness of reason? In your case the Furet effect is massive and it appears you were not embarrassed by his correspondence with Nolte. To appreciate its importance, it suffices to read what you write concerning Thermidor. I cite *in extenso*:

> From the perspective of this reflection of the Revolution on itself, the richest and most poignant moment is the most neglected: Thermidor. It is the moment of freedom rediscovered, but also the moment of the final failure to institutionalize freedom despite the lessons of experience, the moment of impotent self-criticism. There is something pathetic in the inability of the men of Thermidor and the Directory to escape a model whose traps they nonetheless clearly discerned and whose holes they struggled to plug. But to no avail; they were insuperably stuck. It is a sort of intellectual tragedy after the political tragedy. But the effort of reflection of these torn minds is remarkable.[7]

For tragedy and something to admire, to the extent that you agree to leave constitutional history, it seems to me that you are knocking at the wrong door. Indeed, from this point of view it is better to turn to the Revolt of Prairial, the Prairial martyrs brought before a military tribunal reserved for Vendée insurgents (a manifestation of the Thermidorian rule of law, no doubt), to Babeuf and the Conspiracy of Equals. Here we breathe different air than that which emanates from the miasma of Thermidorian venality.

It is this turn to the right, you say, that won you over to "normal politics." How can a mind as fine as yours be satisfied with such a poor concept, if it even is one? What is it, this normal politics? In June 1940, for example, to rally to normal politics, which side would one have joined: Vichy and its ignominies, or revolt and those who cried out against accepting the unacceptable? Today do we need to get our bearings by looking at a fresh episode, the heatwave? Fifteen thousand elderly dead in a few weeks, that is to say a French town wiped out, emptied of its inhabitants as a result of government incompetence and not a natural disaster, contrary to those who confuse nature and history.[8] A parliamentary commission blames the minister's office the better to exculpate the minister. Let me tell you that under the Third or Fourth Republic the minister responsible would immediately have been sent packing for good. A case of normal politics? But enough of such trivial events, as you would see it.

I will grant that you are somewhat tinged by Hans Kelsen and that your understanding of "normal politics" corresponds to the basic law, that is, the constitution. Do I then have to remind you, a scholar of constitutional history, that the 1958 French Constitution, born in a merciless colonial war and a coup d'état, is anything but democratic? And the 1981 change of government did not, like a magic wand, suddenly democratize it. Did not François Mitterrand, the author of *Le Coup d'État permanent*,[9] suddenly find that the shoe fit? This should no doubt be part of the "completely honorable balance sheet of social democracy."[10] Strictly speaking, this Constitution is explicitly counterrevolutionary. Was it not in fact in the republican and democratic tradition (1789–1791, the laws of 1875) that the law was recognized as having a universal jurisdiction, which has since been restricted? To rally to normal politics is thus to accept institutions with openly authoritarian tendencies, born of the revaluation of strong governments, a movement that emerged at the start of the 1930s. Even the Thermidorians would have been troubled. But perhaps you simply want to say that the time has come to convert to normalization. If there is something uncontrollable, unpredictable—in a word, "savage"—in the practice of democracy, it should therefore be normalized, tamed, disciplined, the tumultuous river of democracy should finally be returned to its bed, to its framework, you would say.

For, in the end, what do we find behind the expression "normal politics" (why not "politically normal"?) if not the trigger, the launch of a process of accepting what is, of the established order such that injustices, the unacceptable, fade to the point of seeming a necessary part of the order of the world, as if history were confused with nature. It is a real feat of sleight of hand: thanks to "normal politics," to the idea of the normal political, everything that does not go without saying suddenly seems to go without saying. It is like this and cannot be otherwise. You are on the wrong track. How can you, author of *La condition politique*, master of the study of the political, lose your way on this point? Far from going together with what is normal, politics is an irruption, and this irruption is an interruption. An interruption of domination, politics is the action that breaks off the reign of the normal, of what passes for normal, the apparently "normal" disposition of things. Conversely, the "return to normal" is the end, the extinction, the disappearance of politics. The connection between politics and the event made by an interruption in the name of freedom, of equality, means that there is not always politics, that in fact there is politics only rarely, even if these openings, these "prophecies of freedom" as Saint-Just magnificently called them, give birth to institutions and at the very least leave indelible traces. Everything else is only the management of domination, "police," a thing or machinery, as you like. Yes, you have lost your way. With all due respect, politics is situated on the side of the "revoltism" that you dislike, or that you no longer like; and normality is not on the side of politics that you like or think you like. The "return to normal" that comes after the event of political interruption marks the death of politics.

Moreover, "normal politics" is the other name for the hatred of alterity, of the completely Other social—in a word, it is the contemporary figure of the hatred of utopia. Ultimately, under the cover of "normal politics," a world gradually settles in where the utopian gap would disappear forever, another way of imperceptibly entering into an unprecedented figure of totalitarianism in which human society prides itself on having reached its culmination and claims to have liquidated utopia forever in the name of the rule of law and achieved democracy. This closure of society onto itself, a soft form of voluntary servitude, aside from its ignorance of the persistence of utopia in history, dedicates human society to the repetition of the same. Instead of celebrating the death of utopia like happy imbeciles, the bards of "normal politics" would do better to ask with some anxiety about what a human society that had killed the *vis utopica*, the utopian tendency, would be. Once again what are you doing but taking up the disenchanted lesson, an invitation to common cynicism, of your oracle François Furet? Did he not write in *The Passing of an Illusion: The Idea of Communism in the Twentieth Century*: "The idea of another society has become almost impossible to conceive of, and no one in the world today is offering any advice on the subject or even trying to formulate a new concept. Here we are, condemned to live in the world as it is"?[11] At the start of your magnum opus you declare, repeating the master's lesson, "Democracy has become the unsurpassable horizon of our time," and continue further on: "The perspective has reversed. There is nothing before us but the same. The consecration of individualism that we have just experienced prevents us from conceiving of other principles of personal or collective existence than those we practice. . . . This closes off to us the possibility of imagining a different norm for governing."[12] A word to the wise. Thank you, Marcel Gauchet, you said "norm"? Thanks to you, to your painstaking efforts, "normal politics" has finally been established.

We know you are a clever man. You have a keen sense for which way the wind is blowing. Thus in the February 26, 2004, *Libération* you told us that you burst out laughing when you read the Inrockuptibles petition and immediately added for good measure that "in government and at the Élysée [presidential palace], it is undeniably idiocy in power." You are free to allow yourself a few juvenile caprices, a few rants. But this fools no one. What counts is your definition of democracy as an unsurpassable framework. While you're at it, why not define it as "police" in Jacques Rancière's sense, that is, as "the organization of powers, the distribution of places and roles, and the systems for legitimizing this distribution"?[13] But the term framework speaks volumes: it has to do with shaping, with putting in place, with placing within limits a phenomenon, for example, an action, that spontaneously tends to spill beyond the limits that work precisely to assign it to a framework—a sort of house arrest. Before getting started and ridiculing the idea of savage democracy, you could have recalled some reading from your youth, namely, Marx and his remarkable intuition in an 1843 text that democracy, when it achieves its truth, "true democracy," goes hand in hand with the disappearance of the political state—or, better, is accompanied by a struggle against the state. The adjectives chosen to define this true democracy—"radical," "savage," for my part I prefer "insurgent"—matter little. What these efforts have in common, what their authors know, whether they want to or not, is fidelity to Marx's intuition, or, beyond the name of Marx, sensitivity to the anti-statist impulse, to the struggle against the state that emerges at the heart of every modern revolution. Contrary to what you maintain, democracy is not a crystalized form or a process of crystallization or autonomization that would establish an organization of powers and rules of the game. Rather, it is a continuous movement, a political action that in its very appearance works to undo the state-form, to stop its logic (of domination, totalization, mediation, integration) and replace it with its own, that of the sovereign people struggling against illusory reconciliations and false integrations. Democracy is the determinate institution of a conflictual space, a space *against*, an agonistic scene on which two antagonistic logics face off: that of the autonomization of the state as form, and that of the life of the people as action, political action. At the heart of the revolution, democracy is insurgent twice over, because it struggles on two fronts simultaneously: against the state of the "Old Regime" and its holdovers, and against the new state *in statu nascendi* and its innovations that aim to fix a new division between the grandees and the people. Against the antiquated cadres but also against the newly minted cadres of the new state, against the identification with or reduction of democracy to the rule of law, this is the struggle that turns "the world upside down"—democracy as the continuous institution of the social. If there is a corruption of democracy, it is to let its political action petrify and, at the same time, to the detriment of its insurgence, to leave it to the logic of the state as framework.

I will stop here. You have understood me, Monsieur admirer of Thermidor—*Thermidor mon amour*, as Louis Janover wrote: if there is a revoltist "rabble," I am part of it and happy to be so.

Notes

Introduction

1. For a full list of Abensour's works in French and English, see the bibliography.

2. François Cusset, *French Theory: How Foucault, Derrida, Deleuze, & Co. Transformed the Intellectual Life of the United States* (Minneapolis: University of Minnesota Press, 2008).

3. Étienne Balibar, *On the Dictatorship of the Proletariat*, trans. Grahame Lock (London: New Left Books, 1977).

4. Étienne de La Boétie, *Discourse on Voluntary Servitude* (Indianapolis: Hackett, 2012).

5. Miguel Abensour, *La communauté politique des tous-uns* (Paris: Les Belles-Lettres, 2014), 12.

6. Abensour, *La communauté politique des tous-uns*, 13.

7. Abensour, *La communauté politique des tous-uns*, 14.

8. Abensour, *La communauté politique des tous-uns*, 14.

9. Miguel Abensour, "Insistances démocratiques: Entretien avec Miguel Abensour, Jean-Luc Nancy & Jacques Rancière: Entretien réalisé par Stany Grelet, Jérôme Lèbre, Sophie Wahnich," *Vacarme* 48, no. 3 (2009): 16.

10. Dominique Janicaud, *Heidegger in France*, trans. François Raffoul and David Pettigrew (Bloomington: Indiana University Press, 2015), 476n74.

11. Joseph Ferrari, *Les philosophes salariés* (Paris: Payot, 1983).

12. Jérôme Melançon, "Note critique—Partir des textes avec Miguel Abensour," *Cahiers Société*, no. 2 (2020): 269.

13. Martin Breaugh, "Critique de la domination, pensée de l'émancipation: Sur la philosophie politique de Miguel Abensour," *Politique et sociétés* 22, no. 3 (2003): 45–69; Anne Kupiec and Étienne Tassin, *Critique de la politique: Autour de Miguel Abensour* (Paris: Sens & Tonka, 2006); Manuel Cervera-Marzal, *Miguel Abensour, critique de la domination, pensée de l'émancipation* (Paris: Sens & Tonka,

2013); Gilles Labelle, *L'écart absolu: Miguel Abensour* (Paris: Sens & Tonka, 2017); Manuel Cervera-Marzal and Nicolas Poirier, *Désir d'utopie: Politique et émancipation avec Miguel Abensour* (Paris: Editions L'Harmattan, 2018); Patrice Vermeren, *Penser contre: Essais sur la philosophie critique de Miguel Abensour* (Paris: Sens & Tonka, 2019).

14. As some commentators have pointed out, this proclamation is often overstated. R. Bruce Douglass, "John Rawls and the Revival of Political Philosophy: Where Does He Leave Us?," *Theoria* 59, no. 133 (2012): 81–83.

15. David Easton, "The Decline of Modern Political Theory," *Journal of Politics* 13, no. 2 (1951): 36–58; Alfred Cobban, "The Decline of Political Theory," *Political Science Quarterly* 68, no. 3 (1953): 321–37; Leo Strauss, "What Is Political Philosophy?," *Journal of Politics* 19, no. 3 (1957): 343–68; Peter Laslett, introduction to *Philosophy, Politics and Society*, ed. Peter Laslett (Cambridge: Blackwell, 1956); Robert A. Dahl, "Political Theory: Truth and Consequences," *World Politics* 11, no. 2 (1958): 89–102; Gilles Labelle and Daniel Tanguay, "Le retour de la philosophie politique en France," *Politique et sociétés* 22, no. 3 (2003): 3–7; Franck Fischbach, "Le déni du social: Deux exemples contemporains—Rancière et Abensour," *Recherches sur la Philosophie et le Langage*, no. 28 (2012): 29–46; Christopher Holman, Martin Breaugh, Rachel Magnusson, Paul Mazzocchi, and Devin Penner, "Introduction: Radical Democracy and Twentieth Century French Thought," in *Thinking Radical Democracy: The Return to Politics in Postwar France*, ed. Martin Breaugh, Christopher Holman, Rachel Magnusson, Paul Mazzocchi, and Devin Penner (Toronto: University of Toronto Press, 2015), 3–30.

16. Pierre Manent, "The Return of Political Philosophy," *First Things*, May 2000, 15–22; Martha Nussbaum, "The Enduring Significance of John Rawls," *Chronicle of Higher Education*, July 20, 2001.

17. Strauss, "What Is Political Philosophy?," 245–46.

18. Easton, "The Decline of Modern Political Theory," 40.

19. Dahl, "Political Theory," 89.

20. Nussbaum, "The Enduring Significance of John Rawls."

21. Douglass, "John Rawls and the Revival of Political Philosophy," 83–84.

22. John Rawls, *A Theory of Justice* (Cambridge, MA: Belknap Press of Harvard University Press, 1971).

23. Brian Barry, "The Strange Death of Political Philosophy," *Government and Opposition* 15, no. 3/4 (1980): 284; Nussbaum, "The Enduring Significance of John Rawls." Barry notes that 1971 also marked the first issue of *Philosophy and Social Affairs*.

24. Cited in Labelle and Tanguay, "Le retour de la philosophie politique en France," 3–4.

25. See both Labelle and Tanguay, "Le retour de la philosophie politique en France," 3–6, and Manent, "The Return of Political Philosophy."

26. Miguel Abensour, "What Kind of Return?," 37.

27. Abensour, "What Kind of Return?," 38.

28. Manent, "The Return of Political Philosophy."
29. Bonnie Honig, *Political Theory and the Displacement of Politics* (Ithaca, NY: Cornell University Press, 1993), 10.
30. Marcel Gauchet, *The Disenchantment of the World: A Political History of Religion*, trans. Oscar Borge (Princeton, NJ: Princeton University Press, 1997), 192.
31. Holman et al., "Introduction," 14–18.
32. Samuel Moyn, "Modernity and the Specter of Totalitarianism," in *The Cambridge History of Modern Thought*, vol. 2, *The Twentieth Century*, ed. Peter E. Gordon and Warren Breckman (Cambridge: Cambridge University Press, 2019), 417.
33. Miguel Abensour, "Avant-propos," in *Pour une philosophie politique critique* (Paris: Sens & Tonka, 2009), 27–30; Labelle, *L'écart absolu*, 16–19.
34. Abensour, "Avant-propos," 27.
35. Miguel Abensour, "Hannah Arendt against Political Philosophy?," 104.
36. Labelle, *L'écart absolu*, 13, 21.
37. Miguel Abensour, "Manifesto for the 'Critique de la Politique' Book Series, Éditions Payot (1974)," 27
38. Miguel Abensour, "Le choix du petit," in *Minima moralia: Réflexions sur la vie mutilée* (Paris: Payot, 1991), 335–53. Although the literal translation of "du petit" would be rendered as "the little one," "the negligible" more closely approximates Abensour's deployment of the term.
39. Abensour, "Le choix du petit," 340–41, 349.
40. Christopher Holman, "Abensour and the Political Legacy of Critical Theory" (paper presented at "The Politics of Emancipation: Utopia, Insurgent Democracy, and the Legacy of Miguel Abensour," York University, Toronto, 2022).
41. Miguel Abensour, "Machiavel: Le grand penseur du désordre, entretien avec Miguel Abensour," *Le Monde*, October 4, 2008; Martin Breaugh, "From a Critique of Totalitarian Domination to the Utopia of Insurgent Democracy: On the 'Political Philosophy' of Miguel Abensour," in *Thinking Radical Democracy: The Return to Politics in Postwar France* (Toronto: University of Toronto Press, 2015), 237.
42. Miguel Abensour, *La communauté politique des tous-uns*, 13–14.
43. Miguel Abensour, "Letter from a 'Revoltist' to Marcel Gauchet, Convert to 'Normal Politics,'" 254–56.
44. Abensour, "For a Critical Political Philosophy?" 155.
45. Claude Lefort, "The Question of Democracy," in *Democracy and Political Theory*, trans. David Macey (Cambridge, UK: Polity, 1988), 9–20.
46. Abensour, "For a Critical Political Philosophy?," 156.
47. As argued in Fischbach, "Le déni du social," 34–37.
48. James D. Ingram, "The Politics of Claude Lefort's Political: Between Liberalism and Radical Democracy," *Thesis Eleven*, no. 87 (2006): 36.
49. Miguel Abensour, "On Compactness: Architecture and Totalitarian Regimes," 73.

50. Claude Lefort, *The Political Forms of Modern Society: Bureaucracy, Democracy, Totalitarianism*, ed. John Thompson (Cambridge, UK: Polity, 1986), 305.

51. Miguel Abensour, "To Think Utopia Otherwise," trans. Bettina Bergo, *Graduate Faculty Philosophy Journal* 20/21, no. 2/1 (1998): 251–79.

52. Abensour, "On Compactness," 93.

53. Miguel Abensour, "Is There a Proper Way to Use the Voluntary Servitude Hypothesis?," *Journal of Political Ideologies* 16, no. 3 (2011): 345.

54. Abensour, "On Compactness," 95.

55. Abensour, "On a Misinterpretation of Totalitarianism and Its Effects," 62.

56. Abensour, "Avant-propos," 19.

57. Abensour, 29, and "Manifesto for the 'Critique de la Politique' Book Series, Éditions Payot (1974)," See also, Jacques Rancière, *Hatred of Democracy*, trans. Steve Corcoran (New York: Verso, 2014), ch. 4.

58. Miguel Abensour, "For a Critical Political Philosophy?," 128.

59. Ingram, "The Politics of Claude Lefort's Political," 46.

60. After having articulated different labels for his approach to political philosophy, including critical political philosophy, Abensour finally opted for "critical-utopian political philosophy," to signify not only the critique of domination and its conditions of possibility, but also the utopian demand to think politics otherwise. For an overview of this, see Abensour "Avant-propos."

61. Abensour, "New Manifesto for the 'Critique de la Politique' Book Series, Éditions Klincksieck (2016)," 29.

62. While Abensour presents this impasse in the more generalized terms of critical theory and philosophy, it also reflects an impasse—the Bourdieu-Rancière debate—within the French academy between sociology and philosophy. See Pierre Bourdieu, *La distinction* (Paris: Les Editions de Minuit, 1970); Jacques Rancière, *The Philosopher and His Poor*, trans. John Drury, Corinne Oster, and Andrew Parker (Durham, NC: Duke University Press, 2003); Luc Boltanski, "Sociologie critique et sociologie de la critique," *Politix* 3, no. 10–11 (1990): 124–34; Claude Grignon and Jean-Claude Passeron, *Le savant et le populaire, misérabilisme et populisme en sociologie et en littérature* (Paris: Seuil, 1990); Philippe Corcuff, *Où est passée la critique sociale? Penser le global au croisement des savoirs* (Paris: La Découverte, 2012); Charlotte Nordmann, *Bourdieu/Rancière: La politique entre sociologie et philosophie* (Paris: Editions Amsterdam, 2006). For an overview of the debate in relation to Abensour's work, see Cervera-Marzal, *Miguel Abensour, critique de la domination, pensée de l'émancipation*, 13–42.

63. On Abensour's method of reading texts, see Horacio Gonzalez, "Le processus de libération des textes," in *Critique de la philosophie: Autour de Miguel Abensour*, ed. Anne Kupiec and Étienne Tassin (Paris, 2006); Christopher Holman, "History of Political Thought at a Standstill: Abensour, Constellations and Textual Alterity," *Philosophy and Social Criticism*, 49, no. 9 (2023): 1079–1106.

64. Abensour, "For a Critical Political Philosophy?," 138.
65. Herbert Marcuse, *An Essay on Liberation* (Boston: Beacon, 1969), 3. Marcuse notes this tendency while laying out his own attempt to transcend it.
66. Abensour, "For a Critical Political Philosophy?," 142.
67. Abensour, "For a Critical Political Philosophy?," 159.
68. Abensour, "For a Critical Political Philosophy?," 166.
69. E. P Thompson, "Postscript: 1976," *William Morris: Romantic to Revolutionary* (New York: Pantheon, 1976).
70. Lars Tønder and Lasse Thomassen, eds., *Radical Democracy: Politics between Abundance and Lack* (Manchester: Manchester University Press, 2005); Adrian Little and Moya Lloyd, eds., *The Politics of Radical Democracy* (Edinburgh: Edinburgh University Press, 2009); Martin Breaugh et al., *Thinking Radical Democracy*; Alexandros Kioupkiolis and Giorgos Katsambekis, eds., *Radical Democracy and Collective Movements Today: The Biopolitics of the Multitude versus the Hegemony of the People* (London: Routledge, 2016).
71. James D. Ingram, *Radical Cosmopolitics: The Ethics and Politics of Democratic Universalism* (New York: Columbia University Press, 2013), 199.
72. Paul Mazzocchi, "Insurgent Democracy and the German Councils," in *The German Revolution and Political Theory*, ed. Gaard Kets and James Muldoon (Cham, Switzerland: Palgrave Macmillan, 2019), 278–79.
73. Miguel Abensour, *Democracy against the State: Marx and the Machiavellian Moment*, trans. Max Blechman and Martin Breaugh (Cambridge, UK: Polity, 2011), 96–97.
74. Abensour, *Democracy against the State*, 96.
75. For an analysis of the London Corresponding Society's contribution to modern politics, see Martin Breaugh, *The Plebeian Experience: A Discontinuous History of Political Freedom* (New York: Columbia University Press, 2013), 142–72.
76. Raymond Williams, "Utopia and Science Fiction," *Science Fiction Studies* 5, no. 3 (1978): 203–14.
77. Phillip E. Wegner, "Escaping the Repetition of Catastrophe: On Abensour's Utopianism," *Cultural Critique* 111, no. 1 (2021): 168.
78. See, for example, Tom Moylan, *Demand the Impossible: Science Fiction and the Utopian Imagination* (London: Methuen, 1986); Ruth Levitas, *The Concept of Utopia* (Oxford: Peter Lang, 2011). For overviews of the trajectory of utopian studies, including Abensour's relationship to it, see Christine Nadir, "Utopian Studies, Environmental Literature, and the Legacy of an Idea: Educating Desire in Miguel Abensour and Ursula K. Le Guin," *Utopian Studies* 21, no. 1 (2010): 24–56; Michael E. Gardiner, *Weak Messianism: Essays in Everyday Utopianism* (Bern: Peter Lang, 2012), 1–39.
79. For example, see Karl Popper, *The Open Society and Its Enemies* (Princeton, NJ: Princeton University Press, 1945); Jacob Talmon, *Utopianism and Politics* (London: Conservative Political Centre, n.d.); Judith Shklar, "The Political Theory of Utopia: From Melancholy to Nostalgia," *Daedalus* 94, no. 2 (1965): 367–81.

80. Miguel Abensour, "The History of Utopia and the Destiny of Its Critique," in *Political Uses of Utopia: New Marxist, Anarchist, and Radical Democratic Perspectives*, ed. S. D. Chrostowska and James D. Ingram (New York: Columbia University Press, 2016), 3–56; Miguel Abensour, "Pierre Leroux et l'utopie," in *Utopiques I: Le procès des maîtres rêveurs* (Paris: Sens & Tonka, 2013), 129–30

81. Miguel Abensour, "William Morris: The Politics of Romance," in *Revolutionary Romance*, ed. Max Blechman (San Francisco: City Lights, 1999), 145–46.

82. Nadir, "Utopian Studies, Environmental Literature, and the Legacy of an Idea," 32.

83. Miguel Abensour and Marcel Gauchet, "Les leçons de la servitude et leur destin," in *Discours de la servitude volontaire*, ed. Pierre Leonard (Paris: Payot, 1976), vii–xxix; Abensour, "Is There a Proper Way to Use the Voluntary Servitude Hypothesis?"

84. Miguel Abensour, "The New Utopian Spirit," 199.

85. Tom Moylan, *Becoming Utopian: The Culture and Politics of Radical Transformation* (London: Bloomsbury, 2020), 5.

86. Abensour, "The Utopian Conversion," 222.

87. For the suggestion that Abensour is too focused on literary texts and utopia, see Ruth Levitas, "For Utopia: The (Limits of the) Utopian Function in Late Capitalist Society," *Critical Review of International Social and Political Philosophy* 3, no. 2–3 (2007): 25–43; Ruth Levitas, *Utopia as Method: The Imaginary Reconstitution of Society* (London: Palgrave Macmillan UK, 2013), 120, 124; Gardiner, *Weak Messianism*, 30.

88. Abensour, "The Utopian Conversion," 226.

89. For a more detailed elaboration of this argument, see Paul Mazzocchi, "Excavating Abensour: The Dialectics of Democracy and Utopia at a Standstill," *Constellations* 22, no. 2 (2015): 290–301.

90. Miguel Abensour, "Persistent Utopia," *Constellations* 15, no. 3 (2008): 417.

91. Abensour, 417.

92. Marcel Gauchet, *La condition historique* (Paris: Stock, 2003), 160; Robin Celikates, review of *Pour une philosophie politique critique*, by Miguel Abensour, *European Journal of Philosophy* 18, no. 4 (2010): 608; Christopher Holman, review of *Democracy against the State: Marx and the Machiavellian Moment*, by Miguel Abensour, *Rethinking Marxism* 26, no. 3 (2014): 439–42; Oliver Marchart, *Thinking Antagonism: Political Ontology after Laclau* (Edinburgh: Edinburgh University Press, 2018), 201–2; Roberto Esposito, "The Creative Force of Institutions: A Reply to Benoît Dillet's, Vanessa Lemm's, and Robert Nichols's Responses to 'Three Paradigms of Political Ontology,'" *Cultural Critique* 115, no. 1 (2022): 148. Simon Critchley directs this criticism at 'Rancière and many others" in "Five Problems in Levinas's View of Politics and the Sketch of a Solution to Them," in *Radicalizing Levinas*, ed. Atterton and Matthew Calarco (Albany: State University of New York Press, 2010), 52.

93. Ruth Levitas, "For Utopia," 40. For these lines of criticism, see also Ruth Levitas, *Utopia as Method*, ch. 6; Ruth Levitas, "Educated Hope: Ernst Bloch on Abstract and Concrete Utopia," in *Not Yet: Reconsidering Ernst Bloch*, ed. Jamie Owen and Tom Moylan (New York: Verso, 1997), 75–78. For an overview of this response to critical utopias, see Gardiner, *Weak Messianism*, 29–30.

94. Manuel Cervera-Marzal, "Miguel Abensour, Cornelius Castoriadis: Un conseillisme français?," *Revue du MAUSS* 40, no. 2 (2012): 300–320.

95. Abensour, "Persistent Utopia," 413.

96. Abensour, "The Utopian Conversion," 223.

97. Andreas Kalyvas, *Democracy and the Politics of the Extraordinary: Max Weber, Carl Schmitt, and Hannah Arendt* (Cambridge: Cambridge University Press, 2008), ch. 9.

98. Abensour, *Democracy against the State*, xxviii.

99. Niklas Plätzer, "How to Make the Moment Last? On Rupture and Institutions in Massimiliano Tomba's *Insurgent Universality*," *Historical Materialism* 30, no. 4 (2022): 119–21.

100. William Morris, cited in Abensour, "E. P. Thompson's Passion," 188.

101. Abensour, *Democracy against the State*, xxiv; "The Utopian Conversion"; "Letter from a 'Revoltist.'"

102. Abensour, *Democracy against the State*, 84–88.

103. Miguel Abensour and Louis Janover, preface to *Le mythe bolchevik: Journal 1920–1922* by Alexander Berkman (Paris: Klincksieck, 2017).

104. Abensour, *Democracy against the State*, 71–72.

105. Abensour, *La communauté politique des tous-uns*, 13–14.

106. Abensour, "Insistances démocratiques," 16.

107. For an articulation of this project, see Martin Breaugh and Dean Caivano, "A Living Critique of Domination: Exemplars of Radical Democracy from Black Lives Matter to #MeToo," *Philosophy and Social Criticism* 50, no. 3 (2024): 447–72.

108. Labelle, *L'écart absolu*, 24–25.

109. Holman, "History of Political Thought at a Standstill"; Paul Mazzocchi, "Desire, Friendship, and the Politics of Refusal: The Utopian Afterlives of La Boétie's *Discourse on Voluntary Servitude*," *Utopian Studies* 29, no. 2 (2018): 248–66.

110. Abensour, "Pierre Leroux et l'utopie," 133–34.

111. Melançon, "Note critique," 284.

112. Abensour, "The Politics of Romance," 145–46.

Chapter 2

1. Jean-Jacques Rousseau, *The Confessions*, trans. J. M. Cohen (New York: Penguin, 1953), book 9. Translation modified.—Trans.

2. Theodor W. Adorno, *Metaphysics: Concept and Problems*, ed. Rolf Tiedemann, trans. Edmund Jephcott (Stanford, CA: Stanford University Press, 2001), 104.—Trans.

3. Françoise Proust, *L'histoire à contretemps: Le temps historique chez Walter Benjamin* (Paris: Éditions du Cerf, 1994), 121.—Trans.

Chapter 3

1. Leo Strauss, "What Is Political Philosophy?," *Journal of Politics* 19, no. 3 (1957): 345–46.

2. On that point, see my article with Michel-Pierre Edmond, "Leo Strauss," *Encyclopædia universalis* (1983).

3. Maurice Merleau-Ponty, "Man and Adversity," in *Signs* (Evanston, IL: Northwestern University Press, 1964), 240.

4. Jean-Jacques Rousseau, *The Confessions*, trans. J. M. Cohen (New York: Penguin, 1953), book 9. Translation modified.—Trans.

Chapter 4

1. Ludwig Feuerbach, "The Necessity of a Reform of Philosophy," in *The Fiery Brook: Selected Writings*, trans. Zawar Hanfi (London: Verso, 2013), 145.

Chapter 5

1. Simon Leys, *The Chairman's New Clothes: Mao and the Cultural Revolution* (New York: St. Martin's, 1977); Simon Leys, *Chinese Shadows* (New York: Viking, 1977).

2. Simon Leys, *Orwell ou l'horreur de la politique* (Paris: Hermann, 1984).

3. Leys, *Orwell ou l'horreur de la politique*, 34.

4. Leys, *Orwell ou l'horreur de la politique*, 35.

5. Leys, *Orwell ou l'horreur de la politique*, 36.

6. George Orwell, *Homage to Catalonia* (New York: Penguin, 1970), 8, 10.

7. Jean-Jacques Rousseau, *The Confessions*, trans. J. M. Cohen (New York: Penguin, 1953), book 9. Translation modified.—Trans.

8. Benjamin Constant, *Mélanges de littérature et de politique* (Paris: Pichon et Didier, 1829).

9. Miguel Abensour, "Réflexions sur les deux interprétations du totalitarisme chez Claude Lefort," in *La démocratie à l'oeuvre: Autour de Claude Lefort*, ed. Claude Habib and Claude Mouchard (Paris: Esprit, 1993), 70–136.—Trans.

10. Hannah Arendt, "On the Nature of Totalitarianism: An Essay in Understanding," in *Essays in Understanding, 1930–1954*, ed. Jerome Kohn (New York: Schocken, 1994), 336.
11. Hannah Arendt, "Introduction into Politics," in *The Promise of Politics*, ed. Jerome Kohn (New York: Schocken, 2005), 108.
12. Arendt, "Introduction into Politics," 126.
13. Arendt, "On the Nature of Totalitarianism," 342.
14. Arendt, "On the Nature of Totalitarianism," 342.
15. Arendt, "On the Nature of Totalitarianism," 342.
16. Arendt, "On the Nature of Totalitarianism," 342
17. Arendt, "On the Nature of Totalitarianism," 343.
18. Hannah Arendt, *The Origins of Totalitarianism* (New York: Penguin, 2017), 452.
19. Aristotle, *Politics*, trans. Ernest Barker (Oxford: Oxford University Press, 1995), 39–41.
20. Arendt, "On the Nature of Totalitarianism," 359.
21. Hannah Arendt, "On the Nature of Totalitarianism: An Essay in Understanding," Essays and Lectures, Hannah Arendt Papers: Speeches and Writings File, 1923–1975, Library of Congress, https://www.loc.gov/item/mss1105601268/.
22. Arendt, "On the Nature of Totalitarianism," 338.
23. Léon Krier, ed., *Albert Speer: Architecture, 1932–1942* (Bruxelles: Archives d'Architecture Moderne, 1985). On this point, see ch. 5, "On Compactness: Architecture and Totalitarian Regimes."
24. Hannah Arendt, Hannah Arendt Papers: Speeches and Writings File, 1923–1975, Miscellany, Outlines and Research Memoranda, 1946, undated, https://www.loc.gov/item/mss1105601418/.
25. Arendt, "On the Nature of Totalitarianism," 355.
26. Arendt, *The Origins of Totalitarianism*, 450.
27. Arendt, "On the Nature of Totalitarianism," 344.
28. Arendt, *The Origins of Totalitarianism*, 452.
29. Arendt, "On the Nature of Totalitarianism," 348–49.
30. Arendt, "On the Nature of Totalitarianism," 357.
31. Arendt, "On the Nature of Totalitarianism," 356.
32. On this point, see Miguel Abensour, "Hannah Arendt: La critique du totalitarisme et la servitude volontaire," in *Pour une philosophie politique critique* (Paris: Sens & Tonka, 2006), 137–65.
33. Immanuel Kant, *Critique of Judgement*, trans. James Creed Meredith (Oxford: Oxford University Press, 2007), sec. 40, 125.
34. Cf. Hannah Arendt, *Lectures on Kant's Political Philosophy*, ed. Ronald Beiner (Chicago: University of Chicago Press, 1989).
35. Arendt, "On the Nature of Totalitarianism: An Essay in Understanding," Hannah Arendt Papers.

36. Hannah Arendt, epilogue to *The Promise of Politics*, ed. Jerome Kohn (New York: Schocken, 2005), 202.

37. Arendt, *The Origins of Totalitarianism*, 461.

38. Christian Meier, *Introduction à l'anthropologie politique de l'Antiquité classique*, trans. Pierre Blanchaud (Paris: PUF, 1984), 30. [Our translation.]

39. Hannah Arendt, "Walter Benjamin: 1892–1940," in *Men in Dark Times*, trans. Harry Zorn (New York: Harvest, 1968), 204.

40. Arendt, "On the Nature of Totalitarianism," 360.

41. Hannah Arendt, "On Humanity in Dark Times: Thoughts about Lessing," in *Men in Dark Times*, trans. Harry Zorn (New York: Harvest, 1968), 10.

Chapter 6

1. Friedrich Nietzsche, "Twilight of the Idols," in *The Anti-Christ, Ecce Homo, Twilight of the Idols and Other Writings*, ed. Aaron Ridley and Judith Norman, trans. Judith Norman (Cambridge: Cambridge University Press, 2005), 197.

2. Theodor W. Adorno, *Negative Dialectics*, trans. E. B. Ashton (New York: Continuum, 1973), 365.

3. See in particular Lars Olof Larsson, *Albert Speer: Le plan de Berlin, 1937–1943* (Brussels: Archives d'Architecture Moderne, 1983); Léon Krier, "An Architecture of Desire," in *Albert Speer: Architecture, 1932–1942* (New York: Monacelli, 2013), 217–31.

4. Quoted in Eric Michaud, *The Cult of Art in Nazi Germany*, trans. Janet Lloyd (Stanford, CA: Stanford University Press, 2004), 36–37.

5. Abensour invents the French word "indifférentisme," which is translated here by the neologism "indifferentism."—Trans.

6. Krier, "An Architecture of Desire," 227.

7. Krier, "An Architecture of Desire," 227.

8. Barbara Miller Lane, *Architecture and Politics in Germany, 1918–1945* (Cambridge, MA: Harvard University Press, 1968), 9.

9. Krier, "An Architecture of Desire," 223.

10. Leo Strauss, *Natural Right and History* (Chicago: University of Chicago Press, 1953), 136.

11. Claude Lefort, "The Permanence of the Theological-Political?," in *Democracy and Political Theory*, trans. David Macey (Cambridge, UK: Polity, 1988), 218–19.

12. George Mosse, *The Nationalization of the Masses: Political Symbolism and Mass Movements in Germany from the Napoleonic Wars through the Third Reich* (New York: Fertig, 1975).

13. Franz Neumann, *Behemoth: The Structure and Practice of National Socialism 1933–1944* (New York: Oxford University Press, 1944).

14. Throughout this work the term "la masse" has been translated as "the mass" rather than "the crowd," even though Canetti's influential work *Masse und*

Macht (1960) has been translated into English as *Crowds and Power*. There is an important difference between "mass" and "crowd," which is particularly significant here due to the nature of Abensour's argument: "mass" implies that a group of people has cohered together into one body, whereas "crowd" implies a group of dissociated individuals who have merely congregated together in the same area.—Trans.

15. On this point, see proposition 5 regarding the strategy of disjunction, which directs attention to the dangers of dogmatic affirmations of a conjunction between two phenomena.

16. Albert Speer, *Inside the Third Reich: Memoirs*, trans. Richard Winston and Clara Winston (New York: Macmillan, 1970), 27–28.

17. Speer, *Inside the Third Reich*, 28. Emphasis added.

18. Alexandre Kojève, "Tyranny and Wisdom," in *On Tyranny*, by Leo Strauss, rev. and exp. ed. (Chicago: University of Chicago Press, 2000), 135–76.

19. Lane, *Architecture and Politics in Germany, 1918–1945*, 161.

20. Lane, *Architecture and Politics in Germany, 1918–1945*, 179–80.

21. Eric Michaud, *Un art de l'éternité* (Paris: Gallimard, 1996), 37, 56.

22. Quoted in Lane, *Architecture and Politics in Germany, 1918–1945*, 162–63.

23. Hannah Arendt, "Introduction into Politics," in *The Promise of Politics*, ed. Jerome Kohn (New York: Schocken, 2005), 114–24.

24. Speer, *Inside the Third Reich*, 134.

25. Speer, *Inside the Third Reich*, 134–35.

26. Mosse, *The Nationalization of the Masses*, 4.

27. François Guizot, *History of the Origin of Representative Government in Europe*, trans. Andrew Scoble (London: Henry G. Bohn, 1861), lecture 16.

28. Krier, "An Architecture of Desire," 219, 223. Emphasis added.

29. Elias Canetti, *Crowds and Power*, trans. Carol Stewart (New York: Seabury, 1978), 15. [The English translation of Canetti's work has been used, but all references to "crowd" have been changed to "mass." See note 14.]

30. Canetti, *Crowds and Power*, 15–16.

31. Canetti, *Crowds and Power*, 18. Original emphasis.

32. Elias Canetti, *The Conscience of Words*, trans. Joachim Neugroschel (New York: Seabury, 1979), 146–47. Original emphasis.

33. Canetti, *The Conscience of Words*, 147–48. Original emphasis.

34. Siegfried Kracauer, "The Mass Ornament," in *The Mass Ornament: Weimar Essays*, ed. and trans. Thomas Y. Levin (Cambridge: Harvard University Press, 1995), 85.—Trans.

35. Max Weber, *Economy and Society: An Outline of Interpretive Sociology*, ed. Guenther Roth and Claus Wittich (Berkeley: University of California Press, 1978), 241.

36. Hitler quoted in Speer, *Inside the Third Reich*, 114.

37. Speer, *Inside the Third Reich*, 79.

38. Canetti, *The Conscience of Words*, 148. Emphasis added.

39. Canetti, *The Conscience of Words*, 148.

40. Krier, "An Architecture of Desire," 223.
41. Speer, *Inside the Third Reich*, 69.
42. Canetti, *The Conscience of Words*, 148.
43. Canetti, *The Conscience of Words*, 148–49. Emphasis added.
44. Miguel Abensour, "On a Misinterpretation of Totalitarianism and Its Effects."
45. Hannah Arendt, *The Human Condition*, 2nd ed. (Chicago: University of Chicago Press, 1998), 52–53.
46. Albert Speer, *L'immortalité du pouvoir* (Paris: La Table Ronde, 1981), 266–68. Emphasis added.
47. Speer, *L'immortalité du pouvoir*, 266–68. Emphasis added.
48. Speer, *L'immortalité du pouvoir*, 266–68. Emphasis added.
49. Speer, *L'immortalité du pouvoir*, 243–44. Emphasis added.
50. Roger Caillois, *Quatre essais de sociologie contemporaine* (Paris: O. Perrin, 1951), 63.
51. Caillois, *Quatre essais de sociologie contemporaine*, 66–67.
52. Walter Benjamin and Asja Lacis, "Naples," in *Reflections: Essays, Aphorisms, Autobiographical Writing*, ed. Peter Demetz, trans. Edmund Jephcott (New York: Schocken Books, 1986), 165–66.
53. Krier, "An Architecture of Desire," 222.
54. Hannah Arendt, "Hannah Arendt on Hannah Arendt," in *Hannah Arendt: The Recovery of the Public World*, ed. Melvyn Hill (New York: St. Martin's, 1979), 309.—Trans.
55. For an account of the historical development of this title, see Annette Wieviorka, *Déportation et génocide: Entre la mémoire et l'oubli* (Paris: Plon, 1992), 223–29.
56. Claude Lefort, *The Political Forms of Modern Society: Bureaucracy, Democracy, Totalitarianism*, ed. John Thompson (Cambridge, UK: Polity, 1986), 298.
57. Lefort, *The Political Forms of Modern Society*, 298.
58. Lefort, *The Political Forms of Modern Society*, 306.
59. Paul Nizan, "Du problème de la monumentalité, 1934," *VH* 101, no. 7–8 (1972): 206.
60. Hannah Arendt, *The Origins of Totalitarianism* (New York: Harcourt, 1994), 465–66.
61. Caillois, *Quatre essais de sociologie contemporaine*, 65.

Chapter 7

1. Hannah Arendt, "'What Remains? The Language Remains': A Conversation with Günter Gaus," in *The Portable Hannah Arendt*, ed. Peter Baehr (New York: Penguin, 2000), 3–22.
2. Arendt, "'What Remains? The Language Remains': A Conversation with Günter Gaus," 3–4.

3. Quoted in Hannah Arendt, *Lectures on Kant's Political Philosophy*, ed. Ronald Beiner (Chicago: University of Chicago Press 1989), 22.

4. Hannah Arendt, "Concern with Politics in Recent European Philosophical Thought," in *Essays in Understanding, 1930–1954*, ed. Jerome Kohn (New York: Harcourt Brace, 1994).—Trans.

5. Hannah Arendt, *The Life of the Mind*, one-volume ed. (New York: Harcourt, 1978), 152–53.—Trans.

6. Hannah Arendt, "'Philosophy and Politics: What Is Political Philosophy?' Lectures and Seminar, 1969, New School for Social Research, New York, N.Y.," Courses, Hannah Arendt Papers, Subject File, 1949–1975, Library of Congress, undated, http://hdl.loc.gov/loc.mss/ms001004.mss11056.00971.—Trans.

7. Blaise Pascal, *Pensées*, trans. A. J. Krailsheimer (London: Penguin, 1995), 487.

8. Hannah Arendt, "Philosophy and Politics," *Social Research* 57, no. 1 (1990): 73.

9. Reiner Schürmann, *Heidegger on Being and Acting: From Principles to Anarchy* (Bloomington: Indiana University Press, 1987), 37.

10. Schürmann, *Heidegger on Being and Acting*, 37.

11. Schürmann, *Heidegger on Being and Acting*, 41.—Trans.

12. Hannah Arendt, "Tradition and the Modern Age," in *Between Past and Future: Eight Exercises in Political Thought* (New York: Viking, 1961), 28–29.

13. Hannah Arendt, "Introduction into Politics," in *The Promise of Politics*, ed. J. Kohn (New York: Schocken, 2005), 130.

14. Arendt, "Philosophy and Politics," 103.

15. Plato, *Phaedo*, in *The Portable Plato*, ed. Scott Buchanan, trans. Benjamin Jowett (New York: Penguin, 2009), 201–2.

16. Plato, *Phédon*, trans. Monique Dixsaut (Paris: Flammarion, 1991), note 94 by Dixsaut, 333.

17. Arendt, *The Life of the Mind*, 79.

18. Plato, *Phaedo*, 226.

19. Nicole Loraux, "Donc Socrate est immortel," *Le temps de la réflexion* 3 (1982): 36.

20. Loraux, "Donc Socrate est immortel," 45.

21. Arendt, "Philosophy and Politics: What Is Political Philosophy?," 024445.

22. Arendt, "Philosophy and Politics: What Is Political Philosophy?," 024445.

23. Hannah Arendt, *The Origins of Totalitarianism* (New York: Harcourt, 1994), 479.

24. Arendt, "Philosophy and Politics: What Is Political Philosophy?," 24446.

25. Leo Strauss, "On the Intention of Rousseau," *Social Research* 14, no. 4 (1947): 485.

26. Strauss, "On the Intention of Rousseau," 486.

27. Arendt, *Lectures on Kant's Political Philosophy*, 27.—Trans.

28. Arendt, *Lectures on Kant's Political Philosophy*, 28.

29. Arendt, *Lectures on Kant's Political Philosophy*, 28.

30. Immanuel Kant, *Observations on the Feeling of the Beautiful and Sublime and Other Writings*, trans. Patrick Frierson and Paul Guyer (Cambridge: Cambridge University Press, 2011), 96.

31. Arendt, *Lectures on Kant's Political Philosophy*, 29.

32. Éric Weil, *Problèmes kantiens* (Paris: Vrin, 1970), 140–41.

33. Weil, *Problèmes kantiens*, 140–41

34. Jacques Rancière, *Disagreement: Politics and Philosophy*, trans. Julie Rose (Minneapolis: University of Minnesota Press, 2004), from ch. 4, "From Archipolitics to Metapolitics," 61–93.

35. Hannah Arendt, *The Human Condition* (Chicago: University of Chicago Press, 1998), 186.

36. Arendt, "Introduction into Politics," 122.

37. Arendt, "Introduction into Politics," 124.

38. Arendt, *The Life of the Mind*, 72.

39. Hannah Arendt, "Action and the Pursuit of Happiness," in *Politische Ordnung und menschliche Existenz: Festgabe für Eric Voegelin zum 60. Geburtstag*, ed. Alois Dempf, Hannah Arendt, and Friedrich Engel-Janosi (Munich: Beck, 1962), 1–16.

40. Maurice Blanchot, *The Infinite Conversation*, trans. Susan Hanson (Minneapolis: University of Minnesota Press, 1993), 374.

41. Hannah Arendt, "Zionism Reconsidered," in *The Jewish Writings*, ed. Jerome Kohn and Ron H. Feldman (New York: Schocken, 2008), 343–74.

Chapter 8

1. Ludwig Feuerbach, "'The Necessity of a Reform of Philosophy,'" in *The Fiery Brook: Selected Writings*, trans. Zawar Hanfi (London: Verso, 2013), 145.

2. Max Horkheimer, "Authority and the Family," in *Critical Theory: Selected Essays*, trans. Matthew J. O'Connell (New York: Continuum, 1975), 69.

3. George Friedman, *The Political Philosophy of the Frankfurt School* (Ithaca, NY: Cornell University Press, 1981).

4. Friedman, *The Political Philosophy of the Frankfurt School*.

5. Max Horkheimer and Theodor W. Adorno, *Dialectic of Enlightenment*, trans. Edmund Jephcott (Stanford, CA: Stanford University Press, 2002), 1.

6. Horkheimer and Adorno, *Dialectic of Enlightenment*, xvi.

7. Herbert Marcuse, *Reason and Revolution: Hegel and the Rise of Social Theory* (London: Routledge, 2000), 258.

8. Marcuse, *Reason and Revolution*, 258.

9. Marcuse, *Reason and Revolution*, 258.

10. Karl Korsch, *Marxism and Philosophy*, trans. Fred Halliday (London: Verso, 2013).

11. Theodor W. Adorno, *Minima Moralia: Reflections on a Damaged Life*, trans. Edmund Jephcott (London: Verso, 2005), 15.

12. Max Horkheimer, "Egoism and Freedom Movements: On the Anthropology of the Bourgeois Era," in *Between Philosophy and Social Science: Selected Early Writings*, trans. G. Frederick Hunter, Matthew S. Kramer, and John Torpey (Cambridge, MA: MIT Press, 1993), 49–110.

13. Max Horkheimer, "The End of Reason," in *The Essential Frankfurt School Reader*, ed. Andrew Arato and Elike Gerhardt (New York: Continuum, 1982), 26–48.

14. Max Horkheimer, "The Authoritarian State," *Telos*, no. 15 (1973): 3–20.

15. Max Horkheimer, *Eclipse of Reason* (London: Continuum, 2004).

16. Theodor W. Adorno et al., *The Authoritarian Personality* (London: Verso, 2019).

17. Norbert Guterman and Leo Löwenthal, *Prophets of Deceit: A Study of the Techniques of the American Agitator* (London: Verso, 2021).

18. Leo Lowenthal, *False Prophets: Studies on Authoritarianism* (London: Routledge, 2015).

19. Herbert Marcuse, "The Struggle against Liberalism in the Totalitarian View of the State," in *Negations: Essays in Critical Theory* (Boston: Beacon, 1968), 3–42.

20. Herbert Marcuse, "Some Social Implications of Modern Technology," in *The Essential Frankfurt School Reader*, 138–62.

21. Herbert Marcuse, "State and Individual under National Socialism," in *Technology, War and Fascism: Collected Papers of Herbert Marcuse*, ed. Douglas Kellner (London: Routledge, 2004), 1:67–92.

22. Theodor W. Adorno, *The Stars Down to Earth and Other Essays on the Irrational in Culture*, ed. Stephen Crook (London: Routledge, 1994).

23. Franz Neumann, *Behemoth: The Structure and Practice of National Socialism, 1933–1944* (New York: Oxford University Press, 1944).

24. William E. Scheuerman, *Between the Norm and the Exception: The Frankfurt School and the Rule of Law* (Cambridge, MA: MIT Press, 1997); Franz Neumann and Otto Kirchheimer, *The Rule of Law under Siege: Selected Essays of Franz L. Neumann and Otto Kirchheimer*, ed. William E. Scheuerman (Berkeley: University of California Press, 1996).

25. Friedrich Pollock, *The Economic and Social Consequences of Automation*, trans. W. O. Henderson and W.H. Chaloner (Oxford: Blackwell, 1957).

26. Friedrich Pollock, "State Capitalism: Its Possibilities and Limitations," in *The Essential Frankfurt School Reader*, 71–94.

27. Max Horkheimer, "Beginnings of the Bourgeois Philosophy of History," in *Between Philosophy and Social Science*, 316.

28. Horkheimer, "Beginnings of the Bourgeois Philosophy of History," 316.

29. Theodor W. Adorno, *Negative Dialectics*, trans. E. B. Ashton (New York: Continuum, 1973), 321–23.

30. Adorno, *Negative Dialectics*, 323.

31. Horkheimer, "Authority and the Family," 53.
32. Horkheimer, "Authority and the Family," 54.
33. Horkheimer, "Authority and the Family," 53.
34. Horkheimer, "Authority and the Family," 55.
35. Horkheimer, "Authority and the Family," 55.
36. Friedrich Nietzsche, "On the Genealogy of Morals," in *On the Genealogy of Morals and Ecce Homo*, trans. Walter Kaufmann and R. J. Hollingdale (New York: Vintage, 1989), 61.
37. Horkheimer, "Authority and the Family," 57.
38. Horkheimer, "Authority and the Family," 57.
39. Horkheimer, "Authority and the Family," 66.
40. Horkheimer, "Authority and the Family," 66.
41. Horkheimer, "Authority and the Family," 69.
42. Horkheimer, "Authority and the Family," 68.
43. Horkheimer, "Authority and the Family," 69.
44. Horkheimer, "Authority and the Family," 67–68.
45. Max Horkheimer, "La philosophie de la concentration absolue," in *Théorie critique* (Paris: Payot, 1978).
46. Horkheimer, "La philosophie de la concentration absolue," 324.
47. Horkheimer, "La philosophie de la concentration absolue," 324.
48. Moses Hess, "The Philosophy of the Act," in *Socialist Thought: A Documentary History*, rev. ed., ed. Albert Fried and Ronald Sanders (New York: Columbia University Press, 1992), 249–75.
49. Benedict de Spinoza, *Theological-Political Treatise*, trans. Michael Silverthorne and Jonathan Israel (Cambridge: Cambridge University Press, 2007), 252.
50. Herbert Marcuse, "Philosophy and Critical Theory," in *Negations: Essays in Critical Theory* (Boston: Beacon, 1968), 145.
51. Jacques Rancière, *Disagreement: Politics and Philosophy*, trans. Julie Rose (Minneapolis: University of Minnesota Press, 2004), 30.
52. Rancière, *Disagreement: Politics and Philosophy*, 31.
53. Hannah Arendt, "What Is Freedom," in *Between Past and Future: Eight Exercises in Political Thought* (New York: Viking, 1961), 146.
54. Karl Korsch et al., *La contre-révolution bureaucratique* (Paris: UGE, 1973).
55. On this point see the very valuable work of William David Jones, *The Lost Debate: German Socialist Intellectuals and Totalitarianism* (Champaign: University of Illinois Press, 1999), which shows that the question of totalitarianism was not limited to the confrontations of the Cold War.
56. Horkheimer, "The Authoritarian State," 16.
57. Horkheimer, "The Authoritarian State," 20.
58. Horkheimer, "The Authoritarian State," 20.
59. Horkheimer, "La Philosophie de La Concentration Absolue," 322. See also 298 and 323.
60. Horkheimer, "The Authoritarian State," 11.

61. Luc Ferry and Alain Renaut, eds., *Why We Are Not Nietzscheans*, trans. Robert de Loaiza (Chicago: University of Chicago Press, 1997).—Trans.

62. Luc Ferry and Alain Renaut were coresponsible for an edition of *Archives de philosophie* (45, no. 2 [1982]) dedicated to the Frankfurt School.

63. Guy Petitdemange, "L'Aufklärung: Un mythe, une tâche," *Recherches de science religieuse*, July–September 1984, 426. See also, Rolf Wiggershaus, *L'Ecole de Francfort: Histoire, développement, signification*, trans. L. Deroche-Gurcel (Paris: Presses Universitaires France, 1993), 320–21.

64. Horkheimer, *Eclipse of Reason*, 120.
65. Horkheimer and Adorno, *Dialectic of Enlightenment*, 185.
66. Horkheimer and Adorno, *Dialectic of Enlightenment*, 2.
67. Horkheimer and Adorno, *Dialectic of Enlightenment*, 42–43.
68. Horkheimer, "Beginnings of the Bourgeois Philosophy of History," 332.
69. Horkheimer and Adorno, *Dialectic of Enlightenment*, 192.
70. Horkheimer, *Eclipse of Reason*, 64.
71. G. W. F. Hegel, *Phenomenology of Spirit*, trans. A. V. Miller (Oxford: Oxford University Press, 1977), 110.
72. Herbert Marcuse, *Hegel's Ontology and the Theory of Historicity*, trans. Seyla Benhabib (Cambridge, MA: MIT Press, 1987); Marcuse, *Reason and Revolution*, 114–20.
73. Horkheimer and Adorno, *Dialectic of Enlightenment*, 27.
74. Horkheimer and Adorno, *Dialectic of Enlightenment*, 27.
75. Horkheimer, "The End of Reason," 35.
76. Friedrich Nietzsche, *Beyond Good and Evil*, trans. Judith Norman (Cambridge: Cambridge University Press, 2002), 123.
77. Nietzsche, "On the Genealogy of Morals," 61.
78. Nietzsche, "On the Genealogy of Morals," 62.
79. Nietzsche, "On the Genealogy of Morals," 86–87.
80. Claude Lefort and Marcel Gauchet, "Sur la democratie: Le politique et l'institution du social," *Textures*, no. 2–3 (1971): 8.
81. Lefort and Gauchet, "Sur la démocratie," 8–9.
82. Claude Lefort, "The Permanence of the Theologico-Political?," in *Political Theologies: Public Religions in a Post-Secular World*, ed. Hent de Vries and Lawrence Eugene Sullivan (New York: Fordham University Press, 2006), 152.
83. Hannah Arendt, *The Human Condition*, 2nd ed. (Chicago: University of Chicago Press, 1998), 32n22.
84. Arendt, *The Human Condition*, 32.
85. Hannah Arendt, "Introduction into Politics," in *The Promise of Politics*, ed. Jerome Kohn (New York: Schocken, 2005), 120.
86. Karl Marx, *Critique of Hegel's "Philosophy of Right,"* trans. Joseph O'Malley and Annette Jolin (Cambridge: Cambridge University Press, 1977), 27.
87. Arendt, *The Human Condition*, 35.

88. Immanuel Kant, "What Does It Mean to Orient Oneself in Thinking?," in *Religion and Rational Theology*, trans. Allen W. Wood and George di Giovanni, rev. ed. (Cambridge: Cambridge University Press, 2001), 16.

89. Claude Lefort, "Machiavelli and the Verità Effetuale," in *Writing, the Political Test*, trans. David Ames Curtis (Durham, NC: Duke University Press, 2000), 133.

90. Georges Navet, "Le temps de l'émancipation," MHDR, Université Paris 7–Denis Diderot, 2001–2002.

91. Neumann, *Behemoth*, 479; also Herbert Marcuse, ed., *The Democratic and the Authoritarian State* (New York: Free Press, 1957); also Neumann and Kirchheimer, *The Rule of Law under Siege*.

92. Adorno, *Minima Moralia*, 67.

Chapter 9

1. Walter Benjamin, "Theses on the Philosophy of History," in *Illuminations*, ed. Hannah Arendt, trans. Harry Zohn (New York: Schocken, 1968), 254.—Trans.

2. Cornelius Castoriadis, "On the History of the Workers' Movement," *Telos*, no. 30 (1976): 3–42; Patrick Fridenson, "La formation de la classe ouvrière anglaise," *Le Débat* 3, no. 3 (1980): 175–88. [Maximilien Rubel, "Non-market Socialism in the Nineteenth Century," in *Non-market Socialism in the Nineteenth and Twentieth Centuries*, ed. John Crump and Maximilien Rubel (New York: Palgrave Macmillan, 1987), 10–34.]

3. E. P. Thompson, "An Open Letter to Leszek Kolakowski (1973)," in *The Poverty of Theory: Or an Orrery of Errors* (London: Merlin, 1978), 93–192.

4. William Morris, *William Morris on Art and Socialism*, ed. Norman Kelvin (New York: Dover, 1999).

5. E. P. Thompson, *William Morris: Romantic to Revolutionary* (New York: Pantheon, 1976).

6. On the controversy as a whole, see Perry Anderson, "Origins of the Present Crisis," *New Left Review*, 1st ser., no. 23 (1964): 26–53; Tom Nairn, "The English Working Class," *New Left Review*, 1st ser., no. 24 (1964): 43–57; E. P. Thompson, "The Peculiarities of the English," *Socialist Register* 2 (1965): 35–91.

7. E. P. Thompson, "An Interview with E. P. Thompson," *Radical History Review*, no. 12 (1976): 24–25. See also E. P. Thompson, "Romanticism, Utopianism and Moralism: The Case of William Morris," *New Left Review*, 1st ser., no. 99 (1976): 83–111.

8. E. P. Thompson, *The Making of the English Working Class* (Harmondsworth, UK: Penguin, 1980), 14.

9. Thompson, *The Making of the English Working Class*, 214.

10. Claude Lefort, "L'experience prolétarienne," *Socialisme ou barbarie*, no. 11 (1952); reprinted in *Éléments d'une critique de la bureaucratie* (Paris-Geneva: Droz, 1971).

11. Thompson, *The Making of the English Working Class*, 8.
12. Thompson, *The Making of the English Working Class*, 10.
13. E. P. Thompson, "Eighteenth-Century English Society: Class Struggle without Class?," *Social History* 3, no. 2 (1978): 146–50.
14. Karl Marx, *The Poverty of Philosophy*, trans. Harry Quelch (New York: Prometheus, 1995), 190.
15. Thompson, *The Making of the English Working Class*, 883.
16. Karl Marx and Friedrich Engels, *The Holy Family*, trans. R. Dixon (Moscow: Foreign Languages Publishing House, 1956), 53.
17. Thompson, *The Making of the English Working Class*, 487.
18. Thompson, *The Making of the English Working Class*, 217–18.
19. Thompson, *The Making of the English Working Class*, 487.
20. Thompson, *The Making of the English Working Class*, 231.
21. Thompson, *The Making of the English Working Class*, 231.
22. Thompson, *The Making of the English Working Class*, 487–88.
23. Thompson, *The Making of the English Working Class*, 12.
24. E. P. Thompson, "Time, Work-Discipline, and Industrial Capitalism," *Past & Present*, no. 38 (1967): 95.
25. Thompson, *The Making of the English Working Class*, 215–16.
26. Quoted in Thompson, *The Making of the English Working Class*, 200.
27. Thompson, *The Making of the English Working Class*, 110.
28. Thompson, *The Making of the English Working Class*, 194–95.
29. Thompson, *The Making of the English Working Class*, 915.
30. Jürgen Habermas, *The Structural Transformation of the Public Sphere: An Inquiry into a Category of Bourgeois Society*, trans. Thomas Burger and Frederick Lawrence (Cambridge, MA: MIT Press, 1991), xviii.
31. Thompson, *The Making of the English Working Class*, 24.
32. Hannah Arendt, *The Human Condition* (Chicago: University of Chicago Press, 1998), 215.
33. Thompson, *The Making of the English Working Class*, 203.
34. Thompson, "Romanticism, Utopianism and Moralism," 109.
35. William Morris, "A Dream of John Ball," in *Selected Writings*, ed. G. D. H. Cole (London: Nonesuch, 1948), 214.

Chapter 10

1. Theodor W. Adorno, *Negative Dialectics*, trans. E. B. Ashton (New York: Continuum, 1973), 145.—Trans.
2. Paul Bénichou, *Le temps des prophètes: Doctrines de l'âge romantique* (Paris: Gallimard, 1977).
3. See Jean-Jacques Rousseau, *Politics and the Arts: Letter to M. D'Alembert on the Theatre*, trans. Allan Bloom (Ithaca, NY: Cornell University Press, 1968), 66.—Trans.

4. Bronislaw Baczko, *Les imaginaires sociaux: Mémoires et espoirs collectifs* (Paris: Payot, 1984), 127–48.

5. In fact, we might ask if our contemporaries know how to read utopia. Some Christian and Marxist interpretations of Thomas More, for example, suggest not. Both neglect that More's utopia is one of the greatest rhetorical inventions ever—that *Utopia* should not be read literally, but rather that we should first look at the issue of indirect ways and thus recognize that indirectness as defined in book 1 provides the key for interpreting book 2.

6. Adorno, *Negative Dialectics*, 3.

7. Miguel Abensour, "The History of Utopia and the Destiny of Its Critique," in *Political Uses of Utopia: New Marxist, Anarchist, and Radical Democratic Perspectives*, ed. S. D. Chrostowska and James D. Ingram (New York: Columbia University Press, 2016), 3–56. [This article was originally published in two parts in 1973–1974. See Miguel Abensour, "L'histoire de l'utopie et le destin de sa critique I," *Textures*, no. 6–7 (1973): 3–26; Miguel Abensour, "L'histoire de l'utopie et le destin de sa critique II," *Textures*, no. 8–9 (1974): 55–81.]

8. William Morris, *News from Nowhere*, ed. Krishan Kumar (Cambridge: Cambridge University Press, 1995).

9. Joseph Dejacque, "L'humanisphère," in *La question révolutionnaire; L'humanisphère; À bas les chefs; La libération des noirs américains*, ed. Valentin Pelosse (Paris: Champ Libre, 1971), 85–207.

10. Lucien Goldmann, *Sciences humaines et philosophie*, Nouvelle encyclopédie philosophique (Paris: Presses universitaires de France, 1952), 40–41.

11. Karl Marx and Friedrich Engels, *Manifesto of the Communist Party*, in *The Marx-Engels Reader*, ed. Robert C. Tucker, 2nd ed. (New York: Norton, 1978), 498–99.—Trans.

12. Karl Marx, "Letter to Dr. Kugelmann, October 9, 1866," in *Letters to Dr. Kugelmann* (London: Lawrence and Wishart, 1941), 40.—Trans.

13. Karl Marx, "Marx to Friedrich Adolph Sorge in Hoboken, October 19, 1877," in *Karl Marx and Frederick Engels: Selected Correspondence*, 2nd ed. (Moscow: Progress, 1965), 291. Original emphasis.

14. In English, this tradition is most often referred to as the council or councilist tradition. On the distinction between the communalist/councilist and Jacobin traditions, see Oskar Anweiler, *The Soviets: The Russian Workers, Peasants, and Soldiers Councils, 1905–1921*, trans. Ruth Hein (New York: Pantheon, 1975).—Trans.

15. Theodor W. Adorno, "Progress," in *Critical Models: Interventions and Catchwords*, trans. Henry Pickford (New York: Columbia University Press, 1998), 143–60.

16. Theodor W. Adorno, *Minima Moralia*, trans. Edmund Jephcott (London: Verso, 2005), sec. 100. Abensour translates Adorno's "Fluchtlinien" into French as "lignes de fuite." Although Jephcott translates "Fluchtlinien" into English as "vanishing-lines," we use "lines of flight," which better captures Abensour's use of the term.—Trans.

17. Emmanuel Levinas, *Humanism of the Other*, trans. Nidra Poller (Urbana: University of Illinois Press, 2003), 60. We also encounter in Levinas a dialectic of emancipation in relation to the revolutions in which "disalienation itself is alienated." See Emmanuel Levinas, "No Identity," in *Collected Philosophical Papers* (Dordrecht: Nijhoff, 1987), 143. This dialectic of emancipation is also connected to another conception of utopia. See Miguel Abensour, "To Think Utopia Otherwise," trans. Bettina Bergo, *Graduate Faculty Philosophy Journal* 20/21, no. 2/1 (1998): 251–79.

18. Friedrich Nietzsche, *Human, All Too Human: A Book for Free Spirits*, trans. R. J. Hollingdale (Cambridge: Cambridge University Press, 1996), 173.

19. Georg Lukács, *The Destruction of Reason*, trans. Peter Palmer (Atlantic Highlands, NJ: Humanities Press, 1981).—Trans.

20. Max Horkheimer and Theodor W. Adorno, *Dialectic of Enlightenment*, trans. Edmund Jephcott (Stanford, CA: Stanford University Press, 2002), xvi.

21. Horkheimer and Adorno, *Dialectic of Enlightenment*, xviii.

22. Horkheimer and Adorno, *Dialectic of Enlightenment*, 8.—Trans.

23. Horkheimer and Adorno, *Dialectic of Enlightenment*, 1.

24. Horkheimer and Adorno, *Dialectic of Enlightenment*, 6.

25. Horkheimer and Adorno, *Dialectic of Enlightenment*, 11.

26. Theodor W. Adorno, *Hegel: Three Studies* (Cambridge, MA: MIT Press, 1993), 74.

27. Adorno, *Minima Moralia*, 192.

28. Horkheimer and Adorno, *Dialectic of Enlightenment*, 32–33.

29. Walter Benjamin, "Paris, the Capital of the Nineteenth Century: Exposé of 1935," in *The Arcades Project*, ed. Rolf Tiedemann, trans. Howard Eiland and Kevin McLaughlin (Cambridge, MA: Belknap Press of Harvard University Press, 2002), 4.

30. Benjamin, "Paris, the Capital of the Nineteenth Century: Exposé of 1935," 4.

31. Theodor W. Adorno, "Wiesengrund-Adorno and Gretel Karplus to Benjamin: Hornberg, 2–4 and 5.8.1935," in *The Complete Correspondence, 1928–1940*, ed. Henri Lonitz, trans. Nicholas Walker (Cambridge, MA: Harvard University Press, 1999), 104.

32. Adorno, "Wiesengrund-Adorno and Gretel Karplus to Benjamin: Hornberg, 2–4 and 5.8.1935," 106.

33. Adorno, *Negative Dialectics*, 323.—Trans.

34. Adorno, *Negative Dialectics*, 320.

35. Adorno, *Minima Moralia*, 234, 236.—Trans.

36. Gretel Adorno and Walter Benjamin, *Correspondence, 1930–1940*, ed. Henri Lonitz and Christoph Gödde, trans. Wieland Hoban (Cambridge, UK: Polity, 2008), 155.

37. Georges Henein, *Prestige de la terreur* (La Caire: Éditions Champollion, 1945).

38. Here I draw on the discussion of the dialectical problem of emancipation and utopia in Miguel Abensour, "W. Benjamin entre mélancolie et révolution—Pas-

sages Blanqui," in *Walter Benjamin à Paris* (Paris: Éditions du Cerf, 1986), 219–47.

39. Walter Benjamin, *The Correspondence of Walter Benjamin, 1910–1940* (Chicago: University of Chicago Press, 1994), 549.

40. Auguste Blanqui, *Eternity by the Stars: An Astronomical Hypothesis*, trans. Frank Chouraqui (New York: Contra Mundum, 2013).—Trans.

41. Benjamin, *The Correspondence of Walter Benjamin, 1910–1940*, 549.

42. Walter Benjamin, "Paris, Capital of the Nineteenth Century: Exposé of 1939," in *The Arcades Project*, ed. Rolf Tiedemann, trans. Howard Eiland and Kevin McLaughlin (Cambridge, MA: Belknap Press of Harvard University Press, 2002), 26.—Trans.

43. Benjamin, "Paris, Capital of the Nineteenth Century: Exposé of 1939," 26.—Trans.

44. Benjamin, "Paris, Capital of the Nineteenth Century: Exposé of 1939," 15.

45. Walter Benjamin, *The Arcades Project*, ed. Rolf Tiedemann, trans. Howard Eiland and Kevin McLaughlin (Cambridge, MA: Belknap Press of Harvard University Press, 2002), 21.—Trans.

46. Adorno, *Negative Dialectics*, 323.

47. Walter Benjamin, *Charles Baudelaire: Un poète lyrique à l'apogée du capitalisme*, ed. Rolf Tiedemann, trans. Jean Lacoste (Paris: Payot, 1990), 242. [Translated from the French edition.]

48. Walter Benjamin, "Sur le concept d'histoire," *Les Temps modernes*, no. 25 (1947). [Translated from the French edition.]

49. Benjamin, "Theses on the Philosophy of History," 259 (thesis 11).

50. Benjamin, "Theses on the Philosophy of History," 263–264 (thesis 18B). I take the term "two days after dialectics" ("surlendemain des dialectiques") from Levinas. See Emmanuel Levinas, "Le surlendemain des dialectiques," in *Emmanuel Levinas: Cahiers de la nuit surveillée* (Paris: Verdier, 1984), 322–24. This lesson on utopia does not follow critical theory or Benjamin, even if they help us to explain it better. Similar movements—transformations of the utopia-form or new creative practices—which draw from close analyses of the reversal of emancipation, can be found in the utopian movement. Pierre Leroux and William Morris both belong to the little-known or ignored tradition of the new utopian spirit that we are trying to draw out. Leroux had the role of determining the true field of utopia—the life of the "I" and the "we" as intersubjective relations but also as relations to humanity, to the human bond—and also delimited utopia through the relation it necessarily maintains to the infinite. Utopia no longer means a good society that is fully reconciled with itself, but is rather defined as the opening of the topos to the call and experience of nowhere, the opening of a place to a nonplace that prohibits a given historical community from closing in on itself in the illusion of mastery or sovereignty, making it possible to preserve a notion of otherness. For his part, William Morris transformed the utopian narrative by superimposing what could be

called an experimental utopia on a classic utopia. In the process, he fought against the model of production and devised a utopian theory—leisure time—which tries to ward off the specter of repetition by suspending time and the practice of forgetting. The Morrisian utopia, which forges a new relation with finitude, can be read as the very test of separation. Instead of denying the encroachment of the past on the present, the emancipated society is constituted in support of the suffering of lost generations, a debt that can never be remedied, as if in its very fragility this society felt permanently exposed to the burden of the past and the threat of repetition. I take the liberty of referring the interested reader to the texts in which I developed these ideas. On Leroux, see Miguel Abensour, "Pierre Leroux et l'utopie socialiste," *Cahiers de l'ISEA* 15 (1972): 2201–83; Miguel Abensour, "L'utopie socialiste: Une nouvelle alliance de la politique et de la religion," *Le temps de la réflexion II* (1981): 61–112; Miguel Abensour, "Pierre Leroux, 'De l'humanité,' " in *Dictionnaire des oeuvres politiques* (Paris: PUF, 1989), 551–56. On Morris, see Miguel Abensour, "The History of Utopia and the Destiny of Its Critique," 3–56; Miguel Abensour, "William Morris, utopie libertaire et novation technique," in *L'imaginaire subversif: interrogations sur l'utopie* (Geneva: Éditions Noir, 1982), 113–14.

51. This phrase is from Baudelaire. See Charles Baudelaire, "My Heart Laid Bare," in *Baudelaire: His Prose and Poetry*, ed. T. R. Smith (New York: Boni and Liveright, 1919), 245.—Trans.

52. Emmanuel Levinas, *Proper Names* (London: Athlone, 1996), 44.—Trans.

Chapter 11

1. André Prévost, *L'Utopie de Thomas More* (Paris: Mame, 1978), 158.

2. James C. Scott, *Domination and the Arts of Resistance: Hidden Transcripts* (New Haven, CT: Yale University Press, 1992), 147.

3. "L'utopie des livres" is a recent essay by Abensour on Levinas, included in the collection for which the present one was composed, *Utopiques II: L'homme est un animal utopique* (Paris: Sens & Tonka, 2013).—Trans.

4. Aristotle, *Politics*, trans. Ernest Barker (Oxford: Oxford University Press, 1995), 39.

5. Miguel Abensour, *Utopia from Thomas More to Walter Benjamin* (Minneapolis: Univocal, 2017).

6. Charles Fourier, *The Theory of the Four Movements*, ed. Gareth Stedman Jones and Ian Patterson (Cambridge: Cambridge University Press, 1996), 8.

7. Emmanuel Levinas, preface to *Utopie et socialisme*, by Martin Buber (Paris: Aubier Montaigne, 1977), 10–11.

8. J. G. Fichte, *Contribution to the Correction of the Public's Judgments on the French Revolution*, trans. Jeffrey Church and Anna Marisa Schön (Albany: State University of New York Press, 2021), 16.

9. Fichte, *Contribution to the Correction of the Public's Judgments on the French Revolution*, 25.

10. Alexis Philonenko, *Théorie et praxis dans la pensée morale et politique de Kant et de Fichte en 1793* (Paris: Vrin, 1968).

11. Edgar Quinet, *Le christianisme et la Révolution française* (Paris: Fayard, 1984), 278–79.

12. Max Horkheimer and Theodor Adorno, *Dialectic of Enlightenment* (Stanford, CA: Stanford University Press, 2002), 192.

13. Friedrich Nietzsche, *On the Genealogy of Morals*, in *On the Genealogy of Morals and Ecce Homo* (New York: Vintage, 1989), 59.

14. Emmanuel Levinas, "Philosophy and Awakening," in *Entre Nous: Essays on Thinking-of-the-Other*, trans. Michael Smith and Barbara Harshav (New York: Columbia University Press, 1998), 83.—Trans.

15. Jules Michelet, *History of the French Revolution*, ed. Gordon Wright, trans. Charles Cocks (Chicago: University of Chicago Press, 1967), 444.

16. Marc Richir, *Du sublime en politique* (Paris: Payot, 1991), 19.

17. Ronald Creagh, *Laboratoires de l'utopie: Les communautés libertaires aux États-Unis* (Paris: Payot, 1983).—Trans.

18. Emmanuel Levinas, *Of God Who Comes to Mind*, trans. Bettina Bergo (Stanford, CA: Stanford University Press, 1998), 9. In the same text, Levinas asks whether the separation between the subject and reality or the void between the subject and being makes a rapprochement between the nonplace of utopia and the interval of the epoché opened by disinterestedness (see 5 and esp. 185n3).

19. Levinas, "Philosophy and Awakening," 83.

20. Emmanuel Levinas, *Time and the Other*, trans. Richard A. Cohen (Pittsburgh: Duquesne University Press, 1987), 77.

21. Emmanuel Levinas, *God, Death, and Time*, trans. Bettina Bergo (Stanford, CA: Stanford University Press, 2000), 99.

22. Walter Benjamin, *The Arcades Project*, ed. Rolf Tiedemann, trans. Howard Eiland and Kevin McLaughlin (Cambridge, MA: Belknap Press of Harvard University Press, 2002), 392.

23. Benjamin, *The Arcades Project*, 391.

24. Benjamin, *The Arcades Project*, 456–57.

25. Rolf Tiedemann, "Dialectics at a Standstill: Approaches to the Passegen-Werk," in Benjamin, *The Arcades Project*, 935.

26. Walter Benjamin, "Materials for the Exposé of 1935," in *The Arcades Project*, 908.

27. Antonia Birnbaum, *Bonheur justice, Walter Benjamin: Le détour grec* (Paris: Payot, 2008), 62.

28. Benjamin, *The Arcades Project*, 460.

29. Walter Benjamin, "Paris, the Capital of the Nineteenth Century: Exposé of 1935," in *The Arcades Project*, 4

30. Benjamin, "Paris, the Capital of the Nineteenth Century: Exposé of 1935," 5.
31. Benjamin, "Paris, the Capital of the Nineteenth Century: Exposé of 1935," 13.
32. Benjamin, "Paris, the Capital of the Nineteenth Century: Exposé of 1935," 10.
33. Benjamin, *The Arcades Project*, 475.
34. Theodor W. Adorno, "Letter to Benjamin, Aug. 2–4, 1935," in *Walter Benjamin: Selected Writings*, vol. 3, *1958–1938*, ed. Howard Eiland and Michael William Jennings, trans. Edmund Jephcott and Howard Eiland (Cambridge, MA: Belknap Press of Harvard University Press, 2006), 54.—Trans.
35. Walter Benjamin, "Letter to Gretel Adorno, Aug. 16, 1935," in *Gretel Adorno and Walter Benjamin: Correspondence, 1930–1940*, ed. Christoph Gödde, trans. Wieland Hoban (Cambridge, UK: Polity, 2008), 155.
36. Benjamin, "Letter to Gretel Adorno, Aug. 16, 1935," 155.
37. Benjamin, *The Arcades Project*, 474.
38. Benjamin, *The Arcades Project*, 422.
39. Benjamin, *The Arcades Project*, 388.
40. Benjamin, *The Arcades Project*, 390.
41. Benjamin, *The Arcades Project*, 391.
42. Benjamin, *The Arcades Project*, 392.
43. Benjamin, *The Arcades Project*, 473.
44. Levinas, *Time and the Other*, 73.
45. Levinas, *Of God Who Comes to Mind*, 99.
46. Levinas, *God, Death, and Time*, 171.
47. Levinas, *God, Death, and Time*, 208–9.
48. Levinas, *God, Death, and Time*, 209. [Translation modified.]
49. Levinas, *Of God Who Comes to Mind*, 30.
50. Levinas, *Of God Who Comes to Mind*, 32. [Translation modified.]
51. Emmanuel Levinas, "Is Ontology Fundamental?," trans. Peter Atterton, *Philosophy Today* 33, no. 2 (1989): 127.
52. Levinas, *Of God Who Comes to Mind*, 31. [Translation modified.]
53. Levinas, *God, Death, and Time*, 99. Also, Levinas, *Of God Who Comes to Mind*, 38.
54. Levinas, *God, Death, and Time*, 99.
55. Levinas, *God, Death, and Time*, 99.—Trans.
56. Levinas, *God, Death, and Time*, 99.—Trans.
57. Levinas, *God, Death, and Time*, 100.—Trans.
58. Levinas, *God, Death, and Time*, 101. [Translation modified.]
59. Levinas, *God, Death, and Time*, 95.
60. Levinas, *God, Death, and Time*, 96.
61. Levinas, *God, Death, and Time*, 103.

62. Levinas, *God, Death, and Time*, 98–99.
63. Benjamin, "Paris, the Capital of the Nineteenth Century: Exposé of 1935," 10.
64. Susan Buck-Morss, *The Dialectics of Seeing: Walter Benjamin and the Arcades Project* (Cambridge, MA: MIT Press, 1989), 144.
65. Thomas More, *Utopia*, ed. George M. Logan, trans. Robert M. Adams (Cambridge: Cambridge University Press, 1989), 50.
66. More, *Utopia*, 76.
67. More, *Utopia*, 50.
68. Karl Marx, *Capital*, vol. 3, *A Critique of Political Economy*, trans. David Fernbach (New York: Penguin, 1993), ch. 48.
69. Levinas, *God, Death, and Time*, 93. [Translation modified.]

Chapter 12

1. Marcel Gauchet, *La condition historique* (Paris: Stock, 2003), 160.—Trans.
2. Miguel Abensour and Marcel Gauchet, "Les leçons de la servitude et leur destin," in *Etienne de La Boétie, Le discours de la servitude volontaire*, ed. Miguel Abensour (Paris: Payot, 1976).—Trans.
3. Gauchet, *La condition historique*, 160.—Trans.
4. Miguel Abensour, "'Savage Democracy' and 'Principle of Anarchy,'" *Philosophy and Social Criticism* 28, no. 6 (2002): 703–26.
5. Oskar Anweiler, *The Soviets: The Russian Workers, Peasants, and Soldiers Councils, 1905–1921*. Trans. Ruth Hein (New York: Pantheon, 1975).
6. Marcel Gauchet, *La démocratie contre elle-même* (Paris: Gallimard, 2002), 15.
7. Gauchet, *La condition historique*, 280–81.
8. The 2003 European heatwave, which saw the highest temperatures since the sixteenth century, brought crop failures and mass casualties across the continent, but hit France much harder than any other country.—Trans.
9. François Mitterrand, *Le Coup d'État permanent* (Paris: Plon, 1964).—Trans.
10. Gauchet, *La condition historique*, 269.—Trans.
11. François Furet, *The Passing of an Illusion: The Idea of Communism in the Twentieth Century*, trans. Deborah Furet (Chicago: University of Chicago Press, 1999), 502.
12. Marcel Gauchet, *L'avènement de la démocratie*, vol. 1, *La révolution moderne* (Paris: Gallimard, 2007), 16, 18.
13. Jacques Rancière, *Disagreement: Politics and Philosophy*, trans. Julie Rose (Minneapolis: University of Minnesota Press, 2004), 28.

Bibliography

Abensour's Publications

COMPLETE LIST OF ABENSOUR'S PUBLICATIONS (AUTHORED AND EDITED)—FRENCH

Authored Books

De la compacité: Architectures et régimes totalitaires. Paris: Sens & Tonka, 1997. Republished as *De la compacité: Architectures et régimes totalitaires, le cas Albert Speer.* Paris: Sens & Tonka, 2006.
Emmanuel Levinas, l'intrigue de l'humain: Entre métapolitique et politique, entretiens avec Danielle Cohen-Levinas. Paris: Hermann, 2012.
Hannah Arendt contre la philosophie politique? Paris: Sens & Tonka, 2006.
La Boétie prophète de la liberté. Paris: Sens & Tonka, 2018.
La communauté politique des tous-uns: Entretien avec Michel Enaudeau. Paris: Les Belles-Lettres, 2014.
La démocratie contre l'état: Marx et le moment machiavélien. Paris: PUF, 1997. Republished by Le Félin, 2004; Sens & Tonka, 2019.
La lumière et la boue: "Le rouge et le noir" à l'ombre de 1793. Paris: Sens & Tonka, 2019.
Le contre Hobbes de Pierre Clastres. Paris: Sens & Tonka, 2023.
Les formes de l'utopie socialiste-communiste: Essai sur le communisme critique et l'utopie. Thèse d'état completed at the Université Paris I, Science politique, under the supervision of Charles Eisenmann and Gilles Deleuze. 2 vols. 1973. Forthcoming publication, Sens & Tonka.
Les passages Blanqui: Walter Benjamin entre mélancolie et révolution. Paris: Sens & Tonka, 2013.
Levinas. Paris: Sens & Tonka, 2021.
Libérer l'enfermé: Auguste Blanqui. With Valentin Pelosse. Paris: Sens & Tonka, 2014.

Pour une philosophie politique critique. Paris: Sens & Tonka, 2009.
Rire des lois, du magistrat et des dieux: L'impulsion Saint-Just. Lyon: Horlieu, 2005.
Utopiques I: Le procès des maîtres rêveurs. Paris: Sens & Tonka, 2013. Previously published as *Le procès des maîtres rêveurs.* Arles: Éditions Sulliver, 2000.
Utopiques II: L'homme est un animal utopique. Paris: Sens & Tonka, 2013. Previously published as *L'homme est un animal utopique.* Arles: Éditions de la Nuit, 2010.
Utopiques III: L'utopie de Thomas More à Walter Benjamin. Paris: Sens & Tonka, 2009. Previously published as *L'utopie de Thomas More à Walter Benjamin.* Paris: Sens & Tonka, 2000.
Utopiques IV: L'histoire de l'utopie et le destin de sa critique. Paris: Sens & Tonka, 2016.
Utopiques V: Le nouvel esprit utopique. Paris: Sens & Tonka, 2020.

Articles, Chapters, and Interviews

"Adorno, Theodor Wiesengrund (1903–1969)." *Encyclopaedia universalis*, 23–26. Paris: Albin Michel, 2006.
"*A New View of Society* de Robert Owen." In *Dictionnaire des oeuvres politiques.* Edited by François Châtelet, Olivier Duhamel, and Evelyne Pisier, 619–32. Paris: PUF, 1986.
"Architecture et régimes totalitaires." *La part de l'oeil*, no. 12 (1996): 1–19.
"Au-delà de *la fluctuatio animi* marrane: Spinoza en quête de l'universel." *Tumultes*, no. 21–22 (2003): 107–39.
"Avant-propos." With Catherine Chalier. In *Cahier de l'Herne: Emmanuel Levinas*, edited by Miguel Abensour and Catherine Chalier, 9–13. Paris: Éditions de L'Herne, 1991.
"Avant-propos." With Étienne Tassin. *Épokhè* 6 (1996): 7–10.
"Avant-propos: Pierre Clastres et nous: La révolution copernicienne et la question de l'état." In *Pierre Clastres*, edited by Miguel Abensour and Anne Kupiec, 11–13. Paris: Sens & Tonka, 2011.
"Benjamin, Walter." In *Dictionnaire des utopies*, edited by Michèle Riot-Sarcey, Thomas Bouchet, and Antoine Picon, 22–28. Paris: Larousse, 2002.
"Ça se passe bien! Pour François Châtelet." *La Mazarine*, March 1988, 11–15.
"Comment penser le politique avec Hannah Arendt?" In *La question de l'état: Données et débats: actes du XXIXe Colloque des intellectuels juifs de langue française*, edited by Jean Halpérin and Georges Lévitte, 183–211. Paris: Denoël, 1989.
"Comment une philosophe de l'humanité peut-elle être une philosophie politique moderne?" In *Aux philosophes, aux artistes, aux politiques: Trois discours et autres textes*, by Pierre Leroux, 295–320. Edited by Jean-Pierre Lacassagne. Paris: Payot, 1994. Republished in *Pour une philosophie politique critique*, 201–30. Paris: Sens & Tonka, 2009.
"Comprendre ou provoquer l'histoire?" *Magazine littéraire*, no. 479 (2008): 59–62.

"Contre la souveraineté de la philosophie sur la politique. La lecture arendtienne du mythe de la caverne." In *Hannah Arendt: Crises de l'état-nation*, edited by Anne Kupiec, Martine Leibovici, Géraldine Muhlmann, and Étienne Tassin, 341–65. Paris: Sens & Tonka, 2007.

"Conversation autour du Collège international de philosophie: Miguel Abensour, Jacques Derrida, Élisabéth Fontenay, Marie-Louise Mallet, Étienne Tassin." *Lignes* 35 (1998): 121–36.

"Critique de la politique." In *Éclipse de la raison*, by Max Horkheimer, 7–8. Paris: Payot, 1974. Republished in *Pour une philosophie politique critique*, 49–51. Paris: Sens & Tonka, 2009.

"Critique de la politique." Éditions Klincksieck, 2016. https://www.klincksieck.com/les-livres/collection/95-critique-de-la-politique.

"*De la nature* de Saint-Just." In *Dictionnaire des oeuvres politiques*, edited by François Châtelet, Olivier Duhamel, and Évelyne Pisier. Paris: PUF, 1986, 711–25.

"*De l'humanité* de Pierre Leroux." In *Dictionnaire des oeuvres politiques*, edited by François Châtelet, Olivier Duhamel, and Évelyne Pisier, 610–21. Paris: PUF, 1989.

"De l'intraitable." In *Jean-François Lyotard: L'exercice du différend*, edited by Dolorès Lyotard, Jean-Claude Milner, and Gérald Sfez, 241–61. Paris: PUF, 2001.

"'Démocratie insurgeante' et institution." In *La démocratie au-delà du libéralisme: Perspectives critiques*, edited by Martin Breaugh and Francis Dupuis-Déri, 185–93. Outremont, QC: Athéna éditions, 2009.

"Démocratie insurgeante et institution." *De(s)générations*, no. 11 (2010): 5–14.

"'Démocratie sauvage' et 'principe d'anarchie.'" *Revue européenne de sciences sociales* 97 (1993): 225–41. Revised and republished in *Les cahiers de philosophie* 18 (1994): 125–48. And in *La démocratie contre l'état: Marx et le moment machiavélien*, 161–90. Paris: Le Félin, 2004.

"De quel retour s'agit-il?" *Les cahiers de philosophie*, no. 18 (1994): 5–8. Republished in *Pour une philosophie politique critique*, 59–63. Paris: Sens & Tonka, 2009.

"Du bon usage de l'hypothèse de la servitude volontaire." *Réfractions* 17 (2006): 65–84.

"D'une mésinterprétation du totalitarisme et de ses effets." *Tumultes*, no. 8 (1996): 11–44. Revised and republished in *Le totalitarisme*, edited by Enzo Traverso, 749–79. Paris: Seuil, 2001. And in *Pour une philosophie politique critique*, 167–98. Paris: Sens & Tonka, 2009.

"Edmond El Maleh ou l'impatiente subversion." In *Entretiens avec Edmond El Maleh*, interviews by Marie Redonnet. Grenoble: La Pensée sauvage, 2005.

"Entretien." *Revue philosophiae scientae* 11 (2016).

"Entretien (avec Jean-Claude Poizat)." *Le philosophoire* 44 (2015): 11–37.

"Entretien réalisé par Edmond El Maleh sur l'École de Francfort." In *Entretiens avec Le Monde 1: Philosophies*, 209–19. Paris: La Découverte/Journal Le Monde, 1984.

"Hannah Arendt: La critique du totalitarisme et la servitude volontaire." In *Le goût de l'altérité*, edited by Eugène Enriquez, 29–52. Paris: Desclée de Brouwer, 1999. Republished in *Pour une philosophie politique critique*, 137–165. Paris: Sens & Tonka, 2006.

"Hannah Arendt contre la philosophie politique?" In *Hannah Arendt: L'humaine condition politique*, edited by Étienne Tassin, 11–46. Paris: L'Harmattan, 2001. Republished in *Lire Hannah Arendt aujourd'hui: Pouvoir, guerre, pensée, jugement politique*, edited by Marie-Claire Caloz-Tschop, 151–59. Paris: L'Harmattan, 2008. And in *Pour une philosophie politique critique*, 231–63 Paris: Sens & Tonka, 2009.

"Hannah Arendt et le sionisme en question." *Passé présent*, no. 3 (1984): 17–23.

"Héroïsme et modernité." *Le magazine littéraire*, no. 408 (2002): 44–46

"Il faut placer l'utopie du côté du réveil et non de l'illusion." *Le magazine littéraire*, no. 521 (2012): 12.

"Insistances démocratiques: Entretien avec Miguel Abensour, Jean-Luc Nancy & Jacques Rancière: Entretien réalisé par Stany Grelet, Jérôme Lèbre, Sophie Wahnich." *Vacarme* 48, no. 3 (2009): 8–17.

"La conversion utopique: L'utopie et l'éveil." In *Utopiques II: L'homme est un animal utopique*, 13–60. Paris: Sens & Tonka, 2013.

"La disposition héroïque et son aliénation." *Tumultes*, no. 2–3 (1993): 59–87.

"L'affaire Schelling: Une controverse entre Pierre Leroux et les jeunes hégéliens." *Corpus*, no. 18–19 (1991): 117–42.

"L'an-archie entre métapolitique et politique." *Les cahiers philosophiques de Strasbourg* 14 (2002): 109–31.

"La philosophie politique de Saint-Just: Problématique et cadres sociaux." *Annales historiques de la Révolution française*, no. 183 (1966): 1–32. And "La philosophie politique de Saint-Just: Problématique et cadres sociaux (suite et fin)," *Annales historiques de la Révolution française*, no. 185 (1966): 341–58.

"La protection est l'archétype de la domination" / "Généalogie de la domination" / "Là où on ne voyait rien, on discerne quelque chose." *Prismes: Théorie critique* 4 (2022). Republication of extracts from *La communauté politique des tous-uns: Entretien avec Michel Enaudeau*. Paris: Les Belles Lettres, 2014.

"La théorie critique et la question politique." *Prismes: Théorie critique* 1 (2018): 17–23.

"La théorie critique, une pensée de l'Exil?" *Archives de philosophie* 45, no. 2 (1982): 179–200. Republished in *L'imagination dialectique: L'École de Francfort, 1923-1950*, by Martin Jay, 231–43. Paris: Payot, 2001.

"La théorie des institutions et les relations du législateur et du peuple selon Saint-Just." In *Actes du Colloque Saint-Just*, 239–90. Paris: Société des études robespierristes, 1968.

"L'autre tâche du traducteur." *Quinzaine littéraire*, March 16–31, 2003, 19–20.

"La voix de Pierre Castres." In *Entretien avec l'Anti-mythes (1974)*, Pierre Clastres. Paris: Sens & Tonka, 2012.

"Le bonheur, une idée fanée en Europe?" In *Où est le bonheur?*, edited by Roger-Pol Droit, 234–54. Paris: Le Monde éditions, 1994.
"Le choix du petit." *Passé présent*, no. 1 (1982): 59–72. Republished in Theodor W. Adorno, *Minima moralia: Réflexions sur la vie mutilée*, 335–53. Paris: Payot, 1991.
"Le contre-Hobbes d'Emmanuel Levinas." In *Difficile Justice: Dans la trace d'Emmanuel Levinas*, edited by Jean Halpérin and Nelly Hansson, 120–33. Paris: Albin Michel, 1998.
"Le contre-Hobbes d'Emmanuel Lévinas (entretien avec Philippe Roux)." *De(s) générations*, no. 11 (2010): 15–18.
"Le contre-Hobbes de Pierre Clastres." In *L'esprit des lois sauvages: Pierre Clastres ou une nouvelle anthropologie politique*, edited by Miguel Abensour, 115–44. Paris: Seuil, 1987.
"Le destin du rire dans la Révolution." *Mirmanda*, no. 1 (2006): 65–80.
"Le double visage de l'héroïsme révolutionnaire." In *La philosophie et la Révolution française*, edited by Bernard Bourgeois and Jacques D'Hondt, 121–41. Paris: Vrin, 1993.
"Le guetteur de rêves: Walter Benjamin et l'utopie." *Tumultes*, no. 12 (1999): 81–119.
"Le mal élémental." In *Quelques réflexions sur la philosophie de l'hitlérisme*, by Emmanuel Levinas, 27–108. Paris: Rivages, 1997.
"L'énigme du révolutionnaire moderne et la dimension de l'héroïsme." Sao Paulo: Musée d'art moderne, 1992.
"Le nouvel esprit utopique." *Cahiers Bernard Lazare*, no. 128 (1991): 132–63. Republished in *Utopiques II: L'homme est un animal utopique*, 191–226. Paris: Sens & Tonka, 2013.
"Le nouvel esprit utopique." *Le cahier*, no. 3 (1987): 111–14.
"Le pari de la démocratie." *Le Monde des débats*, January 1995.
"Le procès des maîtres-rêveurs." *Libre* 4 (1978): 207–30.
"*Le rouge et le noir* à l'ombre de 1793." In *Critique de la politique: Autour de Miguel Abensour*, edited by Anne Kupiec and Étienne Tassin, 553–92. Paris: Sens & Tonka, 2006.
"Les leçons de la servitude et leur destin." With Marcel Gauchet. In *Discours de la servitude volontaire*, edited by Pierre Leonard, vii–xxix. Paris: Payot, 1976.
"L'état de la justice." *Magazine littéraire*, no. 419 (2003): 54–57.
"L'état de la justice chez Levinas." In *Utopies: Entre droit et politique, études en hommage à Claude Courvoisier*, edited by Patrick Charlot. Dijon: Éditions universitaires de Dijon, 2005.
"Lettre d'un 'révoltiste' à Marcel Gauchet converti à la 'politique normale." *Réfractions*, no. 12 (2004): 159–64. Revised and republished as *Lettre d'un "révoltiste" à Marcel Gauchet converti à la "politique normale."* Paris: Sens & Tonka, 2008.
"Lettre et notes inédites sur La Boétie," "Du bon usage de l'hypothèse de la servitude volontaire," and "Spinoza et l'épineuse question de la servitude volontaire." In

La Boétie, *Le Discours de la servitude volontaire*, text established by Malcolm Smith. Paris: éditions Klincksieck, 2022.

"Lettre-préface." In David Munnich, *L'art de l'amitié: Rousseau et la servitude volontaire*, 9–25. Paris: Sens & Tonka, 2012.

"L'extravagante hypothèse." *Rue Descartes*, no. 19 (1998): 55–84. Revised and republished in *Emmanuel Levinas et l'histoire*, edited by Natalie Frogneux and Françoise Mies, 161–88. Paris: Éditions du Cerf, 1998. And in *Pour une philosophie politique critique*, 363–400. Paris: Sens & Tonka, 2009.

"L'héroïsme et l'énigme du révolutionnaire moderne." In *Les aventures de la raison politique*, edited by Adauto Novaes. Paris: Anne-Marie Métailié, 2006.

"L'histoire de l'utopie et le destin de sa critique I." *Textures*, no. 6–7 (1973): 3–26. And "L'histoire de l'utopie et le destin de sa critique II." *Textures*, no. 8–9 (1974): 55–81. Republished in *Utopiques IV: L'histoire de l'utopie et le destin de sa critique*. Paris: Sens & Tonka, 2016.

"L'homme est un animal utopique: Entretien avec Miguel Abensour." *Mouvements*, no. 45–46 (2006): 72–86.

"Libérer l'enfermé." With Valentin Pelosse. *Instructions pour une prise d'armes; L'éternité par les astres*, by Auguste Blanqui. Edited by Miguel Abensour and Valentin Pelosse. Paris: Ed. de la Tête de feuille (Futur antérieur), 1973. Republished in *Instructions pour une prise d'armes; L'éternité par les astres*, by Auguste Blanqui, 373–442. Paris: Sens & Tonka, 2000.

"Lire Pierre Clastres à la lumière de Nietzsche." In *Pierre Clastres*, edited by Miguel Abensour and Anne Kupiec, 249–57. Paris: Sens & Tonka, 2011.

"Lire Saint-Just." In *Oeuvres completes*, by Antoine-Louis de Saint-Just, 9–100. Paris: Gallimard, 2004.

"L'utopie des livres." In *Emmanuel Levinas, la question du livre*, edited by Miguel Abensour and Anne Kupiec, 67–87. Saint-Germain la Blanche-Herbe: IMEC, 2008. Republished in *Utopiques II: L'homme est un animal utopique*, 61–96. Paris: Sens & Tonka, 2013.

"*L'Utopie* de Thomas More." *Dictionnaire des oeuvres politiques*, edited by François Châtelet, Olivier Duhamel, and Evelyne Pisier, 798–815. Paris: PUF, 1986.

"L'utopie ou la transformation du monde." In *Le nouvel observateur*, October–November 2003, 90–93.

"L'utopie socialiste: Une nouvelle alliance de la politique et de la religion." *Le temps de la réflexion*, no. 2 (1981): 61–112.

"Machiavel: La politique comme expérience de la liberté: Entretien avec Miguel Abensour." In *Philosophes d'hier et d'aujourd'hui: Trente entretiens du Monde des livres*, edited by Jean Birnbaum, 113–17. Paris: Flammarion, 2008.

"Machiavel: Le grand penseur du désordre, entretien avec Miguel Abensour." *Le Monde* October 4, 2008. Republished as "Sur le chemin de Machiavelli." In *Pour une philosophie politique critique*, 65–68. Paris: Sens & Tonka, 2009.

"Malheureux comme Adorno en France." *Variations*, no. 6 (2005): 17–30.

"Manifeste de la collection 'Critique de la politique.'" In *Critique de la politique: Autour de Miguel Abensour*, edited by Anne Kupiec and Étienne Tassin, 613–15. Paris: Sens & Tonka, 2006. Republished in *Pour une philosophie politique critique*, 49–51. Paris: Sens & Tonka, 2009.

"Marx et le moment machiavélien: 'Vraie démocratie' et modernité." In *Phénoménologie et politique: Mélanges offerts à Jacques Taminiaux*, edited by Danielle Lories and Bernard Stevens, 17–114. Brussels: Ousia, 1989.

"Marx: Quelle critique de l'utopie?" *Lignes*, no. 17 (1992): 43–65. Republished in *Rencontres autour de Pierre Fougeyrollas*, edited by Pierre Ansart, 27–45. Paris: L'Harmattan, 1993.

"Maximilien Rubel, une oeuvre à l'écart." With Louis Janover. In *Maximilien Rubel: Pour redécouvrir Marx*, 9–23. Paris: Sens & Tonka, 2008.

"Oser rire." *Textures*, no. 10–11 (1975): 47–56. Republished in *Pour une philosophie politique critique*, 71–82. Paris: Sens & Tonka, 2009.

"Overture." In *Emmanuel Levinas, la question du livre*, edited by Miguel Abensour and Anne Kupiec, 6–8. Saint-Germain la Blanche-Herbe: IMEC, 2008.

"Parasites appointés qu'avez-vous fait de la vérité?" With Pierre-Jean Labarrière. In *Contre la philosophie universitaire*, by Arthur Schopenhauer, 7–36. Paris: Rivages-Payot, 1993.

"Penser l'utopie autrement." *L'Herne*, no. 60 (1991): 477–96.

"Persistance de l'utopie: Entretien avec Miguel Abensour." Interviewed by Sophie Wahnich. *Vacarme*, no. 53 (2010): 34–37.

"Persistante utopie." *Mortibus*, no. 1 (2006): 37–58.

"Philosophie de l'humanité et philosophie politique moderne: Pierre Leroux." In *Écrivains de la dissidence: Pierre Leroux, Charles Péguy, Boris Souvarine*, edited by Julie Bertrand-Sabiani, 11–34. Orléans: Centre Charles-Péguy, 1987.

"Philosophie politique et socialisme, Pierre Leroux ou du 'style barbare' en philosophie." *Le cahier du Collège international de philosophie*, no. 1 (1985): 9–24.

"Philosophie politique critique et émancipation." In *Philosophie politique et état de la démocratie*, edited by Julie Dotti, Laura Brondino, and Patrice Vermeren. Paris: L'Harmattan, 2007. Republished in *Lignes*, no. 23–24 (2007): 86–118. And in *Politiques et sociétés* 22, no. 3 (2003): 119–42. Revised and republished as "Pour une philosophie politique critique?" In *Pour une philosophie politique critique*, 265–318. Paris: Sens & Tonka, 2009.

"Pierre Leroux, 'De l'humanité.'" In *Dictionnaire des oeuvres politiques*, edited by François Châtelet, Olivier Duhamel, and Evelyne Pisier, 551–56. Paris: PUF, 1989.

"Pierre Leroux et l'utopie socialiste." *Cahiers de l'ISEA* 15 (1972): 2201–45. Republished in *Utopiques I: Le procès des maîtres rêveurs*, 91–136. Paris: Sens & Tonka, 2013.

"Pierre Leroux, le prophète enragé." *Le nouvel observateur*, April–May 2010, 24–25.

"Pour lire Marx." *Revue française de science politique* 20, no. 4 (1970): 772–88. Republished in *Maximilien Rubel: Pour redécouvrir Marx*. Paris: Sens & Tonka, 2008.

"Pourquoi la théorie critique?" In *Le souci du droit: Où en est la Théorie critique?* edited by Hourya Bentouhami, Ninon Grangé, Anne Kupiec, and Julie Saada, 15–28. Paris: Sens & Tonka, 2009.

"Pour une philosophie politique critique?" *Tumultes*, no. 17–18 (2002): 207–58. Republished in *Pour une philosophie politique critique*, 265–318. Paris: Sens & Tonka, 2009.

"Préface: Le bolchevisme sans mythe." With Louis Janover. In *Le mythe bolchevik: Journal, 1920–1922*, by Alexander Berkman, vii–xxix. Paris: Klincksieck, 2017.

"Présentation." *Cahiers de philosophie politique*, no. 1 (1983): 3–8. Republished as "Philosophie politique moderne et émancipation." In *Pour une philosophie politique critique*, 53–58. Paris: Sens & Tonka, 2009.

"Présentation." In *La Révolution par l'état: Une nouvelle classe dirigeante en Amérique latine*, by Louis Mercier-Vega, 3–6. Paris: Payot, 1978.

"Présentation." In *L'esprit des lois sauvages: Pierre Clastres ou une nouvelle anthropologie politique*, edited by Miguel Abensour, 7–18. Paris: Seuil, 1987.

"Présentation." With Géraldine Muhlmann. *Tumultes*, no. 17–18 (2001–2002): i–iv.

"Présentation: La passion d'Edward P. Thompson." In *La formation de la classe ouvrière anglaise*, by Edward P. Thompson, xxvii–xlviii. Paris: Seuil-Gallimard, 1998.

"Réflexions sur les deux interprétations du totalitarisme chez Claude Lefort." In *La démocratie à l'oeuvre: Autour de Claude Lefort*, edited by Claude Habib and Claude Mouchard, 70–136. Paris: Esprit, 1993. Republished in *Pour une philosophie politique critique*, 83–135. Paris: Sens & Tonka, 2009.

"Rencontre, silence." In *Heidegger questions ouvertes*, 247–54. Paris: Osiris, 1988.

Review of *Coleridge and the Idea of the Modern State*, by David P. Calleo. *Revue française de science politique* 18, no. 4 (1968): 779–81.

Review of *The Enragés: Socialists of the French Revolution*, by R. B. Rose. *Revue française de science politique* 17, no. 1 (1967): 147–48.

"Rire des lois, du magistrat et des dieux." In *Jean Borreil: La raison de l'autre*, edited by Christine Glucksmann, Geneviève Fraisse, and Jacques Rancière, 79–140. Paris: L'Harmattan, 1995. Revised and republished as *Rire des lois, du magistrat et des dieux: L'impulsion Saint-Just*. Paris: Horlieu éditions, 2005. Republished in *Le coeur de Brutus*, 255–329. Paris: Sens & Tonka, 2019.

"Saint-Just: Les paradoxes de l'héroïsme révolutionnaire." *Esprit* 147, no. 2 (1989): 60–81.

"Spinoza et l'épineuse question de la servitude volontaire." *Astérion*, no. 13 (2015).

"Strauss, Leo (1899–1973)." With Michel-Pierre Edmond. *Encyclopædia universalis*. Paris: Albin Michel, 1983. Republished in *Cahiers de philosophie politique*, no. 2–3 (1984): 230–39.

"T. W. Adorno: La philosophie à l'épreuve de la théorie critique." *Universalia* (2005): 322–24.
"Une biographie de la classe ouvrière. Entretien avec Miguel Abensour." With François Jarrige. *Le Monde des livres*, April 6, 2012.
"Utopie." In *Cinquante idées qui ébranlèrent le monde*, edited by Youri Afanassiev and Marc Ferro, 233–39. Paris: Payot, 1989.
"Utopie: Futur et/ou altérité." In *L'oeuvre du phénomène: Mélanges de philosophie offerts à Marc Richir*, edited by Pierre Kerszberg, Antonio Mazzù, and Alexandre Schnell, 215–40. Brussels: Ousia, 2009.
"Utopie et démocratie." *Raison présente*, no. 121 (1997): 29–41. Republished in *L'utopie en questions*, edited by Michèle Riot-Sarcey, 245–56. Saint-Denis: Presses universitaires de Vincennes, 2001. And in *Pour une philosophie politique critique*, 349–62. Paris: Sens & Tonka, 2009.
"Utopie et émancipation." *L'inactuel* 8 (2003): 61–70.
"Utopie socialiste: Une nouvelle alliance de la politique et de la religion." *Le temps de la réflexion*, no. 1 (1981): 61–112.
"Walter Benjamin entre mélancolie et révolution—Passages Blanqui." In *Walter Benjamin et Paris*, edited by Heinz Wismann, 219–47. Paris: Éditions du Cerf, 1986. Abridged version published in *Passé présent*, no. 4 (1984): 71–100.
"William Morris, utopie et romance." *Europe: Revue littéraire mensuelle* 900 (2004): 130–63.
"William Morris, utopie libertaire et novation technique." In *L'Imaginaire subversif: interrogations sur l'utopie*, 113–60. Geneva: Édition Noir, 1982.

Books and Journals Edited

Blanqui, Auguste. *Instructions pour une prise d'armes/L'éternité par les astres*. Edited with Valentin Pelosse. Paris: Sens & Tonka, 2000. Previously published with Éditions de la Tête des Feuilles, 1973.
Emmanuel Levinas. Edited with Catherine Chalier. Cahier de l'Herne. Paris: Éditions de L'Herne, 1991.
Emmanuel Levinas: La question du livre. Edited with Anne Kupiec. Saint-Germain la Blanche-Herbe: IMEC, 2008.
"L'animal politique." Edited with Étienne Tassin. Special issue, *Épokhè*, no. 6 (1996).
"L'École de Francfort: La théorie critique entre philosophie et sociologie." Edited with Géraldine Muhlmann. Special issue, *Tumultes*, no. 17–18 (2001–2002).
Leroux, Pierre. *De l'humanité*. Edited with Patrice Vermeren. Paris: Corpus, 1985.
"Les choses politiques." Edited with Étienne Tassin. Special issue, *Les cahiers de philosophie* 18 (1994).
L'esprit des lois sauvages: Pierre Clastres ou une nouvelle anthropologie politique. Paris: Seuil, 1987.

Levinas, Emmanuel. *Quelques réflexions sur la philosophie de l'hitlérisme*. Paris: Rivages, 1997.
Maximilien Rubel: Pour redécouvrir Marx. Edited with Louis Janover. Paris: Sens & Tonka, 2008.
Ontologie et politique: Actes du Colloque Hannah Arendt. Paris: Tierce, 1989. Republished as *Politique et pensée: Colloque Hannah Arendt*. Paris: Payot, 1996.
Pierre Clastres. Edited with Anne Kupiec. Paris: Sens & Tonka, 2011.
Saint-Just, Louis Antoine Léon de. *Oeuvres complètes*. Edited with Anne Kupiec. Paris: Gallimard, 2004.
Schopenhauer, Arthur. *Contre la philosophie universitaire*. Edited with Pierre-Jean Labarrière. Paris: Rivages-Payot, 1993.

Books Published in the "Critique de la Politique" Series under Abensour's Supervision (1974–2017)

Adorno, Theodor. *Beaux passages: Écouter la musique*. Edited, translated, and with presentation by Jean Lauxerois. Paris: Payot & Rivages, 2013.
———. *Contribution à une métacritique de la théorie de la connaissance: Études sur Husserl et les antinomies de la phénoménologie*. Translated by Christophe David and Alexandra Richter. Paris: Payot & Rivages, 2011.
———. *Dialectique négative*. Translated by the Translation Group of the Collège de philosophie. Postface by Hans-Günther Holl. Paris: Payot, 1978.
———. *Jargon de l'authenticité: De l'idéologie allemande*. Translated and with preface by Éliane Escoubas. Postface by Guy Petitdemange. Paris: Payot, 1989.
———. *Kierkegaard: Construction de l'esthétique*. Translated and with preface by Éliane Escoubas. Paris: Payot & Rivages, 1995.
———. *Le Conflit des sociologies: Théorie critique et sciences sociales*. Translated by Pierre Arnoux, Jacques-Olivier Bégot, Julia Christ, et al. Paris: Payot & Rivages, 2016.
———. *Métaphysique: Concept et problèmes*. Translated and with presentation by Christophe David. Paris: Payot & Rivages, 2006.
———. *Minima Moralia: Réflexions sur la vie mutilée*. Translated by Eliane Kaufhoiz and Jean-René Ladmiral. Paris: Payot, 1980.
———. *Modèles critiques: Interventions répliques*. Translated by Marc Jimenez and Eliane Kaufholz. Paris: Payot, 1984.
———. *Prismes: Critique de la culture et société*. Translated by Geneviève Rochlitz and Rainer Rochlitz. Paris: Payot, 1986.
———. *Société: Intégration, désintégration: Écrits sociologiques*. Translated by Pierre Arnoux, Julia Christ, Georges Felten, et al. Preface by Axel Honneth. Paris: Payot & Rivages, 2011.
———. *Trois études sur Hegel*. Translated by the Translation Seminar of the Collège de philosophie. Paris: Payot, 1979.

Agamben, Giorgio. *Enfance et histoire: Destruction de l'expérience et origine de l'histoire.* Translated by Yves Hersant. Paris: Payot, 1989.
Ansart-Dourlen, Michèle. *Freud et les Lumières: Individu, raison et société.* Paris: Payot, 1985.
Authier, Denis, and Jean Barrot. *La gauche communiste en Allemagne, 1918–1921.* Paris: Payot, 1976.
Bachofen, Blaise. *La condition de la liberté: Rousseau, critique des raisons politiques.* Paris: Payot & Rivages, 2002.
Baczko, Bronislaw. *Les imaginaires sociaux: Mémoire et espoirs collectifs.* Paris: Payot, 1984.
———. *Lumières de l'utopie.* Paris: Payot, 1978.
Benjamin, Walter. *Charles Baudelaire: Un poète lyrique à l'apogée du capitalisme.* Translated by Jean Lacoste. Paris: Payot, 1982.
———. *Romantisme et critique de la civilisation.* Translated by Christophe David and Alexandra Richter. Preface by Michael Löwy. Paris: Payot & Rivages, 2010.
Beradt, Charlotte. *Rêver sous le IIIe Reich.* Translated by Pierre Saint-Germain. Preface by Martine Leibovici. Postface by Reinhart Koselleck and François Gantheret. Paris: Payot-Rivages, 2002.
Berkman, Alexander. *Le mythe bolchevik: Journal, 1920–1922.* Translated by Pascale Haas. Preface by Miguel Abensour and Louis Janover. Paris: Éditions Klincksieck, 2017.
Birnbaum, Antonia. *Bonheur justice, Walter Benjamin: Le détour grec.* Paris: Payot & Rivages, 2009.
———. *Nietzsche: Les aventures de l'héroïsme.* Paris: Payot & Rivages, 2000.
Bloch, Ernst. *Droit naturel et dignité humaine.* Translated by Denis Authier and Jean Lacoste. Paris: Payot, 1976.
———. *Experimentum mundi: Question, catégories de l'élaboration, praxis.* Translated and with notes by Gérard Raulet. Paris: Payot, 1981.
———. *Héritage de ce temps.* Translated by Jean Lacoste. Paris: Payot, 1978.
Borreil, Jean. *La raison nomade.* Texts coedited by Christine Buci-Glucksmann, Geneviève Fraisse, and Jacques Rancière. Postface by Jacques Rancière. Paris: Payot & Rivages, 1993.
Breaugh, Martin. *L'expérience plébéienne: Une histoire discontinue de la liberté politique.* Paris: Payot & Rivages, 2007.
Cohen-Halimi, Michèle. *Stridence spéculative: Adorno, Lyotard, Derrida.* Paris: Payot & Rivages, 2014.
Collective, *Utopie, marxisme selon Ernst Bloch: Un système de l'inconstructible—hommage à Ernst Bloch pour son 90e anniversaire.* Edited by Gérard Raulet. Paris: Payot, 1976.
Cousin de Grainville, Jean-Baptiste. *Le dernier homme.* Edited and postface by Anne Kupiec. Preface by Jules Michelet. Paris: Payot & Rivages, 2010.

Creagh, Ronald. *Laboratoires de l'utopie: Les communautés libertaires aux États-Unis*. Paris: Payot, 1983.
Debout-Oleszkiewicz, Simone. *"Griffe au nez": Fourier, Burroughs*. Paris: Payot & Rivages, 1999.
Domela Nieuwenhuis, Ferdinand. *Le socialisme en danger*. Edited by Jean-Yves Bériou. Paris: Payot, 1975.
Donaggio, Enrico. *Karl Lowith et la philosophie: Une sobre inquiétude*. Translated by Philippe Audegean. Paris: Payot & Rivages, 2013.
Dubigeon, Yohan. *La démocratie des conseils: Aux origines modernes de l'autogouvernement*. Paris: Éditions Klincksieck, 2017.
Edmond, Michel-Pierre. *Aristote: La politique des citoyens et la contingence*. Paris: Payot & Rivages, 2000.
———. *Le philosophe-roi: Platon et la politique*. Paris: Payot, 1991.
Ferrari, Joseph. *Les philosophes salariés*. Preface by Stéphane Douailler and Patrice Vermeren. Paris: Payot, 1983.
———. *Machiavel, juge des révolutions de notre temps*. Preface by Georges Navet. Paris: Payot & Rivages, 2003.
Ferrié, Christian. *La politique de Kant: Un réformisme révolutionnaire*. Paris: Payot & Rivages, 2016.
Fichte, J. G. *Considérations sur la Révolution française*. Translated by Jules Barni. Preface by Marc Richir. Paris: Payot, 1974.
———. *Machiavel et autres écrits philosophiques et politiques*. Translated and with presentation by Luc Ferry and Alain Renaut. Paris: Payot, 1981.
Genel, Katia. *Autorité et emancipation: Horkheimer et la théorie critique*. Paris: Payot & Rivages, 2013.
Guyau, Jean-Marie. *Esquisse d'une morale sans obligation ni sanction*. With biography, preface, and postface by Jordi Riba. Paris: Payot & Rivages, 2012.
Habermas, Jürgen. *L'espace public: Archéologie de la publicité comme dimension constitutive de la société bourgeoise*. Translated by Marc B. de Launay Paris: Payot, 1978.
———. *Raison et Légitimité: Problèmes de légitimation dans le capitalisme avancé*. Translated by Jean Lacoste. Paris: Payot, 1978.
———. *Théorie et pratique*. 2 vols. Translated by Gerard Raulet. Paris: Payot, 1975.
Hegel, Georg W. F. *Système de la vie éthique*. Translated and with presentation by Jacques Taminiaux. Paris: Payot, 1976.
Hill, Christopher. *Le monde à l'envers: Les idées radicales au cours de la Révolution anglaise*. Translated by Simone Chambon and Rachel Ertel. Paris: Payot, 1977.
Horkheimer, Max. *Crépuscule: Notes en Allemagne, 1926–1931*. Translated by Sabine Cornille and Philippe Ivernel. Paris: Payot & Rivages, 1994.
———. *Éclipse de la raison*. Translated by Jacques Debouzy and Jacques Laizé. Paris: Payot, 1974.
———. *Les débuts de la philosophie bourgeoise de l'histoire*. Translated by Denis Authier. Payot: Paris, 1974.

———. *Notes critiques: 1949–1969: Sur le temps présent*. Translated by Sabine Cornille and Philippe Ivernel. Paris: Payot & Rivages, 1993.

———. *Théorie critique*. Translated by the Translation Group of the Collège de philosophie. Paris: Payot, 1978.

Israël, Nicolas. *Spinoza: Le temps de la vigilance*. Paris: Payot & Rivages, 2001.

Israël, Nicolas, with Laurent Gryn. *Généalogie du droit moderne: L'état de nécessité*. Paris: Payot & Rivages, 2006.

Janover, Louis. *La révolution surréaliste*. Paris: Éditions Klincksieck, 2016.

Jay, Martin. *L'imagination dialectique: L'École de Francfort, 1923–1950*. Translated by E. E. Moreno and Alain Spiquel. Paris: Payot, 1977.

Kant, Immanuel. *Le conflit des facultés et autres textes sur la Révolution*. Translated and with notes and preface by Christian Ferrié. Paris: Payot & Rivages, 2015.

Kleist, Heinrich von. *Anecdotes et petits écrits*. Translated by Jean Ruffet. Paris: Payot, 1981.

Kracauer, Siegfried. *Le roman policier: Un traité philosophique*. Translated by Geneviève Rochlitz and Rainer Rochlitz. Preface by Rainer Rochlitz. Paris: Payot, 1981.

La Boétie, Étienne de. *Le Discours de la servitude volontaire*. Edited by Pierre Leonard and Miguel Abensour. Introduction by Miguel Abensour and Marcel Gauchet. Paris: Payot, 1976.

Leroux, Pierre. *Aux philosophes, aux artistes, aux politiques: Trois discours et autres textes*. Edited and with preface by Jean-Pierre Lacassagne. Postface by Miguel Abensour. Paris: Payot & Rivages, 1994.

Loraux, Nicole. *La cité divisée: L'oubli dans la mémoire d'Athènes*. Paris: Payot & Rivages, 1997.

———. *L'invention d'Athènes: Histoire de l'oraison funèbre dans la cité classique*. Paris: Payot & Rivages, 1993.

Löwith, Karl. *Max Weber et Karl Marx*. Translated by Marianne Dautrey. Preface by Enrico Donaggio. Paris: Payot & Rivages, 2009.

Löwy, Michael, and Robert Sayre. *Révolte et mélancolie: Le romantisme à contre-courant de la modernité*. Paris: Payot, 1992.

Manent, Pierre. *Naissances de la politique moderne: Machiavel, Hobbes, Rousseau*. Paris: Payot, 1977.

Mercier-Vega, Louis. *La Révolution par l'état: Une nouvelle classe dirigeante en Amérique latine*. Presentation by Miguel Abensour. Paris: Payot, 1978.

Moutot, Gilles. *Essai sur Adorno*. Paris: Payot & Rivages, 2010.

Muhlmann, Géraldine. *Du journalisme en démocratie*. Paris: Payot & Rivages, 2004.

Negt, Oskar. *L'espace public oppositionnel*. Translated and with preface by Alexander Neumann. Paris: Payot & Rivages, 2007.

Neumann, Franz. *Béhémoth: Structure et pratique du national-socialisme, 1933–1944*. Translated by Gilles Dauvé, with Jean-Louis Boireau. Paris: Payot, 1987.

Oehler, Dolf. *Le spleen contre l'oubli, juin 1848: Baudelaire, Flaubert, Heine, Herzen*. Translated by Guy Petitdemange, with Sabine Cornille. Paris: Payot & Rivages, 1996.

Pelli, Giuseppe. *Contre la peine de mort: Précédé de correspondance avec Beccaria.* Translated and with presentation by Philippe Audegean. Paris: Éditions Klincksieck, 2016.
Perrier, Florent. *Topeaugraphies de l'utopie: Esquisses sur l'art, l'utopie et le politique.* Paris: Payot & Rivages, 2014.
Philosophies de l'université: L'idéalisme allemand et la question de l'université. Contributions by Friedrich Wilhelm Joseph von Schelling, Johann Gottlieb Fichte, Georg Wilhelm Friedrich Hegel, Friedrich Schleiermacher, and Wilhelm Freiherr von Humboldt. Translated by the Translation Seminar of the Collège de Philosophie. Presentation by Luc Ferry, Jean-Pierre Pesron, and Alain Renaut. Paris: Payot, 1979.
Poirier, Nicolas. *L'ontologie politique de Castoriadis: Création et institution.* Paris: Payot & Rivages, 2011.
Proust, Françoise. *Kant, le ton de l'histoire.* Paris: Payot, 1991.
Quinet, Edgar. *Philosophie de l'histoire de France.* Postface by Jean-Michel Rey. Paris: Payot & Rivages, 2009.
Richir, Marc. *Du sublime en politique.* Paris: Payot, 1991.
———. *La Contingence du despote.* Paris: Payot & Rivages, 2014.
Riviale, Philippe. *Johann Fichte, éveil à l'autonomie, le moi et le monde.* Paris: Payot & Rivages, 2012.
———. *L'impatience du bonheur: Apologie de Gracchus Babeuf.* Paris: Payot & Rivages, 2001.
Rubel, Maximilien. *Karl Marx, essai de biographie intellectuelle.* Preface by Louis Janover. Paris: Éditions Klincksieck, 2016.
———. *Marx, critique du marxisme: Essais.* Paris: Payot, 1974.
Schelling, Friedrich W. J. von. *Recherches sur la liberté humaine.* Translated and with notes, introduction, and comments by Marc Richir. Paris: Payot, 1977.
Schroyer, Trent. *Critique de la domination: Origines et développement de la théorie critique.* Translated by Jacques Debouzy. Paris: Payot, 1980.
Simmel, Georg. *Esthétique et modernité, conflit et modernité, testament philosophique.* Vol. 2 of *Philosophie de la modernité.* Translated and with introduction by Jean-Louise Vieillard-Barron. Paris: Payot, 1990.
———. *La femme, la ville, l'individualisme.* Vol. 1 of *Philosophie de la modernité* 1. Translated and with introduction by Jean-Louise Vieillard-Barron. Paris: Payot, 1988.
Strauss, Leo. *Pensées sur Machiavel.* Translated by Michel-Pierre Edmond and Thomas Stern. Introduction by Michel-Pierre Edmond. Paris: Payot, 1982.
Strayer, Joseph Reese *Les origines médiévales de l'état moderne.* Translated by Michèle Clément. Paris: Payot, 1979.
Taminiaux, Jacques. *La fille de Thrace et le penseur professionnel: Arendt et Heidegger.* Paris: Payot, 1992.
———. *Naissance de la philosophie hégélienne de l'état: Commentaire et traduction de la "Realphilosophie d'Iéna," 1805–1806.* Paris: Payot, 1984.

Tassin, Étienne. *Le trésor perdu: Hannah Arendt, l'intelligence de l'action politique.* Paris: Payot & Rivages, 1999.
Villa, Dana. *Arendt et Heidegger: Le destin du politique.* Translated by Christophe David and David Munnich. Paris: Payot & Rivages, 2008.
Wahnich, Sophie. *La longue patience du peuple: 1792, naissance de la République.* Paris: Payot & Rivages, 2008.
———. *La Révolution française n'est pas un mythe.* Paris: Éditions Klincksieck, 2017.
Walzer, Michael. *Régicide et révolution: Le procès de Louis XVI.* Translated by Jacques Debouzy and Anne Kupiec. Paris: Payot, 1989.

COMPLETE LIST OF ABENSOUR'S PUBLICATIONS—
ENGLISH TRANSLATIONS

Books

Democracy against the State: Marx and the Machiavellian Moment (including "Preface to the Italian Edition [2008]: Insurgent Democracy and Institution"; "Foreward to the Second French Edition [2004]: Of Insurgent Democracy"; and "Appendix: 'Savage Democracy' and the 'Principle of Anarchy'"). Translated by Max Blechman and Martin Breaugh. Cambridge, UK: Polity, 2011.
Utopia from Thomas More to Walter Benjamin. Translated by Raymond N. MacKenzie. Minneapolis: Univocal, 2017.

Articles and Chapters

"Against the Sovereignty of Philosophy over Politics: Arendt's Reading of Plato's Cave Allegory." Translated by Martin Breaugh. *Social Research* 74, no. 4 (2007): 955–82.
"An-archy between Metapolitics and Politics." Translated by Martin Breaugh. *Parallax* 8, no. 3 (2002): 5–18. Republished in *The Anarchist Turn*, edited by Jacob Blumenfeld, Chiara Bottici, and Simon Critchley, 80–97. London: Pluto Press, 2013.
"The Appeal to Vigilance by Forty Intellectuals [Abensour et al.]." *Telos*, no. 98–99 (1993): 135–36.
"The Counter-Hobbes of Pierre Clastres." Translated by Martin Breaugh and Devin Penner. In *Thinking Radical Democracy: The Return to Politics in Post-war France*, edited by Martin Breaugh, Christopher Holman, Rachel Magnusson, Paul Mazzocchi, and Devin Penner, 89–118. Toronto: University of Toronto Press, 2015.
"The History of Utopia and the Destiny of Its Critique." Translated by James D. Ingram. In *Political Uses of Utopia: New Marxist, Anarchist, and Radical Democratic Perspectives*, edited by S. D. Chrostowska and James D. Ingram, 3–56. New York: Columbia University Press, 2016.

"Is There a Proper Way to Use the Voluntary Servitude Hypothesis?" Translated by Ronald Creagh. *Journal of Political Ideologies* 16, no. 3 (2011): 329–48.

"Persistent Utopia." Translated by James D. Ingram. *Constellations* 15, no. 3 (2008): 406–21.

"Saint-Just and the Problem of Heroism in the French Revolution." *Social Research* 56, no. 1 (1989): 187–211.

"'Savage Democracy' and 'Principle of Anarchy.'" Translated by Max Blechman. *Philosophy and Social Criticism* 28, no. 6 (2002): 703–26.

"To Think Utopia Otherwise." Translated by Bettina Bergo. *Graduate Faculty Philosophy Journal* 20/21, no. 2/1 (1998): 251–79.

"Utopia and Democracy." Translated by Matthew Lorenzen. In *The Weariness of Democracy: Confronting the Failure of Liberal Democracy*, edited by Obed Frausto, Jason Powell, and Sarah Vitale, 27–38. Cham, Switzerland: Palgrave Macmillan, 2020.

"Utopia: Future and/or Alterity?" Translated by Trinanjan Chakraborty. In *The Politics of the (Im)Possible: Utopia and Dystopia Reconsidered*, edited by Barnita Bagchi, 23–46. Thousand Oaks, CA: Sage, 2012.

"The Voice of Pierre Clastres." Translated by Helen Arnold. In *The Question of Power: An Interview with Pierre Clastres*, by Peirre Clastres, 5–13. South Pasadena: Semiotext(e), 2015.

"William Morris: The Politics of Romance." Translated by Max Blechman. In *Revolutionary Romance*, edited by Max Blechman, 125–59. San Francisco: City Lights, 1999.

Secondary Sources

Adorno, Gretel, and Walter Benjamin. *Correspondence, 1930–1940*. Edited by Henri Lonitz and Christoph Gödde. Translated by Wieland Hoban. Cambridge, UK: Polity, 2008.

Adorno, Theodor. *Hegel: Three Studies*. Cambridge, MA: MIT Press, 1993.

———. "Letter to Benjamin, Aug. 2–4, 1935." In *Selected Writings*, vol. 3, *1958–1938*, by Walter Benjamin, 53–62. Edited by Howard Eiland and Michael William Jennings. Translated by Edmund Jephcott and Howard Eiland. Cambridge, MA: Belknap Press of Harvard University Press, 2006.

———. *Metaphysics: Concept and Problems*. Edited by Rolf Tiedemann. Translated by Edmund Jephcott. Stanford, CA: Stanford University Press, 2001.

———. *Minima Moralia: Reflections on a Damaged Life*. Translated by Edmund Jephcott. London: Verso, 2005.

———. *Negative Dialectics*. Translated by E. B. Ashton. New York: Continuum, 1973.

———. "Progress." In *Critical Models: Interventions and Catchwords*, translated by Henry Pickford, 143–60. New York: Columbia University Press, 1998.

———. *The Stars Down to Earth and Other Essays on the Irrational in Culture*. Edited by Stephen Crook. London: Routledge, 1994.

Adorno, Theodor, and Walter Benjamin. *The Complete Correspondence, 1928–1940*. Edited by Henri Lonitz. Translated by Nicholas Walker. Cambridge, MA: Harvard University Press, 1999.

Adorno, Theodor, Else Frenkel-Brunswik, Daniel J. Levinson, and R. Nevitt Sanford. *The Authoritarian Personality*. London: Verso, 2019.

Anderson, Perry. "Origins of the Present Crisis." *New Left Review*, 1st ser., no. 23 (1964): 26–53.

Anweiler, Oskar. *The Soviets: The Russian Workers, Peasants, and Soldiers Councils, 1905–1921*. Translated by Ruth Hein. New York: Pantheon, 1975.

Arendt, Hannah. "Action and the Pursuit of Happiness." In *Politische Ordnung und menschliche Existenz: Festgabe für Eric Voegelin zum 60. Geburtstag*, edited by Alois Dempf, Hannah Arendt, and Friedrich Engel-Janosi, 1–16. Munich: Beck, 1962.

———. *Between Past and Future*. Edited by Jerome Kohn. New York: Viking, 1961.

———. "Concern with Politics in Recent European Philosophical Thought." In *Essays in Understanding, 1930–1954*, edited by Jerome Kohn, 399–417. New York: Harcourt Brace, 1994.

———. Epilogue to *The Promise of Politics*, edited by Jerome Kohn, 201–4. New York: Schocken, 2005.

———. "Hannah Arendt on Hannah Arendt." In *Hannah Arendt: The Recovery of the Public World*, edited by Melvyn Hill, 301–39. New York: St. Martin's, 1979.

———. *The Human Condition*. 2nd ed. Chicago: University of Chicago Press, 1998.

———. "Introduction into Politics." In *The Promise of Politics*, edited by Jerome Kohn, 93–200. New York: Schocken, 2005.

———. *Lectures on Kant's Political Philosophy*. Edited by Ronald Beiner. Chicago: University of Chicago Press, 1989.

———. *The Life of the Mind*. One-volume ed. New York: Harcourt, 1978.

———. "Miscellany; Outlines and Research Memoranda, 1946, undated." Hannah Arendt Papers: Speeches and Writings File, 1923–1975, Library of Congress. https://www.loc.gov/item/mss11056014l8/.

———. "On Humanity in Dark Times: Thoughts about Lessing." In *Men in Dark Times*, translated by Harry Zorn, 3–32. New York: Harvest, 1968.

———. "On the Nature of Totalitarianism: An Essay in Understanding." Essays and Lectures, Hannah Arendt Papers: Speeches and Writings File, 1923–1975, Library of Congress, undated. https://www.loc.gov/item/mss11056012 68/.

———. "On the Nature of Totalitarianism: An Essay in Understanding." In *Essays in Understanding, 1930–1954*, edited by Jerome Kohn, 328–60. New York: Schocken, 1994.

———. *The Origins of Totalitarianism*. New York: Harcourt, 1994.

———. "Philosophy and Politics." *Social Research* 57, no. 1 (1990): 73–103.

———. "Philosophy and Politics: What Is Political Philosophy?" Lectures and Seminar, 1969, New School for Social Research, New York. Courses, Hannah Arendt Papers: Subject File, 1949–1975, Library of Congress. http://hdl.loc.gov/loc.mss/ms001004.mss11056.00971.

———. "Tradition and the Modern Age." In *Between Past and Future: Eight Exercises in Political Thought*, 17–40. New York: Viking, 1961.

———. "Walter Benjamin: 1892–1940." In *Men in Dark Times*, translated by Harry Zorn, 153–206. New York: Harvest, 1968.

———. "What Is Freedom." In *Between Past and Future: Eight Exercises in Political Thought*, 143–71. New York: Viking Press, 1961.

———. "'What Remains? The Language Remains': A Conversation with Günter Gaus." In *The Portable Hannah Arendt*, edited by Peter Baehr, 3–22. New York: Penguin, 2000.

———. "Zionism Reconsidered." In *The Jewish Writings*, edited by Jerome Kohn and Ron H. Feldman, 343–74. New York: Schocken, 2008.

Aristotle. *Politics*. Translated by Ernest Barker. Oxford: Oxford University Press, 1995.

Baczko, Bronislaw. *Les imaginaires sociaux: Mémoires et espoirs collectifs*. Paris: Payot, 1984.

Balibar, Étienne. *On the Dictatorship of the Proletariat*. Translated by Grahame Lock. London: New Left Books, 1977.

Barry, Brian. "The Strange Death of Political Philosophy." *Government and Opposition* 15, no. 3/4 (1980): 276–88.

Baudelaire, Charles. "My Heart Laid Bare." In *Baudelaire: His Prose and Poetry*, edited by T. R. Smith, 225–48. New York: Boni and Liveright, 1919.

Bénichou, Paul. *Le temps des prophètes: Doctrines de l'âge romantique*. Paris: Gallimard, 1977.

Benjamin, Walter. *The Arcades Project*. Edited by Rolf Tiedemann. Translated by Howard Eiland and Kevin McLaughlin. Cambridge, MA: Belknap Press of Harvard University Press, 2002.

———. *Charles Baudelaire: A Lyric Poet in the Era of High Capitalism*. London: Verso, 1983.

———. *Charles Baudelaire: Un poète lyrique à l'apogée du capitalisme*. Edited by Rolf Tiedemann. Translated by Jean Lacoste. Paris: Payot, 1990.

———. *The Correspondence of Walter Benjamin, 1910–1940*. Chicago: University of Chicago Press, 1994.

———. "Letter to Gretel Adorno, Aug. 16, 1935." In *Gretel Adorno and Walter Benjamin: Correspondence, 1930–1940*, edited by Christoph Gödde. Translated by Wieland Hoban. Cambridge, UK: Polity, 2008.

———. "Materials for the Exposé of 1935." In *The Arcades Project*, edited by Rolf Tiedemann, 899–918. Translated by Howard Eiland and Kevin McLaughlin. Cambridge, MA: Belknap Press of Harvard University Press, 2002.

———. "Paris, the Capital of the Nineteenth Century: Exposé of 1935." In *The Arcades Project*, edited by Rolf Tiedemann, 3–13. Translated by Howard

Eiland and Kevin McLaughlin. Cambridge, MA: Belknap Press of Harvard University Press, 2002.
———. "Paris, Capital of the Nineteenth Century: Exposé of 1939." In *The Arcades Project*, edited by Rolf Tiedemann, 14–26. Translated by Howard Eiland and Kevin McLaughlin. Cambridge, MA: Belknap Press of Harvard University Press, 2002.
———. "Sur le concept d'histoire." Translated by Pierre Missac. *Les temps modernes*, no. 25 (1947): 623–34.
———. "Theses on the Philosophy of History." In *Illuminations*, edited by Hannah Arendt, 253–64. Translated by Harry Zohn. New York: Schocken, 1968.
Benjamin, Walter, and Asja Lacis. "Naples." In *Reflections: Essays, Aphorisms, Autobiographical Writing*, edited by Peter Demetz, 163–73. Translated by Edmund Jephcott. New York: Schocken, 1986.
Birnbaum, Antonia. *Bonheur justice, Walter Benjamin: Le détour grec*. Paris: Payot, 2008.
Blanchot, Maurice. *The Infinite Conversation*. Translated by Susan Hanson. Minneapolis: University of Minnesota Press, 1993.
Blanqui, Auguste. *Eternity by the Stars: An Astronomical Hypothesis*. Translated by Frank Chouraqui. New York: Contra Mundum, 2013.
Boltanski, Luc. "Sociologie critique et sociologie de la critique." *Politix* 3, no. 10–11 (1990): 124–34.
Bourdieu, Pierre. *La distinction*. Paris: Les Editions de Minuit, 1970.
Breaugh, Martin. "Critique de la domination, pensée de l'émancipation: Sur la philosophie politique de Miguel Abensour." *Politique et sociétés* 22, no. 3 (2003): 45–69.
———. "From a Critique of Totalitarian Domination to the Utopia of Insurgent Democracy: On the 'Political Philosophy' of Miguel Abensour." In *Thinking Radical Democracy: The Return to Politics in Post-war France*, edited by Breaugh et al., 234–54. Toronto: University of Toronto Press, 2015.
———. *The Plebeian Experience: A Discontinuous History of Political Freedom*. New York: Columbia University Press, 2013.
Breaugh, Martin, and Dean Caivano. "A Living Critique of Domination: Exemplars of Radical Democracy from Black Lives Matter to #MeToo." *Philosophy and Social Criticism. Philosophy & Social Criticism* 50, no. 3 (2024): 447–72.
Breaugh, Martin, Christopher Holman, Rachel Magnusson, Paul Mazzocchi, and Devin Penner, eds. *Thinking Radical Democracy: The Return to Politics in Post-war France*. Toronto: University of Toronto Press, 2015.
Buck-Morss, Susan. *The Dialectics of Seeing: Walter Benjamin and the Arcades Project*. Cambridge, MA: MIT Press, 1989.
Caillois, Roger. *Quatre essais de sociologie contemporaine*. Paris: O. Perrin, 1951.
Canetti, Elias. *The Conscience of Words*. Translated by Joachim Neugroschel. New York: Seabury, 1979.
———. *Crowds and Power*. Translated by Carol Stewart. New York: Seabury, 1978.

Castoriadis, Cornelius. "On the History of the Workers' Movement." *Telos*, no. 30 (1976): 3–42.
Celikates, Robin. Review of *Pour une philosophie politique critique*, by Miguel Abensour. *European Journal of Philosophy* 18, no. 4 (2010): 605–9.
Cervera-Marzal, Manuel. "Miguel Abensour, Cornelius Castoriadis: Un conseillisme français?" *Revue du MAUSS* 40, no. 2 (2012): 300–320.
———. *Miguel Abensour, critique de la domination, pensée de l'émancipation*. Paris: Sens & Tonka, 2013.
Cervera-Marzal, Manuel, and Nicolas Poirier. *Désir d'utopie: Politique et émancipation avec Miguel Abensour*. Paris: L'Harmattan, 2018.
Cobban, Alfred. "The Decline of Political Theory." *Political Science Quarterly* 68, no. 3 (1953): 321–37.
Constant, Benjamin. *Mélanges de littérature et de politique*. Paris: Pichon et Didier, 1829.
Corcuff, Philippe. *Où est passée la critique sociale? Penser le global au croisement des savoirs*. Paris: La Découverte, 2012.
Creagh, Ronald. *Laboratoires de l'utopie: Les communautés libertaires aux États-Unis*. Paris: Payot, 1983.
Critchley, Simon. "Five Problems in Levinas's View of Politics and the Sketch of a Solution to Them." In *Radicalizing Levinas*, edited by Peter Atterton and Matthew Calarco, 41–55. Albany: State University of New York Press, 2010.
Cusset, François. *French Theory. How Foucault, Derrida, Deleuze, & Co. Transformed the Intellectual Life of the United States*. Minneapolis: University of Minnesota Press, 2008.
Dahl, Robert A. "Political Theory: Truth and Consequences." *World Politics* 11, no. 2 (1958): 89–102.
Dejacque, Joseph. "L'humanisphere." In *La question révolutionnaire; L'humanisphère; À bas les chefs; La libération des noirs américains*, edited by Valentin Pelosse, 85–207. Paris: Champ Libre, 1971.
Douglass, R. Bruce. "John Rawls and the Revival of Political Philosophy: Where Does He Leave Us?" *Theoria* 59, no. 133 (2012): 81–97.
Easton, David. "The Decline of Modern Political Theory." *Journal of Politics* 13, no. 2 (1951): 36–58.
Esposito, Roberto. "The Creative Force of Institutions: A Reply to Benoît Dillet's, Vanessa Lemm's, and Robert Nichols's Responses to 'Three Paradigms of Political Ontology.'" *Cultural Critique* 115, no. 1 (2022): 143–49.
Ferrari, Joseph. *Les philosophes salariés*. Paris: Payot, 1983.
Ferry, Luc, and Alain Renaut, eds. *Archives de philosophie* 45, no. 2 (1982).
———. eds. *Why We Are Not Nietzscheans*. Translated by Robert de Loaiza. Chicago: University of Chicago Press, 1997.
Feuerbach, Ludwig. "The Necessity of a Reform of Philosophy." In *The Fiery Brook: Selected Writings*, translated by Zawar Hanfi, 145–52. London: Verso, 2013.

Fichte, J. G. *Contribution to the Correction of the Public's Judgments on the French Revolution*. Translated by Jeffrey Church and Anna Marisa Schön. Albany: State University of New York Press, 2021.
Fischbach, Franck. "Le déni du social: Deux exemples contemporains: Rancière et Abensour." *Recherches sur la philosophie et le langage*, no. 28 (2012): 29–46.
Fourier, Charles. *The Theory of the Four Movements*. Edited by Gareth Stedman Jones and Ian Patterson. Cambridge: Cambridge University Press, 1996.
Fridenson, Patrick. "La formation de la classe ouvrière anglaise." *Le Débat* 3, no. 3 (1980): 175–88.
Friedman, George. *The Political Philosophy of the Frankfurt School*. Ithaca, NY: Cornell University Press, 1981.
Furet, François. *The Passing of an Illusion: The Idea of Communism in the Twentieth Century*. Translated by Deborah Furet. Chicago: University of Chicago Press, 1999.
Gardiner, Michael E. *Weak Messianism: Essays in Everyday Utopianism*. Bern: Peter Lang, 2012.
Gauchet, Marcel. *La condition historique*. Paris: Stock, 2003.
———. *La démocratie contre elle-même*. Paris: Gallimard, 2002.
———. *L'avènement de la démocratie I: La révolution moderne*. Paris: Gallimard, 2007.
———. *The Disenchantment of the World: A Political History of Religion*. Translated by Oscar Borge. Princeton, NJ: Princeton University Press, 1997.
Geffroy, Gustave. *L'enfermé*. Paris: Bibliothèque-Charpentier, 1897.
Goldmann, Lucien. *The Human Sciences and Philosophy*. Translated by Hayden White and Robert Anchor. London: Cape, 1969.
———. *Sciences humaines et philosophie*. Nouvelle encyclopédie philosophique. Paris: Presses universitaires de France, 1952.
Gonzalez, Horacio. "Le processus de libération des textes." In *Critique de la philosophie: Autour de Miguel Abensour*, edited by Anne Kupiec and Étienne Tassin. Paris, 2006.
Grignon, Claude, and Jean-Claude Passeron. *Le savant et le populaire, misérabilisme et populisme en sociologie et en littérature*. Paris: Seuil, 1990.
Guizot, François. *History of the Origin of Representative Government in Europe*. Translated by Andrew Scoble. London: Henry G. Bohn, 1861.
Guterman, Norbert, and Leo Löwenthal. *Prophets of Deceit: A Study of the Techniques of the American Agitator*. London: Verso, 2021.
Habermas, Jürgen. *The Structural Transformation of the Public Sphere: An Inquiry into a Category of Bourgeois Society*. Translated by Thomas Burger and Frederick Lawrence. Cambridge, MA: MIT Press, 1991.
Hegel, G. W. F. *Phenomenology of Spirit*. Translated by A. V. Miller. Oxford: Oxford University Press, 1977.
Henein, Georges. *Prestige de la terreur*. La Caire: Éditions Champollion, 1945.

Hess, Moses. "The Philosophy of the Act." In *Socialist Thought: A Documentary History*, edited by Albert Fried and Ronald Sanders, 249–75. Rev. ed. New York: Columbia University Press, 1992.

Holman, Christopher. "Abensour and the Political Legacy of Critical Theory." Paper presented at "The Politics of Emancipation: Utopia, Insurgent Democracy, and the Legacy of Miguel Abensour," York University, Toronto, 2022.

———. "History of Political Thought at a Standstill: Abensour, Constellations and Textual Alterity." *Philosophy and Social Criticism* 49, no. 9 (2022): 1079–1106.

———. Review of *Democracy against the State: Marx and the Machiavellian Moment*, by Miguel Abensour." *Rethinking Marxism* 26, no. 3 (2014): 434–42.

Holman, Christopher, Martin Breaugh, Rachel Magnusson, Paul Mazzocchi, and Devin Penner. "Introduction: Radical Democracy and Twentieth-Century French Thought." In *Thinking Radical Democracy: The Return to Politics in Postwar France*, edited by Breaugh et al., 3–30. Toronto: University of Toronto Press, 2015.

Honig, Bonnie. *Political Theory and the Displacement of Politics*. Ithaca, NY: Cornell University Press, 1993.

Horkheimer, Max. "The Authoritarian State." *Telos*, no. 15 (1973): 3–20.

———. "Authority and the Family." In *Critical Theory: Selected Essays*, translated by Matthew J. O'Connell. New York: Continuum, 1975.

———. "Beginnings of the Bourgeois Philosophy of History." In *Between Philosophy and Social Science: Selected Early Writings*, translated by G. Frederick Hunter, Matthew S. Kramer, and John Torpey, 49–110. Cambridge, MA: MIT Press, 1993.

———. *Eclipse of Reason*. London: Continuum, 2004.

———. "Egoism and Freedom Movements: On the Anthropology of the Bourgeois Era." In *Between Philosophy and Social Science: Selected Early Writings*, translated by G. Frederick Hunter, Matthew S. Kramer, and John Torpey, 49–110. Cambridge, MA: MIT Press, 1993.

———. "The End of Reason." In *The Essential Frankfurt School Reader*, edited by Andrew Arato and Elike Gerhardt, 26–48. New York: Continuum, 1982.

———. "La philosophie de la concentration absolue." In *Théorie critique*. Paris: Payot, 1978.

Horkheimer, Max, and Theodor Adorno. *Dialectic of Enlightenment*. Translated by Edmund Jephcott. Stanford, CA: Stanford University Press, 2002.

Ingram, James D. "The Politics of Claude Lefort's Political: Between Liberalism and Radical Democracy." *Thesis Eleven*, no. 87 (2006): 33–50.

———. *Radical Cosmopolitics: The Ethics and Politics of Democratic Universalism*. New York: Columbia University Press, 2013.

Janicaud, Dominique. *Heidegger in France*. Translated by François Raffoul and David Pettigrew. Bloomington: Indiana University Press, 2015.

Jones, William David. *The Lost Debate: German Socialist Intellectuals and Totalitarianism*. Champaign: University of Illinois Press, 1999.

Kalyvas, Andreas. *Democracy and the Politics of the Extraordinary: Max Weber, Carl Schmitt, and Hannah Arendt.* Cambridge: Cambridge University Press, 2008.
Kant, Immanuel. *Critique of Judgement.* Translated by James Creed Meredith. Oxford: Oxford University Press, 2007.
———. *Observations on the Feeling of the Beautiful and Sublime and Other Writings.* Translated by Patrick Frierson and Paul Guyer. Cambridge: Cambridge University Press, 2011.
———. "What Does It Mean to Orient Oneself in Thinking?'" In *Religion and Rational Theology*, translated by Allen W. Wood and George di Giovanni, 7–18. Rev. ed. Cambridge: Cambridge University Press, 2001.
Kioupkiolis, Alexandros, and Giorgos Katsambekis, eds. *Radical Democracy and Collective Movements Today: The Biopolitics of the Multitude versus the Hegemony of the People.* London: Routledge, 2016.
Kojève, Alexandre. "Tyranny and Wisdom." In *On Tyranny*, by Leo Strauss, 135–76. Rev. and exp. ed. Chicago: University of Chicago Press, 2000.
Korsch, Karl. *Marxism and Philosophy.* Translated by Fred Halliday. London: Verso, 2013.
Korsch, Karl, et al. *La contre-révolution bureaucratique.* Paris: UGE, 1973.
Kracauer, Siegfried. "The Mass Ornament." In *The Mass Ornament: Weimar Essays*, edited and translated by Thomas Y. Levin, 75–86. Cambridge, MA: Harvard University Press, 1995.
Krier, Léon, ed. *Albert Speer: Architecture, 1932–1942.* Brussels: Archives d'Architecture Moderne, 1985.
———. "An Architecture of Desire." In *Albert Speer: Architecture, 1932–1942*, 217–31. New York: Monacelli, 2013.
Kupiec, Anne, David Munnich, and Hubert Tonka, eds. *La bibliothèque de Miguel Abensour.* Paris: Sens & Tonka, 2018.
Kupiec, Anne, and Étienne Tassin. *Critique de la politique: Autour de Miguel Abensour.* Paris: Sens & Tonka, 2006.
La Boétie, Étienne de. *Discourse on Voluntary Servitude.* Indianapolis: Hackett, 2012.
Labelle, Gilles. *L'écart absolu: Miguel Abensour.* Paris: Sens & Tonka, 2017.
Labelle, Gilles, and Daniel Tanguay. "Le retour de la philosophie politique en France." *Politique et sociétés* 22, no. 3 (2003): 3–7.
Lane, Barbara Miller. *Architecture and Politics in Germany, 1918–1945.* Cambridge, MA: Harvard University Press, 1968.
Larsson, Lars Olof. *Albert Speer: Le plan de Berlin, 1937–1943.* Brussels: Archives d'architecture moderne, 1983.
Laslett, Peter. Introduction to *Philosophy, Politics and Society*, edited by Peter Laslett. Cambridge, UK: Blackwell, 1956.
Lefort, Claude. *Éléments d'une critique de la bureaucratie.* Geneva: Droz, 1971.
———. "L'experience prolétarienne." *Socialisme ou barbarie*, no. 11 (1952): 1–19.
———. "Machiavelli and the verità effetuale." In *Writing, the Political Test*, translated by David Ames Curtis. Durham, NC: Duke University Press, 2000.

———. "The Permanence of the Theological-Political?" In *Democracy and Political Theory*, translated by David Macey, 213–55. Cambridge, UK: Polity, 1988.

———. *The Political Forms of Modern Society: Bureaucracy, Democracy, Totalitarianism*. Edited by John Thompson. Cambridge, UK: Polity, 1986.

———. "The Question of Democracy." In *Democracy and Political Theory*, translated by David Macey, 9–20. Cambridge, UK: Polity, 1988.

Lefort, Claude, and Marcel Gauchet. "Sur la democratie: Le politique et l'institution du social." *Textures*, no. 2–3 (1971): 7–78.

Levinas, Emmanuel. *God, Death, and Time*. Translated by Bettina Bergo. Stanford, CA: Stanford University Press, 2000.

———. *Humanism of the Other*. Translated by Nidra Poller. Urbana: University of Illinois Press, 2003.

———. "Is Ontology Fundamental?" Translated by Peter Atterton. *Philosophy Today* 33, no. 2 (1989): 121–29.

———. "Le surlendemain des dialectiques." In *Emmanuel Levinas: Cahiers de la nuit surveillée*, 322–24. Paris: Verdier, 1984.

———. "No Identity." In *Collected Philosophical Papers*, 141–52. Dordrecht: Nijhoff, 1987.

———. *Of God Who Comes to Mind*. Translated by Bettina Bergo. Stanford, CA: Stanford University Press, 1998.

———. "Philosophy and Awakening." In *Entre Nous: Essays on Thinking-of-the-Other*, 77–90. Translated by Michael Smith and Barbara Harshav. New York: Columbia University Press, 1998.

———. Preface to *Utopie et socialisme*, by Martin Buber. Paris: Aubier Montaigne, 1977.

———. *Proper Names*. London: Athlone, 1996.

———. *Time and the Other*. Translated by Richard A. Cohen. Pittsburgh: Duquesne University Press, 1987.

Levitas, Ruth. *The Concept of Utopia*. Oxford: Peter Lang, 2011.

———. "Educated Hope: Ernst Bloch on Abstract and Concrete Utopia." In *Not Yet: Reconsidering Ernst Bloch*, edited by Jamie Owen and Tom Moylan, 65–79. New York: Verso, 1997.

———. "For Utopia: The (Limits of the) Utopian Function in Late Capitalist Society." *Critical Review of International Social and Political Philosophy* 3, no. 2–3 (2007): 25–43.

———. *Utopia as Method: The Imaginary Reconstitution of Society*. London: Palgrave Macmillan, 2013.

Leys, Simon. *The Chairman's New Clothes: Mao and the Cultural Revolution*. New York: St. Martin's, 1977.

———. *Chinese Shadows*. New York: Viking, 1977.

———. *Orwell ou l'horreur de la politique*. Paris: Hermann, 1984.

Little, Adrian, and Moya Lloyd, eds. *The Politics of Radical Democracy*. Edinburgh: Edinburgh University Press, 2009.

Loraux, Nicole. "Donc Socrate est immortel." In *Le temps de la réflexion*. Paris: Gallimard, 1982.
Lowenthal, Leo. *False Prophets: Studies on Authoritarianism*. London: Routledge, 2015.
Lukács, Georg. *The Destruction of Reason*. Translated by Peter Palmer. Atlantic Highlands, NJ: Humanities Press, 1981.
Manent, Pierre. "The Return of Political Philosophy." *First Things*, May 2000, 15–22.
Marchart, Oliver. *Thinking Antagonism: Political Ontology after Laclau*. Edinburgh: Edinburgh University Press, 2018.
Marcuse, Herbert, ed. *The Democratic and the Authoritarian State*. New York: Free Press, 1957.
———. *An Essay on Liberation*. Boston: Beacon, 1969.
———. *Hegel's Ontology and the Theory of Historicity*. Translated by Seyla Benhabib. Cambridge, MA: MIT Press, 1987.
———. "Philosophy and Critical Theory." In *Negations: Essays in Critical Theory*, 134–58. Boston: Beacon, 1968.
———. *Reason and Revolution: Hegel and the Rise of Social Theory*. London: Routledge, 2000.
———. "State and Individual under National Socialism." In *Technology, War and Fascism*, edited by Douglas Kellner, 67–92. Vol. 1 of *Collected Papers of Herbert Marcuse*. London: Routledge, 2004.
———. "The Struggle against Liberalism in the Totalitarian View of the State." In *Negations: Essays in Critical Theory*, 3–42. Boston: Beacon, 1968.
Marx, Karl. *Capital*. Vol. 3, *A Critique of Political Economy*, translated by David Fernbach. New York: Penguin, 1993.
———. *Critique of Hegel's "Philosophy of Right."* Translated by Joseph O'Malley and Annette Jolin. Cambridge: Cambridge University Press, 1977.
———. "Letter to Dr. Kugelmann, October 9, 1866." In *Letters to Dr. Kugelmann*, 39–40. London: Lawrence and Wishart, 1941.
———. "Marx to Friedrich Adolph Sorge in Hoboken, October 19, 1877." In *Karl Marx and Frederick Engels: Selected Correspondence*, 290–91. 2nd ed. Moscow: Progress, 1965.
———. *The Poverty of Philosophy*. Translated by Harry Quelch. New York: Prometheus, 1995.
Marx, Karl, and Friedrich Engels. *Manifesto of the Communist Party*. In *The Marx-Engels Reader*, edited by Robert C. Tucker, 469–500. 2nd ed. New York: Norton, 1978.
———. *The Holy Family*. Translated by R. Dixon. Moscow: Foreign Languages Publishing House, 1956.
Mazzocchi, Paul. "Desire, Friendship, and the Politics of Refusal: The Utopian Afterlives of La Boétie's *Discourse on Voluntary Servitude*." *Utopian Studies* 29, no. 2 (2018): 248–66.

———. "Excavating Abensour: The Dialectics of Democracy and Utopia at a Standstill." *Constellations* 22, no. 2 (2015): 290–301.

———. "Insurgent Democracy and the German Councils." In *The German Revolution and Political Theory*, edited by Gaard Kets and James Muldoon, 277–98. Cham, Switzerland: Palgrave Macmillan, 2019.

Meier, Christian. *Introduction à l'anthropologie politique de l'antiquité classique*. Translated by Pierre Blanchaud. Paris: PUF, 1984.

Melançon, Jérôme. "Note critique—Partir des textes avec Miguel Abensour." *Cahiers Société*, no. 2 (2020): 269–84.

Merleau-Ponty, Maurice. "Man and Adversity." In *Signs*, 224–43. Evanston, IL: Northwestern University Press, 1964.

Michaud, Eric. *The Cult of Art in Nazi Germany*. Translated by Janet Lloyd. Stanford, CA: Stanford University Press, 2004.

———. *Un art de l'éternité*. Paris: Gallimard, 1996.

Michelet, Jules. *History of the French Revolution*. Edited by Gordon Wright. Translated by Charles Cocks. Chicago: University of Chicago Press, 1967.

Mitterrand, François. *Le Coup d'État permanent*. Paris: Plon, 1964.

More, Thomas. *Utopia*. Edited by George M. Logan. Translated by Robert M. Adams. Cambridge: Cambridge University Press, 1989.

Morris, William. "A Dream of John Ball." In *Selected Writings*, edited by G. D. H. Cole. London: Nonesuch, 1948.

———. *News from Nowhere*. Edited by Krishan Kumar. Cambridge: Cambridge University Press, 1995.

———. *William Morris on Art and Socialism*. Edited by Norman Kelvin. New York: Dover, 1999.

Mosse, George. *The Nationalization of the Masses: Political Symbolism and Mass Movements in Germany from the Napoleonic Wars through the Third Reich*. New York: Fertig, 1975.

Moylan, Tom. *Becoming Utopian: The Culture and Politics of Radical Transformation*. London: Bloomsbury, 2020.

———. *Demand the Impossible: Science Fiction and the Utopian Imagination*. London: Methuen, 1986.

Moyn, Samuel. "Modernity and the Specter of Totalitarianism." In *The Cambridge History of Modern Thought*, vol. 2, *The Twentieth Century*, edited by Peter E. Gordon and Warren Breckman, 417–37. Cambridge: Cambridge University Press, 2019.

Nadir, Christine. "Utopian Studies, Environmental Literature, and the Legacy of an Idea: Educating Desire in Miguel Abensour and Ursula K. Le Guin." *Utopian Studies* 21, no. 1 (2010): 24–56.

Nairn, Tom. "The English Working Class." *New Left Review*, 1st ser., no. 24 (1964): 43–57.

Navet, Georges. "Le temps de l'émancipation." MHDR, Université Paris 7–Denis Diderot, 2001.

Neumann, Franz. *Behemoth: The Structure and Practice of National Socialism, 1933–1944*. New York: Oxford University Press, 1944.
Neumann, Franz, and Otto Kirchheimer. *The Rule of Law under Siege: Selected Essays of Franz L. Neumann and Otto Kirchheimer*. Edited by William E. Scheuerman. Berkeley: University of California Press, 1996.
Nietzsche, Friedrich. *Beyond Good and Evil*. Translated by Judith Norman. Cambridge: Cambridge University Press, 2002.
———. *Human, All Too Human: A Book for Free Spirits*. Translated by R. J. Hollingdale. Cambridge: Cambridge University Press, 1996.
———. "On the Genealogy of Morals." In *On the Genealogy of Morals and Ecce Homo*, translated by Walter Kaufmann and R. J. Hollingdale, 15–163 New York: Vintage, 1989.
———. "Twilight of the Idols." In *The Anti-Christ, Ecce Homo, Twilight of the Idols and Other Writings*, edited by Aaron Ridley and Judith Norman, 153–230. Translated by Judith Norman. Cambridge: Cambridge University Press, 2005.
Nizan, Paul. "Du problème de la monumentalité, 1934." Translated by Françoise Esselier. *VH 101*, no. 7–8 (1972).
Nordmann, Charlotte. *Bourdieu/Rancière: La politique entre sociologie et philosophie*. Paris: Editions Amsterdam, 2006.
Nussbaum, Martha. "The Enduring Significance of John Rawls." *Chronicle of Higher Education* 47, no. 45 (2001): B7.
Orwell, George. *Homage to Catalonia*. New York: Penguin, 1970.
Pascal, Blaise. *Pensées*. Translated by A. J. Krailsheimer. London: Penguin, 1995.
Petitdemange, Guy. "L'Aufklärung: Un mythe, une tâche." *Recherches de science religieuse* 72, no. 3 (1984): 420–49.
Philonenko, Alexis. *Théorie et praxis dans la pensée morale et politique de Kant et de Fichte en 1793*. Paris: Vrin, 1968.
Plato. "Phaedo." In *The Portable Plato*, edited by Scott Buchanan. Translated by Benjamin Jowett. New York: Penguin, 2009.
———. *Phédon*. Translated by Monique Dixsaut. Paris: Flammarion, 1991.
Plätzer, Niklas. "How to Make the Moment Last? On Rupture and Institutions in Massimiliano Tomba's *Insurgent Universality*." *Historical Materialism* 30, no. 4 (2022): 108–24.
Pollock, Friedrich. *The Economic and Social Consequences of Automation*. Translated by W. O. Henderson and W. H. Chaloner. Oxford: Blackwell, 1957.
———. "State Capitalism: Its Possibilities and Limitations." In *The Essential Frankfurt School Reader*, edited by Andrew Arato and Elike Gerhardt, 71–94. New York: Continuum, 1982.
Popper, Karl. *The Open Society and Its Enemies*. Princeton, NJ: Princeton University Press, 1945.
Prévost, André. *L'Utopie de Thomas More*. Paris: Mame, 1978.
Proust, Françoise. *L'histoire à contretemps: Le temps historique chez Walter Benjamin*. Paris: Éditions du Cerf, 1994.

Quinet, Edgar. *Le christianisme et la Révolution française*. Paris: Fayard, 1984.
Rancière, Jacques. *Disagreement: Politics and Philosophy*. Translated by Julie Rose. Minneapolis: University of Minnesota Press, 2004.
———. *Hatred of Democracy*. Translated by Steve Corcoran. New York: Verso, 2014.
———. *The Philosopher and His Poor*. Translated by John Drury, Corinne Oster, and Andrew Parker. Durham, NC: Duke University Press, 2003.
Rawls, John. *A Theory of Justice*. Cambridge, MA: Belknap Press of Harvard University Press, 1971.
Richir, Marc. *Du sublime en politique*. Paris: Payot, 1991.
Rousseau, Jean-Jacques. *The Confessions*. Translated by J.M. Cohen. New York: Penguin, 1953.
———. *Politics and the Arts: Letter to M. D'Alembert on the Theatre*. Translated by Allan Bloom. Ithaca, NY: Cornell University Press, 1968.
Rubel, Maximilien. "Non-market Socialism in the Nineteenth Century." In *Non-market Socialism in the Nineteenth and Twentieth Centuries*, edited by John Crump and Maximilien Rubel, 10–34. New York: Palgrave Macmillan, 1987.
Scheuerman, William E. *Between the Norm and the Exception: The Frankfurt School and the Rule of Law*. Cambridge, MA: MIT Press, 1997.
Schürmann, Reiner. *Heidegger on Being and Acting: From Principles to Anarchy*. Bloomington: Indiana University Press, 1987.
Scott, James C. *Domination and the Arts of Resistance: Hidden Transcripts*. New Haven, CT: Yale University Press, 1992.
Shklar, Judith. "The Political Theory of Utopia: From Melancholy to Nostalgia." *Daedalus* 94, no. 2 (1965): 367–81.
Speer, Albert. *Inside the Third Reich: Memoirs*. Translated by Richard Winston and Clara Winston. New York: Macmillan, 1970.
———. *L'immortalité du pouvoir*. Paris: La Table Ronde, 1981.
Spinoza, Benedict de. *Spinoza: Theological-Political Treatise*. Translated by Michael Silverthorne and Jonathan Israel. Cambridge: Cambridge University Press, 2007.
Strauss, Leo. *Natural Right and History*. Chicago: University of Chicago Press, 1953.
———. "On the Intention of Rousseau." *Social Research* 14, no. 4 (1947): 455–87.
———. "What Is Political Philosophy?" *Journal of Politics* 19, no. 3 (1957): 343–68.
Talmon, Jacob. *Utopianism and Politics*. London: Conservative Political Centre, n.d.
Thompson, E. P. "Eighteenth-Century English Society: Class Struggle without Class?" *Social History* 3, no. 2 (1978): 133–65.
———. "An Interview with E. P. Thompson." *Radical History Review*, no. 12 (1976): 4–25.
———. *The Making of the English Working Class*. Harmondsworth, UK: Penguin, 1980.
———. "An Open Letter to Leszek Kolakowski (1973)." In *The Poverty of Theory: Or an Orrery of Errors*, 93–192. London: Merlin, 1978.
———. "The Peculiarities of the English." *Socialist Register* 2 (1965): 35–91.

———. "Romanticism, Utopianism and Moralism: The Case of William Morris." *New Left Review*, 1st ser., no. 99 (1976): 83–111.

———. "Time, Work-Discipline, and Industrial Capitalism." *Past and Present*, no. 38 (1967): 56–97.

———. *William Morris: Romantic to Revolutionary*. New York: Pantheon, 1976.

Tiedemann, Rolf. "Dialectics at a Standstill: Approaches to the Passegen-Werk." In *The Arcades Project*, 929–45. Cambridge, MA: Belknap Press of Harvard University Press, 2002.

Tønder, Lars, and Lasse Thomassen, eds. *Radical Democracy: Politics between Abundance and Lack*. Manchester: Manchester University Press, 2005.

Vermeren, Patrice. *Penser contre: Essais sur la philosophie critique de Miguel Abensour*. Paris: Sens & Tonka, 2019.

Weber, Max. *Economy and Society: An Outline of Interpretive Sociology*. Edited by Guenther Roth and Claus Wittich. Berkeley: University of California Press, 1978.

Wegner, Phillip E. "Escaping the Repetition of Catastrophe: On Abensour's Utopianism." *Cultural Critique* 111, no. 1 (2021): 168–81.

Wieviorka, Annette. *Déportation et génocide: Entre la mémoire et l'oubli*. Paris: Plon, 1992.

Wiggershaus, Rolf. *L'Ecole de Francfort: Histoire, développement, signification*. Translated by L. Deroche-Gurcel. Paris: Presses Universitaires France, 1993.

Williams, Raymond. "Utopia and Science Fiction." *Science Fiction Studies* 5, no. 3 (1978): 203–14.

Index

Abensour, Miguel: academic career of, 3–4; Algerian War experiences of, 3–4; Anglophone reception of, 16–17; birth and upbringing of, 2; caution on using ideas of, 22; central themes in thought of, 4; contemporary relevance of, 21–22; critical-utopian political philosophy of, 4, 11–23, 30; on critique of domination, 13–14; experimental journal participation of, 4; flight from the Nazis of, 2; intimate encounter with a tragic century of, 2–4; legacy of, 1–23; May '68 protests and, 3; as not yet fully discovered, 1–2; overview of, 1–23; political institution of the social and, 9–10; political philosophy overview of, 5–20; radical democratic turn contributed to by, 3, 14–15; totalitarianism critique overview of, 7–11; on utopia, 16, 19; World War II experiences of, 2–3. *See also specific works*
Adorno, Gretel, 235, 246
Adorno, Theodor: authoritarian personality and, 134, 143; Benjamin critiqued by, 205–206, 231–235, 247; critique of domination and, 136–138, 150–152, 166, 206; dialectic of emancipation and, 200; dialectic of enlightenment and, 131, 200–201; difference and, 189; domination differentiated from exploitation and, 135–136; emancipation and, 209; Jewish question and, 195; lines of flight and, 199; Marxism and, 136; master-slave dialectic and, 151; myth and, 201, 205; negative dialectics and, 20, 192; negative utopia and, 210; philosophy of history and, 150; politics of emancipation and, 166; progress and, 210; self-destructive reason and, 131; self-reflection and, 202; task of philosophy and, 133–134; utopia and, 30, 204–209, 231
all One, 10, 15, 29, 80, 94, 97, 158, 161
all ones, 10, 15, 29, 80, 89, 158–159, 161
Althusser, Louis, 173, 194
Anderson, Perry, 173, 176
Arcades Project, The (Benjamin), 232, 236, 241, 246
Arendt, Hannah: action principle of totalitarian regimes and, 40, 52, 58–59; architecture and, 96; classical political philosophy and, 7, 13, 48,

Arendt, Hannah *(continued)*
143, 157–158; concentration camps and, 56; confusion of politics and domination and, 55–56; critique of domination and, 13, 38, 50–66, 144–146, 157–158; definition of totalitarianism and, 43, 50–52, 56–57, 79, 145–146; desertification and, 62–63; destruction of the political and, 51–53; downfall of totalitarian regimes and, 64; everything is political and, 55; exercises in political thought and, 39; function of law and, 52–53; ideology and, 56–63; language and, 64; logic of inclusion and exclusion and, 96; mass society and, 89; miracle of being and, 45; multiplicity and, 54–56; natality and, 51, 53; negation of politics and, 52; nonthinking and, 94; opposition to political philosophy and, 13, 48, 162; power and, 55–56; public space and, 78, 88–89; regime types and, 50–51; return of political things and, 103; self-identification as "political writer" of, 38; status as philosopher of, 101–106; system of councils and, 162; terror and, 53–60, 96; tyranny and, 55–56, 62; workers' movement and, 187. *See also* "Hannah Arendt against Political Philosophy?"
Aristotle, 44, 54–55, 106, 190
"Art as Foundation for the Creative Force of Politics" *(Völkischer Beobachter)*, 69
"Authoritarian State, The" (Horkheimer), 134, 143–145
awakening, 206, 220, 224, 226–244, 247–248

Bachelard, Gaston, 194

Baczko, Bronislaw, 191
Baudelaire, Charles, 204
Bauhaus, 77
Beginnings of the Bourgeois Philosophy of History (Horkheimer), 154, 164
Behemoth (Neumann), 74, 81, 134, 143, 146, 164
Being and Time (Heidegger), 115
Benjamin, Walter: Adorno's critiques of, 205–206, 231–235, 247; ambiguity and, 233; awakening and, 228, 246; cathartic-redemptive aim of, 229; conditions of life and, 228; conversion to utopia and, 229–231; dialectical image and, 17, 224, 228, 232–238, 245–247; dream images and, 230–232, 237, 245–247; emancipation and, 185, 207–210, 229–230; esoteric doctrine and, 229; eternal return of the same and, 208; face of the Other and, 240–242; hermeneutic of suspicion and, 245–246; historical awakening and, 235–239; masses and, 92–93; mode of production and, 231; mythology and, 230; originality of, 229–230; passions and, 210; phantasmagoria and, 209; phenomenological epoché and, 228; prehistory and, 231; primal terror and, 153; progress and, 160, 209–211; secret agreement between past and present generations and, 171; utopia and, 198, 201, 204–210, 224, 228–232, 240–241, 246–248
Billy Budd (Melville), 181
Blanchot, Maurice, 123–124
Blanqui, Auguste, 160, 197, 207–210, 215, 238
Bloch, Ernst, 241–245, 248, 250
Bodei, Remo, 61
bond of division, 15, 142
Bourdieu-Rancière debate, 264n62

Buber, Martin, 241–243
Buck-Morss, Susan, 246

Caillois, Roger, 84, 92, 98
Canetti, Elias, 74, 82–87, 89, 92
capitalism: democracy and, 155; industrial capitalism, 174, 177–179, 184; political economy and, 174; revolution and, 180–181; state capitalism, 144–146; utopia and, 19, 230–232
Castoriadis, Cornelius, 2, 171
catastrophism, 13, 21, 130, 149, 159, 167
Clastres, Pierre, 2, 4
Communards, 3
Confessions, The (Rousseau), 47–48, 155
Constant, Benjamin, 7, 49, 80, 187
Counter-Hobbes, 227–228
Creagh, Ronald, 224
critical theory: critique of domination and, 12–14, 19, 30, 129–130, 141, 143, 148–149; democracy and, 166; development of, 131–133; emancipation and, 12–14, 127–129, 132–134, 147, 160; myth and, 200–201; as political philosophy, 130–147; political philosophy and, 12–13; political things and, 127–129, 143–144, 156–157. *See also* "For a Critical Political Philosophy?"
critical-utopian political philosophy, 4, 11–23, 30. *See also* "For a Critical Political Philosophy?"; "Hannah Arendt against Political Philosophy"
critique of domination: Abensour on, 13–14; catastrophism and, 149, 159; critical theory and, 12–13, 19, 30, 129–130, 141, 143, 148–149; democracy and, 162–163; domination-emancipation, 12, 14, 142, 147; emancipation and, 2, 12–14, 19, 21–23, 142, 147, 159; levels of, 12; Marxism and, 13; option of articulation and, 13–14; political philosophy and, 8, 12–13, 35, 50–66, 128, 141, 164–167; political things and, 7–11, 21, 44, 49–50, 148; social critique and, 28; utopia and, 17–18. *See also* "For a Critical Political Philosophy?"; "On a Misinterpretation of Totalitarianism and Its Effects"; totalitarianism
Critique of Hegel's Philosophy of Right (Marx), 190
Critique of Politics series, 27–30; aims of, 27–29; "Critique de la Politique," Éditions Klincksieck, 29–30; "Critique de la Politique," Éditions Payot, 27–28; critique of political economy and reason in, 27–28; definition of, 27–29; domination-slavery as central object of, 27–28; main directions of, 28–30; political knowledge in, 30; reconstruction of the practical critiques of politics in, 28; social critique of domination in, 28; totalitarianism in, 29; utopia and, 30
Critique of Pure Reason (Kant), 117–118
crowd, the, 80–81, 84, 93
Cumming, Robert, 105–106

de Gaulle, Charles, 3
Déjacque, Joseph, 193, 197
Deleuze, Gilles, 4
democracy: Abensour's contribution to radical democratic turn, 3, 14–15; capitalism and, 155; council democracy, 19, 21, 147; critical theory and, 166; critique of domination and, 162–163; crowd and, 80; democratic-utopian,

democracy *(continued)*
18–20; emancipation and, 14–20, 174; hypercriticism and, 252–253; institutions and, 20; insurgent democracy, 15, 18–20, 253; legitimacy of regimes and, 182; liberal democracy, 7–8, 11; libertarian idea of, 66, 187, 252; overview of, 14–20; plebeian democracy, 15–16, 186–187; political institution of the social and, 10; political philosophy and, 14–20; revolution and, 18–19, 253–254; savage democracy, 66, 252–253, 258; social democracy, 256; State's relation to demos in, 15; totalitarianism's relation to, 7–10, 14, 95, 144, 164–165; utopia and, 17–20, 189–191, 212–213, 257
Democracy against the State (Abensour), 14–15
Derrida, Jacques, 4
Descartes, René, 220
Destruction of Reason, The (Lukács), 200
Dialectic of Enlightenment, The (Horkheimer and Adorno), 131, 134, 151, 193, 201
Discourse on Voluntary Servitude (La Boétie), 29
Dixsaut, Monique, 112
domination. *See* critique of domination
Domination and the Arts of Resistance (Scott), 216
Dream of John Ball, A (Morris), 20, 188

education of desire, 14, 16–17, 23
Eisenmann, Charles, 4
Elias, Nobert, 139
emancipation: blind spots of, 192; conditions for possibility of a politics of, 30; critical theory and, 12–14, 127–129, 132–134, 147, 160; critique of domination and, 2, 12–14, 19, 21–23, 142, 147, 159; democracy and, 14–20, 174; dialectic of, 193, 198–204; domination-emancipation, 12, 14, 142, 147; as at heart of human history, 164; modernity and, 33, 172, 185; option of articulation and, 13–14; political liberalism and, 190; political philosophy and, 12–20, 31–35; politics of, 3, 14–20, 132, 166; possibility of, 12; utopia and, 14–20, 190–191, 197–204, 207–211, 229, 239. *See also* "Letter from a 'Revoltist' to Marcel Gauchet, Convert to Normal Politics"; "Modern Political Philosophy and Emancipation"
"End of Reason, The" (Horkheimer), 152
Engels, Friedrich, 135–136, 173, 194–195
epoché (phenomenology), 17, 223–227, 239–242
"E. P. Thompson's Passion" (Abensour), 171–188; class and, 175–176; communism and, 172–173; distinctness of Thompson and, 172; exploitation and, 179; exterminism and, 172; Industrial Revolution's impact on society and, 175–180; influence of Thompson and, 174; Jacobinism and, 181–183; Marxism and, 172–176; modernization and, 178; New Left and, 173; overview of, 15, 171–177, 185–188; political affiliations of Thompson and, 172–173; political resistance and, 176–177; popular radicalism and, 181–183; proletarian experience and, 175; quality of daily life and, 178–180; social reform and, 172–

173, 178–184; Stalinism and, 173; working class as greatest productive power and, 176; WWII experiences of Thompson and, 172–173
Essay on Man (Cassirer), 218
Essay on Wagner (Adorno), 195
Eternity by the Stars (Blanqui), 160, 210
everything is political, 47–50, 55, 155
"Exposé of 1935" (Benjamin), 201, 204, 207, 230, 232–233

Ferry, Luc, 148
Feuerbach, Ludwig, 39–40, 128, 132
Few, the, 15
Fichte, J. G., 220
"For a Critical Political Philosophy?" (Abensour), 127–167; all One and all ones and, 158–161; classical political philosophy and, 157–158; critical theory as political philosophy, 130–147; critique of domination and, 129, 134–136, 141–143, 147–155, 159–161; critique of politics and, 134–136, 140; development of critical theory and, 131–133; deviations and, 141–144; emancipation and, 142, 164; Enlightenment thought and, 131; exploitation and, 135–136; formation of paradigm of domination and, 151–152; Hegelian scheme and, 151–153; hermeneutics of suspicion and, 128–129; Marxism and, 135–137, 145–146, 152–153; nature and, 149–151; option of articulation and, 162–165; overview of, 12, 127–130, 165–167; political question and, 132–133, 147–149, 155–162; reform of thought and, 128; return of political things and, 128; totalitarianism and, 143–146; two paradigms and, 147–149; unilateral presentation of politics and, 159–161
Fourier, Charles, 191, 193, 197, 211, 219–220, 224, 229, 231, 234, 239
Frankfurt School, 4, 12, 28, 130, 132, 138, 147–150, 166
French Communist Party, 2–3, 79
French Revolution, 19, 21, 79, 119, 186, 220–221
Fridenson, Patrick, 171
Friedman, George, 131
Furet, François, 254

Gauchet, Marcel, 6–7, 18, 155–156, 257
Gaus, Günther, 103
Geffroy, Gustave, 207
Genealogy of Morals, The (Nietzsche), 137–138, 153, 222
grandees, 162–163, 258
Guizot, François, 79

Habermas, Jürgen, 15, 34, 186, 200
"Hannah Arendt against Political Philosophy?" (Abensour), 101–126; characteristics of the political, 109–110; classical political philosophy in, 101–111, 117; death's relation to philosophy in, 112–116; denial of action and, 105–111; functionalism and, 101; heroic conception of politics and, 121–126; intellectual landscape and, 101–102; Kantian reversal and, 116–120; Marxism and, 101; natality and, 114–116; overview of, 101–105, 120–126; philosophers and, 105–111; political question and, 112–116; question of equality and, 116–120; return of political things and, 102–103; schemes for, 109–110; status of Arendt as philosopher, 101–106; task of thinking and, 109

Hegel (Adorno), 201
Hegel, G. W. F.: concept of science and, 196; critical theory and, 12–13, 132–133; critique of domination and, 151; historical necessity and, 135; master-slave dialectic and, 151–152; philosophy of history and, 119–120, 135, 145; social theory and, 132–133; theory of religion and, 195
Heidegger, Martin, 108, 112, 115, 121–122, 242–245
Henein, Georges, 207
Hess, Moses, 141
"History of Utopia and the Destiny of Its Critique, The" (Abensour), 192
Hitler, Adolf, 67–71, 76, 83–87, 92, 94, 98, 145
Hobbes, Thomas, 33, 98, 226–228
Homage to Catalonia (Orwell), 46
Homer, 122–123, 190
Horkheimer, Max: authority and, 129, 137; critique of domination and, 135–144, 147, 150–151, 166; dialectic of emancipation and, 200; division and, 154; embodiment and, 150; liberalism and, 145; Marxism and, 137, 141; master-slave dialectic and, 151; myth and, 201; Nazism and, 144–145; philosophy of history and, 135, 150; progress and, 139; science of politics and, 154; self-destructive reason and, 131, 201; skepticism of political philosophy and, 140–141; totalitarianism and, 143–146; violence in human history and, 138; voluntary servitude and, 151
Hugo, Victor, 201
Human, All Too Human (Nietzsche), 200
Human Condition, The (Arendt), 125, 143, 161
Human Sciences and Philosophy, The (Goldmann), 194

Hundred Flowers Campaign, 62–63
Husserl, Edmund, 226, 240, 242

ideology, 9, 31, 50–51, 56–63, 80, 160, 174, 176, 185, 191
Industrial Revolution, 175–180
Ingram, James D., 9–10
Inside the Third Reich (Speer), 83
institutions, 12, 20, 80, 107, 137–138, 175, 186, 213, 256–257
insurgence, 15, 18–20, 253, 259
insurgent democracy, 15, 18–20, 253
I-Thou relation, 227, 241–243

Jacobinism, 181–183, 187
Janover, Louis, 259
Jewish question, 195
Jünger, Ernest, 88–89

Kant, Immanuel, 39–40, 61, 104, 106, 116–120, 156, 161
Kelsen, Hans, 256
Kirchheimer, Otto, 166
Klossowski, Pierre, 229
Kojève, Alexandre, 76
Kolakowski, Leszek, 132, 192
Korsch, Karl, 133, 144, 196
Krier, Léon, 70–71, 73–74, 80, 83, 86, 88, 94

La Boétie, Étienne de, 2, 12, 28–29, 34, 61, 74, 128, 158, 252
La fille de Thrace et le penseur professionnel (Taminiaux), 122
Landauer, Gustav, 223
Lane, Barbara Miller, 72, 76
"La philosophie de la concentration absolue" (Horkheimer), 140, 145
Le Coup d'État permanent (Mitterrand), 256
Lefort, Claude: body and, 146; capitalism and, 155; critique of

domination and, 38–40, 50, 72, 144; democracy and, 10, 66, 187; inclusion/exclusion and, 96; literary investigation and, 45; logic of political regimes and, 156; People-as-One and, 95; political freedom and, 163; political institution of the social and, 9–10, 13, 34, 143, 161; political philosophy and, 38–39; principle of anarchy and, 252–253; proletarian experience and, 175; restoration of political philosophy and, 6; savage democracy and, 252–253; totalitarianism and, 146
"Le Pouvoir Charismatique: Adolf Hitler comme idole" (Caillois), 92
Leroux, Pierre, 212, 219, 282n50
Le temps des prophètes (Benichou), 190
L'éternité par les astres (Blanqui), 160, 197, 208
"Letter from a 'Revoltist' to Marcel Gauchet, Convert to 'Normal Politics,'" 251–259; accusation of revoltism and, 251–252; alterity and, 257; anarchy principle and, 252–253; definition of democracy and, 258; definition of revoltism and, 252; freedom and, 256–257; Furet effect and, 254–255; Gauchet and Abensour's prior relationship and, 252; Marxism and, 258; normal politics and, 256–257; opening of, 251–252; overview of, 18, 20; savage democracy and, 252–253; separation of democracy from revolution and, 253–254; Thermidor and, 255, 259; utopia and, 257
Leviathan (Hobbes), 228
Levinas, Emmanuel: attitude of defiance of politics and, 48–49; awakening and, 242–244; common sense and, 228; death and, 243; dogma and, 222; ethics and politics distinguished by, 49; face of the Other and, 240–242; freedom and, 199; importance of the political and, 49; nothingness and, 227, 243; phenomenological epoché and, 17, 224–226, 240–242; post-totalitarian era and, 49; reception of, 48–49; reversal of reasonable projects and, 200; time and, 244–245; utopia and, 213, 217, 219, 224–227, 242–248, 282n50
Leys, Simon, 45–47
"L'humanisphère" (Déjacque), 193, 197
Life of the Mind, The (Arendt), 106, 123
London Corresponding Society, 16, 186
Loraux, Nicole, 113–114, 142
Lyotard, Jean-François, 4

Machiavelli, Niccolò, 15, 33–34, 39, 101, 122, 135, 154, 158–159, 162–163
Making of the English Working Class, The (Thompson), 15, 171, 173–174, 183–184, 187–188
Manifesto for the "Critique de la Politique" Book Series. See Critique of Politics series
Many, the, 46, 172, 230
Marck, Siegfried, 140
Marcuse, Herbert, 131, 142, 150
Martin, R. M., 177
Marx, Karl: anarchy and, 136; atheism and, 136; critical theory and, 133, 229; critique of politics and, 27; deification of history and, 136; emancipation and, 190; Hegel's influence on, 133, 145; historical necessity and, 135, 145; Jewish question and, 195; proletariat and, 177; quietism of, 152

Marxism: Bauhaus as cathedral of, 77; classless society and, 206–207; critical theory and, 13, 131; critique of domination and, 13; critique of politics and, 27; exclusion and, 192; French Marxism, 6; new scientific spirit of, 194; philosophy of history and, 13, 153; political philosophy challenged by, 5; theory and, 173; utopia and, 193–199, 247–249
Marxism and Philosophy (Korsch), 133
masses, the, 60–61, 79, 81, 88, 90–93, 96, 138, 145, 177, 270n14
Masse und Macht (Canetti), 270n14
Mass Ornament, The (Kracauer), 84
May '68 protests, 3, 21
Meier, Christian, 64
Memoirs (Speer), 76, 78, 85
Merleau-Ponty, Maurice, 20, 33
Minima Moralia (Adorno), 133–134
"Modern Political Philosophy and Emancipation" (Abensour), 31–35; Ancients and the Moderns and, 32–34; crisis of modernity and, 32–33; crisis of political philosophy and, 31–32; critique of domination and, 35; ethical critique and, 31; reconstruction of the political and, 34; scientific knowledge and, 31; scientization of the political and, 34
Montesquieu (Charles Louis de Secondat), 47, 50, 57–58, 108
More, Thomas, 218, 224, 247, 280n5
Morris, William, 15–17, 20, 173–174, 178, 198, 224, 282n50
Mosse, George, 79
Moylan, Tom, 17
Moyn, Samuel, 7

Nadir, Christine, 16
Navet, George, 164

Nazism, 49, 56, 67–77, 79, 81, 87–90, 134–135, 144, 164. *See also* "On Compactness"
Necessity for a Reform of Philosophy, The (Feuerbach), 128
need of humanity, 102, 128
negative dialectics, 20, 192
Negative Dialectics (Adorno), 135, 192
Neumann, Franz, 81, 84, 143–144
News from Nowhere (Morris), 234
new utopian spirit, 16–18, 192–199, 203–204, 209–212, 247
"New Utopian Spirit, The" (Abensour), 189–213; autonomy of new utopian spirit and, 193, 199, 203; beyond of politics and, 212–213; blind spots of emancipation and, 192; circle of repetition disrupted and, 199; complicity of reason and myth and, 201; critical theory and, 200–201; definition of new utopian spirit and, 193; definition of utopia and, 191–192; demythologization and, 201, 207; dialectic of emancipation and, 193, 198–204; dialectic of enlightenment and, 200–203; difficult utopia and, 199–200; displacement approach and, 192–193; emancipation and, 190–192, 195–197; forms of new utopian spirit and, 193; freedom and, 199; "Jewish idea" and, utopia as, 195–196, 200; main currents in new utopian spirit and, 197–198; Marxism and, 189–190, 192–198, 199, 206; May '68 protests and, 189; Morrisian utopia and, 194, 198; multiple passionality and, 197–198; overview of, 17–18, 189–193; Paris Commune and, 197, 208; plurality of utopian traditions and,

193–198; progress and, 209–211; reconciliation and, 191; rediscovery of utopia and, 189–192; repetition and, 204–213; totalitarianism and, 190–192; traditions of utopia and, 192–193; utopia-science opposition and, 194–195
Nietzsche, Friedrich, 67, 68, 124
1984 (Orwell), 63
Nizan, Paul, 95–96

"On a Misinterpretation of Totalitarianism and Its Effects" (Abensour), 43–66; action principle of totalitarian regimes and, 58–59; apoliticism and, 44–45; concentration camps and, 56; definition of totalitarianism and, 43; desertification and, 62–63; destruction of the political and, 50–66; dictatorship and, 43–44; domination identified with politics itself and, 44; downfall of totalitarian regimes and, 64; everything is political and, 47–50, 55; excess of the political and, 45–49, 64–66; function of law and, 52–53; horrors of politics and, 44–47; ideology and, 56–63; language and, 64; meaning of politics and, 65–66; modernity and, 43; multiplicity and, 54–55; overview of, 9; paradox and, 43; power and, 55–56; terror and, 53–60; total domination and, 50–66; voluntary servitude and, 61
"On Compactness" (Abensour), 67–98; aestheticization of the political and, 88–93; alienation and, 80; cathedral of light and, 94–98; charismatic domination and, 84–88; classical architecture and, 68–71; concentration camps and, 94; constitution of People-as-One and, 95; depoliticization of the political and, 88–93; direction of the daemonic and, 84–85; effects of compactness and, 82–83; entrapping charisma and, 85–88; five propositions encapsulating strategy of disjunction and, 70–71; gigantism and, 90–92; grand position and, 75–90; Hitler as architect and, 76–77; idols of the marketplace and, 79; inclusion/exclusion and, 94–98; logic of totalitarian regimes and, 94; magical power and, 80–81; mass society and, 89–90; mobilization of the masses and, 79–84; modern architecture and, 67–68; monumental art and, 88–93; necessity of displacement and, 75; neutrality of architecture thesis and, 70–71; new politics and, 79–84; night and fog and, 94–98; no univocal relation and, 75; overpoliticization and, 88, 92–93; overview of, 10; philosophical interpretations of totalitarianism and, 72–73; political intelligence and, 73–75; public space and, 88–89; question of the status of architecture and, 75–77; question of the threshold and, 77–79; research hypothesis and, 71–72; social bonds and, 79–88; space of political mobilization and, 92–93; Speer's role in Nazi Germany and, 67–69; strategy of disjunction and, 69–71, 94; three critical demands for analysis of architecture and, 71–75; time and, 85–88; totalitarian logic

"On Compactness" (Abensour) *(continued)*
  and, 88–98; unity and diversity and, 72–73; voluntary servitude and, 74–75
One-Dimensional Man (Marcuse), 150
On the Concept of History (Benjamin), 193
On the Jewish Question (Marx), 190
originary division of the social, 9, 156, 161
Origins of Totalitarianism, The (Arendt), 54, 145
Orwell, George, 45–46

Papon, Maurice, 3
Paris Commune (1871), 21, 187, 197, 208
Pascal, Blaise, 106–111
Passing of an Illusion, The (Furet), 257
Pensées (Pascal), 106
Petitdemange, Guy, 149
Phaedo (Plato), 112–113, 116
phenomenological epoché, 17, 223–227, 239–242
"Philosophy and Critical Theory" (Marcuse), 142
"Philosophy and Politics" (Arendt), 113–114
philosophy of history, 120, 135, 150
Philosophy of the Act, The (Hess), 141
"Philosophy of Wakefulness" (Levinas), 225–226
political bonds, 11, 29, 44, 62, 97, 142–143, 158–159
political institution of the social, 9–10, 13, 34, 47, 72, 79, 97, 143, 156, 161, 254
political philosophy: Abensour as instigator of return to, 5–11; challenging the tradition of, 5–7; classical political philosophy, 7, 11, 13, 48, 143, 157–158; crisis of modern form of, 31–35; critical theory as, 12–13, 130–147; critical-utopian political philosophy and, 4, 11–23, 30; critique of domination and, 8, 12–13, 35, 50–66, 128, 141, 164–167; democracy and, 14–20; emancipation and, 12–20, 31–35; normative inquiry and, 5–7; overview of Abensour's contributions to, 5–20; philosophy's relation to politics and, 7–13; political institution of the social and, 9–10, 13; political things distinguished from, 7–11, 22–23, 37–38, 107–108, 127–129; Quarrel of the Ancients and the Moderns and, 32–34; return of, 5–7, 11; return of political things and, 4, 6–8, 11, 21–22, 37–38, 102–103, 128–129, 148, 167; scientization of, 5; totalitarianism as subject of, 6–11; utopia and, 14–20. *See also* "Modern Political Philosophy and Emancipation"; "What Kind of Return?"
Political Philosophy of the Frankfurt School, The (Friedman), 130
political things: critical theory and, 127–129, 143–144, 156–157; critical-utopian political philosophy and, 4, 11–23, 30; critique of domination and, 7–11, 21, 44, 49–50, 148; heterogeneity of, 166; irreducibility of, 21, 156–157; normal politics challenged by return of, 7; phenomenology of, 7; political philosophy distinguished from, 7–11, 22–23, 37–38, 107–108, 127–129; return of, 4, 6–8, 11, 21–22, 37–38, 102–103, 128–129, 148, 167; totalitarianism and, 7–11.

See also Critique of Politics series; "Modern Political Philosophy and Emancipation"; "What Kind of Return?"
politics of emancipation, 2–3, 14–20, 132, 166
Popper, Karl, 55
Posen Conference, 68
Prévost, André, 216
Problèmes kantiens (Weil), 119
progress, 106, 139, 144, 160, 164, 177, 200, 209–211
Promise of Politics, The (Arendt), 111, 123
"Provisional Theses for the Reformation of Philosophy" (Feuerbach), 39

Quarrel of the Ancients and the Moderns, 32–34

Rancière, Jacques, 120, 142, 187, 258
Reason and Revolution (Marcuse), 132, 151
Renaut, Alain, 148
Republic (Plato), 54–55, 57, 217
return of political things, 4, 6–8, 11, 21–22, 37–38, 102–103, 128–129, 148, 167
Revolution (Landauer), 219
Richir, Marc, 223, 239
Rousseau, Jean-Jacques, 2, 9, 30, 32, 34, 40, 47, 117–118, 155, 190, 220
Rozensweig, Franz, 39
Rubel, Maximilien, 171, 249
rule of law, 164, 255–258

salvage by transplant, 133, 139, 147
savage democracy, 66, 252–253, 258
Saville, John, 173
Schopenhauer, Arthur, 132
Schürmann, Reiner, 108, 252

self-destructive reason, 131
sentry of dreams, the, 204–205, 228–229, 236–239
social bonds, 10–12, 14, 16, 19, 34, 72, 74, 79–81, 97, 180, 224
Socialism (Engels), 194
Socrates, 32, 48, 107–108, 119, 122–123, 126
Speer, Albert: architecture of desire and, 74; civilizing facade of architecture of, 70; as expert liar, 68; fundamental transformation and, 90; imprisonment of, 68; legacy of, 68–69; lies of, 68; literary career of, 68; magical power of architecture and, 80–81; masses and, 93; nonthinking and, 94; on project of domination, 91; question of the threshold and, 78; role in Nazi regime of, 67–68; on words of Hitler, 85
Spinoza, Benedict de, 12, 29, 74, 116, 128, 141, 148
Stalinism, 46, 49, 71, 173, 255
Strauss, Leo, 32–33, 101–102, 117, 119–120
"Sur la démocratie: Le politique et l'institution du social" (Lefort and Gauchet), 155–156

Taminiaux, Jacques, 124
Thelwall, John, 187
Theory of Justice, A (Rawls), 5
"Theses on the Concept of History" (Benjamin), 210
Thompson, E. P. *See* "E. P. Thompson's Passion"
Timaeus (Plato), 57
Time and the Other (Levinas), 244
totalitarianism: Abensour's critique of, 7–11; definition of, 43, 45–49, 50–52, 56–57, 79, 145–146;

totalitarianism *(continued)*
democracy's relation to, 7–10, 14, 95, 144, 164–165; destruction of the political and, 50–66; as excess of the political, 45–49, 64–66; forms of, 51–52; philosophical interpretations of, 72–73; political philosophy, as subject of, 6–11; political things and, 7–11; politicization thesis of, 9–10. *See also* critique of domination; "On a Misinterpretation of Totalitarianism and Its Effects"; "On Compactness"

utopia: Abensour on, 16, 19; capitalism and, 19, 230–232; critical-utopian political philosophy and, 4, 11–23, 30; critique of domination and, 17–18; democracy and, 17–20, 189–191, 212–213, 257; democratic-utopian, 18–20; dialectical image and, 17; education of desire and, 16–17; emancipation and, 14–20, 190–191, 197–204, 207–211, 229, 239; institutions and, 20; Marxism and, 193–199, 247–249; Morrisian utopia, 194, 198, 283n50; myth of reconciled society of, 16; negative utopia, 210; new utopian spirit, 16; phenomenological epoché and, 17; political philosophy and, 14–20; utopian animal, 217–219, 227, 250; utopian human, 217, 219, 227, 244, 250. *See also* "E. P. Thompson's Passion"; "Letter from a 'Revoltist' to Marcel Gauchet, Convert to 'Normal Politics'"; "New Utopian Spirit, The"; "Utopian Conversion, The"
Utopia (More), 216, 218, 248–249, 280n5
"Utopian Conversion, The" (Abensour), 215–250; ambiguity and, 233; awakening and, 220, 224, 226–244, 247–248; border between utopia and utopian conversion and, 247; definition of utopian conversion and, 218–220; dialectical image and, 224–226, 232–240; dogmatism and, 222–223; French Revolution and, 220–222; golden age and, 220, 231–232; historical wisdom rejected and, 220–223; how of utopian conversion and, 224; I-Thou relation and, 227; linguistic struggle around term utopia and, 215–216; Marxism and, 249; metanoia and, 216, 248; Morrisian utopia and, 223; motivations for writing on utopia and, 215–216; mythology and, 218; nothingness and, 243–244; ontological eruption and, 224–225; overview of, 17, 215–224, 248–250; phantasmagoria and, 229–230; phenomenological epoché and, 224–227, 239–242; philosophy's relation to utopia and, 247–248; studious Utopians and, 249; symbolic animal and, 218; totalitarian utopia and, 216; utopian animal and, 227; utopian human and, 217
"Utopia of Books, The" (Levinas), 217

Vico, Giambattista, 125, 164, 190, 216
voluntary servitude, 2, 29, 34, 40, 61, 74–75, 151, 203, 257

Weber, Max, 5, 74, 84–85, 87
Weil, Éric, 119
"What Kind of Return?" (Abensour), 37–40; critique of domination and, 38–40; definition of return and, 37–38; overview of, 6; political things and, 37–38; restoration of

political philosophy and, 37–39;
totalitarianism and, 38–40
Why We Are Not Nietzscheans (Ferry and Renaut), 148

William Morris (Thompson), 173, 188
Williams, Raymond, 16

Zinoniev, Alexander, 192

www.ingramcontent.com/pod-product-compliance
Lightning Source LLC
Chambersburg PA
CBHW031705230426
43668CB00006B/114